Ex Libris

. . . .

The Arden Dictionary of Shakespeare Quotations

compiled by
Jane Armstrong

Arden Shakespeare

1 3 5 7 9 10 8 6 4 2

This edition of *The Arden Dictionary of Shakespeare Quotations*
first published 2010 by Methuen Drama

Editorial matter copyright © Jane Armstrong 1999

Arden Shakespeare is an imprint of Methuen Drama

Methuen Drama
A & C Black Publishers Limited
36 Soho Square
London WID 3QY

www.methuendrama.com
www.ardenshakespeare.com

A CIP catalogue record for this book is available
from the British Library

ISBN 978 1 408 12897 8

Typeset by Country Setting, Kingsdown, Kent
Printed and bound in Great Britain by Clays Limited

For Joe, Eddo, Nick and Jim

Contents

Preface   xi

QUOTATIONS   1

Life of Shakespeare   325

Glossary   329

Topic Index   342

Keyword Index   347

Index of References to Plays   392

JANE ARMSTRONG was born and brought up in North London. Her first encounter with Shakespeare was through music, at an early performance of Benjamin Britten's opera *A Midsummer Night's Dream*. She has worked with the Arden Shakespeare as commissioning editor and editorial series manager, and more recently with volume editors as copy-editor on a number of individual plays. She is the author of the forthcoming *Arden Shakespeare Miscellany*.

❧ Preface ❧

A dictionary of Shakespeare hovers somewhere in an alternative world of quoted or quotable Shakespeare: alongside a collection of the proverbial wisdom which Shakespeare uses so frequently; *Hamlet*, almost entirely 'quotation'; and the innumerable references made by later authors in their book titles, their chapter headings and their prose (the works of P. G. Wodehouse are practically a dictionary in themselves). It is part of the function of a book such as this to enable the reader to check out where all those quoted or half-remembered lines come from, exactly how they run, and perhaps what their role was in their original context. Lines which are essentially proverbial, or which contain a single strikingly expressed thought or resonant phrase, are the obvious candidates for inclusion, and make up a large part of the content of the book.

Other aspects of the plays are less easily conveyed in extract but are nonetheless a central part of our sense and recollection of 'Shakespeare'. The overwhelming beauty of his poetry, expressed over the flow of a paragraph or the whole verse of a song, as well as in a single phrase; the fluidity and complexity of thought which moves through a complete soliloquy; the sense of dramatic play within a speech; the counterpoint of language between the vernacular and the elevated: all require space and extent for their expression. Conversely, some of the moments of most intense emotion, where language is reduced to a minimum or even falls silent in the face of experience – some of the most memorable moments for a Shakespeare audience – are hard (or indeed impossible) to convey adequately in the context of a topic-based dictionary. I have quoted some passages at length, therefore, not only because they are stuffed with familiar phrases, but also because their complete form and structure are familiar or outstanding in themselves. Other phrases are included which can never, in extract, have the impact that they have in context, but which are nonetheless often remembered, with their context luminous around them.

The book is organized by topic – as were the 'commonplace books' in which Shakespeare's contemporaries recorded memorable extracts from their reading. A few passages appear in more than one place where appropriate, and shorter passages or phrases are occasionally extracted from longer extracts and quoted additionally elsewhere. Cross-references often direct the reader to related passages. The organization by topic provides minor interests in itself. It often clearly reveals the concentration round a subject in a particular play; and on another dimension it sometimes shows ideas recurring through Shakespeare's work, either in similar form or in a progression from the more straightforwardly expressed to the increasingly complex and embedded. Each entry is briefly annotated, normally with a text reference and identification of the speaker and addressee.

A keyword index gives locations for readers searching for a particular phrase, and a separate index lists all the entries by play title. A glossary is also provided at the end of the text.

Note on the text

The text and act/scene/line references are taken from the Arden Shakespeare *Complete Works* (1998). Some speech prefixes have been altered to make it clearer who is speaking (the King in *Hamlet*, for example, appears as 'Claudius'); and -ed endings, which are abbreviated (-'d) in verse when unstressed in the majority of the plays in that volume, have been expanded to their full form in line with the current style for the Arden Shakespeare series. The spacing of minor abbreviations (such as i'th') has also been regularized (though they have not been expanded). Where an extract begins well into the second half of a line the first line is indented; a half-line appearing by itself is not.

Jane Armstrong

A

ABSENCE

1   This great gap of time
My Antony is away.
Antony and Cleopatra 1.5.5–6, CLEOPATRA TO CHARMIAN

2 I shall be loved when I am lacked.
Coriolanus 4.1.15, CORIOLANUS TO HIS WIFE AND MOTHER

3 How like a winter hath my absence been
From thee, the pleasure of the fleeting year!
Sonnet 97.1–2

4 From you have I been absent in the spring.
Sonnet 98.1

ACTION AND DEEDS

5 Action is eloquence.
Coriolanus 3.2.76, VOLUMNIA

6   We must not stint
Our necessary actions in the fear
To cope malicious censurers.
Henry VIII 1.2.76–8, CARDINAL WOLSEY TO HENRY

7 I have done the deed.
Macbeth 2.2.14, LADY MACBETH

8 Was not that nobly done? Ay, and wisely too.
Macbeth 3.6.14, LENOX TO ANOTHER LORD

9 PORTIA Good sentences, and well pronounced.
NERISSA They would be better if well followed.
Merchant of Venice 1.2.10–11

10 If to do were as easy as to know what were good to do, chapels had
been churches, and poor men's cottages princes' palaces.
Merchant of Venice 1.2.12–14, PORTIA continues the conversation

1 O, what men dare do! What men may do! What men daily do, not
knowing what they do!
Much Ado About Nothing 4.1.17–18, CLAUDIO to the assembled company

2   This is the night
That either makes me or fordoes me quite.
Othello 5.1.128–9, IAGO TO EMILIA

3 Talkers are no good doers.
Richard III 1.3.351, SECOND MURDERER TO RICHARD

4 What you cannot as you would achieve,
You must perforce accomplish as you may.
Titus Andronicus 1.1.606–7, AARON TO DEMETRIUS AND CHIRON, referring to rape

5 Things won are done; joy's soul lies in the doing.
Troilus and Cressida 1.2.287, CRESSIDA TO PANDARUS

ACTION, immediate

6   That we would do,
We should do when we would.
Hamlet 4.7.118–19, CLAUDIUS TO LAERTES

7 If it were done, when 'tis done, then 'twere well
It were done quickly.
Macbeth 1.7.1–2, MACBETH; *more at* **CRIMES**

8   From this moment,
The very firstlings of my heart shall be
The firstlings of my hand.
Macbeth 4.1.146–8, MACBETH

9 Come, to the forge with it, then; shape it: I would not have things
cool.
Merry Wives of Windsor 4.2.213–14, MISTRESS PAGE TO MISTRESS FORD

ADVERSITY

10 O how full of briars is this working-day world!
As You Like It 1.3.11–12, ROSALIND TO CELIA

11 Sweet are the uses of adversity,
Which like the toad, ugly and venomous,
Wears yet a precious jewel in his head.
As You Like It 2.1.12–14, DUKE SENIOR TO HIS COMPANIONS in the Forest of Arden

1 A wretched soul bruised with adversity,
  We bid be quiet when we hear it cry;
  But were we burdened with like weight of pain,
  As much, or more, we should ourselves complain.
  Comedy of Errors 2.1.34–7, ADRIANA TO LUCIANA

2 Who would bear the whips and scorns of time,
  Th'oppressor's wrong, the proud man's contumely,
  The pangs of disprized love, the law's delay,
  The insolence of office . . .
  Hamlet 3.1.70–3, HAMLET; *more at* **SUICIDE**

3 Let me embrace thee, sour Adversity,
  For wise men say it is the wisest course.
  3 Henry VI 3.1.24–5, HENRY, about to be taken prisoner

4 Misery acquaints a man with strange bed-fellows.
  Tempest 2.2.38–9, TRINCULO

  See also **MISFORTUNE; TROUBLE**

ADVICE

5   Love all, trust a few,
  Do wrong to none. Be able for thine enemy
  Rather in power than use, and keep thy friend
  Under thy own life's key.
  All's Well That Ends Well 1.1.63–6, COUNTESS OF ROSSILLION TO BERTRAM

6 He that commends me to mine own content
  Commends me to the thing I cannot get.
  Comedy of Errors 1.2.33–4, ANTIPHOLUS OF SYRACUSE TO A MERCHANT

7 These few precepts in thy memory
  Look thou character. Give thy thoughts no tongue,
  Nor any unproportioned thought his act.
  Be thou familiar, but by no means vulgar;
  Those friends thou hast, and their adoption tried,
  Grapple them unto thy soul with hoops of steel,
  But do not dull thy palm with entertainment
  Of each new-hatched, unfledged courage. Beware
  Of entrance to a quarrel, but being in,
  Bear't that th'opposed may beware of thee.
  Give every man thy ear, but few thy voice;
  Take each man's censure, but reserve thy judgment.

Costly thy habit as thy purse can buy,
But not expressed in fancy; rich, not gaudy;
For the apparel oft proclaims the man, . . .
Neither a borrower nor a lender be,
For loan oft loses both itself and friend,
And borrowing dulls the edge of husbandry.
This above all: to thine own self be true,
And it must follow as the night the day
Thou canst not then be false to any man.
Hamlet 1.3.58–72, 75–80, POLONIUS' advice to LAERTES

1 Be something scanter of your maiden presence.
Hamlet 1.3.121, POLONIUS' advice to OPHELIA

2 No! – I defy all counsel.
King John 3.3.23, CONSTANCE to PHILIP, KING OF FRANCE

3 Have more than thou showest,
Speak less than thou knowest,
Lend less than thou owest.
King Lear 1.4.116–18, FOOL to LEAR

4 Let not the creaking of shoes, nor the rustling of silks, betray thy poor heart to woman. Keep thy foot out of brothels, thy hand out of plackets, thy pen from lenders' books, and defy the foul fiend.
King Lear 3.4.93–7, EDGAR, disguised as Poor Tom, to LEAR

5 Good counsellors lack no clients.
Measure for Measure 1.2.106–7, POMPEY to MISTRESS OVERDONE

6   Men
Can counsel and speak comfort to that grief
Which they themselves not feel; but tasting it,
Their counsel turns to passion.
Much Ado About Nothing 5.1.20–3, LEONATO to ANTONIO

AGE *see* **OLD AGE; YOUTH**

ALIENATION

7 I am myself alone.
3 Henry VI 5.6.83, RICHARD OF GLOUCESTER

See also **IDENTITY**

ALLIANCE

1 The heart of brothers govern in our loves
   And sway our great designs!
   Antony and Cleopatra 2.2.156–7, ANTONY TO OCTAVIUS CAESAR

2 You shall find the band that seems to tie their friendship together will
   be the very strangler of their amity.
   Antony and Cleopatra 2.6.120–3, ENOBARBUS TO MENAS, of Mark Antony and Caesar

3 Never so few, and never yet more need.
   2 Henry IV 1.1.215, NORTHUMBERLAND TO MORTON

4 One for all or all for one we gage.
   Lucrece 144

   See also **FRIENDS AND FRIENDSHIP**

AMBITION

5 He married but his occasion here.
   Antony and Cleopatra 2.6.131, ENOBARBUS assessing Antony's marriage to Octavia

6 Wilt thou be lord of the whole world?
   Antony and Cleopatra 2.7.62, MENAS TO POMPEY

7 Who does i'th' wars more than his captain can,
   Becomes his captain's captain.
   Antony and Cleopatra 3.1.21–2, VENTIDIUS TO SILIUS

8 Thou art not for the fashion of these times,
   Where none will sweat but for promotion.
   As You Like It 2.3.59–60, ORLANDO to the faithful retainer ADAM

9   Who doth ambition shun
              And loves to live i'th' sun.
   As You Like It 2.5.35–6, AMIENS's song

10 The very substance of the ambitious is merely the shadow of a dream.
   Hamlet 2.2.259–60, GUILDENSTERN TO HAMLET

11   A . . . prince,
   Whose spirit, with divine ambition puffed,
   Makes mouths at the invisible event,
   Exposing what is mortal and unsure
   To all that fortune, death, and danger dare,
   Even for an eggshell.
   Hamlet 4.4.48–53, HAMLET, tormented by the example of Fortinbras

1   O foolish youth!
Thou seek'st the greatness that will overwhelm thee.
2 Henry IV 4.5.96–7, HENRY TO PRINCE HAL

2 I spy advantage.
2 Henry VI 1.1.243, RICHARD OF YORK

3 Be that thou hop'st to be, or what thou art
Resign to death; it is not worth th'enjoying.
2 Henry VI 3.1.333–4, RICHARD OF YORK

4 For a kingdom any oath may be broken.
3 Henry VI 1.2.16, EDWARD TO RICHARD OF YORK

5   I do but dream on sovereignty;
Like one that stands upon a promontory
And spies a far-off shore where he would tread.
3 Henry VI 3.2.134–6, RICHARD OF GLOUCESTER

6   No man's pie is freed
From his ambitious finger.
Henry VIII 1.1.52–3, BUCKINGHAM TO NORFOLK, of Cardinal Wolsey

7   Fling away ambition,
By that sin fell the angels.
Henry VIII 3.2.440–1, CARDINAL WOLSEY TO CROMWELL

8   He was a man
Of an unbounded stomach, ever ranking
Himself with princes; . . .
His own opinion was his law: i'th' presence
He would say untruths, and be ever double
Both in his words and meaning.
Henry VIII 4.2.33–5, 37–9, KATHERINE OF ARAGON TO GRIFFITH, an usher, of Cardinal Wolsey

9 Lowliness is young ambition's ladder
Whereto the climber-upward turns his face;
But when he once attains the upmost round,
He then unto the ladder turns his back,
Looks in the clouds, scorning the base degrees
By which he did ascend.
Julius Caesar 2.1.22–7, BRUTUS TO LUCIUS

1 As Caesar loved me, I weep for him; as he was fortunate, I rejoice at it; as he was valiant, I honour him; but, as he was ambitious, I slew him.
Julius Caesar 3.2.24–7, BRUTUS' oration on the death of Julius Caesar

2 Ambition should be made of sterner stuff.
Julius Caesar 3.2.93, MARK ANTONY's oration on the death of Julius Caesar

3 I grow, I prosper.
King Lear 1.2.21, EDMUND

4 In venturing ill we leave to be
The things we are.
Lucrece 148–9

5   That is a step
On which I must fall down, or else o'erleap.
For in my way it lies.
Macbeth 1.4.48–50, MACBETH

6 Glamis thou art, and Cawdor; and shalt be
What thou art promised. – Yet do I fear thy nature:
It is too full o'th' milk of human kindness,
To catch the nearest way. Thou wouldst be great;
Art not without ambition, but without
The illness should attend it: what thou wouldst highly,
That wouldst thou holily; wouldst not play false,
And yet wouldst wrongly win.
Macbeth 1.5.14–21, LADY MACBETH, of Macbeth

7 Vaulting ambition, which o'erleaps itself.
Macbeth 1.7.27, MACBETH

8   Arm thy heart and fit thy thoughts
To mount aloft.
Titus Andronicus 1.1.511–12, AARON

9 He rises on the toe; that spirit of his
In aspiration lifts him from the earth.
Troilus and Cressida 4.5.15–16, ULYSSES TO AGAMEMNON, of Diomedes

ANGER

10 This tiger-footed rage.
Coriolanus 3.1.311, MENENIUS TO BRUTUS

1 Come not between the dragon and his wrath!
King Lear 1.1.123, LEAR TO KENT, self-dramatizingly

2   Let grief
Convert to anger; blunt not the heart, enrage it.
Macbeth 4.3.228–9, MALCOLM TO MACDUFF

3 There is no following her in this fierce vein.
Midsummer Night's Dream 3.2.82, DEMETRIUS, of Hermia

4 I understand a fury in your words
But not the words.
Othello 4.2.32–3, DESDEMONA TO OTHELLO

5 Who is man that is not angry?
Timon of Athens 3.5.59, ALCIBIADES TO TWO SENATORS

6 Come not within the measure of my wrath.
Two Gentlemen of Verona 5.4.125, VALENTINE TO THURIO

ANIMALS

7 Pray you no more of this, 'tis like the howling of Irish wolves against
the moon.
As You Like It 5.2.109–10, ROSALIND TO ORLANDO, PHOEBE and SILVIUS all vying to
declare their love

8 They will out of their burrows, like conies after rain.
Coriolanus 4.5.217–18; A SERVANT suggests that Coriolanus' friends will reappear
when his fortunes improve

9   The fox,
Who, never so tame, so cherished and locked up,
Will have a wild trick of his ancestors.
1 Henry IV 5.2.9–11, WORCESTER TO VERNON; he compares treason to a fox

10   So work the honey-bees,
Creatures that by a rule in nature teach
The act of order to a peopled kingdom.
They have a king and officers of sorts,
Where some like magistrates correct at home,
Others like merchants venture trade abroad,
Others like soldiers, armed in their stings,
Make boot upon the summer's velvet buds,
Which pillage they with merry march bring home
To the tent-royal of their emperor,
Who busied in his majesty surveys

The singing masons building roofs of gold,
The civil citizens kneading up the honey,
The poor mechanic porters crowding in
Their heavy burdens at his narrow gate,
The sad-eyed justice, with his surly hum,
Delivering o'er to executors pale
The lazy yawning drone.

Henry V 1.2.187–204, ARCHBISHOP OF CANTERBURY TO HENRY AND EXETER

1 It is the bright day that brings forth the adder,
And that craves wary walking.
Julius Caesar 2.1.14–15; BRUTUS fears the rise of Julius Caesar

2 The poor beetle that we tread upon
In corporal sufferance finds a pang as great
As when a giant dies.
Measure for Measure 3.1.78–80, ISABELLA TO CLAUDIO

3 To hold opinion with Pythagoras,
That souls of animals infuse themselves
Into the trunks of men.
Merchant of Venice 4.1.131–3, GRATIANO

4 How he outruns the wind, and with what care
He cranks and crosses with a thousand doubles.
Venus and Adonis 681–2, of the hare

5 *Exit, pursued by a bear.*
Winter's Tale 3.3.58, describing Antigonus on the desert shore of Bohemia. Possibly the best-known stage direction in English drama.

See also **BIRDS; CATS; DOGS; HORSES**

ANTICIPATION

6 Time goes on crutches till love hath all his rites.
Much Ado About Nothing 2.1.336–7, CLAUDIO TO DON PEDRO, saying he plans to marry Hero on the following day

7 Gallop apace, you fiery-footed steeds,
Towards Phoebus' lodging.
Romeo and Juliet 3.2.1–2, JULIET

8 I am giddy: expectation whirls me round.
Troilus and Cressida 3.2.16, TROILUS, about to be brought to Cressida by Pandarus

ANTONY *see* **MARK ANTONY**

ANXIETY

1 Doubting things go ill often hurts more
  Than to be sure they do.
  Cymbeline 1.7.95–6, IMOGEN TO IACHIMO

2 O polished perturbation! golden care!
  That keep'st the ports of slumber open wide
  To many a watchful night!
  2 Henry IV 4.5.22–4, PRINCE HAL, watching his father sleeping

3 Care is no cure, but rather corrosive,
  For things that are not to be remedied.
  1 Henry VI 3.3.3–4, PUCELLE (JOAN OF ARC) TO THE BASTARD

4 Each substance of a grief hath twenty shadows,
  Which shows like grief itself.
  Richard II 2.2.14–15, BUSHY TO QUEEN ISABEL

5   Fearful commenting
  Is leaden servitor to dull delay.
  Richard III 4.3.51–2, RICHARD TO RATCLIFFE

6 A troubled mind drove me to walk abroad.
  Romeo and Juliet 1.1.120, BENVOLIO TO ROMEO'S PARENTS

  See also **CARES; CONFUSION; FEAR; FOREBODING; MISGIVINGS**

APPARITIONS

7 What, has this thing appeared again tonight?
  Hamlet 1.1.24, HORATIO TO BARNARDO AND MARCELLUS

8 What art thou that usurp'st this time of night?
  Hamlet 1.1.49, HORATIO questioning the ghost of Hamlet's father

9 But soft, behold. Lo, where it comes again.
  I'll cross it though it blast me.
  Hamlet 1.1.128–9, HORATIO on the reappearance of the ghost

10 BARNARDO It was about to speak when the cock crew.
  HORATIO And then it started like a guilty thing
  Upon a fearful summons. I have heard
  The cock, that is the trumpet to the morn,
  Doth with his lofty and shrill-sounding throat
  Awake the god of day, and at his warning,
  Whether in sea or fire, in earth or air,

Th'extravagant and erring spirit hies
To his confine.
Hamlet 1.1.152–60

1 HORATIO   Look, my lord, it comes.
HAMLET Angels and ministers of grace defend us!
Be thou a spirit of health or goblin damned,
Bring with thee airs from heaven or blasts from hell,
Be thy intents wicked or charitable,
Thou com'st in such a questionable shape
That I will speak to thee. I'll call thee Hamlet,
King, father, royal Dane.
Hamlet 1.4.38–45

2   I am thy father's spirit,
Doomed for a certain term to walk the night,
And for the day confined to fast in fires,
Till the foul crimes done in my days of nature
Are burnt and purged away.
Hamlet 1.5.9–13, GHOST TO HAMLET; *more at* **STORIES**

3 Rest, rest, perturbed spirit.
Hamlet 1.5.190, HAMLET TO THE GHOST

4   Live you? or are you aught
That man may question?
Macbeth 1.3.42–3, BANQUO TO THE WITCHES

5 Is this a dagger, which I see before me,
The handle toward my hand? Come, let me clutch thee: –
I have thee not, and yet I see thee still.
Macbeth 2.1.33–5, MACBETH

See also **FAIRIES; OMENS AND PORTENTS; SPIRITS; SUPERNATURAL, the; WITCHES**

APPEARANCE

6 An eye like Mars to threaten and command,
A station like the herald Mercury
New-lighted on a heaven-kissing hill.
Hamlet 3.4.57–9, HAMLET reminds HIS MOTHER of his dead father's qualities

7 Thou art our admiral, thou bearest the lantern in the poop, but 'tis in
the nose of thee; thou art the Knight of the Burning Lamp.
1 Henry IV 3.3.25–7, FALSTAFF to the red-nosed BARDOLPH

1 Let me have men about me that are fat,
Sleek-headed men, and such as sleep a-nights.
Julius Caesar 1.2.189–90, JULIUS CAESAR TO MARK ANTONY

2 Sir, 'tis my occupation to be plain:
I have seen better faces in my time
Than stands on any shoulder that I see
Before me at this instant.
King Lear 2.2.93–6, KENT TO CORNWALL

3 Your face, my Thane, is as a book, where men
May read strange matters.
Macbeth 1.5.61–2, LADY MACBETH TO MACBETH

4 His face is the worst thing about him.
Measure for Measure 2.1.152–3, POMPEY TO ESCALUS, of Froth

5 Mislike me not for my complexion.
Merchant of Venice 2.1.1, PRINCE OF MOROCCO TO PORTIA

6 Thou painted maypole.
Midsummer Night's Dream 3.2.296, HERMIA TO HELENA

7 Though she be but little, she is fierce.
Midsummer Night's Dream 3.2.325, HELENA'S retort

8   Why, what's the matter,
That you have such a February face,
So full of frost, of storm, and cloudiness?
Much Ado About Nothing 5.4.40–2, DON PEDRO TO BENEDICK

9   Was this face the face
That every day under his household roof
Did keep ten thousand men?
Richard II 4.1.281–3, RICHARD TO BOLINGBROKE AND NORTHUMBERLAND – a rather
poor echo of Christopher Marlowe's description of Helen of Troy in *Doctor Faustus*
(5.1.107): 'Was this the face that launched a thousand ships?'; *see also* **SORROW**

10 I, that am rudely stamped, and want love's majesty.
Richard III 1.1.16, RICHARD

11 His complexion is perfect gallows.
Tempest 1.1.29–30, GONZALO TO HIS COMPANIONS, of a boatswain

1 There's nothing ill can dwell in such a temple:
   If the ill spirit have so fair a house,
   Good things will strive to dwell with 't.
   Tempest 1.2.460–2, MIRANDA TO FERDINAND

2 Item, two lips indifferent red; item, two grey eyes, with lids to them;
   item, one neck, one chin, and so forth.
   Twelfth Night 1.5.241–3, OLIVIA's 'schedule' of herself to VIOLA

APPEARANCES

3 I took this lark for a bunting.
   All's Well That Ends Well 2.5.5–6, LAFEW TO BERTRAM

4 Seems, madam? Nay, it is. I know not 'seems'.
   Hamlet 1.2.76, HAMLET TO GERTRUDE

5   The devil hath power
   T'assume a pleasing shape.
   Hamlet 2.2.601–2, HAMLET

6 Ye have angels' faces, but heaven knows your hearts.
   Henry VIII 3.1.144, KATHERINE OF ARAGON TO CARDINAL WOLSEY AND CARDINAL
   CAMPEIUS

7   There's no art
   To find the mind's construction in the face.
   He was a gentleman on whom I built
   An absolute trust.
   Macbeth 1.4.11–14, DUNCAN TO MALCOLM, of the Thane of Cawdor – a title which
   ironically will now be given to Macbeth

8 Sleek o'er your rugged looks;
   Be bright and jovial among your guests to-night.
   Macbeth 3.2.27–8, LADY MACBETH TO MACBETH

9 Let's write good angel on the devil's horn.
   Measure for Measure 2.4.16, ANGELO

10 All that glisters is not gold.
   Merchant of Venice 2.7.65, PRINCE OF MOROCCO

11 The world is still deceived with ornament.
   Merchant of Venice 3.2.74, BASSANIO, while choosing a casket

12 I will wear my heart upon my sleeve.
   Othello 1.1.63, IAGO TO RODERIGO

1   I am not merry, but I do beguile
    The thing I am by seeming otherwise.
    Othello 2.1.122–3, DESDEMONA TO IAGO

2   By his face straight shall you know his heart.
    Richard III 3.4.53, HASTINGS TO STANLEY AND THE BISHOP OF ELY, of Richard

3   O in what sweets dost thou thy sins enclose!
    Sonnet 95.4

4   Degree being vizarded,
    Th'unworthiest shows as fairly in the mask.
    Troilus and Cressida 1.3.83–4, ULYSSES TO THE GREEK PRINCES; 'degree' here means
    'rank', and 'vizarded', 'masked'

5   *Cucullus non facit monachum*; that's as much to say, as I wear not
    motley in my brain.
    Twelfth Night 1.5.52–4, FESTE TO OLIVIA; 'the hood does not make the monk' was
    proverbial

6   I do believe thee:
    I saw his heart in 's face.
    Winter's Tale 1.2.446–7, POLIXENES TO CAMILLO

    See also **HYPOCRISY**

ARGUMENT

7   O sir, we quarrel in print, by the book; as you have books for good
    manners. I will name you the degrees. The first, the Retort Courteous;
    the second, the Quip Modest; the third, the Reply Churlish; the fourth,
    the Reproof Valiant; the fifth, the Countercheck Quarrelsome; the
    sixth, the Lie with Circumstance; the seventh, the Lie Direct. All these
    you may avoid but the Lie Direct; and you may avoid that too, with
    an If.
    As You Like It 5.4.88–96, TOUCHSTONE TO JAQUES

8   He draweth out the thread of his verbosity finer than the staple of his
    argument.
    Love's Labour's Lost 5.1.16–17, HOLOFERNES TO NATHANIEL

    See also **QUARRELS**

ARMIES

9   From camp to camp through the foul womb of night
    The hum of either army stilly sounds,
    That the fixed sentinels almost receive

The secret whispers of each other's watch.
Fire answers fire, and through their paly flames
Each battle sees the other's umbered face.
Henry V 4.0.4–9, CHORUS; this passage and the following one describe the English army before Agincourt

1   The poor condemned English,
Like sacrifices, by their watchful fires
Sit patiently and inly ruminate
The morning's danger.
Henry V 4.0.22–5, CHORUS

2 We are but warriors for the working-day;
Our gayness and our gilt are all besmirched
With rainy marching in the painful field.
Henry V 4.3.109–11, HENRY TO MONTJOY

See also **SOLDIERS; WAR**

ART

3 Art made tongue-tied by authority.
Sonnet 66.9

4 O, had I but followed the arts!
Twelfth Night 1.3.93, SIR ANDREW AGUECHEEK TO SIR TOBY BELCH

5   What fine chisel
Could ever yet cut breath?
Winter's Tale 5.3.78–9, LEONTES TO PAULINA

See also **POETRY**

AUTHORITY

6 KENT You have that in your countenance which I would fain call master.
LEAR What's that?
KENT Authority.
King Lear 1.4.27–30

7 Thou hast seen a farmer's dog bark at a beggar? . . . And the creature run from the cur – there thou mightst behold the great image of authority – a dog's obeyed in office.
King Lear 4.6.150–1, 153–5, LEAR TO GLOUCESTER

8 The demi-god, Authority.
Measure for Measure 1.2.120, CLAUDIO TO THE PROVOST

AUTUMN

1 The teeming autumn big with rich increase.
   Sonnet 97.6

BABIES

2   The infant,
   Mewling and puking in the nurse's arms.
   As You Like It 2.7.143–4, from JAQUES's 'Seven Ages of Man' speech

3 Poor inch of nature!
   Pericles 3.1.34, PERICLES OF MARINA, born at sea in a storm

   See also **BIRTH AND CHILDBEARING**

BAD BEHAVIOUR

4   Harsh rage,
   Defect of manners, want of government,
   Pride, haughtiness, opinion, and disdain,
   The least of which haunting a nobleman
   Loseth men's hearts.
   1 Henry IV 3.1.177–81, WORCESTER admonishing HOTSPUR

5   To persist
   In doing wrong extenuates not wrong,
   But makes it much more heavy.
   Troilus and Cressida 2.2.187–9, HECTOR TO TROJAN PRINCES

BAD NEWS *see* **NEWS, bad**

BAD PEOPLE

6 He will steal an egg out of a cloister.
   All's Well That Ends Well 4.3.245, PAROLLES TO SOLDIERS

7 I fear your disposition.
   King Lear 4.2.32, ALBANY TO GONERIL

8 I know thee well; a serviceable villain.
   King Lear 4.6.247, EDGAR TO OSWALD

1 Which is the villain? Let me see his eyes,
That when I note another man like him
I may avoid him.
Much Ado About Nothing 5.1.251–3, LEONATO

See also **EVIL PEOPLE**

BAD TIMES

2 The time is out of joint. O cursed spite,
That ever I was born to set it right.
Hamlet 1.5.196–7, HAMLET TO THE GHOST

3   These days are dangerous.
Virtue is choked with foul Ambition,
And Charity chased hence by Rancour's hand.
2 Henry VI 3.1.142–4, GLOUCESTER TO HENRY

4 None but in this iron age would do it.
King John 4.1.60, the boy ARTHUR TO HUBERT, who has admitted that he has sworn to put out his eyes

5 The weight of this sad time we must obey,
Speak what we feel, not what we ought to say.
The oldest hath borne most; we that are young
Shall never see so much, nor live so long.
King Lear 5.3.322–5, EDGAR

6 This is the time that the unjust man doth thrive.
Winter's Tale 4.4.675–6, AUTOLYCUS

See also **DECLINE AND FALL**

BEARDS

7 Nay, faith, let not me play a woman: I have a beard coming.
Midsummer Night's Dream 1.2.44–5, FRANCIS FLUTE, horrified at the idea of having to act a female role

8 Lord, I could not endure a husband with a beard on his face! I had rather lie in the woollen.
Much Ado About Nothing 2.1.26–8, BEATRICE TO LEONATO

9 Now Jove, in his next commodity of hair, send thee a beard!
Twelfth Night 3.1.45–6, FESTE TO VIOLA, disguised as the boy Cesario

See also **MEN AND WOMEN**

BEAUTY

1   O beauty,
Till now I never knew thee.
Henry VIII 1.4.75–6; HENRY catches sight of Anne Bullen (Boleyn)

2 Beauty itself doth of itself persuade
The eyes of men without an orator.
Lucrece 29–30

3   Look on beauty,
And you shall see 'tis purchased by the weight.
Merchant of Venice 3.2.88–9, BASSANIO

4 Beauty is a witch.
Much Ado About Nothing 2.1.170, CLAUDIO

5 He hath a daily beauty in his life.
Othello 5.1.19, IAGO TO RODERIGO, of Cassio; *see also* **RESENTMENT**

6 O momentary grace of mortal men,
Which we more hunt for than the grace of God.
Richard III 3.4.96–7, HASTINGS TO RATCLIFFE

7 O, she doth teach the torches to burn bright.
It seems she hangs upon the cheek of night
As a rich jewel in an Ethiop's ear –
Beauty too rich for use, for earth too dear.
Romeo and Juliet 1.5.44–7, ROMEO catching sight of Juliet for the first time

8 Beauty herself is black.
Sonnet 132.13; Shakespeare's beloved is popularly known as the 'Dark Lady'

9 I see you what you are, you are too proud:
But if you were the devil, you are fair.
Twelfth Night 1.5.244–5, VIOLA TO OLIVIA

10 Beauty dead, black Chaos comes again.
Venus and Adonis 1020

See also **APPEARANCE**

BEGGARS

11 Bedlam beggars, who, with roaring voices,
Strike in their numbed and mortified bare arms
Pins, wooden pricks, nails, sprigs of rosemary;
And with this horrible object, from low farms,
Poor pelting villages, sheepcotes and mills,

Sometime with lunatic bans, sometime with prayers,
Enforce their charity.
King Lear 2.2.188–94, EDGAR

1 Poor naked wretches, wheresoe'er you are,
That bide the pelting of this pitiless storm,
How shall your houseless heads and unfed sides,
Your looped and windowed raggedness, defend you
From seasons such as these? O, I have ta'en
Too little care of this.
King Lear 3.4.28–33, LEAR

2   His poor self,
A dedicated beggar to the air,
With his disease of all-shunned poverty,
Walks like contempt, alone.
Timon of Athens 4.2.12–15, SERVANT TO OTHERS, of Timon

See also **POVERTY**

BETRAYAL

3 I know thee not, old man.
2 Henry IV 5.5.47, the new KING HENRY V to his former friend FALSTAFF

4 *Et tu, Brute?*
Julius Caesar 3.1.77, CAESAR TO BRUTUS: 'You too, Brutus?'

5 This was the most unkindest cut of all.
Julius Caesar 3.2.184, MARK ANTONY's oration on the death of Julius Caesar

6   Take, o take those lips away
        That so sweetly were forsworn.
Measure for Measure 4.1.1–2, song

7 The private wound is deepest.
Two Gentlemen of Verona 5.4.71, VALENTINE TO PROTEUS

8 Him I do not love that tells close offices
The foulest way nor names concealments in
The boldest language.
Two Noble Kinsmen 5.1.122–4, PALAMON

See also **INFIDELITY; TREASON AND TREACHERY**

BETTER DAYS

1 If ever you have looked on better days;
    If ever been where bells have knolled to church;
    If ever sat at any good man's feast;
    If ever from your eyelids wiped a tear,
    And know what 'tis to pity and be pitied,
    Let gentleness my strong enforcement be.
    As You Like It 2.7.113–18, ORLANDO TO DUKE SENIOR AND COMPANIONS

2 We have seen better days.
    As You Like It 2.7.120, DUKE SENIOR TO ORLANDO

3 We have seen the best of our time.
    King Lear 1.2.112, GLOUCESTER TO EDMUND; *more at* **DECLINE AND FALL**

4   I feel
    The best is past.
    Tempest 3.3.50–1, ALONSO TO GONZALO

5   Let's shake our heads, and say, . . .
    'We have seen better days'.
    Timon of Athens 4.2.25, 27, STEWARD TO SERVANTS

    See also **DECLINE AND FALL; PAST, the**

BIRDS

6   Hark, hark, the lark at heaven's gate sings,
       And Phoebus gins arise.
    Cymbeline 2.3.20–1, song

7 This bird of dawning singeth all night long.
    Hamlet 1.1.165, HORATIO's description of the cock crowing at the holy time of Christmas; *more at* **CHRISTMAS**

8 The croaking raven doth bellow for revenge.
    Hamlet 3.2.256, HAMLET, encouraging the dumb show

9   A summer bird,
    Which ever in the haunch of winter sings
    The lifting up of day.
    2 Henry IV 4.4.91–3, HENRY TO WESTMORELAND, who has just brought him good news

10   This guest of summer,
    The temple-haunting martlet.
    Macbeth 1.6.3–4, BANQUO TO DUNCAN

1 It was the owl that shrieked, the fatal bellman,
  Which gives the stern'st good-night.
  Macbeth 2.2.3–4, LADY MACBETH

2 A falcon, towering in her pride of place,
  Was by a mousing owl hawked at, and killed.
  Macbeth 2.4.12–13, OLD MAN TO ROSSE

3   Light thickens; and the crow
  Makes wing to th' rooky wood.
  Macbeth 3.2.50–1, MACBETH TO LADY MACBETH

4   The poor wren,
  The most diminitive of birds, will fight,
  Her young ones in her nest, against the owl.
  Macbeth 4.2.9–11, LADY MACDUFF TO ROSSE

5 As wild geese that the creeping fowler eye,
  Or russet-pated choughs, many in sort,
  Rising and cawing at the gun's report,
  Sever themselves, and madly sweep the sky.
  Midsummer Night's Dream 3.2.20–3, PUCK TO OBERON

6 Let the bird of loudest lay
  On the sole Arabian tree
  Herald sad and trumpet be.
  Phoenix and Turtle 1–3

7 Night-owls shriek where mounting larks should sing.
  Richard II 3.3.183, RICHARD TO NORTHUMBERLAND

8   The lark at break of day arising,
  From sullen earth sings hymns at heaven's gate.
  Sonnet 29.11–12

See also **MUSIC; OMENS AND PORTENTS**

BIRTH AND CHILDBEARING

9 The pleasing punishment that women bear.
  Comedy of Errors 1.1.46, EGEON TO THE DUKE OF EPHESUS

10 We came crying hither.
  King Lear 4.6.174, LEAR TO GLOUCESTER

11 When we are born we cry that we are come
  To this great stage of fools.
  King Lear 4.6.178–9, LEAR TO GLOUCESTER

1   I have given suck, and know
How tender 'tis to love the babe that milks me.
Macbeth 1.7.54–5, LADY MACBETH TO MACBETH; *see also, however,* **CRUELTY**

2 She came in great with child; and longing . . . for stewed prunes.
Measure for Measure 2.1.87–8, POMPEY TO ESCALUS, of Mistress Elbow

3 But she, being mortal, of that boy did die.
Midsummer Night's Dream 2.1.135, TITANIA TO OBERON

4 A grievous burden was thy birth to me;
Tetchy and wayward was thy infancy.
Richard III 4.4.168–9, DUCHESS OF YORK TO RICHARD

See also **BABIES; MOTHERS**

BLOOD

5 He today that sheds his blood with me
Shall be my brother, be he ne'er so vile.
Henry V 4.3.61–2, HENRY TO WESTMORLAND

6 Will all great Neptune's ocean wash this blood
Clean from my hand? No, this my hand will rather
The multitudinous seas incarnadine,
Making the green one red.
Macbeth 2.2.59–62, MACBETH TO LADY MACBETH

7 Out, damned spot! out, I say!
Macbeth 5.1.36, LADY MACBETH

8 Yet who would have thought the old man to have had so much blood in him?
Macbeth 5.1.40–1, LADY MACBETH

9 Here's the smell of the blood still: all the perfumes of Arabia will not sweeten this little hand.
Macbeth 5.1.51–3, LADY MACBETH

BODY, the

10   On her left breast
A mole cinque-spotted: like the crimson drops
I'th' bottom of a cowslip.
Cymbeline 2.2.37–9, IACHIMO, illicitly observing Imogen in her sleep

11 O that this too too sullied flesh would melt.
Hamlet 1.2.129, HAMLET; *more at* **SUICIDE**

1 Our bodies are gardens, to the which our wills are gardeners.
Othello 1.3.322–3, Iago to Roderigo

See also **MIND, the**

BOLDNESS

2 They follow him / . . . with no less confidence
Than boys pursuing summer butterflies,
Or butchers killing flies.
Coriolanus 4.6.93–6, Cominius to Menenius, describing the Volscians following Coriolanus in battle

3 Boldness be my friend!
Cymbeline 1.7.18, Iachimo

4   Young Fortinbras,
Of unimproved mettle, hot and full,
Hath . . .
Sharked up a list of lawless resolutes
For food and diet to some enterprise
That hath a stomach in it.
Hamlet 1.1.98–103, Horatio to Barnardo

5 By heaven, I'll make a ghost of him that lets me.
Hamlet 1.4.85, Hamlet to Horatio and Marcellus ('lets' here means 'hinders')

6 Imitate the action of the tiger:
Stiffen up the sinews, conjure up the blood.
Henry V 3.1.7–8, Henry to his forces

7 Be stirring as the time, be fire with fire,
Threaten the threat'ner.
King John 5.1.48–9, Philip the Bastard to John

8 Be bloody, bold, and resolute.
Macbeth 4.1.79, Second apparition to Macbeth

9 Have you no modesty, no maiden shame,
No touch of bashfulness?
Midsummer Night's Dream 3.2.285–6, Helena to Hermia

10 Things out of hope are compassed oft with venturing.
Venus and Adonis 567

BOOKS

1 Painfully to pore upon a book
   To seek the light of truth.
   Love's Labour's Lost 1.1.73–4, BEROWNE TO HIS FRIENDS; he continues, 'while truth the
   while / Doth falsely blind the eyesight of his look'

2 How well he's read, to reason against reading!
   Love's Labour's Lost 1.1.94, KING OF NAVARRE TO HIS FRIENDS

3 For where is any author in the world
   Teaches such beauty as a woman's eye?
   Love's Labour's Lost 4.3.308–9, BEROWNE TO HIS FRIENDS

4 Knowing I loved my books, he furnished me
   From mine own library with volumes that
   I prize above my dukedom.
   Tempest 1.2.166–8, PROSPERO TO MIRANDA

5 Burn his books.
   Tempest 3.2.97, CALIBAN's advice to STEPHANO, as the way to overcome Prospero

6 I love a ballad in print, . . . for then we are sure they are true.
   Winter's Tale 4.4.261–2, the unsophisticated MOPSA to the SHEPHERD'S SON

   See also **EDUCATION; POETRY; READING; WRITING**

BRAGGADOCIO

7 He speaks plain cannon, fire, and smoke, and bounce;
   He gives the bastinado with his tongue.
   King John 2.1.462–3, PHILIP THE BASTARD, of Hubert, a citizen of Angers

8 Thou coward, art thou bragging to the stars?
   Midsummer Night's Dream 3.2.407, PUCK, imitating Lysander, to DEMETRIUS

9 ABRAM Do you bite your thumb at us, sir?
   SAMPSON I do bite my thumb, sir.
   Romeo and Juliet 1.1.44–5, bickering between Montagues and Capulets

BRAVADO

10   I'll set my teeth
   And send to darkness all that stop me.
   Antony and Cleopatra 3.13.186–7, ANTONY TO CLEOPATRA

11   The next time I do fight
   I'll make Death love me, for I will contend
   Even with his pestilent scythe.
   Antony and Cleopatra 3.13.197–9, ANTONY TO CLEOPATRA

1 I dare damnation.
   Hamlet 4.5.133, LAERTES TO CLAUDIUS

2 Men's eyes were made to look, and let them gaze.
   I will not budge for no man's pleasure, I.
   Romeo and Juliet 3.1.53–4, MERCUTIO TO BENVOLIO AND TYBALT

   See also **BOLDNESS; BRAGGADOCIO; BRAVERY; COURAGE**

BRAVERY

3   He did look far
   Into the service of the time, and was
   Discipled of the bravest.
   All's Well That Ends Well 1.2.26–8, KING OF FRANCE TO BERTRAM

4   It is held
   That valour is the chiefest virtue and
   Most dignifies the haver: if it be,
   The man I speak of cannot in the world
   Be singly counter-poised.
   Coriolanus 2.2.83–7, COMINIUS TO MENENIUS; the man spoken of is Coriolanus

5 O noble English, that could entertain
   With half their forces the full pride of France
   And let another half stand laughing by,
   All out of work and cold for action!
   Henry V 1.2.111–14, ARCHBISHOP OF CANTERBURY TO THE BISHOP OF ELY

6 His soldiers, spying his undaunted spirit,
   'A Talbot! a Talbot!' cried out amain,
   And rushed into the bowels of the battle.
   1 Henry VI 1.1.127–9, MESSENGER TO THE BISHOP OF WINCHESTER

7   A breathing valiant man
   Of an invincible unconquered spirit.
   1 Henry VI 4.2.31–2, GENERAL OF BORDEAUX admiring Talbot

8   I had rather have
   Such men my friends than enemies.
   Julius Caesar 5.4.28–9, MARK ANTONY TO LUCILIUS, of a prisoner taken on the battlefield

9 His horse is slain, and all on foot he fights,
   Seeking for Richmond in the throat of death.
   Richard III 5.4.4–5, CATESBY TO NORFOLK, of Richard at the battle of Bosworth

   See also **BOLDNESS; BRAVADO; COURAGE**

BRIBERY *see* **CORRUPTION**

BRITAIN

1 Britain's a world by itself, and we will nothing pay for wearing our own noses.
   Cymbeline 3.1.13–14, the slow-witted CLOTEN to his mother the QUEEN

2 To you, the liver, heart and brain of Britain.
   Cymbeline 5.5.14, CYMBELINE, TO BELARIUS, GUIDERIUS and ARVIRAGUS

   See also **ENGLAND AND THE ENGLISH; SCOTLAND AND THE SCOTS; WALES AND THE WELSH**

BROTHERS

3 OLIVER I never loved my brother in my life.
   DUKE FREDERICK More villain thou.
   As You Like It 3.1.14–15

4 We came into the world like brother and brother,
   And now let's go hand in hand, not one before another.
   Comedy of Errors 5.1.425–6, DROMIO OF EPHESUS TO DROMIO OF SYRACUSE, closing the play

5 I loved Ophelia. Forty thousand brothers
   Could not with all their quantity of love
   Make up my sum.
   Hamlet 5.1.269–71, HAMLET challenging LAERTES in Ophelia's grave

6 More than our brother is our chastity.
   Measure for Measure 2.4.184; ISABELLA toughs it out, as her brother faces a death sentence

BUSINESS

7 Sell when you can.
   As You Like It 3.5.60, ROSALIND TO PHEBE

8 What with the war, what with the sweat, what with the gallows, and what with poverty, I am custom-shrunk.
   Measure for Measure 1.2.81–3, MISTRESS OVERDONE; her business is a brothel

9 Farewell: Othello's occupation's gone.
   Othello 3.3.360, OTHELLO, with Iago

10 [He] ruminates like an hostess that hath no arithmetic bu. her brain to set down her reckoning.
    Troilus and Cressida 3.3.250–2, THERSITES TO ACHILLES, of Ajax

1   You do as chapmen do,
Dispraise the thing that they desire to buy.
Troilus and Cressida 4.1.76–7, PARIS TO DIOMEDES

2 Let me have no lying: it becomes none but tradesmen.
Winter's Tale 4.4.724–5, AUTOLYCUS TO THE SHEPHERD'S SON

See also **CONTRACTS; WORK**

C

CAESAR *see* **JULIUS CAESAR**

CARES

3 So shaken as we are, so wan with care.
1 Henry IV 1.1.1, HENRY TO LORDS, opening the play

4 It keeps on the windy side of care.
Much Ado About Nothing 2.1.295–6, BEATRICE TO DON PEDRO, describing her 'merry heart'

5 What though care killed a cat, thou hast mettle enough in thee to kill care.
Much Ado About Nothing 5.1.133–4, CLAUDIO TO DON PEDRO

See also **ANXIETY**

CATS

6 I could endure anything before but a cat.
All's Well That Ends Well 4.3.233, BERTRAM

7 I am as vigilant as a cat to steal cream.
1 Henry IV 4.2.57–8, FALSTAFF TO WESTMORELAND

8 I come, Graymalkin!
Macbeth 1.1.8, SECOND WITCH; *more at* **WITCHES**

9 Thrice the brinded cat hath mewed.
Macbeth 4.1.1, FIRST WITCH

10 A harmless necessary cat.
Merchant of Venice 4.1.55, SHYLOCK

CAUSES

1 What need we any spur but our own cause
To prick us to redress?
Julius Caesar 2.1.122–4, BRUTUS TO CASSIUS

CAUTION

2   Some craven scruple
Of thinking too precisely on th'event.
Hamlet 4.4.40–1, HAMLET ('event' here means outcome)

3 Show me one scar charactered on thy skin:
Men's flesh preserved so whole do seldom win.
2 Henry VI 3.1.300–1, RICHARD OF YORK TO SOMERSET

CEREMONY

4 What have kings that privates have not too,
Save ceremony, save general ceremony?
Henry V 4.1.234–5, HENRY; *more below, and at* **KINGSHIP AND RULE; SLEEP AND SLEEPLESSNESS**

5 'Tis not the balm, the sceptre and the ball,
The sword, the mace, the crown imperial,
The intertissued robe of gold and pearl,
The farced title running 'fore the king,
The throne he sits on, nor the tide of pomp
That beats upon the high shore of this world,
No, not all these, thrice-gorgeous ceremony.
Henry V 4.1.256–62, HENRY; *more at* **SLEEP AND SLEEPLESSNESS**

6   Ceremony was but devised at first
To set a gloss on faint deeds.
Timon of Athens 1.2.15–16, TIMON TO LORDS

See also **CUSTOM**

CERTAINTY

7 Certainties / . . . are past remedies.
Cymbeline 1.7.96–7, IMOGEN TO IACHIMO

8 Be sure of it, give me the ocular proof.
Othello 3.3.363, the desperate OTHELLO TO IAGO

CHANCE

1 If Chance will have me King, why, Chance may crown me
   Without my stir.
   Macbeth 1.3.144–5, MACBETH

2   The slaves of chance, and flies
   Of every wind that blows.
   Winter's Tale 4.4.542–3, FLORIZEL TO CAMILLO, of himself and Perdita

   See also **FORTUNE; LUCK**

CHANGE

3 Presume not that I am the thing I was.
   2 Henry IV 5.5.56, the new KING HENRY V to FALSTAFF

4 The case is altered.
   3 Henry VI 4.3.31, WARWICK 'the Kingmaker', changing allegiance

5 Bless thee, Bottom, bless thee! Thou art translated.
   Midsummer Night's Dream 3.1.112–13, PETER QUINCE TO BOTTOM

6   Sure this robe of mine
   Does change my disposition.
   Winter's Tale 4.4.134–5, PERDITA TO FLORIZEL; she is dressed as the queen of the
   sheep-shearing feast

CHASTITY

7   I thought her
   As chaste as unsunned snow.
   Cymbeline 2.4.164–5, POSTHUMUS, of Imogen

8 Keep you in the rear of your affection
   Out of the shot and danger of desire.
   The chariest maid is prodigal enough
   If she unmask her beauty to the moon.
   Hamlet 1.3.34–7, LAERTES TO OPHELIA

9 Be thou as chaste as ice, as pure as snow, thou shalt not escape
   calumny.
   Hamlet 3.1.137–8, HAMLET TO OPHELIA

10 Th'impression of keen whips I'd wear as rubies,
   And strip myself to death as to a bed
   That longing have been sick for, ere I'd yield
   My body up to shame.
   Measure for Measure 2.4.101–4, ISABELLA TO ANGELO, defending herself in somewhat
   ambiguous language

1 Earthlier happy is the rose distilled
Than that which, withering on the virgin thorn,
Grows, lives, and dies, in single blessedness.
Midsummer Night's Dream 1.1.76–8, THESEUS TO HERMIA, recommending marriage
in preference to virginity

2 The nobleman would have dealt with her like a nobleman, and she sent
him away as cold as a snowball.
Pericles 4.6.136–8, BOULT TO THE BAWD

3 Beauty starved with her severity
Cuts beauty off from all posterity.
Romeo and Juliet 1.1.219–20, ROMEO TO BENVOLIO

4   I am bride-habited,
But maiden-hearted.
Two Noble Kinsmen 5.1.150–1, EMILIA

CHILDHOOD

5 Two lads that thought there was no more behind,
But such a day to-morrow as to-day,
And to be boy eternal.
Winter's Tale 1.2.63–5, POLIXENES TO HERMIONE, of his childhood friendship with
Leontes

CHILDREN

6 Then, the whining school-boy with his satchel
And shining morning face, creeping like snail
Unwillingly to school.
As You Like It 2.7.145–7, from JAQUES's 'Seven Ages of Man' speech

7 The limbs of Limehouse.
Henry VIII 5.3.61, A PORTER TO HIS MAN, of young troublemakers

8 How sharper than a serpent's tooth it is
To have a thankless child.
King Lear 1.4.280–1, LEAR TO ALBANY, angered by Goneril

9 Pitchers have ears.
Richard III 2.4.37, QUEEN ELIZABETH TO THE DUCHESS OF YORK, in the presence of the
boy Duke of York; proverbial (*see also* **RUMOUR**)

10 Thou art thy mother's glass, and she in thee
Calls back the lovely April of her prime.
Sonnet 3.9–10

1 He makes a July's day as short as December.
   Winter's Tale 1.2.169, POLIXENES TO LEONTES, of his boy Florizel, who keeps him busy

   See also **BIRTH AND CHILDBEARING; DAUGHTERS; FATHERS; MOTHERS; PARENTS AND CHILDREN**

CHILDREN, having or not having

2 Get thee to a nunnery. Why, wouldst thou be a breeder of sinners?
   Hamlet 3.1.121–2, HAMLET TO OPHELIA

3 The world must be peopled.
   Much Ado About Nothing 2.3.232–3, BENEDICK, coming round to the idea of marriage

4 From fairest creatures we desire increase,
   That thereby beauty's rose might never die.
   Sonnet 1.1–2

5 Die single, and thine image dies with thee.
   Sonnet 3.14

6 Herein lives wisdom, beauty and increase;
   Without this, folly, age and cold decay.
   Sonnet 11.5–6, on having children

7 You are the cruellest she alive
   If you will lead these graces to the grave
   And leave the world no copy.
   Twelfth Night 1.5.235–7, VIOLA TO OLIVIA

CHOICE

8 Since my dear soul was mistress of her choice
   And could of men distinguish her election,
   Sh'ath sealed thee for herself.
   Hamlet 3.2.64–6, HAMLET TO HORATIO

9 Take her or leave her.
   King Lear 1.1.206, LEAR TO BURGUNDY, offering him Cordelia without a dowry

10 Who chooseth me, shall gain what many men desire.
   Who chooseth me, shall get as much as he deserves.
   Who chooseth me, must give and hazard all he hath.
   Merchant of Venice 2.7.5, 7, 9, PRINCE OF MOROCCO, reading the inscriptions on the gold, silver and lead caskets, one of which will award him Portia's hand in marriage

CHRISTIANS

1   What these Christians are,
Whose own hard dealings teaches them suspect
The thoughts of others!
Merchant of Venice 1.3.159–61, SHYLOCK

CHRISTMAS

2 Some say that ever 'gainst that season comes
Wherein our Saviour's birth is celebrated,
This bird of dawning singeth all night long;
And then, they say, no spirit dare stir abroad,
The nights are wholesome, then no planets strike,
No fairy takes, nor witch hath power to charm,
So hallowed and so gracious is that time.
Hamlet 1.1.163–9, MARCELLUS TO HORATIO

CITIES

3 They say this town is full of cozenage,
As nimble jugglers that deceive the eye,
Dark-working sorcerers that change the mind,
Soul-killing witches that deform the body,
Disguised cheaters, prating mountebanks,
And many such-like liberties of sin.
Comedy of Errors 1.2.97–102, ANTIPHOLUS OF SYRACUSE TO DROMIO OF EPHESUS, of the city of Ephesus

4 Cloud-kissing Ilion.
Lucrece 1370; Ilion is Troy

5   Here in Vienna,
Where I have seen corruption boil and bubble
Till it o'errun the stew.
Measure for Measure 5.1.315–17, DUKE, disguised as a friar, to ESCALUS

6 Two households both alike in dignity
In fair Verona, where we lay our scene.
Romeo and Juliet Prologue 1–2, CHORUS

7 Fair Padua, nursery of arts.
Taming of the Shrew 1.1.2, LUCENTIO TO TRANIO

See also **DEMOCRACY; ROME AND THE ROMANS**

CLASS, social

1 Lord Hamlet is a prince out of thy star.
   Hamlet 2.2.141, POLONIUS reports to CLAUDIUS how he advised Ophelia

2 If this had not been a gentlewoman, she should have been buried out
   o' Christian burial.
   Hamlet 5.1.23–5, GRAVEDIGGER; suicides such as Ophelia were not normally permitted
   to be buried in sacred ground

3 Dost know this waterfly? . . . He hath much land and fertile . . . 'Tis a
   chuff, but, as I say, spacious in the possession of dirt.
   Hamlet 5.2.83–4, 87, 89–90; HAMLET categorizes Osric as a useless member of the
   landed gentry

4 It never was merry world in England since gentlemen came up.
   2 Henry VI 4.2.8–9, JOHN HOLLAND TO GEORGE BEVIS, both participators in Jack
   Cade's rebellion

5 That in the captain's but a choleric word,
   Which in the soldier is flat blasphemy.
   Measure for Measure 2.2.131–2, ISABELLA TO ANGELO

6 The wealthy, curled darlings of our nation.
   Othello 1.2.68, BRABANTIO TO OTHELLO, describing the superior persons Desdemona
   shunned, in her dislike of the idea of marriage

   See also **EDUCATION; EQUALITY; PEOPLE, the; WORKING PEOPLE**

CLEANLINESS

7   Bid them wash their faces
   And keep their teeth clean.
   Coriolanus 2.3.60–1, CORIOLANUS TO MENENIUS, of the citizenry

8 A little water clears us of this deed.
   Macbeth 2.2.66, LADY MACBETH TO MACBETH, not knowing what is in store

9 What, will these hands ne'er be clean?
   Macbeth 5.1.44, LADY MACBETH; *more at* **BLOOD**

CLEOPATRA

10 ANTONY She is cunning past man's thought.
   ENOBARBUS Alack, sir, no; her passions are made of nothing but the
   finest part of pure love.
   Antony and Cleopatra 1.2.150–2

11 My serpent of old Nile.
   Antony and Cleopatra 1.5.26, CLEOPATRA, recalling what Antony calls her

1   Think on me
That am with Phoebus' amorous pinches black
And wrinkled deep in time. Broad-fronted Caesar,
When thou wast here above the ground, I was
A morsel for a monarch.
Antony and Cleopatra 1.5.28–32, Cleopatra to Charmian

2   The barge she sat in, like a burnished throne
Burned on the water; the poop was beaten gold;
Purple the sails, and so perfumed that
The winds were love-sick with them; the oars were silver,
Which to the tune of flutes kept stroke, and made
The water which they beat to follow faster,
As amorous of their strokes. For her own person,
It beggared all description: she did lie
In her pavilion, cloth-of-gold of tissue,
O'erpicturing that Venus where we see
The fancy outwork nature. On each side her
Stood pretty dimpled boys, like smiling cupids,
With divers-coloured fans, whose wind did seem
To glow the delicate cheeks which they did cool,
And what they undid did.
Antony and Cleopatra 2.2.201–15, Enobarbus describing Cleopatra

3   Rare Egyptian!
Antony and Cleopatra 2.2.228, Agrippa to Enobarbus; at 2.6.126 she is described by
Enobarbus as Antony's 'Egyptian dish'

4   Age cannot wither her, nor custom stale
Her infinite variety. Other women cloy
The appetites they feed, but she makes hungry,
Where most she satisfies.
Antony and Cleopatra 2.2.245–8, Enobarbus to Maecenas

5   She looks like sleep,
As she would catch another Antony
In her strong toil of grace.
Antony and Cleopatra 5.2.344–6, Octavius Caesar

COLD

6   'Tis bitter cold,
And I am sick at heart.
Hamlet 1.1.8–9, Francisco to Barnardo

1 HAMLET The air bites shrewdly, it is very cold.
  HORATIO It is a nipping and an eager air.
  Hamlet 1.4.1–2

2 Poor Tom's a-cold.
  King Lear 3.4.143, EDGAR, disguised as Poor Tom, to GLOUCESTER

3 This place is too cold for Hell.
  Macbeth 2.3.16–17, PORTER

   See also **WEATHER; WINTER**

COMFORT

4 That comfort comes too late,
  'Tis like a pardon after execution.
  Henry VIII 4.2.120–1, KATHERINE OF ARAGON TO CAPUCHIUS

5   I do not ask you much,
  I beg cold comfort.
  King John 5.7.41–2, JOHN TO PRINCE HENRY; in a similar but more down-to-earth
  phrase, Sebastian says of Gonzalo (*Tempest* 2.1.10–11), 'He receives comfort like cold
  porridge.'

6 Let no comforter delight mine ear
  But such a one whose wrongs do suit with mine.
  Much Ado About Nothing 5.1.6–7, LEONATO TO ANTONIO

COMMUNICATION

7   If our virtues
  Did not go forth of us, 'twere all alike
  As if we had them not.
  Measure for Measure 1.1.33–5, DUKE TO ANGELO

8 No man is the lord of anything,
  Though in and of him there be much consisting,
  Till he communicate his parts to others.
  Troilus and Cressida 3.3.115–17, ULYSSES TO ACHILLES

COMPARISONS

9 So excellent a king, that was to this
  Hyperion to a satyr.
  Hamlet 1.2.139–40, HAMLET's comparison of his father with Claudius

10 My father's brother – but no more like my father
   Than I to Hercules.
   Hamlet 1.2.152–3, HAMLET

1 Comparisons are odorous.
   Much Ado About Nothing 3.5.15, DOGBERRY TO VERGES AND LEONATO

2 My mistress' eyes are nothing like the sun;
   Coral is far more red than her lips' red.
   Sonnet 130.1–2; the poet rejects standard poetic comparisons

COMPASSION

3   I have suffered
   With those that I saw suffer!
   Tempest 1.2.5–6, MIRANDA TO PROSPERO

COMPROMISE

4 I would dissemble with my nature where
   My fortunes and my friends at stake required
   I should do so in honour.
   Coriolanus 3.2.62–4, VOLUMNIA TO CORIOLANUS; an ambitious mother's advice to her son

COMRADESHIP

5 Gallants, lads, boys, hearts of gold, all the titles of good fellowship come to you! What, shall we be merry?
   1 Henry IV 2.4.273–5, FALSTAFF TO HIS COMPANIONS

6 We few, we happy few, we band of brothers.
   Henry V 4.3.60, HENRY TO WESTMORLAND

CONFUSION

7 My thoughts are whirled like a potter's wheel:
   I know not where I am, nor what I do.
   1 Henry VI 1.5.19–20, TALBOT

8 My mind is troubled, like a fountain stirred,
   And I myself see not the bottom of it.
   Troilus and Cressida 3.3.306–7, ACHILLES TO THERSITES; Thersites comments, 'I had rather be a tick in a sheep than such a valiant ignorance.'

CONSCIENCE

9 Conscience does make cowards of us all.
   Hamlet 3.1.83, HAMLET

10 A peace above all earthly dignities,
   A still and quiet conscience.
   Henry VIII 3.2.379–80, WOLSEY TO CROMWELL

1   Disputation
'Tween frozen conscience and hot burning will.
Lucrece 246–7

2 We will proceed no further in this business.
Macbeth 1.7.31, MACBETH TO LADY MACBETH, referring to the 'business' of murdering Duncan

3 The worm of conscience still begnaw thy soul.
Richard III 1.3.222, QUEEN MARGARET TO RICHARD

4 Some certain dregs of conscience are yet within me.
Richard III 1.4.120–1, SECOND MURDERER TO FIRST MURDERER; these dregs of conscience are, however, overcome a moment later: 'Zounds, he dies! I had forgot the reward.'

5 It makes a man a coward. A man cannot steal but it accuseth him; a man cannot swear but it checks him; a man cannot lie with his neighbour's wife but it detects him. 'Tis a blushing, shamefaced spirit, that mutinies in a man's bosom. It fills a man full of obstacles; it made me once restore a purse of gold that by chance I found. It beggars any man that keeps it.
Richard III 1.4.132–9, SECOND MURDERER TO FIRST MURDERER

6 Every man's conscience is a thousand men.
Richard III 5.2.17, OXFORD TO COMPANIONS IN ARMS

7 Coward conscience.
Richard III 5.3.180, RICHARD after dreaming of the ghosts of those he has murdered

8 My conscience hath a thousand several tongues,
And every tongue brings in a several tale,
And every tale condemns me for a villain.
Richard III 5.3.194–6, RICHARD after dreaming of the ghosts of those he has murdered

9 Conscience is but a word that cowards use,
Devised at first to keep the strong in awe.
Richard III 5.3.310–11, RICHARD TO NORFOLK

CONTENTMENT

10 I seek not to wax great by others' waning,
Or gather wealth I care not with what envy.
2 Henry VI 4.10.20–1, IDEN, a gentleman of Kent

1   My crown is called content;
A crown it is that seldom kings enjoy.
3 Henry VI 3.1.64–5, HENRY to two keepers who are taking him prisoner; they reply that he must therefore 'be contented / To go along with us'

2 All places that the eye of heaven visits
Are to a wise man ports and happy havens.
Richard II 1.3.275–6, JOHN OF GAUNT TO BOLINGBROKE

See also **COUNTRY LIFE; HAPPINESS; HUMBLE LIFE**

CONTRACTS

3 If you repay me not on such a day
In such a place, such sum or sums as are
Expressed in the condition, let the forfeit
Be nominated for an equal pound
Of your fair flesh, to be cut off and taken
In what part of your body pleaseth me.
Merchant of Venice 1.3.145–50, SHYLOCK's agreement with ANTONIO

4 I like not fair terms, and a villain's mind.
Merchant of Venice 1.3.178, BASSANIO TO ANTONIO

5 Let him look to his bond! he was wont to call me usurer, let him look to his bond!
Merchant of Venice 3.1.43–4, SHYLOCK TO SALERIO

6 I cannot find it, 'tis not in the bond.
Merchant of Venice 4.1.260, SHYLOCK TO PORTIA

7 Let every eye negotiate for itself,
And trust no agent.
Much Ado About Nothing 2.1.169–70, CLAUDIO

8 I have no joy of this contract tonight:
It is too rash, too unadvised, too sudden.
Romeo and Juliet 2.2.117–18, JULIET TO ROMEO

CORRUPTION

9 Something is rotten in the state of Denmark.
Hamlet 1.4.90, MARCELLUS TO HORATIO

10 In the corrupted currents of this world
Offence's gilded hand may shove by justice,
And oft 'tis seen the wicked prize itself
Buys out the law.
Hamlet 3.3.57–60, CLAUDIUS

1 It will but skin and film the ulcerous place,
Whiles rank corruption, mining all within,
Infects unseen.
Hamlet 3.4.149–51, HAMLET TO GERTRUDE, advising against self-delusion

2 Corruption wins not more than honesty.
Henry VIII 3.2.444, CARDINAL WOLSEY TO CROMWELL

3 Who so firm that cannot be seduced?
Julius Caesar 1.2.308, CASSIUS TO BRUTUS

4   You yourself
Are much condemned to have an itching palm,
To sell and mark your offices for gold
To undeservers.
Julius Caesar 4.3.9–12, BRUTUS to his brother-in-law CASSIUS

5   Shall we now
Contaminate our fingers with base bribes,
And sell the mighty space of our large honours
For so much trash as may be grasped thus?
I had rather be a dog, and bay the moon,
Than such a Roman.
Julius Caesar 4.3.23–8, BRUTUS TO CASSIUS

6 There's not a one of them but in his house
I keep a servant fee'd.
Macbeth 3.4.130–1, MACBETH TO LADY MACBETH

7 I have supped full with horrors:
Direness, familiar to my slaughterous thoughts,
Cannot once start me.
Macbeth 5.5.13–15, MACBETH TO SEYTON, describing his moral corruption

8 Preferment goes by letter and affection
And not by old gradation.
Othello 1.1.35–6, IAGO TO RODERIGO

9 Lilies that fester smell far worse than weeds.
Sonnet 94.14

10 Though authority be a stubborn bear, yet he is oft led by the nose with gold.
Winter's Tale 4.4.804–5, SHEPHERD'S SON TO THE SHEPHERD

COUNSEL, keeping your own
1 I hear, yet say not much, but think the more.
   3 Henry VI 4.1.82, RICHARD OF GLOUCESTER

COUNTRY LIFE
2 I am a woodland fellow, that always loved a great fire.
   All's Well That Ends Well 4.5.46–7, LAVATCH

3 Hath not old custom made this life more sweet
   Than that of painted pomp? Are not these woods
   More free from peril than the envious court? . . .
   And this our life, exempt from public haunt,
   Finds tongues in trees, books in the running brooks,
   Sermons in stones, and good in everything.
   As You Like It 2.1.2–4, 15–17, DUKE SENIOR TO HIS COMPANIONS in the Forest of Arden

4   Under the greenwood tree,
           Who loves to lie with me,
       And turn his merry note
           Unto the sweet bird's throat,
       Come hither, come hither, come hither.
           Here shall he see
           No enemy,
       But winter and rough weather.

       Who doth ambition shun,
           And loves to live i'th' sun,
       Seeking the food he eats,
           And pleased with what he gets,
       Come hither, come hither, come hither.
   As You Like It 2.5.1–8, 35–9, AMIENS's song

5 Let us every one go home,
   And laugh this sport o'er by a country fire.
   Merry Wives of Windsor 5.5.237–8, MISTRESS PAGE TO HER HUSBAND

6 The queen of curds and cream.
   Winter's Tale 4.4.161, CAMILLO's description to POLIXENES of Perdita

See also **HUMBLE LIFE**

COURAGE

1 Like an eagle in a dove-cote, I
   Fluttered your Volscians in Corioles.
   Alone I did it.
   Coriolanus 5.6.114–16, CORIOLANUS TO THE VOLSCIANS

2 Confident against the world in arms.
   1 Henry IV 5.1.117, PRINCE HAL describes Douglas and Hotspur to his father KING HENRY

3 We are ready to try our fortunes
   To the last man.
   2 Henry IV 4.2.43–4, MOWBRAY TO HASTINGS

4 Cowards die many times before their deaths;
   The valiant never taste of death but once.
   Julius Caesar 2.2.32–3, JULIUS CAESAR TO CALPHURNIA

5 Courage mounteth with occasion.
   King John 2.1.82, DUKE OF AUSTRIA TO PHILIP, KING OF FRANCE; 'with occasion' means 'when it is needed'

6 MACBETH   If we should fail?
   LADY MACBETH We fail?
   But screw your courage to the sticking-place,
   And we'll not fail.
   Macbeth 1.7.59–62

7 Infirm of purpose!
   Give me the daggers.
   Macbeth 2.2.51–2, LADY MACBETH TO MACBETH

8 To horse, to horse! urge doubts to them that fear.
   Richard II 2.1.299, ROSS TO LORDS

9   But one fiend at a time,
   I'll fight their legions o'er.
   Tempest 3.3.102–3, SEBASTIAN TO ALONSO

10 She did show favour to the youth . . . only to exasperate you, to awake
   your dormouse valour, to put fire in your heart, and brimstone in your
   liver.
   Twelfth Night 3.2.17–20, FABIAN TO SIR ANDREW AGUECHEEK

11 Never dream on infamy, but go.
   Two Gentlemen of Verona 2.7.64, LUCETTA TO JULIA; 'infamy' meaning getting a bad name

COURTIERS

1 I have trod a measure, I have flattered a lady, I have been politic with
my friend, smooth with mine enemy, I have undone three tailors, I
have had four quarrels, and like to have fought one.
As You Like It 5.4.43–6, TOUCHSTONE TO JAQUES

2 ROSENCRANTZ Take you me for a sponge, my lord?
HAMLET Ay, sir, that soaks up the King's countenance, his rewards, his
authorities.
Hamlet 4.2.14–16

3   O how wretched
Is that poor man that hangs on princes' favours!
There is betwixt that smile we would aspire to,
That sweet aspect of princes, and their ruin,
More pangs and fears than wars or women have.
Henry VIII 3.2.366–70, CARDINAL WOLSEY, on his fall from favour

4   You shall mark
Many a duteous and knee-crooking knave,
That, doting on his own obsequious bondage,
Wears out his time much like his master's ass,
For nought but provender, and when he's old, cashiered.
Othello 1.1.43–7, IAGO TO RODERIGO

See also **FLATTERY; POLITICS AND POLITICIANS**

COWARDICE

5 I am pigeon-livered and lack gall
To make oppression bitter.
Hamlet 2.2.579–80, HAMLET

6 There's no more valour in that Poins than in a wild duck.
1 Henry IV 2.2.99–100, FALSTAFF, encouraging thieves

7 He which hath no stomach to this fight,
Let him depart.
Henry V 4.3.35–6, HENRY TO WESTMORLAND

8   Would'st thou have that
Which thou esteem'st the ornament of life,
And live a coward in thine own esteem,
Letting 'I dare not' wait upon 'I would,'
Like the poor cat i'th' adage?
Macbeth 1.7.41–5, LADY MACBETH TO MACBETH

1 Foul-spoken coward, that thunderest with thy tongue,
   And with thy weapon nothing dar'st perform.
   Titus Andronicus 1.1.557–8, CHIRON TO DEMETRIUS

CRIMES

2   All is not well.
   I doubt some foul play.
   Hamlet 1.2.255–6, HAMLET

3   Foul deeds will rise,
   Though all the earth o'erwhelm them, to men's eyes.
   Hamlet 1.2.257–8, HAMLET

4 'Tis given out that, sleeping in my orchard,
   A serpent stung me – so the whole ear of Denmark
   Is by a forged process of my death
   Rankly abused – but know, thou noble youth,
   The serpent that did sting thy father's life
   Now wears his crown.
   Hamlet 1.5.35–40, GHOST TO HAMLET

5 These pickers and stealers.
   Hamlet 3.2.337, HAMLET TO ROSENCRANTZ (refers to the Church catechism; 'To keep my hands from picking and stealing')

6   Now could I drink hot blood
   And do such bitter business as the day
   Would quake to look on.
   Hamlet 3.2.391–3, HAMLET

7 With all his crimes broad-blown, as flush as May.
   Hamlet 3.3.81, HAMLET, of Claudius

8   The work we have in hand,
   Most bloody, fiery, and most terrible.
   Julius Caesar 1.3.129–30, CASSIUS TO CASCA

9 Between the acting of a dreadful thing
   And the first motion, all the interim is
   Like a phantasma, or a hideous dream: . . .
              and the state of man,
   Like to a little kingdom, suffers then
   The nature of an insurrection.
   Julius Caesar 2.1.63–5, 67–9, BRUTUS

1 What you have charged me with, that have I done,
And more, much more, the time will bring it out.
'Tis past and so am I.
King Lear 5.3.160–2, EDMUND TO ALBANY

2 Now stole upon the time the dead of night: . . .
            pure thoughts are dead and still,
While lust and murder wakes to stain and kill.
Lucrece 162, 167–8

3   If th'assassination
Could trammel up the consequence, and catch
With his surcease success; that but this blow
Might be the be-all and the end-all.
Macbeth 1.7.2–5, MACBETH

4   Thou sure and firm-set earth,
Hear not my steps, which way they walk, for fear
Thy very stones prate of my where-about.
Macbeth 2.1.56–8, MACBETH

5 I go, and it is done: the bell invites me.
Hear it not, Duncan; for it is a knell
That summons thee to Heaven, or to Hell.
Macbeth 2.1.62–4, MACBETH

6   Ere the bat hath flown
His cloistered flight; ere to black Hecate's summons
The shard-born beetle, with his drowsy hums,
Hath rung Night's yawning peal, there shall be done
A deed of dreadful note.
Macbeth 3.2.40–4, MACBETH TO LADY MACBETH

7   I am in blood
Stepped in so far, that, should I wade no more,
Returning were as tedious as go o'er.
Macbeth 3.4.135–7, MACBETH TO LADY MACBETH

8 That would hang us, every mother's son.
Midsummer Night's Dream 1.2.74, MECHANICALS; the envisaged crime being frightening the ladies of the court

9 When rich villains have need of poor ones, poor ones may make what price they will.
Much Ado About Nothing 3.3.110–12, BORACHIO TO CONRADE

1 This will out.
Richard III 1.4.279, FIRST MURDERER TO SECOND MURDERER

2   I am in
So far in blood that sin will pluck on sin.
Richard III 4.2.63–4, RICHARD

See also ACTION AND DEEDS; LIES; MURDER; THIEVES; TYRANNY

CRITICISM

3 That's an ill phrase, a vile phrase, 'beautified' is a vile phrase.
Hamlet 2.2.110–11, POLONIUS commenting on Hamlet's love letter to Ophelia

4 FIRST PLAYER *But who – ah woe! – had seen the mobbled queen –*
HAMLET 'The mobbled queen'.
POLONIUS That's good.
Hamlet 2.2.503–5; a rare moment of disinterested harmony between Polonius and Hamlet

5 Better a little chiding than a great deal of heartbreak.
Merry Wives of Windsor 5.3.9–10, MISTRESS PAGE TO DOCTOR CAIUS

CRUELTY

6 Let me be cruel, not unnatural.
I will speak daggers to her, but use none.
Hamlet 3.2.396–7, HAMLET, preparing to confront Gertrude

7 Why, madam, if I were your father's dog
You should not use me so.
King Lear 2.2.136–7, KENT TO REGAN

8   Out, vile jelly,
Where is thy lustre now?
King Lear 3.7.82–3, CORNWALL, tearing out Gloucester's eye

9   Come, you Spirits
That tend on mortal thoughts, unsex me here,
And fill me, from the crown to the toe, top-full
Of direst cruelty! . . .
        Come to my woman's breasts,
And take my milk for gall, you murth'ring ministers,
Wherever in your sightless substances
You wait on Nature's mischief! Come, thick Night,
And pall thee in the dunnest smoke of Hell,
That my keen knife see not the wound it makes,

Nor Heaven peep through the blanket of the dark,
To cry, 'Hold, hold!'
Macbeth 1.5.39–42, 46–53, LADY MACBETH

1   I have given suck, and know
How tender 'tis to love the babe that milks me:
I would, while it was smiling in my face,
Have plucked my nipple from his boneless gums,
And dashed the brains out, had I so sworn
As you have done to this.
Macbeth 1.7.54–9, LADY MACBETH TO MACBETH

CURSES

2 Melt Egypt into Nile, and kindly creatures
Turn all to serpents!
Antony and Cleopatra 2.5.78–9, CLEOPATRA TO CHARMIAN

3 You common cry of curs! whose breath I hate
As reek o'th' rotten fens, whose loves I prize
As the dead carcasses of unburied men
That do corrupt my air: I banish you!
Coriolanus 3.3.120–3, CORIOLANUS TO THE PLEBEIANS

4 For you, be that you are, long; and your misery increase with your age!
Coriolanus 5.2.104–5, MENENIUS TO WATCHMEN

5 The south-fog rot him!
Cymbeline 2.3.132, CLOTEN

6 Hang thyself in thine own heir-apparent garters!
1 Henry IV 2.2.43–4, FALSTAFF TO PRINCE HAL

7 Die and be damned, and *fico* for thy friendship!
Henry V 3.6.57, PISTOL TO FLUELLEN

8 Hear, Nature, hear, dear Goddess, hear:
Suspend thy purpose if thou didst intend
To make this creature fruitful.
Into her womb convey sterility,
Dry up in her the organs of increase,
And from her derogate body never spring
A babe to honour her.
King Lear 1.4.267–73, LEAR curses Goneril

1 The devil damn thee black, thou cream-faced loon!
  Where gott'st thou that goose look?
  Macbeth 5.3.11–12, MACBETH TO A SERVANT bringing bad news

2 Go thou and fill another room in hell.
  Richard II 5.5.107, RICHARD TO HIS MURDERER

3 Despair and die.
  Richard III 5.3, a number of times, as a succession of GHOSTS curses RICHARD before
  the battle of Bosworth

4 A plague o' both your houses.
  Romeo and Juliet 3.1.92, MERCUTIO, having received his death wound (*see*
  WOUNDS), to CAPULETS and MONTAGUES alike

5 All the infections that the sun sucks up
  From bogs, fens, flats, on Prosper fall, and make him
  By inch-meal a disease!
  Tempest 2.2.1–3, CALIBAN

6 War and lechery confound all!
  Troilus and Cressida 2.3.77, THERSITES TO ACHILLES

CUSTOM

7 What custom wills, in all things should we do't,
  The dust on antique time would lie unswept
  And mountainous error be too highly heaped
  For truth to o'erpeer.
  Coriolanus 2.3.117–20, CORIOLANUS' bitter attack on the stifling effects of custom

8 To my mind, though I am a native here
  And to the manner born, it is a custom
  More honoured in the breach than the observance.
  Hamlet 1.4.14–16, HAMLET TO HORATIO

9 Cover your heads, and mock not flesh and blood
  With solemn reverence; throw away respect,
  Tradition, form and ceremonious duty.
  Richard II 3.2.171–3, RICHARD TO AUMERLE AND SCROOPE

10 Dwellers on form and favour.
   Sonnet 125.5

❧ D ❧

DANCING

1   I am for other than dancing measures.
    As You Like It 5.4.191, JAQUES TO HIS COMPANIONS, retiring from the general celebrations at the end of the play

2   MARGARET God match me with a good dancer!
    BALTHASAR Amen.
    MARGARET   And God keep him out of my sight when the dance is
        done.
    Much Ado About Nothing 2.1.99–102

3   You and I are past our dancing days.
    Romeo and Juliet 1.5.32, CAPULET, Juliet's father, to a COUSIN

4   Faith, I can cut a caper.
    Twelfth Night 1.3.117, SIR ANDREW AGUECHEEK TO SIR TOBY BELCH

5   When you do dance, I wish you
    A wave o'th' sea, that you might ever do
    Nothing but that, . . .
    And own no other function.
    Winter's Tale 4.4.140–3, FLORIZEL TO PERDITA

DANGER

6   Why, man, they did make love to this employment.
    Hamlet 5.2.57, HAMLET telling HORATIO that Rosencrantz and Guildenstern courted their own deaths through their spying activities

7   Wake not a sleeping wolf.
    2 Henry IV 1.2.153–4, LORD CHIEF JUSTICE TO FALSTAFF

8   I must go and meet with danger there,
    Or it will seek me in another place,
    And find me worse provided.
    2 Henry IV 2.3.48–50, NORTHUMBERLAND TO LADY NORTHUMBERLAND AND LADY PERCY

1 'Tis true that we are in great danger;
  The greater therefore should our courage be.
  Henry V 4.1.1–2, HENRY TO GLOUCESTER before the battle of Agincourt

2   Where we are,
  There's daggers in men's smiles.
  Macbeth 2.3.139–40, DONALBAIN TO MALCOLM

3 We have scorched the snake, not killed it.
  Macbeth 3.2.13, MACBETH TO LADY MACBETH; 'scorched', the reading from the First
  Folio, is often amended to 'scotched'

4 There the grown serpent lies; the worm, that's fled,
  Hath nature that in time will venom breed,
  No teeth for th' present.
  Macbeth 3.4.28–30, MACBETH TO A MURDERER: Banquo has been killed, but his son
  Fleance has escaped

5 Men must not walk too late.
  Macbeth 3.6.7, LENOX TO ANOTHER LORD

6 She loved me for the dangers I had passed.
  Othello 1.3.168, OTHELLO TO THE DUKE OF VENICE AND BRABANTIO, of Desdemona

DANGEROUS PEOPLE

7 A dangerous and lascivious boy.
  All's Well That Ends Well 4.3.216, PAROLLES TO SOLDIERS, of Bertram

8 Though I am not splenative and rash,
  Yet have I in me something dangerous.
  Hamlet 5.1.259–60, HAMLET TO LAERTES

9 Yond Cassius has a lean and hungry look;
  He thinks too much: such men are dangerous . . .
              He reads much,
  He is a great observer, and he looks
  Quite through the deeds of men. He loves no plays,
  As thou dost, Antony; he hears no music.
  Seldom he smiles, and smiles in such a sort
  As if he mocked himself, and scorned his spirit
  That could be moved to smile at any thing.
  Such men as he be never at heart's ease
  Whiles they behold a greater than themselves,
  And therefore are they very dangerous.
  Julius Caesar 1.2.191–2, 198–207, JULIUS CAESAR TO MARK ANTONY

1   Thou hast entertained
    A fox, to be shepherd of thy lambs.
    Two Gentlemen of Verona 4.4.90–1, JULIA

DARKNESS

2   By th' clock 'tis day,
    And yet dark night strangles the travelling lamp.
    Macbeth 2.4.6–7, ROSSE TO AN OLD MAN

3 The old fantastical duke of dark corners.
    Measure for Measure 4.3.156–7, LUCIO, of the Duke, to the DUKE, disguised as a friar

4   This thing of darkness I
    Acknowledge mine.
    Tempest 5.1.275–6, PROSPERO, of Caliban

See also **NIGHT**

DAUGHTERS

5 Still harping on my daughter.
    Hamlet 2.2.187–8, POLONIUS

6 Those pelican daughters.
    King Lear 3.4.74, LEAR TO KENT

7 Tigers, not daughters.
    King Lear 4.2.41, ALBANY TO GONERIL

8 My daughter! O my ducats! O my daughter!
    Fled with a Christian! O my Christian ducats!
    Justice, the law, my ducats, and my daughter!
    Merchant of Venice 2.8.15–17, SOLANIO, describing Shylock in a rage

See also **CHILDREN; PARENTS AND CHILDREN**

DAWN *see* MORNING

DEATH

9 She hath such a celerity in dying.
    Antony and Cleopatra 1.2.149, ENOBARBUS, of Cleopatra

10   I will be
    A bridegroom in my death and run into't
    As to a lover's bed.
    Antony and Cleopatra 4.14.100–2, ANTONY TO EROS

1 The crown o'th' earth doth melt . . .
O withered is the garland of the war,
The soldier's pole is fallen; young boys and girls
Are level now with men; the odds is gone
And there is nothing left remarkable
Beneath the visiting moon.
Antony and Cleopatra 4.15.65–70, CLEOPATRA, at the death of Antony

2 Finish, good lady. The bright day is done
And we are for the dark.
Antony and Cleopatra 5.2.192–3, CHARMIAN TO CLEOPATRA

3 A great reckoning in a little room.
As You Like It 3.3.14, TOUCHSTONE TO AUDREY; this phrase may reflect Shakespeare's feelings about the violent early death of his admired contemporary, the poet and playwright Christopher Marlowe

4 Death, that dark spirit.
Coriolanus 2.1.160, VOLUMNIA TO MENENIUS

5 Death by inches.
Coriolanus 5.4.40, MESSENGER

6   All lovers young, all lovers must
Consign to thee and come to dust . . .
Quiet consummation have
And renowned be thy grave!
Cymbeline 4.2.274–5, 280–1, GUIDERIUS' AND ARVIRAGUS' song; *more at* **MORTALITY**

7 The ground that gave them first has them again:
Their pleasures here are past, so is their pain.
Cymbeline 4.2.289–90, BELARIUS

8 The sure physician, Death.
Cymbeline 5.4.7, POSTHUMUS

9   To die – to sleep,
No more; and by a sleep to say we end
The heart-ache and the thousand natural shocks
That flesh is heir to: 'tis a consummation
Devoutly to be wished. To die, to sleep;
To sleep, perchance to dream – ay, there's the rub:
For in that sleep of death what dreams may come,
When we have shuffled off this mortal coil,

Must give us pause – there's the respect
That makes calamity of so long life.
Hamlet 3.1.60–9, HAMLET

1   Death,
The undiscovered country, from whose bourn
No traveller returns.
Hamlet 3.1.78–80, HAMLET

2 How should I your true love know
    From another one?
By his cockle hat and staff
    And his sandal shoon.

He is dead and gone, lady,
    He is dead and gone,
At his head a grass-green turf,
    At his heels a stone.
Hamlet 4.5.23–6, 29–32, a song sung by the mad OPHELIA

3 Down her weedy trophies and herself
Fell in the weeping brook. Her clothes spread wide,
And mermaid-like awhile they bore her up,
Which time she chanted snatches of old lauds, . . .
           But long it could not be
Till that her garments, heavy with their drink,
Pulled the poor wretch from her melodious lay
To muddy death.
Hamlet 4.7.174–7, 180–3, GERTRUDE tells LAERTES of Ophelia's death

4 This fell sergeant, Death.
Hamlet 5.2.344, HAMLET, near death

5 Kings and mightiest potentates must die,
For that's the end of human misery.
1 Henry VI 3.2.137–8, TALBOT TO BURGUNDY

6 Doomsday is near; die all, die merrily.
1 Henry IV 4.1.134, HOTSPUR TO VERNON, before battle

7 Death, as the Psalmist saith, is certain to all, all shall die.
2 Henry IV 3.2.38–9, SHALLOW TO SILENCE; a commonplace, referring to Psalm 89.47

8 A man can die but once, we owe God a death.
2 Henry IV 3.2.233–4, FEEBLE TO BARDOLPH

1 A' parted ev'n just between twelve and one, ev'n at the turning o'th'
tide. For after I saw him fumble with the sheets and play wi'th' flowers
and smile upon his fingers' ends, I knew there was but one way; for his
nose was as sharp as a pen, and a' babbled of green fields. 'How now,
Sir John?' quoth I: 'what, man! be o' good cheer.' So a' cried out 'God,
God, God!' three or four times. Now I, to comfort him, bid him a'
should not think of God; I hoped there was no need to trouble himself
with any such thoughts yet. So a' bade me lay more clothes on his feet.
I put my hand into the bed and felt them, and they were as cold as any
stone. Then felt to his knees, and so up'ard, and up'ard, and all was as
cold as any stone.
Henry V 2.3.12–25, HOSTESS QUICKLY relates the death of Falstaff

2 Death's dishonourable victory.
1 Henry VI 1.1.20, EXETER to assembled LORDS, on the death of Henry V

3 He dies, and makes no sign.
2 Henry VI 3.3.29, HENRY TO WARWICK AND SALISBURY, on the dying Cardinal
Beaufort

4 So bad a death argues a monstrous life.
2 Henry VI 3.3.30, WARWICK's reply

5 Forbear to judge, for we are sinners all.
Close up his eyes, and draw the curtain close;
And let us all to meditation.
2 Henry VI 3.3.31–3, HENRY's conclusion

6 As dead as a door-nail.
2 Henry VI 4.10.39, JACK CADE threatening ALEXANDER IDEN, a country gentleman, in
a common saying

7 The sands are numbered that makes up my life.
3 Henry VI 1.4.25, RICHARD OF YORK

8 Here burns my candle out.
3 Henry VI 2.6.1, CLIFFORD, wounded

9   Of all my lands
Is nothing left me but my body's length.
Why, what is pomp, rule, reign, but earth and dust?
And live we how we can, yet die we must.
3 Henry VI 5.2.25–8, WARWICK TO EDWARD IV

1   Death, a necessary end,
Will come when it will come.
Julius Caesar 2.2.36–7, JULIUS CAESAR TO CALPHURNIA

2 BRUTUS That we shall die, we know; 'tis but the time
And drawing days out, that men stand upon.
CASCA Why, he that cuts off twenty years of life
Cuts off so many years of fearing death.
Julius Caesar 3.1.99–102

3   Live a thousand years,
I shall not find myself so apt to die.
Julius Caesar 3.1.159–60, MARK ANTONY TO BRUTUS

4 When the noble Caesar saw him stab,
Ingratitude, more strong than traitors' arms,
Quite vanquished him: then burst his mighty heart;
And in his mantle muffling up his face,
Even at the base of Pompey's statue
(Which all the while ran blood) great Caesar fell.
O, what a fall was there, my countrymen!
Julius Caesar 3.2.185–91, MARK ANTONY's oration on the death of Julius Caesar

5 An empty casket, where the jewel of life
By some damned hand was robbed and ta'en away.
King John 5.1.40–1, PHILIP THE BASTARD describing the body of the boy Arthur to JOHN

6   'Tis strange that death should sing.
I am the cygnet to this pale faint swan
Who chants a doleful hymn to his own death
And from the organ-pipe of frailty sings
His soul and body to their lasting rest.
King John 5.7.20–4, PRINCE HENRY TO SALISBURY, at the death of his father

7 No further, sir; a man may rot even here.
King Lear 5.2.8, GLOUCESTER TO EDGAR (not recognizing him as his son)

8   Men must endure
Their going hence even as their coming hither.
Ripeness is all.
King Lear 5.2.9–11, EDGAR TO GLOUCESTER

9 I know when one is dead and when one lives;
She's dead as earth.
King Lear 5.3.258–9, LEAR, of Cordelia

1 Is this the promised end?
   King Lear 5.3.261, KENT, with Edgar, Albany and Lear

2 Vex not his ghost; O, let him pass. He hates him
   That would upon the rack of this tough world
   Stretch him out longer.
   King Lear 5.3.312–14, KENT TO EDGAR, of Lear

3 I have a journey, sir, shortly to go;
   My master calls me, I must not say no.
   King Lear 5.3.320–1, KENT TO ALBANY

4 Beat not the bones of the buried; when he breathed, he was a man.
   Love's Labour's Lost 5.2.656–7, ARMADO TO HIS COMPANIONS, of Hector

5   Nothing in his life
   Became him like the leaving it: he died
   As one that had been studied in his death,
   To throw away the dearest thing he owed,
   As 'twere a careless trifle.
   Macbeth 1.4.7–11, MALCOLM TO DUNCAN, of the traitor, the Thane of Cawdor

6 Death and Nature do contend about them,
   Whether they live or die.
   Macbeth 2.2.7–8, LADY MACBETH, of the drugged grooms guarding Duncan

7   Duncan is in his grave;
   After life's fitful fever he sleeps well.
   Macbeth 3.2.22–3, MACBETH TO LADY MACBETH

8 MACBETH   Wherefore was that cry?
   SEYTON The Queen, my Lord, is dead.
   MACBETH She should have died hereafter.
   Macbeth 5.5.15–17

9 Be absolute for death: either death or life
   Shall thereby be the sweeter.
   Measure for Measure 3.1.5–6, DUKE, disguised as a friar, to CLAUDIO

10   Thou art Death's fool;
   For him thou labour'st by thy flight to shun,
   And yet run'st toward him still.
   Measure for Measure 3.1.11–13, DUKE, disguised as a friar, to CLAUDIO

1   Dar'st thou die?
The sense of death is most in apprehension.
Measure for Measure 3.1.76–7, ISABELLA TO CLAUDIO

2   If I must die,
I will encounter darkness as a bride
And hug it in mine arms.
Measure for Measure 3.1.82–4, CLAUDIO TO ISABELLA

3 Ay, but to die, and go we know not where;
To lie in cold obstruction, and to rot;
This sensible warm motion to become
A kneaded clod; and the delighted spirit
To bath in fiery floods, or to reside
In thrilling region of thick-ribbed ice;
To be imprisoned in the viewless winds
And blown with restless violence round about
The pendent world.
Measure for Measure 3.1.117–25, CLAUDIO TO ISABELLA; compare with Hamlet's speech *at* **SUICIDE**

4 O, death's a great disguiser; and you may add to it.
Measure for Measure 4.2.173–4, DUKE, disguised as a friar, to the PROVOST, recommending he falsify a corpse as evidence

5 Put out the light, and then put out the light!
Othello 5.2.7, OTHELLO; *more at* **LIFE**

6   Cold, cold, my girl,
Even like thy chastity.
Othello 5.2.275–6, OTHELLO, of the dead Desdemona

7 More are men's ends marked than their lives before.
The setting sun, and music at the close,
As the last taste of sweets, is sweetest last,
Writ in remembrance more than things long past.
Richard II 2.1.11–14, JOHN OF GAUNT TO YORK

8 The ripest fruit first falls, and so doth he;
His time is spent, our pilgrimage must be.
So much for that.
Richard II 2.1.153–5, RICHARD TO YORK AND NORTHUMBERLAND, of John of Gaunt

9 The worst is death, and death will have his day.
Richard II 3.2.103, RICHARD TO SCROOPE AND AUMERLE

1 Let's talk of graves, of worms, and epitaphs,
  Make dust our paper, and with rainy eyes
  Write sorrow on the bosom of the earth.
  Let's choose executors and talk of wills.
  And yet not so – for what can we bequeath
  Save our deposed bodies to the ground?
  Richard II 3.2.145–50, RICHARD TO AUMERLE AND SCROOPE

2 Nothing can we call our own but death.
  Richard II 3.2.152, RICHARD TO AUMERLE AND SCROOPE

3 For God's sake let us sit upon the ground
  And tell sad stories of the death of kings:
  How some have been deposed, some slain in war,
  Some haunted by the ghosts they have deposed,
  Some poisoned by their wives, some sleeping killed,
  All murthered – for within the hollow crown
  That rounds the mortal temples of a king
  Keeps Death his court, and there the antic sits,
  Scoffing his state and grinning at his pomp,
  Allowing him a breath, a little scene,
  To monarchize, be feared, and kill with looks;
  Infusing him with self and vain conceit,
  As if this flesh which walls about our life
  Were brass impregnable; and, humoured thus,
  Comes at the last, and with a little ʼpin
  Bores thorough his castle wall, and farewell king!
  Richard II 3.2.155–70, RICHARD TO AUMERLE AND SCROOPE

4 Death lies on her like an untimely frost
  Upon the sweetest flower of all the field.
  Romeo and Juliet 4.5.28–9, CAPULET TO LADY CAPULET, of Juliet

5 This sight of death is as a bell
  That warns my old age to a sepulchre.
  Romeo and Juliet 5.3.207–8, LADY CAPULET TO CAPULET

6 Barren rage of death's eternal cold.
  Sonnet 13.12

7 Tired with all these for restful death I cry.
  Sonnet 66.1

1 He that dies pays all debts.
   Tempest 3.2.133, STEPHANO TO TRINCULO

2 Ling'ring perdition – worse than any death
   Can be at once – shall step by step attend
   You.
   Tempest 3.3.77–9, ARIEL TO VILLAINS

3 Hector is dead: there is no more to say.
   Troilus and Cressida 5.10.22, TROILUS TO COMPANIONS, in a phrase that embodies the weary anti-heroics of the play

4   Come away, come away death,
        And in sad cypress let me be laid.
   Twelfth Night 2.4.51–2, FESTE's song

5 Tell me what blessings I have here alive,
   That I should fear to die.
   Winter's Tale 3.2.106–7, HERMIONE TO LEONTES, at her trial

   See also **COURAGE; DYING WORDS; ELEGIES; ENDS AND ENDINGS; GRIEF; LIFE; MORTALITY; SUICIDE**

DECEPTIVENESS

6 Smooth runs the water where the brook is deep.
   2 Henry VI 3.1.53, SUFFOLK TO LORDS; this play is full of secret plotting and machination

DECLINE AND FALL

7 We have seen better days.
   As You Like It 2.7.120, DUKE SENIOR TO ORLANDO

8 O Hamlet, what a falling off was there.
   Hamlet 1.5.47, GHOST TO HAMLET

9 O, what a noble mind is here o'erthrown!
   Hamlet 3.1.151, OPHELIA; *more at* **FASHION**

10 PRINCE HAL Now . . . for a true face and good conscience.
   FALSTAFF Both of which I have had, but their date is out, and therefore I'll hide me.
   1 Henry IV 2.4.494–7

11 When he falls, he falls like Lucifer,
   Never to hope again.
   Henry VIII 3.2.371–2, CARDINAL WOLSEY

1 O mighty Caesar! dost thou lie so low?
  Are all thy conquests, glories, triumphs, spoils,
  Shrunk to this little measure?
  Julius Caesar 3.1.148–50, MARK ANTONY

2 Love cools, friendship falls off, brothers divide: in cities, mutinies; in
  countries, discord; in palaces, treason; and the bond cracked 'twixt son
  and father.
  King Lear 1.2.106–9, GLOUCESTER TO EDMUND

3 We have seen the best of our time. Machinations, hollowness,
  treachery and all ruinous disorders follow us disquietly to our graves.
  King Lear 1.2.112–14, GLOUCESTER TO EDMUND

4 O ruined piece of nature, this great world
  Shall so wear out to naught.
  King Lear 4.6.130–1, GLOUCESTER TO LEAR

5 This land of such dear souls, this dear dear land,
  Dear for her reputation through the world,
  Is now leased out – I die pronouncing it –
  Like to a tenement or pelting farm.
  England, bound in with the triumphant sea,
  Whose rocky shore beats back the envious siege
  Of wat'ry Neptune, is now bound in with shame.
  Richard II 2.1.57–63, JOHN OF GAUNT, on his deathbed, to YORK; *more at*
  ENGLAND AND THE ENGLISH

6 I see thy glory like a shooting star
  Fall to the base earth from the firmament.
  Thy sun sets weeping in the lowly west,
  Witnessing storms to come, woe, and unrest.
  Richard II 2.4.19–22, SALISBURY TO A CAPTAIN

7 Down, down I come, like glist'ring Phaeton,
  Wanting the manage of unruly jades.
  In the base court? Base court, where kings grow base,
  To come at traitors' calls, and do them grace!
  In the base court? Come down? Down, court! down, king
  For night-owls shriek where mounting larks should sing.
  Richard II 3.3.178–83, RICHARD TO NORTHUMBERLAND

8 Every fair from fair sometime declines.
  Sonnet 18.7

See also **BETTER DAYS; FATE; FORTUNE; GREATNESS; ROME AND THE ROMANS; WORLD, the**

DEDICATIONS

1 To the only begetter of these ensuing sonnets, Mr W.H.
Sonnets Dedication, source of much speculation as to Mr W.H.'s identity

2 The pain be mine, but thine shall be the praise.
Sonnet 38.14

DELAY

3   I do not know
Why yet I live to say this thing's to do,
Sith I have cause, and will, and strength, and means
To do't.
Hamlet 4.4.43–6, HAMLET

4 Advantage feeds him fat while men delay.
1 Henry IV 3.2.180, HENRY TO BLUNT ('him' means 'itself')

5 Defer no time, delays have dangerous ends.
1 Henry VI 3.2.34, REIGNIER TO CHARLES, DAUPHIN OF FRANCE, AND THE BASTARD

6 Letting 'I dare not' wait upon 'I would,'
Like the poor cat i'th' adage.
Macbeth 1.7.44–5, LADY MACBETH TO MACBETH

7 Dull not device by coldness and delay.
Othello 2.3.376, IAGO

See also **ACTION, immediate; TIME, wasting**

DELUSION

8 My life stands in the level of your dreams.
Winter's Tale 3.2.80, HERMIONE TO LEONTES; 'my life is at the mercy of your delusions'

DEMOCRACY

9 In Greece . . .
Though there the people had more absolute power –
I say they nourished disobedience, fed
The ruin of the state.
Coriolanus 3.1.114, 116–18, CORIOLANUS' attack on democracy, to MENENIUS

10 What is the city but the people?
Coriolanus 3.1.199, SICINIUS TO SENATORS AND PLEBEIANS

1 The beast with many heads.
Coriolanus 4.1.1–2, CORIOLANUS' description (to HIS WIFE AND MOTHER) of the people, who have rejected him

2 Let desert in pure election shine,
And . . . fight for freedom in your choice.
Titus Andronicus 1.1.16–17, BASSIANUS TO TRIBUNES

See also **PEOPLE, the; PUBLIC OPINION**

DEPRESSION

3 How is it that the clouds still hang on you?
Hamlet 1.2.66, CLAUDIUS TO HAMLET

4   O God! God!
How weary, stale, flat, and unprofitable
Seem to me all the uses of this world!
Hamlet 1.2.132–4, HAMLET; *more at* **WORLD, the**

5 I have of late, but wherefore I know not, lost all my mirth, forgone all custom of exercises; and indeed it goes so heavily with my disposition that this goodly frame the earth seems to me a sterile promontory, this most excellent canopy the air, look you, this brave o'erhanging firmament, this majestical roof fretted with golden fire, why, it appeareth nothing to me but a foul and pestilent congregation of vapours.
Hamlet 2.2.297–305, HAMLET TO ROSENCRANTZ AND GUILDENSTERN; *more at* **HUMANKIND**

6 Cassius is aweary of the world.
Julius Caesar 4.3.94, CASSIUS TO BRUTUS

See also **DESPAIR; WEARINESS**

DESIRES

7 This ambitious foul infirmity,
In having much, torments us with defect
Of that we have: so then we do neglect
The thing we have.
Lucrece 150–3

8 What win I if I gain the thing I seek?
A dream, a breath, a froth of fleeting joy.
Who . . . sells eternity to get a toy?
Lucrece 211–12, 14

1 The sweets we wish for turn to loathed sours
Even in the moment that we call them ours.
Lucrece 867–8

2   Stars, hide your fires!
Let not light see my black and deep desires;
The eye wink at the hand; yet let that be,
Which the eye fears, when it is done, to see.
Macbeth 1.4.50–3, MACBETH

3   Nought's had, all's spent,
Where our desire is got without content.
Macbeth 3.2.4–5, LADY MACBETH TO A SERVANT

4 To have what we would have, we speak not what we mean.
Measure for Measure 2.4.118, ISABELLA TO ANGELO

5   All things that are,
Are more with spirit chased than enjoyed.
Merchant of Venice 2.6.12–13, GRATIANO TO SALERIO

6 Whoever hath her wish, thou hast thy Will,
And Will to boot, and Will in overplus.
Sonnets 135.1–2; Shakespeare puns on his own name

See also **SEX AND LUST**

DESPAIR

7 CLEOPATRA What shall we do, Enobarbus?
ENOBARBUS   Think, and die.
Antony and Cleopatra 3.13.1

8 I found him under a tree like a dropped acorn.
As You Like It 3.2.231–2, CELIA TO ROSALIND, of Orlando

9 Past hope, and in despair, that way past grace.
Cymbeline 1.2.68, IMOGEN TO CYMBELINE

10 All's cheerless, dark and deadly.
King Lear 5.3.288, KENT TO LEAR

11 Never, never, never, never, never.
King Lear 5.3.307, LEAR

12 The king was weeping-ripe for a good word.
Love's Labour's Lost 5.2.274, ROSALINE TO THE PRINCESS OF FRANCE

1   O now for ever
Farewell the tranquil mind, farewell content!
Othello 3.3.350–1, OTHELLO TO IAGO; *more at* **WAR**

2 Call it not patience, . . . it is despair.
Richard II 1.2.29, DUCHESS OF GLOUCESTER TO JOHN OF GAUNT

3 I shall despair. There is no creature loves me,
And if I die, no soul will pity me.
Richard III 5.3.201–2, RICHARD after his dream

4 Tempt not a desperate man.
Romeo and Juliet 5.3.59, ROMEO TO PARIS

DEVIL, the

5 The prince of darkness is a gentleman.
King Lear 3.4.139, EDGAR, disguised as Poor Tom, to GLOUCESTER

6 What! can the Devil speak true?
Macbeth 1.3.107, BANQUO, horrified by the witches

7 The Devil can cite Scripture for his purpose.
Merchant of Venice 1.3.96, ANTONIO TO BASSANIO, referring to Shylock

8 The fiend is at mine elbow, and tempts me.
Merchant of Venice 2.2.2–3, LAUNCELOT GOBBO

DISAPPOINTMENT *see* EXPECTATION

DISCRETION

9 The better part of valour is discretion, in the which better part I have
saved my life.
1 Henry IV 5.4.118–20, FALSTAFF, who has feigned death in battle to avoid injury

DISORDER

10 The times are wild; contention, like a horse
Full of high feeding, madly hath broke loose,
And bears down all before him.
2 Henry IV 1.1.9–11, NORTHUMBERLAND TO LORD BARDOLPH

11 Let order die!
2 Henry IV 1.1.154, NORTHUMBERLAND TO LORD BARDOLPH AND MORTON

12 Shame and confusion! all is on the rout:
Fear frames disorder, and disorder wounds
Where it should guard.
2 Henry VI 5.2.31–3, YOUNG CLIFFORD, in battle

1 Confusion now hath made his masterpiece!
Macbeth 2.3.66, MACDUFF TO MACBETH AND LENOX, at the discovery of Duncan's murder

2 Though you untie the winds, and let them fight
Against the Churches; though the yesty waves
Confound and swallow navigation up;
Though bladed corn be lodged, and trees blown down;
Though castles topple on their warders' heads;
Though palaces, and pyramids, do slope
Their heads to their foundations; though the treasure
Of Nature's germens tumble all together,
Even till destruction sicken, answer me
To what I ask you.
Macbeth 4.1.52–61, MACBETH TO THE WITCHES

3 The ox hath therefore stretched his yoke in vain,
The ploughman lost his sweat, and the green corn
Hath rotted ere his youth attained a beard;
The fold stands empty in the drowned field,
And crows are fatted with the murrion flock;
The nine-men's-morris is filled up with mud,
And the quaint mazes in the wanton green
For lack of tread are undistinguishable.
Midsummer Night's Dream 2.1.93–100, TITANIA TO OBERON, describing the effects of their quarrel; *see also* SEASONS, the

DIVINITY

4 There's a divinity that shapes our ends,
Rough-hew them how we will.
Hamlet 5.2.10–11, HAMLET TO HORATIO

See also FATE; PROVIDENCE

DOCTORS AND MEDICINE

5 A rascally yea-forsooth knave.
2 Henry IV 1.2.36, FALSTAFF, of his doctor

6 Kill thy physician, and thy fee bestow
Upon the foul disease.
King Lear 1.1.164–5, KENT TO LEAR

7 Our foster nurse of nature is repose.
King Lear 4.4.12, A GENTLEMAN's advice to CORDELIA on what Lear needs

1   Let me have surgeons,
I am cut to the brains.
King Lear 4.6.188–9, LEAR TO A GENTLEMAN

2   O you kind gods!
Cure this great breach in his abused nature.
King Lear 4.7.14–15, CORDELIA TO A GENTLEMAN, of Lear

3   Restoration hang
Thy medicine on my lips.
King Lear 4.7.26–7, CORDELIA kisses LEAR

4 This disease is beyond my practice.
Macbeth 5.1.60, DOCTOR TO A GENTLEWOMAN, of Lady Macbeth's affliction

5 Throw physic to the dogs; I'll none of it.
Macbeth 5.3.47, MACBETH TO HIS DOCTOR

6 With the help of a surgeon he might yet recover, and prove an ass.
Midsummer Night's Dream 5.1.305–6, THESEUS TO HIS COMPANIONS, of Bottom performing the part of Pyramus

7 Now put it, God, into the physician's mind
To help him to his grave immediately!
Richard II 1.4.59–60, RICHARD TO BUSHY, of John of Gaunt

8   O true apothecary,
Thy drugs are quick.
Romeo and Juliet 5.3.119–20, ROMEO takes the fatal draught

9 Testy sick men, when their deaths be near,
No news but health from their physicians know.
Sonnet 140.7–8

10   Trust not the physician;
His antidotes are poison.
Timon of Athens 4.3.433–4, TIMON TO BANDITS

See also **ILLNESS AND DISEASE; MADNESS**

DOGS

11 RAMBURES That island of England breeds very valiant creatures: their mastiffs are of unmatchable courage.
ORLEANS Foolish curs, that run winking into the mouth of a Russian bear and have their heads crushed like rotten apples.
Henry V 3.7.142–6

1   The little dogs and all,
Trey, Blanch and Sweetheart, see, they bark at me.
King Lear 3.6.60–1, LEAR TO EDGAR

2 Ask my dog: if he say 'ay', it will; if he say 'no', it will; if he shake his
tail, and say nothing, it will.
Two Gentlemen of Verona 2.5.31–2, LAUNCE TO SPEED

3 Nay, I'll be sworn I have sat in the stocks, for puddings he hath stolen,
otherwise he had been executed.
Two Gentlemen of Verona 4.4.29–31, LAUNCE, of his dog, whom at 4.4.2–3 he
describes as 'One that I brought up of a puppy.'

DREAMS

4 O God, I could be bounded in a nutshell and count myself a king of
infinite space – were it not that I have bad dreams.
Hamlet 2.2.255–7, HAMLET TO ROSENCRANTZ AND GUILDENSTERN

5 There is some ill a-brewing towards my rest,
For I did dream of money-bags tonight.
Merchant of Venice 2.5.17–18, SHYLOCK TO LAUNCELOT GOBBO

6 And by the way let us recount our dreams.
Midsummer Night's Dream 4.1.198, DEMETRIUS TO HIS FRIENDS

7 I have had a most rare vision. I have had a dream, past the wit of man
to say what dream it was. Man is but an ass if he go about to expound
this dream. Methought I was – there is no man can tell what.
Methought I was – and methought I had – but man is but a patched
fool if he will offer to say what methought I had. The eye of man hath
not heard, the ear of man hath not seen, man's hand is not able to
taste, his tongue to conceive, nor his heart to report, what my dream
was. I will get Peter Quince to write a ballad of this dream: it shall be
called 'Bottom's Dream', because it hath no bottom.
Midsummer Night's Dream 4.1.203–14, BOTTOM's dream

8 I have passed a miserable night,
So full of fearful dreams, of ugly sights,
That, as I am a Christian faithful man,
I would not spend another such a night
Though 'twere to buy a world of happy days.
Richard III 1.4.2–6, CLARENCE TO THE KEEPER OF THE TOWER

9 Dream on, dream on.
Richard III 5.3.172, GHOST OF BUCKINGHAM TO RICHARD, continuing, 'of bloody deeds
and death'

1   In dreaming,
The clouds methought would open, and show riches
Ready to drop upon me; that, when I waked,
I cried to dream again.
Tempest 3.2.142–5, CALIBAN TO STEPHANO AND TRINCULO

2   We are such stuff
As dreams are made on.
Tempest 4.1.156–7, PROSPERO TO MIRANDA; *more at* **LIFE; PLAYS, PLAYERS AND PLAYHOUSES**

See also **SLEEP AND SLEEPLESSNESS**

DRINKING

3 Falser than vows made in wine.
As You Like It 3.5.73, ROSALIND TO PHEBE

4 You come in faint for want of meat, depart reeling with too much drink: sorry that you have paid too much, and sorry that you are paid too much: purse and brain, both empty.
Cymbeline 5.4.160–4, GAOLER TO POSTHUMUS

5 We'll teach you to drink deep ere you depart.
Hamlet 1.2.175, HAMLET to his friend HORATIO

6 If sack and sugar be a fault, God help the wicked!
1 Henry IV 2.4.464–5, FALSTAFF TO PRINCE HAL

7 Doth it not show vilely in me to desire small beer?
2 Henry IV 2.2.5–6, PRINCE HAL TO POINS

8 A good sherris-sack . . . ascends me into the brain, dries me there all the foolish and dull and crudy vapours which environ it, makes it apprehensive, quick, forgetive, full of nimble, fiery, and delectable shapes, which delivered o'er to the voice, the tongue, which is the birth, becomes excellent wit.
2 Henry IV 4.3.95–101, part of a much longer speech by FALSTAFF on the benefits of alcohol to the system

9   Was the hope drunk,
Wherein you dressed yourself? Hath it slept since?
Macbeth 1.7.35–6, LADY MACBETH TO MACBETH

10 That which hath made them drunk hath made me bold.
Macbeth 2.2.1, LADY MACBETH

1 Faith, Sir, we were carousing till the second cock.
Macbeth 2.3.23–4, PORTER TO MACBETH

2 [Drink] provokes the desire, but it takes away the performance.
Macbeth 2.3.29–30, PORTER TO MACBETH

3 We'll have a posset for 't soon at night, in faith, at the latter end of a sea-coal fire.
Merry Wives of Windsor 1.4.7–8, MISTRESS QUICKLY TO RUGBY

4 I have very poor and unhappy brains for drinking. I could well wish courtesy would invent some other custom of entertainment.
Othello 2.3.30–2, CASSIO TO IAGO

5 Drunk? and speak parrot? and squabble? swagger? swear? and discourse fustian with one's own shadow?
Othello 2.3.270–2, CASSIO TO IAGO

6 Good wine is a good familiar creature, if it be well used: exclaim no more against it.
Othello 2.3.299–300, IAGO TO CASSIO

7   They were red-hot with drinking;
So full of valour that they smote the air
For breathing in their faces.
Tempest 4.1.171–3, ARIEL TO PROSPERO

8 OLIVIA What's a drunken man like, fool?
FESTE Like a drowned man, a fool, and a madman: one draught above heat makes him a fool, the second mads him, and a third drowns him.
Twelfth Night 1.5.127–30

DUTY

9 Every subject's duty is the King's, but every subject's soul is his own.
Henry V 4.1.174–5, HENRY, incognito, to MICHAEL WILLIAMS and JOHN BATES

10 Never anything can be amiss
When simpleness and duty tender it.
Midsummer Night's Dream 5.1.82–3, THESEUS TO PHILOSTRATE AND HIS COMPANIONS

11 I do perceive here a divided duty.
Othello 1.3.181, DESDEMONA, torn between husband and father, to BRABANTIO

12 We must obey the time.
Othello 1.3.302, OTHELLO TO DESDEMONA

DYING WORDS

1 I am dying, Egypt, dying. Only
   I here importune death awhile until
   Of many thousand kisses the poor last
   I lay upon thy lips.
   Antony and Cleopatra 4.15.19–22, ANTONY TO CLEOPATRA

2   Come, thou mortal wretch,
   With thy sharp teeth this knot intrinsicate
   Of life at once untie.
   Antony and Cleopatra 5.2.301–3, CLEOPATRA to the asp which kills her

3 If thou didst ever hold me in thy heart,
   Absent thee from felicity awhile,
   And in this harsh world draw thy breath in pain
   To tell my story.
   Hamlet 5.2.354–7, HAMLET TO HORATIO

4 The rest is silence.
   Hamlet 5.2.367, HAMLET TO HORATIO

5 An old man, broken with the storms of state,
   Is come to lay his weary bones among ye.
   Give him a little earth for charity.
   Henry VIII 4.2.21–3, GRIFFITH, an usher, to KATHERINE OF ARAGON, repeating the
   words of Cardinal Wolsey

6 *Et tu, Brute?*
   Julius Caesar 3.1.77, JULIUS CAESAR TO BRUTUS: 'You too, Brutus?'

7 Heaven take my soul, and England keep my bones.
   King John 4.3.10, the boy ARTHUR, having leaped from his prison walls

8 Now my soul hath elbow-room.
   King John 5.7.28, JOHN TO HIS COMPANIONS

9 There is so hot a summer in my bosom,
   That all my bowels crumble up to dust:
   I am a scribbled form, drawn with a pen
   Upon a parchment, and against this fire
   Do I shrink up.
   King John 5.7.30–4, JOHN TO HIS COMPANIONS

10 Pray you undo this button.
   King Lear 5.3.308, LEAR TO EDGAR

1
>   Now am I dead
>   Now am I fled;
> My soul is in the sky.
>   Tongue, lose thy light;
>   Moon, take thy flight!
> Now die, die, die, die, die.

Midsummer Night's Dream 5.1.295–300, the death of PYRAMUS (BOTTOM); Shakespeare makes fun of his less talented contemporaries

2
>   The tongues of dying men
> Inforce attention like deep harmony.

Richard II 2.1.5–6, JOHN OF GAUNT, near death, to YORK

3 Convey me to my bed, then to my grave –
  Love they to live that love and honour have.

Richard II 2.1.137–8, JOHN OF GAUNT TO RICHARD

4 Mount, mount, my soul! thy seat is up on high,
  Whilst my gross flesh sinks downward, here to die.

Richard II 5.5.111–12, RICHARD

E

EAST, the

5 I'th' East my pleasure lies.

Antony and Cleopatra 2.3.39, ANTONY

6 The beds i'th' East are soft.

Antony and Cleopatra 2.6.50, ANTONY TO OCTAVIUS CAESAR AND POMPEY

EASY LIFE

7
>   Who doth ambition shun
>   And loves to live i'th' sun.

As You Like It 2.5.35–6, AMIENS's song

8 I were better to be eaten to death with a rust than to be scoured to nothing with perpetual motion.

2 Henry IV 1.2.218–20, FALSTAFF TO THE LORD CHIEF JUSTICE

ECCENTRICITY

1   And in his brain,
Which is as dry as the remainder biscuit
After a voyage, he hath strange places crammed
With observation, the which he vents
In mangled forms.
As You Like It 2.7.38–42, JAQUES TO DUKE SENIOR

2 Put thyself into the trick of singularity.
Twelfth Night 2.5.146–7, MALVOLIO reads the anonymous letter which he believes is from Olivia

ECOLOGY

3 My flocks feed not, my ewes breed not,
My rams speed not, all is amiss . . .
Clear wells spring not, sweet birds sing not,
Green plants bring not forth their dye.
Passionate Pilgrim 17.1–2, 25–6

4 You have fed upon my signories,
Disparked my parks and felled my forest woods.
Richard II 3.1.22–3, BOLINGBROKE TO BUSHY AND GREENE

5 Naught so vile that on the earth doth live
But to the earth some special good doth give;
Nor aught so good but, strained from that fair use,
Revolts from true birth, stumbling on abuse.
Romeo and Juliet 2.3.13–16, FRIAR LAURENCE

6 Traffic confound thee!
Timon of Athens 1.1.240, APEMANTUS TO A MERCHANT

7   This is an art
Which does mend nature – change it rather – but
The art itself is nature.
Winter's Tale 4.4.95–7, POLIXENES TO PERDITA; this is the argument for improving ('mending') crops by selective cross-breeding

EDUCATION

8 Thou art a scholar, speak to it, Horatio.
Hamlet 1.1.45, MARCELLUS

9 He can speak French; and therefore he is a traitor.
2 Henry VI 4.2.161–2, JACK CADE TO THE BUTCHER, of Lord Stafford

1 Away with him! away with him! he speaks Latin.
   2 Henry VI 4.7.55, JACK CADE TO THE BUTCHER, of Lord Say

2 He was a scholar, and a ripe and good one,
   Exceeding wise, fair-spoken and persuading.
   Henry VIII 4.2.51–2, GRIFFITH, an usher, to KATHERINE OF ARAGON, of Cardinal
   Wolsey

3   A little academe,
   Still and contemplative in living art.
   Love's Labour's Lost 1.1.13, KING OF NAVARRE TO HIS FRIENDS

4 These are barren tasks, too hard to keep,
   Not to see ladies, study, fast, not sleep.
   Love's Labour's Lost 1.1.48, BEROWNE TO HIS FRIENDS

5 Study is like the heaven's glorious sun,
   That will not be deep-searched with saucy looks;
   Small have continual plodders ever won,
   Save base authority from others' books.
   These earthly godfathers of heaven's lights,
   That give a name to every fixed star,
   Have no more profit of their shining nights
   Than those that walk and wot not what they are.
   Love's Labour's Lost 1.1.84–91, BEROWNE TO HIS FRIENDS

6 He hath never fed of the dainties that are bred in a book. He hath not
   eat paper, as it were; he hath not drunk ink: his intellect is not
   replenished.
   Love's Labour's Lost 4.2.23–4, NATHANIEL TO HOLOFERNES, of Dull

7 I smell false Latin.
   Love's Labour's Lost 5.1.74, HOLOFERNES TO ARMADO

8   Those that do teach young babes
   Do it with gentle means and easy tasks.
   Othello 4.2.113–14, DESDEMONA TO IAGO

9 Study what you most affect.
   Taming of the Shrew 1.1.40, TRANIO TO LUCENTIO; 'affect' here means 'enjoy'

10 Th'art a scholar; let us therefore eat and drink.
   Twelfth Night 2.3.13, SIR TOBY BELCH TO SIR ANDREW AGUECHEEK

ELEGIES

1   His legs bestrid the ocean; his reared arm
    Crested the world; his voice was propertied
    As all the tuned spheres, and that to friends;
    But when he meant to quail and shake the orb,
    He was as rattling thunder. For his bounty,
    There was no winter in't: an autumn it was
    That grew the more by reaping. His delights
    Were dolphin-like: they showed his back above
    The element they lived in. In his livery
    Walked crowns and crownets; realms and islands were
    As plates dropped from his pocket.
    Antony and Cleopatra 5.2.81–91, CLEOPATRA, of Antony

2   Now boast thee, Death, in thy possession lies
    A lass unparalleled.
    Antony and Cleopatra 5.2.313–14, CHARMIAN, of Cleopatra

3   Alas, poor Yorick. I knew him, Horatio, a fellow of infinite jest, of most
    excellent fancy.
    Hamlet 5.1.182–3, HAMLET TO HORATIO, looking at Yorick's skull

4   Lay her i'th' earth,
    And from her fair and unpolluted flesh
    May violets spring. I tell thee, churlish priest,
    A minist'ring angel shall my sister be
    When thou liest howling.
    Hamlet 5.1.236–40, LAERTES to the PRIEST burying Ophelia

5   Now cracks a noble heart. Good night, sweet prince,
    And flights of angels sing thee to thy rest.
    Hamlet 5.2.368–9, HORATIO at the death of Hamlet

6   Friends, Romans, countrymen, lend me your ears;
    I come to bury Caesar, not to praise him.
    The evil that men do lives after them,
    The good is oft interred with their bones;
    So let it be with Caesar.
    Julius Caesar 3.2.74–8, MARK ANTONY's oration on the death of Julius Caesar; despite
    his opening claim, this is the first of a sequence of speeches in which he does indeed
    set out to praise Caesar to the skies, and disparage Brutus

7   This was the noblest Roman of them all.
    Julius Caesar 5.5.68, MARK ANTONY, of Brutus

1 Soft you, a word or two before you go.
  I have done the state some service, and they know't:
  No more of that. I pray you, in your letters,
  When you shall these unlucky deeds relate,
  Speak of me as I am. Nothing extenuate,
  Nor set down aught in malice. Then must you speak
  Of one that loved not wisely, but too well;
  Of one not easily jealous, but being wrought,
  Perplexed in the extreme; of one whose hand,
  Like the base Indian, threw a pearl away
  Richer than all his tribe: of one whose subdued eyes,
  Albeit unused to the melting mood,
  Drops tears as fast as the Arabian trees
  Their medicinable gum. Set you down this,
  And say besides that in Aleppo once,
  Where a malignant and a turbaned Turk
  Beat a Venetian, and traduced the state,
  I took by th' throat the circumcised dog
  And smote him – thus!
  Othello 5.2.338–56; OTHELLO kills himself

2 Beauty, truth and rarity,
  Grace in all simplicity,
  Here enclosed, in cinders lie.
  Phoenix and Turtle 53–5

3 If you read this line, remember not
  The hand that writ it.
  Sonnet 71.5–6

4 This ditty does remember my drowned father.
  Tempest 1.2.408, FERDINAND, listening to Ariel's song (*see* **SEA, the**)

5 When he lived, his breath and beauty set
  Gloss on the rose, smell to the violet.
  Venus and Adonis 935–6, VENUS

ELIZABETH I

6 This royal infant (heaven still move about her)
  Though in her cradle, yet now promises
  Upon this land a thousand thousand blessings,
  Which time shall bring to ripeness: she shall be . . .

A pattern to all princes living with her,
And all that shall succeed.
Henry VIII 5.4.17–20, 22–3, CRANMER TO HENRY, of the infant Elizabeth

1   Truth shall nurse her,
Holy and heavenly thoughts still counsel her;
She shall be loved and feared.
Henry VIII 5.4.28–30, CRANMER TO HENRY, of the infant Elizabeth

2 The bird of wonder . . . the maiden phoenix.
Henry VIII 5.4.40, CRANMER TO HENRY, of the infant Elizabeth

EMOTION

3   Give me that man
That is not passion's slave, and I will wear him
In my heart's core, ay, in my heart of heart,
As I do thee.
Hamlet 3.2.72–5, HAMLET TO HORATIO

4 You are not wood, you are not stones, but men.
Julius Caesar 3.2.143, MARK ANTONY whipping up feeling in the plebeians

5 That deep torture may be called a hell,
When more is felt than one hath power to tell.
Lucrece 1287–8

ENDS AND ENDINGS

6 All's well that ends well; still the fine's the crown.
Whate'er the course, the end is the renown.
All's Well That Ends Well 4.4.35–6, HELENA TO DIANA

7 Unarm, Eros. The long day's task is done
And we must sleep.
Antony and Cleopatra 4.14.35–6, ANTONY TO EROS

8 O sun,
Burn the great sphere thou mov'st in! Darkling stand
The varying shore o'th' world!
Antony and Cleopatra 4.15.10–12, CLEOPATRA TO ANTONY

9 That it should come to this!
Hamlet 1.2.137, HAMLET

10 Let the end try the man.
2 Henry IV 2.2.45, PRINCE HAL TO POINS

1 Let time shape, and there an end.
   2 Henry IV 3.2.326–7, FALSTAFF

2 Is this the promised end?
   King Lear 5.3.261, KENT, with Edgar, Albany and Lear

3 So quick bright things come to confusion.
   Midsummer Night's Dream 1.1.149, LYSANDER TO HERMIA (of love)

4   Jack shall have Jill
       Nought shall go ill;
   The man shall have his mare again, and all shall be well.
   Midsummer Night's Dream 3.2.461–3, PUCK, applying the juice of the magic flower (and quoting two proverbs)

5 The true beginning of our end.
   Midsummer Night's Dream 5.1.111, PETER QUINCE in his prologue

6   Now I want
   Spirits to enforce, Art to enchant;
   And my ending is despair.
   Tempest Epilogue 13–15, PROSPERO; *more at* **PRAYER**

7 The end crowns all.
   Troilus and Cressida 4.5.223, HECTOR TO ULYSSES AND ACHILLES

ENEMIES

8   I do believe
   (Induced by potent circumstances) that
   You are mine enemy, and make my challenge
   You shall not be my judge.
   Henry VIII 2.4.74–7, KATHERINE TO WOLSEY

9 I have been feasting with mine enemy.
   Romeo and Juliet 2.3.45, ROMEO TO FRIAR LAURENCE

ENGLAND AND THE ENGLISH

10 HAMLET Why was he sent into England?
   GRAVEDIGGER Why, because a was mad. A shall recover his wits there.
   Or if a do not, 'tis no great matter there.
   HAMLET Why?
   GRAVEDIGGER 'Twill not be seen in him there. There the men are as
   mad as he.
   Hamlet 5.1.148–54

1 O England, model to thy inward greatness,
Like little body with a mighty heart,
What mightst thou do, that honour would thee do,
Were all thy children kind and natural!
Henry V 2.0.16–19, CHORUS

2   On, on, you noble English!
Whose blood is fet from fathers of war-proof
Fathers that like so many Alexanders
Have in these parts from morn till even fought,
And sheathed their swords for lack of argument.
Dishonour not your mothers; now attest
That those whom you called fathers did beget you.
Henry V 3.1.18–24, HENRY TO HIS FORCES

3 Is not their climate foggy, raw and dull?
Henry V 3.5.16, CONSTABLE OF FRANCE TO THE DUKE OF BRITAIN

4 That island of England breeds very valiant creatures: their mastiffs are
of unmatchable courage.
Henry V 3.7.142–3, RAMBURES TO ORLEANS AND THE CONSTABLE OF FRANCE

5 Give them great meals of beef and iron and steel, they will eat like
wolves and fight like devils.
Henry V 3.7.150–2, CONSTABLE OF FRANCE TO RAMBURES AND ORLEANS

6 How are we parked and bounded in a pale –
A little herd of England's timorous deer,
Mazed with a yelping kennel of French curs!
1 Henry VI 4.2.45–7, TALBOT

7 Let us be backed with God and with the seas
Which he hath given for fence impregnable.
3 Henry VI 4.1.42–3, HASTINGS TO MONTAGUE

8   That pale, that white-faced shore,
Whose foot spurns back the ocean's roaring tides.
King John 2.1.23–4, DUKE OF AUSTRIA TO LEWIS, DAUPHIN OF FRANCE

9 This England never did, nor never shall,
Lie at the proud foot of a conqueror.
King John 5.7.112–13, PHILIP THE BASTARD TO PRINCE HENRY

10   Nought shall make us rue
If England to itself do rest but true!
King John 5.7.117–18, PHILIP THE BASTARD TO PRINCE HENRY

1 Where'er I wander boast of this I can,
Though banished, yet a true-born Englishman.
Richard II 1.3.308–9, BOLINGBROKE TO JOHN OF GAUNT

2 This royal throne of kings, this sceptered isle,
This earth of majesty, this seat of Mars,
This other Eden, demi-paradise,
This fortress built by Nature for herself
Against infection and the hand of war,
This happy breed of men, this little world,
This precious stone set in the silver sea,
Which serves it in the office of a wall,
Or as a moat defensive to a house,
Against the envy of less happier lands;
This blessed plot, this earth, this realm, this England.
Richard II 2.1.40–50, JOHN OF GAUNT, on his deathbed, to YORK

3 This nurse, this teeming womb of royal kings.
Richard II 2.1.51, JOHN OF GAUNT, on his deathbed, to YORK

4 England, that was wont to conquer others,
Hath made a shameful conquest of itself.
Richard II 2.1.65–6, JOHN OF GAUNT, on his deathbed, to YORK; *more at* **DECLINE AND FALL**

See also **BRITAIN**

ENNUI

5 Tomorrow, and tomorrow, and tomorrow,
Creeps in this petty pace from day to day.
Macbeth 5.5.19–20, MACBETH, with Seyton

6 Thou wilt needs thrust thy neck into a yoke . . . and sigh away Sundays.
Much Ado About Nothing 1.1.191–2, BENEDICK TO CLAUDIO, on the tedium of the married state

ENTHUSIASM

7 To business that we love we rise betime
And go to't with delight.
Antony and Cleopatra 4.4.20–1, ANTONY TO A SOLDIER

ENVY

8 When envy breeds unkind division:
There comes the ruin, there begins confusion.
1 Henry VI 4.1.193–4, EXETER

1 Desiring this man's art and that man's scope,
With what I most enjoy contented least.
Sonnet 29.7–8

See also **JEALOUSY; RESENTMENT; RIVALRY**

EQUALITY

2   Our bloods,
Of colour, weight, and heat, poured all together,
Would quite confound distinction . . .
                 Good alone is good,
Without a name.
All's Well That Ends Well 2.3.119–21, 129–30, KING OF FRANCE TO BERTRAM
(by 'a name' is meant an honorific title or ancient name)

3 There's place and means for every man alive.
All's Well That Ends Well 4.3.333, PAROLLES

4 We came into the world like brother and brother,
And now let's go hand in hand, not one before another.
Comedy of Errors 5.1.425–6, DROMIO OF EPHESUS TO DROMIO OF SYRACUSE, closing the
play

5 I think the King is but a man, as I am.
Henry V 4.1.101, HENRY, incognito, to MICHAEL WILLIAMS, a soldier; ironically, since
of course he is indeed the King

6 Distribution should undo excess
And each man have enough.
King Lear 4.1.73–4, GLOUCESTER TO EDGAR (whom he does not recognize)

7 Is black so base a hue?
Titus Andronicus 4.2.73, AARON to his child's NURSE

8 The selfsame sun that shines upon his court
Hides not his visage from our cottage, but
Looks on all alike.
Winter's Tale 4.4.446–8, PERDITA TO POLIXENES

See also **HUMANKIND; PEOPLE, the**

EVENTS

9 We see which way the stream of time doth run,
And are enforced from our most quiet there
By the rough torrent of occasion.
2 Henry IV 4.1.70–2, ARCHBISHOP OF YORK TO WESTMORELAND

EVIL

1 It is not, nor it cannot come to good.
   Hamlet 1.2.158, HAMLET

2 The evil that men do lives after them,
   The good is oft interred with their bones.
   Julius Caesar 3.2.76–7, MARK ANTONY TO PLEBEIANS

3 And oftentimes, to win us to our harm,
   The instruments of Darkness tell us truths;
   Win us with honest trifles.
   Macbeth 1.3.123–5, BANQUO TO MACBETH

4 Things bad begun make strong themselves by ill.
   Macbeth 3.2.55, MACBETH TO LADY MACBETH

5 By the pricking of my thumbs,
   Something wicked this way comes.
   Macbeth 4.1.44–5, SECOND WITCH

6 They that touch pitch will be defiled.
   Much Ado About Nothing 3.3.55–6, DOGBERRY TO THE WATCH; proverbial, drawn
   ultimately from Ecclesiastes 13.1

   See also **CRIMES; EVIL DEEDS; EVIL PEOPLE; TYRANNY; WITCHES**

EVIL DEEDS

7 This is no place: this house is but a butchery.
   As You Like It 2.3.27; ADAM warns ORLANDO that his brother means to kill him

8 A deed without a name.
   Macbeth 4.1.49, WITCHES in reply to MACBETH's question 'What is't you do?'

   See also **CRIMES; MURDER; TYRANNY**

EVIL PEOPLE

9 O villain, villain, smiling damned villain!
   My tables. Meet it is I set it down
   That one may smile, and smile, and be a villain.
   Hamlet 1.5.106–8, HAMLET

10   Bloody, bawdy villain!
   Remorseless, treacherous, lecherous, kindless villain!
   Hamlet 2.2.582–3, HAMLET

11 Why, I can smile, and murder whiles I smile.
   3 Henry VI 3.2.182, RICHARD OF GLOUCESTER; *more at* **HYPOCRISY**

1 This gilded serpent.
   King Lear 5.3.85, ALBANY, of his wife Goneril

2 We are but young in deed.
   Macbeth 3.4.143, MACBETH TO LADY MACBETH; there is worse to come

3   Bloody,
   Luxurious, avaricious, false, deceitful,
   Sudden, malicious, smacking of every sin
   That has a name.
   Macbeth 4.3.57–60, MALCOLM TO MACDUFF, of Macbeth

4   Since I cannot prove a lover, . . .
   I am determined to prove a villain.
   Richard III 1.1.28, 30, RICHARD

5 When he fawns, he bites; and when he bites
   His venom tooth will rankle to the death.
   Richard III 1.3.290–1, QUEEN MARGARET TO BUCKINGHAM, of Richard

6 Her life was beastly and devoid of pity.
   Titus Andronicus 5.3.198, LUCIUS, of Tamora

   See also **BAD PEOPLE; RICHARD III; TYRANNY**

EXCESS

7 That was laid on with a trowel.
   As You Like It 1.2.100, CELIA TO TOUCHSTONE

8 To gild refined gold, to paint the lily,
   To throw a perfume on the violet,
   To smooth the ice, or add another hue
   Unto the rainbow, or with taper-light
   To seek the beauteous eye of heaven to garnish,
   Is wasteful and ridiculous excess.
   King John 4.2.11–16, SALISBURY TO PEMBROKE

9   Boundless intemperance
   In nature is a tyranny; it hath been
   Th'untimely emptying of the happy throne,
   And fall of many kings.
   Macbeth 4.3.66–9, MACDUFF TO MALCOLM

10 They are as sick that surfeit with too much, as they that starve with nothing.
   Merchant of Venice 1.2.5–6, NERISSA TO PORTIA

EXCUSES

1 Nay, pray you seek no colour for your going,
  But bid farewell and go.
  Antony and Cleopatra 1.3.33–4, CLEOPATRA TO ANTONY

2 Lay not that flattering unction to your soul.
  Hamlet 3.4.147, HAMLET TO GERTRUDE

3 I must be cruel only to be kind.
  Hamlet 3.4.180, HAMLET TO GERTRUDE

4 Company, villainous company, hath been the spoil of me.
  1 Henry IV 3.3.9–10, FALSTAFF TO BARDOLPH

5 If his cause be wrong, our obedience to the King wipes the crime of it
  out of us.
  Henry V 4.1.129–31, MICHAEL WILLIAMS TO JOHN BATES; the classic excuse of those
  who serve tyrants

6 Oftentimes excusing of a fault
  Doth make the fault the worse by th'excuse.
  King John 4.2.30–1, PEMBROKE TO SALISBURY

7 My business was great, and in such a case as mine a man may strain
  courtesy.
  Romeo and Juliet 2.4.50–1, ROMEO TO MERCUTIO

8 The excuse that thou dost make in this delay
  Is longer than the tale thou dost excuse.
  Romeo and Juliet 2.5.33–4, JULIET TO HER NURSE

9 'I am,' quoth he, 'expected of my friends.'
  Venus and Adonis 718, ADONIS' excuse for trying to leave Venus

10 I will but look upon the hedge and follow you.
  Winter's Tale 4.4.828–9; AUTOLYCUS uses a call of nature as an excuse to escape the
  company of the shepherd and his son, whom he has just cheated

EXILE

11   Our exiled friends abroad
  That fled the snares of watchful tyranny.
  Macbeth 5.9.32–3, MALCOLM TO THANES

12 Save back to England, all the world's my way.
  Richard II 1.3.207, MOWBRAY TO BOLINGBROKE

13 The bitter bread of banishment.
  Richard II 3.1.21, BOLINGBROKE TO BUSHY AND GREENE

EXPECTATION

1   Oft expectation fails, and most oft there
    Where most it promises.
    All's Well That Ends Well 2.1.141–2, HELENA TO THE KING OF FRANCE

2   To mock the expectation of the world.
    2 Henry IV 5.2.126, HENRY V, in his grief and determination on acceding to the
    throne at his father's death

3   Now sits expectation in the air.
    Henry V 2.0.8, CHORUS

EXPERIENCE

4   To have seen much and to have nothing is to have rich eyes and poor
    hands.
    As You Like It 4.1.22–3, ROSALIND TO JAQUES

5   I had rather have a fool to make me merry than experience to make me
    sad, and to travel for it too!
    As You Like It 4.1.25–7, ROSALIND TO JAQUES

6   I talk of that, that know it.
    Coriolanus 3.3.85, BRUTUS TO CORIOLANUS, referring to his service to Rome

7   O woe is me
    T'have seen what I have seen, see what I see.
    Hamlet 3.1.161–2, OPHELIA

8   Experience is by industry achieved,
    And perfected by the swift course of time.
    Two Gentlemen of Verona 1.3.22–3, ANTONIO TO PANTHINO

9   His years but young, but his experience old.
    Two Gentlemen of Verona 2.4.68, VALENTINE TO THE DUKE

F

FACTION

10 Civil dissension is a viperous worm
    That gnaws the bowels of the commonwealth.
    1 Henry VI 3.1.72–3, HENRY TO LORDS

1 Civil blood makes civil hands unclean.
   Romeo and Juliet Prologue 4, CHORUS

   See also **WAR, civil**

FAILURE

2   We are not the first
   Who with best meaning have incurred the worst.
   King Lear 5.3.3–4, CORDELIA TO EDMUND AND LEAR

3 MACBETH   If we should fail?
   LADY MACBETH We fail?
   But screw your courage to the sticking-place,
   And we'll not fail.
   Macbeth 1.7.59–62

4   Th'attempt and not the deed
   Confounds us.
   Macbeth 2.2.10–11, LADY MACBETH, fearing discovery in a failed attempt

5 A greater power than we can contradict
   Hath thwarted our intents.
   Romeo and Juliet 5.3.153–4, FRIAR LAURENCE TO JULIET

6 How my achievements mock me!
   Troilus and Cressida 4.2.71, TROILUS TO AENEAS

FAIRIES

7 They are fairies; he that speaks to them shall die.
   Merry Wives of Windsor 5.5.48, FALSTAFF

8 Fairies use flowers for their charactery.
   Merry Wives of Windsor 5.5.74, MISTRESS QUICKLY to her team of disguised FAIRIES

9 PUCK   How now, spirit! Whither wander you?
   FAIRY   Over hill, over dale,
      Thorough bush, thorough briar,
   Over park, over pale,
      Thorough flood, thorough fire,
   I do wander everywhere,
   Swifter than the moon's sphere;
   And I serve the Fairy Queen,
   To dew her orbs upon the green.
   The cowslips tall her pensioners be,
   In their gold coats spots you see;

Those be rubies, fairy favours,
   In those freckles live their savours.
I must go seek some dew-drops here,
And hang a pearl in every cowslip's ear.
Midsummer Night's Dream 2.1.1–15

1 I am that merry wanderer of the night.
   Midsummer Night's Dream 2.1.43, PUCK TO A FAIRY

2 And never, since the middle summer's spring,
   Met we on hill, in dale, forest or mead,
   By paved fountain, or by rushy brook,
   Or in the beached margent of the sea,
   To dance our ringlets to the whistling wind,
   But with thy brawls thou has disturbed our sport.
   Midsummer Night's Dream 2.1.82–7, TITANIA TO OBERON

3 I know a bank where the wild thyme blows,
   Where oxlips and the nodding violet grows,
   Quite over-canopied with luscious woodbine,
   With sweet musk-roses, and with eglantine.
   There sleeps Titania sometime of the night,
   Lulled in these flowers with dances and delight;
   And there the snake throws her enamelled skin,
   Weed wide enough to wrap a fairy in.
   Midsummer Night's Dream 2.1.249–56, OBERON TO PUCK

4 FIRST FAIRY You spotted snakes with double tongue,
     Thorny hedgehogs, be not seen;
     Newts and blind-worms, do no wrong,
     Come not near our fairy queen.
   CHORUS   Philomel, with melody,
   Sing in our sweet lullaby.
   Midsummer Night's Dream 2.2.9–14

5 Be kind and courteous to this gentleman;
   Hop in his walks, and gambol in his eyes;
   Feed him with apricocks and dewberries,
   With purple grapes, green figs, and mulberries;
   The honey-bags steal from the humble-bees,
   And for night-tapers crop their waxen thighs,
   And light them at the fiery glow-worms' eyes.
   Midsummer Night's Dream 3.1.156–62, TITANIA TO HER ATTENDANTS

1 We fairies, that do run . . .
Following darkness like a dream,
Now are frolic; not a mouse
Shall disturb this hallowed house.
I am sent with broom before
To sweep the dust behind the door.
Midsummer Night's Dream 5.1.377, 380–4, PUCK

2 O then I see Queen Mab hath been with you.
She is the fairies' midwife, and she comes
In shape no bigger than an agate stone
On the forefinger of an alderman,
Drawn with a team of little atomi
Over men's noses as they lie asleep.
Her chariot is an empty hazelnut
Made by the joiner squirrel or old grub,
Time out o' mind the fairies' coachmakers;
Her waggon-spokes made of long spinners' legs,
The cover of the wings of grasshoppers,
Her traces of the smallest spider web,
Her collars of the moonshine's watery beams,
Her whip of cricket's bone, the lash of film,
Her waggoner a small grey-coated gnat,
Not half so big as a round little worm
Pricked from the lazy finger of a maid;
And in this state she gallops night by night
Through lovers' brains, and then they dream of love;
O'er courtiers' knees, that dream on curtsies straight;
O'er lawyers' fingers who straight dream on fees;
O'er ladies' lips, who straight on kisses dream.
Romeo and Juliet 1.4.53–74, MERCUTIO TO ROMEO

3   This is that very Mab
That plaits the manes of horses in the night
And bakes the elf-locks in foul sluttish hairs,
Which, once untangled, much misfortune bodes.
Romeo and Juliet 1.4.88–91, MERCUTIO TO ROMEO

4 Ye elves of hills, brooks, standing lakes, and groves;
And ye that on the sands with printless foot
Do chase the ebbing Neptune, and do fly him
When he comes back; you demi-puppets that

By moonshine do the green sour ringlets make,
Whereof the ewe not bites; and you whose pastime
Is to make midnight mushrooms.
Tempest 5.1.33–9, PROSPERO

1 Where the bee sucks, there suck I:
  In a cowslip's bell I lie;
  There I couch when owls do cry.
  On the bat's back I do fly
  After summer merrily.
  Merrily, merrily shall I live now
  Under the blossom that hangs on the bough.
  Tempest 5.1.88–94, ARIEL's song

See also **MAGIC; SPIRITS**

FAITHFULNESS

2 Play fast and loose with faith.
  King John 3.1.168, PHILIP, KING OF FRANCE, TO CARDINAL PANDULPH

3 'As true as Troilus.'
  Troilus and Cressida 3.2.179, TROILUS telling CRESSIDA how he would like to be remembered; *see also* **INFIDELITY**

FALSTAFF

4 That trunk of humours, that bolting-hutch of beastliness, that swollen parcel of dropsies, that huge bombard of sack, that stuffed cloak-bag of guts, that roasted Manningtree ox with the pudding in his belly, that reverend vice, that grey iniquity, that father ruffian, that vanity in years.
  1 Henry IV 2.4.443–8, PRINCE HAL TO FALSTAFF

5 Banish plump Jack, and banish all the world.
  1 Henry IV 2.4.473–4, FALSTAFF TO PRINCE HAL; Hal replies, 'I do, I will.'

6 I am not only witty in myself, but the cause that wit is in other men.
  2 Henry IV 1.2.9–10, FALSTAFF TO HIS PAGE

7 Jack Falstaff with my familiars, John with my brothers and sisters, and Sir John with all Europe.
  2 Henry IV 2.2.125–7, FALSTAFF signing off a letter to Prince Hal

8 Nay, sure, he's not in hell; he's in Arthur's bosom, if ever man went to Arthur's bosom.
  Henry V 2.3.9–10, HOSTESS QUICKLY; for more from this speech *see* **DEATH**

FAME

1 Too famous to live long.
   1 Henry VI 1.1.6, BEDFORD TO OTHER LORDS

2 Let those who are in favour with their stars
   Of public honour and proud titles boast.
   Sonnet 25.1–2

3 He lives in fame that died in honour's cause.
   Titus Andronicus 1.1.395, MARCUS' AND TITUS' SONS

   See also **FORTUNE; HONOUR; REPUTATION**

FAMILIARITY

4 Sweets grown common lose their dear delight.
   Sonnet 102.12

FAMILY

5 A little more than kin, and less than kind.
   Hamlet 1.2.65, HAMLET's famous equivocating opening remark to his uncle CLAUDIUS

6   Wife and child
   Those precious motives, those strong knots of love.
   Macbeth 4.3.26–7, MALCOLM TO MACDUFF

   See also **CHILDREN; DAUGHTERS; FATHERS; MOTHERS; PARENTS AND CHILDREN**

FAREWELLS

7   Comforted . . .
   That there is this jewel in the world
   That I may see again.
   Cymbeline 1.2.21–3, IMOGEN, parting from her husband POSTHUMUS

8 Good night, ladies, good night. Sweet ladies, good night, good night.
   Hamlet 4.5.72–3, the mad OPHELIA

9 Good night, sweet prince.
   Hamlet 5.2.366, HORATIO; *more at* **ELEGIES**

10 Come, I'll be friends with thee, Jack, thou art going to the wars, and whether I shall ever see thee again or no there is nobody cares.
   2 Henry IV 2.4.63–6, DOLL TEARSHEET TO FALSTAFF

11 So part we sadly in this troublous world,
   To meet with joy in sweet Jerusalem.
   3 Henry VI 5.5.7–8, QUEEN MARGARET TO HER IMPRISONED ALLIES

1 Whether we shall meet again I know not.
  Therefore our everlasting farewell take.
  Julius Caesar 5.1.115–16, Brutus to Cassius

2 The last of all the Romans, fare thee well!
  Julius Caesar 5.3.99, Brutus to Cato

3 Enough: hold, or cut bow-strings.
  Midsummer Night's Dream 1.2.105, Bottom to his companions

4 Give me your hands, if we be friends,
  And Robin shall restore amends.
  Midsummer Night's Dream 5.1.431–2, Puck, closing the play

5 Farewell, thou art too dear for my possessing,
  And like enough thou knowst thy estimate.
  Sonnet 87.1–2

6 As many farewells as be stars in heaven,
  With distinct breath and consigned kisses to them,
  [Time] fumbles up into a loose adieu,
  And scants us with a single famished kiss
  Distasted with the salt of broken tears.
  Troilus and Cressida 4.4.43–7, Troilus to Cressida; *see also* **TIME**

  See also **DISMISSALS; EXCUSES; PARTINGS**

FASHION

7 The soul of this man is his clothes.
  All's Well That Ends Well 2.5.43–4, Lafew to Bertram, of Parolles

8 What's the new news at the new court?
  As You Like It 1.1.94–5, Oliver to Charles, of the usurper Duke Frederick's court

9 Costly thy habit as thy purse can buy,
  But not expressed in fancy; rich, not gaudy,
  For the apparel oft proclaims the man.
  Hamlet 1.3.70–2, Polonius' advice to Laertes (*more at* **ADVICE**)

10 Th'expectancy and rose of the fair state,
   The glass of fashion and the mould of form,
   Th'observed of all observers.
   Hamlet 3.1.153–5, Ophelia describing Hamlet before his apparent madness

11 Fashion's own knight.
   Love's Labour's Lost 1.1.176, Berowne to the King of Navarre, of Armado

1 He wears his faith but as the fashion of his hat, it ever changes with the next block.
Much Ado About Nothing 1.1.71–3, BEATRICE TO A MESSENGER AND LEONATO, of Benedick; 'faith' is faithfulness in friendship

2 The fashion is the fashion.
Much Ado About Nothing 3.3.119, CONRADE TO BORACHIO

3 What a deformed thief this fashion is.
Much Ado About Nothing 3.3.127–8, BORACHIO TO CONRADE

4 The fashion wears out more apparel than the man.
Much Ado About Nothing 3.3.135–6, CONRADE TO BORACHIO

5 See, where she comes apparelled like the spring.
Pericles 1.1.13, PERICLES, of Antiochus' daughter

6 These strange flies, these fashion-mongers, these 'pardon-me's', who stand so much on the new form that they cannot sit at ease on the old bench.
Romeo and Juliet 2.4.33–6, MERCUTIO TO BENVOLIO

7 Old fashions please me best. I am not so nice
To change true rules for odd inventions.
Taming of the Shrew 3.1.78–9, BIANCA TO HORTENSIO

8 What's this? A sleeve? 'Tis like a demi-cannon.
What, up and down, carved like an apple tart?
Taming of the Shrew 4.3.88–9, PETRUCHIO TO A TAILOR AND KATHERINA

9   Sure this robe of mine
Does change my disposition.
Winter's Tale 4.4.134–5, PERDITA TO FLORIZEL; she is dressed as the queen of the sheep-shearing feast

See also **IDOLS**

FATE

10 My fate cries out.
Hamlet 1.4.81, HAMLET TO HORATIO

11 Our wills and fates do so contrary run
That our devices still are overthrown.
Hamlet 3.2.213–14, PLAYER KING TO PLAYER QUEEN

12 Let Hercules himself do what he may,
The cat will mew, and dog will have his day.
Hamlet 5.1.291–2, HAMLET to the company assembled at Ophelia's grave

1 Not a whit. We defy augury. There is special providence in the fall of a
sparrow. If it be now, 'tis not to come; if it be not to come, it will be
now; if it be not now, yet it will come. The readiness is all.
Hamlet 5.2.218–21, HAMLET TO HORATIO (including an impressively long
monosyllabic sentence)

2 O God, that one might read the book of fate,
And see the revolution of the times
Make mountains level, and the continent,
Weary of solid firmness, melt itself
Into the sea, . . .
　　　　　O, if this were seen,
The happiest youth, viewing his progress through,
What perils past, what crosses to ensue,
Would shut the book and sit him down and die.
2 Henry IV 3.1.45–9, 53–6, HENRY TO WARWICK AND SURREY

3 　　　　　It is the stars,
The stars above us govern our conditions.
King Lear 4.3.33–4, A GENTLEMAN TO KENT

4 The wheel is come full circle.
King Lear 5.3.172, EDMUND TO EDGAR

5 Thou marshall'st me the way that I was going.
Macbeth 2.1.42, MACBETH to the dagger

6 Then I defy you, stars!
Romeo and Juliet 5.1.24, ROMEO, with Balthasar

7 I find my zenith doth depend upon
A most auspicious star.
Tempest 1.2.181–2, PROSPERO TO MIRANDA

8 My stars shine darkly over me.
Twelfth Night 2.1.3–4, SEBASTIAN TO ANTONIO

See also **DIVINITY; FORTUNE; JUSTICE; LIFE**

FATHERS

9 I would thou hadst told me of another father.
As You Like It 1.2.219, DUKE FREDERICK TO ORLANDO, on being told that Orlando's
father was an enemy of his

10 For this the foolish over-careful fathers
Have broke their sleep with thoughts,

Their brains with care, their bones with industry.
2 Henry IV 4.5.67–9, HENRY, incensed at his son's apparent thankless greed for the crown

1   'Tis a happy thing
To be the father unto many sons.
3 Henry VI 3.2.104–5, KING EDWARD TO RICHARD OF GLOUCESTER

2   Had he not resembled
My father as he slept, I had done't.
Macbeth 2.2.12–13, LADY MACBETH, on not murdering Duncan

3   He loves us not:
He wants the natural touch.
Macbeth 4.2.8–9, LADY MACDUFF, of Macduff, who has gone into exile leaving his family unprotected

4 MACDUFF He has no children. – All my pretty ones?
Did you say all? – O Hell-kite! – All?
What, all my pretty chickens, and their dam,
At one fell swoop?
MALCOLM Dispute it like a man.
MACDUFF   I shall do so;
But I must also feel it as a man:
I cannot but remember such things were,
That were most precious to me.
Macbeth 4.3.216–23; Macduff shows 'the natural touch' (see above). His wife and children have been murdered by Macbeth's henchmen; 'he' in l. 216 is Malcolm.

5 He shall not knit a knot in his fortunes with the finger of my substance;
if he take her, let him take her simply: the wealth I have waits on my
consent, and my consent goes not that way.
Merry Wives of Windsor 3.2.69–72, PAGE TO THE HOST OF THE GARTER, speaking his mind about Fenton as a potential suitor for his daughter Anne

6 To you your father should be as a god:
One that composed your beauties, yea, and one
To whom you are but as a form in wax
By him imprinted, and within his power
To leave the figure, or disfigure it.

Midsummer Night's Dream 1.1.47–51, THESEUS TO HERMIA

7 Who would be a father?
Othello 1.1.162, BRABANTIO, Desdemona's father, to RODERIGO

See also **CHILDREN; DAUGHTERS; PARENTS AND CHILDREN**

FAULTS

1 Do you smell a fault?
King Lear 1.1.15, GLOUCESTER TO KENT

2 Men's faults do seldom to themselves appear.
Lucrece 633

FEAR

3 In time we hate that which we often fear.
Antony and Cleopatra 1.3.13; CHARMIAN advises CLEOPATRA not to be too cruel to Antony

4   To be furious
Is to be frighted out of fear.
Antony and Cleopatra 3.13.200–1, ANTONY TO CLEOPATRA

5 How now, Horatio? You tremble and look pale.
Hamlet 1.1.56, BARNARDO TO HORATIO, who has just addressed the ghost

6 ALBANY You may fear too far.
GONERIL Safer than trust too far.
King Lear 1.4.321–2

7 Extreme fear can neither fight nor fly.
Lucrece 230

8 To be thus is nothing, but to be safely thus.
Macbeth 3.1.47, MACBETH; he continues 'Our fears in Banquo / Stick deep'

9 I am cabined, cribbed, confined, bound in
To saucy doubts and fears.
Macbeth 3.4.23–4, MACBETH TO A MURDERER

10   Thou shalt not live;
That I may tell pale-hearted fear it lies,
And sleep in spite of thunder.
Macbeth 4.1.84–6, MACBETH, vowing to kill Macduff

11 Be not afraid of shadows.
Richard III 5.3.216, RATCLIFFE TO RICHARD, after his dream and before the battle of Bosworth

12 I have a faint cold fear thrills through my veins
That almost freezes up the heat of life.
Romeo and Juliet 4.3.15–16, JULIET

See also **ANXIETY; FOREBODING; IMAGINATION; MISGIVINGS**

FIGHTING

1 As two spent swimmers, that do cling together
  And choke their art.
  Macbeth 1.2.8–9, CAPTAIN describing a close-fought battle to DUNCAN and MALCOLM

2   So they
  Doubly redoubled strokes upon the foe:
  Except they meant to bathe in reeking wounds,
  Or memorize another Golgotha,
  I cannot tell.
  Macbeth 1.2.38–42, CAPTAIN TO DUNCAN

3 Point against point, rebellious arm 'gainst arm,
  Curbing his lavish spirit.
  Macbeth 1.2.57–8, ROSSE TO DUNCAN, describing Macbeth's struggle with the King of Norway

4   I have no words;
  My voice is in my sword.
  Macbeth 5.8.6–7, MACDUFF TO MACBETH

5   Lay on, Macduff;
  And damned be him that first cries, 'Hold, enough!'
  Macbeth 5.8.33–4, MACBETH TO MACDUFF

See also **QUARRELS; SOLDIERS; WAR**

FLATTERY

6   Why should the poor be flattered?
  No, let the candied tongue lick absurd pomp,
  And crook the pregnant hinges of the knee
  Where thrift may follow fawning.
  Hamlet 3.2.60–3, HAMLET TO HORATIO

7 This might be my Lord Such-a-one, that praised my Lord Such-a-one's horse when a meant to beg it.
  Hamlet 5.1.83–6, HAMLET TO HORATIO, examining skulls in the graveyard

8 To dance attendance on their lordships' pleasures.
  Henry VIII 5.2.30, HENRY TO DOCTOR BUTTS

9 When I tell him he hates flatterers,
  He says he does, being then most flattered.
  Julius Caesar 2.1.207–8, DECIUS TO FELLOW CONSPIRATORS, of Julius Caesar

1 That which melteth fools – I mean sweet words,
  Low-crooked curtsies, and base spaniel fawning.
  Julius Caesar 3.1.42–3, JULIUS CAESAR TO THE SENATE

2   To deliver
  Sweet, sweet, sweet poison for the age's tooth.
  King John 1.1.212–13, PHILIP THE BASTARD

3 Better thus, and known to be contemned
  Than still contemned and flattered.
  King Lear 4.1.1–2, EDGAR, disguised as Poor Tom

4 Flattery is the bellows blows up sin.
  Pericles 1.2.40, HELICANUS TO PERICLES AND TWO LORDS

5 A thousand flatterers sit within thy crown,
  Whose compass is no bigger than thy head.
  Richard II 2.1.100–1, JOHN OF GAUNT TO RICHARD

6 He that loves to be flattered is worthy o'th' flatterer.
  Timon of Athens 1.1.229–30, APEMANTUS TO A POET AND TIMON

7 O that men's ears should be
  To counsel deaf, but not to flattery.
  Timon of Athens 1.2.256–7, APEMANTUS TO TIMON

8 When the means are gone that buy this praise,
  The breath is gone whereof this praise is made.
  Timon of Athens 2.2.174–5, STEWARD TO TIMON

  See also **COURTIERS**

FLIRTATION AND SEDUCTION

9 She knew her distance and did angle for me,
  Madding my eagerness with her restraint,
  As all impediments in fancy's course
  Are motives of more fancy.
  All's Well That Ends Well 5.3.212–15, BERTRAM TO THE KING OF FRANCE

10 Tricks he hath had in him, which gentlemen have . . . He did love her,
   sir as a gentleman loves a woman . . . He loved her, sir, and loved her
   not.
   All's Well That Ends Well 5.3.239–48 (extracts), PAROLLES TO THE KING OF FRANCE, of
   Bertram

1 CHARMIAN In each thing give him way; cross him in nothing.
CLEOPATRA Thou teachest like a fool, the way to lose him.
Antony and Cleopatra 1.3.10–11

2   O times!
I laughed him out of patience, and that night
I laughed him into patience, and next morn,
Ere the ninth hour, I drunk him to his bed.
Antony and Cleopatra 2.5.18–21, CLEOPATRA TO CHARMIAN

3 I spy entertainment in her: she discourses, she carves, she gives the leer
of invitation.
Merry Wives of Windsor 1.3.42–3, FALSTAFF TO PISTOL, of Mistress Ford

4 There's language in her eye, her cheek, her lip –
Nay, her foot speaks; her wanton spirits look out
At every joint and motive of her body.
Troilus and Cressida 4.5.55–7, ULYSSES TO THE GREEK PRINCES, of Cressida

FLOWERS AND PLANTS

5   And winking Mary-buds begin to ope their golden eyes.
Cymbeline 2.3.24, song

6 A violet in the youth of primy nature,
Forward, not permanent, sweet, not lasting.
Hamlet 1.3.7–8, LAERTES TO OPHELIA, warning her to treat Hamlet's love to her with
caution

7 There's rosemary, that's for remembrance – pray you, love, remember.
And there is pansies, that's for thoughts . . . There's fennel for you, and
columbines. There's rue for you. And here's some for me. We may call
it herb of grace a Sundays. You must wear your rue with a difference.
There's a daisy. I would give you some violets, but they withered all
when my father died . . . For bonny sweet Robin is all my joy.
Hamlet 4.5.173–5, 178–84, OPHELIA distributing flowers in her madness

8 There is a willow grows askant the brook
That shows his hoary leaves in the glassy stream.
Therewith fantastic garlands did she make
Of crow-flowers, nettles, daisies, and long purples,
That liberal shepherds give a grosser name,
But our cold maids do dead men's fingers call them.
Hamlet 4.7.166–71, GERTRUDE TO LAERTES, describing the mad Ophelia; for the rest of
this speech *see* **DEATH**

1 Sweets to the sweet.
Hamlet 5.1.241, GERTRUDE scattering flowers on Ophelia's grave

2 As mad as the vexed sea, singing aloud,
Crowned with rank fumiter and furrow-weeds,
With burdocks, hemlock, nettles, cuckoo-flowers,
Darnel and all the idle weeds that grow
In our sustaining corn.
King Lear 4.4.2–6, CORDELIA describing Lear, in his madness, to a GENTLEMAN

3 When daisies pied and violets blue
    And lady-smocks all silver-white
    And cuckoo-buds of yellow hue
        Do paint the meadows with delight.
Love's Labour's Lost 5.2.887–90, song; *more at* **INFIDELITY; WINTER**

4 Yet marked I where the bolt of Cupid fell:
It fell upon a little western flower,
Before milk-white, now purple with love's wound:
And maidens call it 'love-in-idleness'.
Midsummer Night's Dream 2.1.165–8, OBERON TO PUCK

5 I know a bank where the wild thyme blows,
Where oxlips and the nodding violet grows,
Quite over-canopied with luscious woodbine,
With sweet musk-roses, and with eglantine.
Midsummer Night's Dream 2.1.249–52, OBERON TO PUCK; *more at* **FAIRIES**

6 Rough winds do shake the darling buds of May.
Sonnet 18.3; *more at* **SUMMER**

7 The rose looks fair, but fairer we it deem
For that sweet odour which doth in it live.
Sonnet 54.3–4

8 Primrose, first-born child of Ver,
Merry springtime's harbinger,
        With harebells dim.
    Oxlips in their cradles growing,
    Marigolds on deathbeds blowing,
        Lark's-heels trim.
Two Noble Kinsmen 1.1.7–12, BOY, singing

9 Fair flowers that are not gathered in their prime
Rot, and consume themselves in little time.
Venus and Adonis 131–2; a commonplace

1   For you, there's rosemary, and rue; these keep
    Seeming and savour all the winter long.
    Winter's Tale 4.4.74–5, PERDITA TO CAMILLO AND POLIXENES in disguise

2   The fairest flowers o'th' season
    Are our carnations and streaked gillyvors.
    Winter's Tale 4.4.81–2, PERDITA TO CAMILLO AND POLIXENES in disguise

3   Here's flowers for you:
    Hot lavender, mints, savory, marjoram,
    The marigold, that goes to bed wi'th' sun
    And with him rises, weeping.
    Winter's Tale 4.4.103–6, PERDITA TO CAMILLO AND POLIXENES in disguise

4   O Proserpina,
    For the flowers now that, frighted, thou let'st fall
    From Dis's waggon!
    Winter's Tale 4.4.116–18, PERDITA TO FLORIZEL

5   Daffodils,
    That come before the swallow dares, and take
    The winds of March with beauty.
    Winter's Tale 4.4.118–20, PERDITA TO FLORIZEL

6   Violets, dim,
    But sweeter than the lids of Juno's eyes
    Or Cytherea's breath; pale primroses,
    That die unmarried, ere they can behold
    Bright Phoebus in his strength . . .
                bold oxlips and
    The crown imperial; lilies of all kinds,
    The flower-de-luce being one.
    Winter's Tale 4.4.120–7, PERDITA TO FLORIZEL

See also **FAIRIES; NAMES; SPRING**

FOOD

7   Tie up the libertine in a field of feasts,
    Keep his brain fuming; Epicurean cooks
    Sharpen with cloyless sauce his appetite.
    Antony and Cleopatra 2.1.23–5, POMPEY TO MENAS

8   Eight wild boars roasted whole at a breakfast, and but twelve persons
    there. Is this true?
    Antony and Cleopatra 2.2.189–90, MAECENAS TO ENOBARBUS

1 This is not yet an Alexandrian feast.
Antony and Cleopatra 2.7.95, POMPEY TO COMPANIONS

2 Unquiet meals make ill digestions.
Comedy of Errors 5.1.74, ABBESS TO ADRIANA, her daughter-in-law

3   Sweetness, whereof a little
More than a little is by much too much.
1 Henry IV 3.2.72–3, KING HENRY to his son PRINCE HAL

4 He hath eaten me out of house and home.
2 Henry IV 2.1.74, HOSTESS QUICKLY TO THE LORD CHIEF JUSTICE, in her attempt to have Falstaff arrested

5 Now, good digestion wait on appetite,
And health on both!
Macbeth 3.4.37–8, MACBETH, just before the appearance of Banquo's ghost

6 I will make an end of my dinner; there's pippins and cheese to come.
Merry Wives of Windsor 1.2.11–12, EVANS TO SIMPLE

7 He is a very valiant trencher-man; he hath an excellent stomach.
Much Ado About Nothing 1.1.49–50, BEATRICE, of Benedick

8 The daintiest last, to make the end most sweet.
Richard II 1.3.68, BOLINGBROKE TO RICHARD

9 Things sweet to taste prove in digestion sour.
Richard II 1.3.236, JOHN OF GAUNT TO RICHARD

10 'Tis an ill cook that cannot lick his own fingers.
Romeo and Juliet 4.2.6–7, SERVANT TO CAPULET

11 I am a great eater of beef, and I believe that does harm to my wit.
Twelfth Night 1.3.84–5, SIR ANDREW AGUECHEEK TO SIR TOBY BELCH AND MARIA

12 Though the chameleon Love can feed on the air, I am one that am nourished by my victuals; and would fain have meat.
Two Gentlemen of Verona 2.1.167–9, SPEED TO VALENTINE

13 I must have saffron to colour the warden pies; mace; dates, none – that's out of my note; nutmegs, seven; a race or two of ginger, but that I may beg; four pound of prunes, and as many of raisins o'th' sun.
Winter's Tale 4.3.45–9; the SHEPHERD'S SON goes over his shopping list

See also **DRINKING; HOSPITALITY AND PARTIES**

FOOLS AND FOOLISHNESS

1   I met a fool i'th' forest,
A motley fool.
As You Like It 2.7.12–13, JAQUES TO DUKE SENIOR

2 LEAR Dost thou call me fool, boy?
 FOOL All thy other titles thou hast given away; that thou wast born with.
King Lear 1.4.141–3

3 Better a witty fool than a foolish wit.
Twelfth Night 1.5.34–5, FESTE TO OLIVIA

4 There is no slander in an allowed fool, though he do nothing but rail.
Twelfth Night 1.5.90–2, OLIVIA TO FESTE

5 This fellow is wise enough to play the fool
Twelfth Night 3.1.60, VIOLA, of Feste

FOREBODING

6 The blood weeps from my heart when I do shape
In forms imaginary th'unguided days
And rotten times that you shall look upon
When I am sleeping with my ancestors.
2 Henry IV 4.4.58–61, HENRY to his son THOMAS, DUKE OF CLARENCE

7 O God, I have an ill-divining soul!
Romeo and Juliet 3.5.54, JULIET TO ROMEO

See also **MISGIVINGS; OMENS AND PORTENTS**

FORGETFULNESS

8 Second childishness and mere oblivion.
As You Like It 2.7.165, the state of extreme old age; from JAQUES's 'Seven Ages of Man' speech to DUKE SENIOR AND HIS COMPANIONS in the Forest of Arden

9 And then, sir, does a this – a does – what was I about to say? By the mass, I was about to say something. Where did I leave?
Hamlet 2.1.50–3, POLONIUS TO REYNALDO

10 What we do determine, oft we break.
Purpose is but the slave to memory.
Hamlet 3.2.189–90, PLAYER KING TO PLAYER QUEEN

11 Old men forget.
Henry V 4.3.49, HENRY TO WESTMORLAND; *more at* **WAR**

FORGIVENESS

1 Pray you now, forget and forgive; I am old and foolish.
King Lear 4.7.83–4, LEAR TO CORDELIA

2 Let's purge this choler without letting blood . . .
Deep malice makes too deep incision.
Forget, forgive, conclude and be agreed.
Richard II 1.1.153, 155–6, RICHARD TO MOWBRAY AND BOLINGBROKE

FORTITUDE

3   Blow, wind! come, wrack!
At least we'll die with harness on our back.
Macbeth 5.5.51–2, MACBETH TO SEYTON AND A MESSENGER

FORTUNE

4   My fortunes have
Corrupted honest men!
Antony and Cleopatra 4.5.16–17, ANTONY TO A SOLDIER

5   'Tis paltry to be Caesar.
Not being Fortune, he's but Fortune's knave.
Antony and Cleopatra 5.2.2–3, CLEOPATRA TO HER COMPANIONS

6 In the secret parts of Fortune? O most true, she is a strumpet.
Hamlet 2.2.235–6, HAMLET TO ROSENCRANTZ AND GUILDENSTERN

7 The slings and arrows of outrageous fortune.
Hamlet 3.1.58, HAMLET; *more at* **SUICIDE**

8 A man that Fortune's buffets and rewards
Hast ta'en with equal thanks.
Hamlet 3.2.68–9, HAMLET complimenting HORATIO

9   Blest are those
Whose blood and judgment are so well commeddled
That they are not a pipe for Fortune's finger
To sound what stop she please.
Hamlet 3.2.69–72, HAMLET TO HORATIO

10 The great man down, you mark his favourite flies;
The poor advanced makes friends of enemies.
Hamlet 3.2.206–7, PLAYER KING TO PLAYER QUEEN

1 Ill blows the wind that profits nobody.
   3 Henry VI 2.5.55, A SON who has killed a man but not yet realized that his victim is his father; proverbial

2   Yield not thy neck
   To Fortune's yoke, but let thy dauntless mind
   Still ride in triumph over all mischance.
   3 Henry VI 3.3.16–18, KING LEWIS OF FRANCE TO QUEEN MARGARET

3 He comes upon a wish. Fortune is merry
   And in this mood will give us anything.
   Julius Caesar 3.2.267–8, MARK ANTONY TO A SERVANT

4 The times conspire with you.
   King John 3.3.146, CARDINAL PANDULPH TO LEWIS, DAUPHIN OF FRANCE

5 A good man's fortune may grow out at heels.
   King Lear 2.2.158, KENT TO LEAR

6 Fortune, good night: smile once more; turn thy wheel.
   King Lear 2.2.174, KENT

7 Fortune, that arrant whore,
   Ne'er turns the key to the poor.
   King Lear 2.2.245–6, FOOL

8 Fortune, on his damned quarrel smiling,
   Showed like a rebel's whore.
   Macbeth 1.2.14–15, CAPTAIN TO DUNCAN AND MALCOLM, reporting a battle

9 Some rise by sin, and some by virtue fall.
   Measure for Measure 2.1.38, ESCALUS TO ANGELO

10 Fortune thy foe.
   Merry Wives of Windsor 3.3.61, FALSTAFF TO MISTRESS FORD

11 O, I am fortune's fool.
   Romeo and Juliet 3.1.137, ROMEO TO BENVOLIO

   See also **CHANCE; FATE; LUCK**

FRANCE AND THE FRENCH

12 My thoughts and wishes bend again toward France.
   Hamlet 1.2.55, LAERTES TO CLAUDIUS

13   This best garden of the world,
   Our fertile France.
   Henry V 5.2.36–7, BURGUNDY TO THE KING AND QUEEN OF FRANCE

1 Done like a Frenchman!
1 Henry VI 3.3.85, PUCELLE (JOAN OF ARC), commenting unfavourably on Burgundy's behaviour in defeat; she continues 'Turn and turn again.'

2   Remember where we are:
In France, amongst a fickle wavering nation.
1 Henry VI 4.1.137–8, HENRY TO LORDS

FREEDOM

3   I must have liberty
Withal, as large a charter as the wind,
To blow on whom I please.
As You Like It 2.7.47–9, JAQUES's plea for freedom of speech

4 I had as lief not be as live to be
In awe of such a thing as I myself.
I was born free as Caesar; so were you.
Julius Caesar 1.2.94–6, CASSIUS TO BRUTUS

5 Every bondman in his own hand bears
The power to cancel his captivity.
Julius Caesar 1.3.101–2, CASCA TO CASSIUS; even a slave can take his own life

6 Liberty! Freedom! Tyranny is dead!
Julius Caesar 3.1.78, CINNA's cry on the death of Julius Caesar

7 Who is here so base, that would be a bondman?
Julius Caesar 3.2.29–30, BRUTUS' speech on the death of Julius Caesar

8   'Ban, 'Ban, Cacaliban
    Has a new master: – get a new man.
Freedom, high-day! high-day, freedom! freedom, high-day, freedom!
Tempest 2.2.182–5, CALIBAN

9   To the elements
Be free, and fare thou well!
Tempest 5.1.320–1, PROSPERO's farewell to ARIEL

See also **REBELLION AND REVOLUTION**

FRIENDS AND FRIENDSHIP

10   Keep thy friend
Under thy own life's key.
All's Well That Ends Well 1.1.65–6, COUNTESS OF ROSSILLION TO BERTRAM; *more at* **ADVICE**

1 Those friends thou hast, and their adoption tried,
Grapple them unto thy soul with hoops of steel.
Hamlet 1.3.62–3, POLONIUS TO LAERTES; *more at* **ADVICE**

2 Since my dear soul was mistress of her choice
And could of men distinguish her election,
Sh'ath sealed thee for herself.
Hamlet 3.2.64–6, HAMLET TO HORATIO

3 I could have better spared a better man.
1 Henry IV 5.4.103, PRINCE HAL, mistakenly thinking Falstaff has been killed in battle

4 A friend should bear his friend's infirmities.
Julius Caesar 4.3.85, CASSIUS TO BRUTUS

5 I see, lady, the gentleman is not in your books.
Much Ado About Nothing 1.1.74–5, MESSENGER's response to BEATRICE

6 Friendship is constant in all other things
Save in the office and affairs of love.
Much Ado About Nothing 2.1.166–7, CLAUDIO

7 I count myself in nothing else so happy
As in a soul remembering my good friends.
Richard II 2.3.46–7, BOLINGBROKE TO PERCY

8   I would not wish
Any companion in the world but you.
Tempest 3.1.54–5, MIRANDA TO FERDINAND

FRIENDS, false

9   My two schoolfellows,
Whom I will trust as I will adders fanged.
Hamlet 3.4.204–5, HAMLET TO GERTRUDE, of Rosencrantz and Guildenstern

FUTURE, the

10 We know what we are, but know not what we may be.
Hamlet 4.5.43–4, the mad OPHELIA

11 There are many events in the womb of time, which will be delivered.
Othello 1.3.369–70, IAGO TO RODERIGO

12   The prophetic soul
Of the wide world, dreaming on things to come.
Sonnet 107.1–2

1   You should have feared false times when you did feast.
    Timon of Athens 4.3.516, STEWARD TO TIMON

    See also **PROPHECIES; TOMORROW; UNCERTAINTY**

GARDENS AND GARDENING

2   'Tis an unweeded garden
  That grows to seed; things rank and gross in nature
  Possess it merely.
  Hamlet 1.2.135–7, HAMLET's view of the world

3   Do not spread the compost on the weeds
  To make them ranker.
  Hamlet 3.4.153–4, HAMLET TO GERTRUDE

4   Most subject is the fattest soil to weeds.
  2 Henry IV 4.4.54, HENRY to his son THOMAS, DUKE OF CLARENCE, referring to his
  other son Prince Hal, who, 'the noble image of my youth, / Is overspread with them'

5   Covering discretion with a coat of folly,
  As gardeners do with ordure hide those roots
  That shall first spring and be most delicate.
  Henry V 2.4.39–41, CONSTABLE OF FRANCE TO THE DAUPHIN

6   Now 'tis the spring, and weeds are shallow-rooted;
  Suffer them now, and they'll o'ergrow the garden,
  And choke the herbs for want of husbandry.
  2 Henry VI 3.1.31–3, QUEEN MARGARET TO HENRY

7   Adam was a gardener.
  2 Henry VI 4.2.129, JACK CADE TO STAFFORD AND HIS BROTHER

8   Our bodies are gardens, to the which our wills are gardeners.
  Othello 1.3.322–3, IAGO TO RODERIGO

9   Our sea-walled garden, the whole land,
  Is full of weeds, her fairest flowers choked up,
  Her fruit-trees all unpruned, her hedges ruined,

Her knots disordered, and her wholesome herbs
Swarming with caterpillars.
Richard II 3.4.43–7, GARDENER'S MAN TO THE GARDENER

1   Superfluous branches
We lop away, that bearing boughs may live.
Richard II 3.4.63–4, GARDENER TO HIS MAN

2 Small herbs have grace, great weeds do grow apace.
Richard III 2.4.13, the boy DUKE OF YORK reports his uncle Richard's ominous remark on his rapid growth to his MOTHER and GRANDMOTHER

See also **ECOLOGY**

GENDER

3 I could find in my heart to disgrace my man's apparel and to cry like a woman. But I must comfort the weaker vessel, as doublet and hose ought to show itself courageous to petticoat.
As You Like It 2.4.4–7, ROSALIND TO TOUCHSTONE AND CELIA

4 Alas the day, what shall I do with my doublet and hose?
As You Like It 3.2.216–17, ROSALIND, in love with Orlando but dressed as a man

5 It is not the fashion to see the lady the epilogue; but it is no more unhandsome than to see the lord the prologue.
As You Like It 5.4.197–9, ROSALIND

6 A woman's face with nature's own hand painted
Hast thou, the master mistress of my passion.
Sonnets 20.1–2

See also **MEN AND WOMEN**

GENETICS

7 How hard it is to hide the sparks of Nature!
Cymbeline 3.3.79, BELARIUS, of the royal brothers Guiderius and Arviragus, brought up as peasants

8 So, oft it chances in particular men
That for some vicious mole of nature in them,
As in their birth, wherein they are not guilty
(Since nature cannot choose his origin),
By their o'ergrowth of some complexion,
Oft breaking down the pales and forts of reason,
Or by some habit, that too much o'erleavens
The form of plausive manners – that these men,

Carrying, I say, the stamp of one defect,
Being Nature's livery or Fortune's star,
His virtues else, be they as pure as grace,
As infinite as man may undergo,
Shall in the general censure take corruption
From that particular fault.
Hamlet 1.4.23–36, HAMLET TO HORATIO

1 If I chance to talk a little wild, forgive me;
   I had it from my father.
   Henry VIII 1.4.26–7, LORD SANDS TO ANNE BULLEN (BOLEYN)

2 A devil, a born devil, on whose nature
   Nurture can never stick.
   Tempest 4.1.188–9, PROSPERO's view of Caliban

GHOSTS *see* APPARITIONS

GIFTS AND GIVING

3 Rich gifts wax poor when givers prove unkind.
   Hamlet 3.1.101, OPHELIA returning Hamlet's gifts

4   Dost thou not wish in heart
   The chain were longer and the letter shorter?
   Love's Labour's Lost 5.2.55–6, PRINCESS OF FRANCE TO MARIA, who has been sent a
   pearl necklace with a letter

5 My good will is great, though the gift small.
   Pericles 3.4.17, THAISA TO CERIMON

6 I am not in the giving vein today.
   Richard III 4.2.116, RICHARD, losing himself an ally in Buckingham

7 He's the very soul of bounty.
   Timon of Athens 1.2.212, A LORD, of Timon

GIRLS

8 An unlessoned girl, unschooled, unpractised,
   Happy in this, she is not yet so old
   But she may learn.
   Merchant of Venice 3.2.159–61, PORTIA, TO BASSANIO, of herself

9 In maiden meditation, fancy-free.
   Midsummer Night's Dream 2.1.164, OBERON TO PUCK (of the moon goddess)

1 She was a vixen when she went to school.
Midsummer Night's Dream 3.2.324, HELENA TO DEMETRIUS AND LYSANDER, of Hermia

2 What pushes are we wenches driven to
When fifteen once has found us!
Two Noble Kinsmen 2.4.6–7, JAILER'S DAUGHTER

GOD

3 This all lies within the will of God.
Henry V 1.2.290, HENRY TO HIS COURT AND AMBASSADORS

4 We are in God's hand, brother, not in theirs.
Henry V 3.6.170, HENRY TO GLOUCESTER, 'they' being the French army at Agincourt

5 O God, thy arm was here.
Henry V 4.8.105, HENRY, giving thanks for the unlooked-for survival of his officers
and men at Agincourt

6 God is our fortress.
1 Henry VI 2.1.26, TALBOT TO LORDS; an echo of several biblical references

7 God defend the right!
2 Henry VI 2.3.55, HENRY TO HIS COURT

8 He was the author, thou the instrument.
3 Henry VI 4.6.18, HENRY TO WARWICK

9 God, the widow's champion and defence.
Richard II 1.2.43, JOHN OF GAUNT TO THE DUCHESS OF GLOUCESTER

GOOD AND GOODNESS

10 I never did repent for doing good,
Nor shall not now.
Merchant of Venice 3.4.10–11, PORTIA TO LORENZO

11 That light we see is burning in my hall.
How far that little candle throws his beams!
So shines a good deed in a naughty world.
Merchant of Venice 5.1.89–91, PORTIA TO NERISSA

See also **VIRTUE**

GOOD INTENTIONS

12 I have not kept my square, but that to come
Shall all be done by th' rule.
Antony and Cleopatra 2.3.6–7, ANTONY TO OCTAVIA

GOOD NEWS *see* **NEWS, good**

GOOD TIMES

1 If sack and sugar be a fault, God help the wicked! If to be old and merry be a sin, then many an old host that I know is damned.
1 Henry IV 2.4.464–6, FALSTAFF TO PRINCE HAL

2 Now stand you on the top of happy hours.
Sonnet 16.5

3 Dost thou think because thou art virtuous, there shall be no more cakes and ale?
Twelfth Night 2.3.113–14, SIR TOBY BELCH TO MALVOLIO

4 Not to be abed after midnight, is to be up betimes.
Twelfth Night 2.3.1–2, SIR TOBY BELCH TO SIR ANDREW AGUECHEEK

See also **EASY LIFE; OLD TIMES**

GRAFFITI

5 These trees shall be my books,
And in their barks my thoughts I'll character.
As You Like It 3.2.5–6, ORLANDO

GRAVES

6 With wild wood-leaves and weeds I ha' strewed his grave
And on it said a century of prayers.
Cymbeline 4.2.390–1, IMOGEN TO LUCIUS

7 There is no ancient gentlemen but gardeners, ditchers, and grave-makers – they hold up Adam's profession.
Hamlet 5.1.29–31, ONE GRAVEDIGGER TO ANOTHER

8 The houses he makes last till doomsday.
Hamlet 5.1.59, ONE GRAVEDIGGER TO ANOTHER, of his profession

9 Gaunt am I for the grave, gaunt as a grave.
Richard II 2.1.82, JOHN OF GAUNT TO RICHARD

10 A little little grave, an obscure grave.
Richard II 3.3.154, RICHARD TO AUMERLE

11 Here lies Juliet, and her beauty makes
This vault a feasting presence, full of light.
Romeo and Juliet 5.3.86, ROMEO

1 The earth can yield me but a common grave.
   Sonnet 81.7

2 Lie where the light foam of the sea may beat
   Thy grave-stone daily.
   Timon of Athens 4.3.381–2, TIMON TO APEMANTUS

GREATNESS

3 Give me my robe. Put on my crown. I have
   Immortal longings in me.
   Antony and Cleopatra 5.2.278–9, CLEOPATRA, at her death

4 I have touched the highest point of all my greatness,
   And from that full meridian of my glory
   I haste now to my setting. I shall fall
   Like a bright exhalation in the evening,
   And no man see me more.
   Henry VIII 3.2.223–7, CARDINAL WOLSEY; Shakespeare's contribution to this co-authored play came at the close of his career

5 Farewell? A long farewell to all my greatness.
   This is the state of man; to-day he puts forth
   The tender leaves of hopes, to-morrow blossoms,
   And bears his blushing honours thick upon him:
   The third day comes a frost, a killing frost,
   And when he thinks, good easy man, full surely
   His greatness is a-ripening, nips his root,
   And then he falls as I do. I have ventured
   Like little wanton boys that swim on bladders,
   This many summers in a sea of glory,
   But far beyond my depth: my high-blown pride
   At length broke under me, and now has left me,
   Weary and old with service, to the mercy
   Of a rude stream that must for ever hide me.
   Vain pomp and glory of this world, I hate ye;
   I feel my heart new opened. O how wretched
   Is that poor man that hangs on princes' favours!
   There is betwixt that smile we would aspire to,
   That sweet aspect of princes, and their ruin,
   More pangs and fears than wars or women have;
   And when he falls, he falls like Lucifer,
   Never to hope again.
   Henry VIII 3.2.351–72, CARDINAL WOLSEY

1 Be not afraid of greatness. Some are born great, some achieve greatness, and some have greatness thrust upon 'em.
Twelfth Night 2.5.139–41; MALVOLIO reads the anonymous letter which he believes is from Olivia

See also **JULIUS CAESAR; KINGSHIP AND RULE; TRANSIENCE**

GREED

2 Sweep on you fat and greasy citizens.
As You Like It 2.1.55, JAQUES's reported address to a herd of deer

3   See, sons, what things you are,
How quickly nature falls into revolt
When gold becomes her object.
2 Henry IV 4.5.64–6, HENRY TO HIS SONS THE DUKES OF GLOUCESTER AND CLARENCE

4 THIRD FISHERMAN I marvel how the fishes live in the sea.
FIRST FISHERMAN Why, as men do a-land: the great ones eat up the little ones.
Pericles 2.1.26–9

GREETINGS

5 FIRST WITCH All hail, Macbeth! hail to thee, Thane of Glamis!
SECOND WITCH All hail, Macbeth! hail to thee, Thane of Cawdor!
THIRD WITCH All hail, Macbeth! that shalt be King hereafter.
Macbeth 1.3.48–50

6 Knock, knock, knock. Who's there, i'th' name of Belzebub?
Macbeth 2.3.3–4, PORTER

7 ISABELLA What hoa! Peace here; grace and good company!
PROVOST Who's there? Come in; the wish deserves a welcome
Measure for Measure 3.1.44–5

8 Where are these lads? Where are these hearts?
Midsummer Night's Dream 4.2.25, BOTTOM hearing his friends approach

9 BOLINGBROKE My gracious uncle –
YORK Grace me no grace, nor uncle me no uncle.
Richard II 2.3.85–6

10 To thee no star be dark!
Two Noble Kinsmen 1.4.1, FIRST QUEEN TO TWO OTHERS

11   Welcome hither,
As is the spring to th'earth.
Winter's Tale 5.1.150–1, LEONTES TO FLORIZEL AND PERDITA

GRIEF

1 Moderate lamentation is the right of the dead; excessive grief the enemy to the living.
All's Well That Ends Well 1.1.54–5, LAFEW TO HELENA

2   To persever
In obstinate condolement is a course
Of impious stubbornness, 'tis unmanly grief,
It shows a will most incorrect to heaven,
A heart unfortified, a mind impatient,
An understanding simple and unschooled.
Hamlet 1.2.92–7, CLAUDIUS lectures HAMLET

3 This is the poison of deep grief.
Hamlet 4.5.75, CLAUDIUS, of Ophelia when she has gone mad

4 Honest plain words best pierce the ear of grief.
Love's Labour's Lost 5.2.746, BEROWNE TO THE PRINCESS OF FRANCE

5   Wild,
Like an unpractised swimmer plunging still,
With too much labour drowns for want of skill.
Lucrece 1097–9

6 Every one can master a grief but he that has it.
Much Ado About Nothing 3.2.26–7, BENEDICK TO LEONATO

7 Grief makes one hour ten.
Richard II 1.3.261, BOLINGBROKE TO JOHN OF GAUNT

8 You may my glories and my state depose,
But not my griefs, still I am king of those.
Richard II 4.1.192–3, RICHARD TO BOLINGBROKE

9 Day doth daily draw my sorrows longer,
And night doth nightly make grief's length seem stronger.
Sonnet 28.13–14

10   He's something stained
With grief (that's beauty's canker).
Tempest 1.2.417–18, PROSPERO TO MIRANDA

11   O, grief and time,
Fearful consumers, you will all devour!
Two Noble Kinsmen 1.1.69–70, THESEUS TO FIRST QUEEN

1 Extremity, that sharpens sundry wits,
  Makes me a fool.
  Two Noble Kinsmen 1.1.118–19, THIRD QUEEN TO EMILIA

2   What's gone and what's past help
  Should be past grief.
  Winter's Tale 3.2.220–1, PAULINA TO A LORD

  See also **ELEGIES; FATHERS; GRIEF, expressions of; SORROW**

GRIEF, expressions of

3 I have that within which passes show,
  These but the trappings and the suits of woe.
  Hamlet 1.2.85–6, HAMLET TO GERTRUDE

4 O, pardon me, thou bleeding piece of earth,
  That I am meek and gentle with these butchers.
  Thou art the ruins of the noblest man
  That ever lived in the tide of times.
  Woe to the hand that shed this costly blood!
  Julius Caesar 3.1.254–8, MARK ANTONY mourning Julius Caesar

5 My heart is in the coffin there with Caesar.
  Julius Caesar 3.2.107, MARK ANTONY's oration on the death of Julius Caesar

6 I will instruct my sorrows to be proud,
  For grief is proud an't makes his owner stoop.
  King John 2.2.68–9, CONSTANCE TO SALISBURY

7 Grief fills the room up of my absent child,
  Lies in his bed, walks up and down with me,
  Puts on his pretty looks, repeats his words,
  Remembers me of all his gracious parts,
  Stuffs out his vacant garments with his form.
  King John 3.3.93–7, CONSTANCE TO PHILIP, KING OF FRANCE, AND CARDINAL PANDULPH

8 My old heart is cracked, it's cracked.
  King Lear 2.1.90, GLOUCESTER TO REGAN

9   Better I were distract;
  So should my thoughts be severed from my griefs,
  And woes by wrong imaginations lose
  The knowledge of themselves.
  King Lear 4.6.275–8, GLOUCESTER

1 Howl, howl, howl, howl! O, you are men of stones!
  Had I your tongues and eyes, I'd use them so
  That heaven's vault should crack: she's gone for ever.
  King Lear 5.3.255–7, LEAR, carrying the dead Cordelia

2 And my poor fool is hanged. No, no, no life!
  Why should a dog, a horse, a rat have life
  And thou no breath at all?
  King Lear 5.3.304–6, LEAR TO ALBANY, EDGAR AND KENT

3 I was a journeyman to grief.
  Richard II 1.3.274, BOLINGBROKE TO JOHN OF GAUNT

4   My grief lies all within,
  And these external manners of lament
  Are merely shadows to the unseen grief
  That swells with silence in the tortured soul.
  Richard II 4.1.295–8, RICHARD TO BOLINGBROKE

5 Cry, Trojans, cry.
  Troilus and Cressida 2.2.98, CASSANDRA, foreseeing Troy's fate

6   Cease; thou know'st
  He dies to me again, when talked of.
  Winter's Tale 5.1.118–19, LEONTES TO PAULINA, of his son Mamillius

  See also **ELEGIES**

GUILT

7 And then it started like a guilty thing
  Upon a fearful summons.
  Hamlet 1.1.153–4, HORATIO TO BARNARDO AND MARCELLUS, of the ghost

8   Leave her to heaven,
  And to those thorns that in her bosom lodge
  To prick and sting her.
  Hamlet 1.5.86–8, GHOST TO HAMLET

9 You were sent for, and there is a kind of confession in your looks,
  which your modesties have not craft enough to colour.
  Hamlet 2.2.280–2, HAMLET TO ROSENCRANTZ AND GUILDENSTERN

10 The lady doth protest too much, methinks.
  Hamlet 3.2.232, GERTRUDE TO HAMLET, of the Player Queen in the dumb show

11 What, frighted with false fire?
  Hamlet 3.2.268, HAMLET, of Claudius' reaction to the dumb show

1   O, my offence is rank, it smells to heaven;
    It hath the primal eldest curse upon't –
    A brother's murder.
    Hamlet 3.3.36–8, CLAUDIUS

2   Suspicion always haunts the guilty mind.
    3 Henry VI 5.6.11, RICHARD OF GLOUCESTER TO KING HENRY; he means that a guilty
    person always suspects a trap and fears discovery

3   One cried, 'God bless us!' and, 'Amen,' the other,
    As they had seen me with these hangman's hands.
    Macbeth 2.2.26–7, MACBETH TO LADY MACBETH

4   These deeds must not be thought
    After these ways: so, it will make us mad.
    Macbeth 2.2.32–3, LADY MACBETH TO MACBETH

5   Condemn the fault, and not the actor of it?
    Why, every fault's condemned ere it be done.
    Measure for Measure 2.2.37–8, ANGELO TO ISABELLA

6   They that set you on
    To do this deed will hate you for the deed.
    Richard III 1.4.251–2; CLARENCE tries to dissuade his MURDERERS from their task

7   All several sins, all used in each degree,
    Throng to the bar, crying all, 'Guilty, guilty!'
    Richard III 5.3.199–200, RICHARD, finally a prey to guilt

    See also **BLOOD; CRIMES; MURDER**

GULLIBILITY

8   The Moor is of a free and open nature
    That thinks men honest that but seem to be so,
    And will as tenderly be led by th' nose
    As asses are.
    Othello 1.3.397–400, IAGO, of Othello

9   They'll take suggestion as a cat laps milk.
    Tempest 2.1.289, ANTONIO TO SEBASTIAN

❧ H ❧

HABIT

1   Refrain tonight,
And that shall lend a kind of easiness
To the next abstinence, the next more easy;
For use almost can change the stamp of nature.
Hamlet 3.4.167–70, HAMLET TO GERTRUDE

2 HAMLET Has this fellow no feeling of his business a sings in grave-making?
HORATIO Custom hath made it in him a property of easiness.
Hamlet 5.1.65–8

3 How use doth breed a habit in a man!
Two Gentlemen of Verona 5.4.1, VALENTINE

See also **CUSTOM**

HAIR

4 There's many a man hath more hair than wit.
Comedy of Errors 2.2.81–2, ANTIPHOLUS OF SYRACUSE TO DROMIO OF SYRACUSE

5 Thou canst not say, I did it: never shake
Thy gory locks at me.
Macbeth 3.4.49–50, MACBETH TO BANQUO'S GHOST

6 I am such a tender ass, if my hair do but tickle me, I must scratch.
Midsummer Night's Dream 4.1.25–6, BOTTOM, wearing the ass's head, to Titania's FAIRIES

HAPPINESS

7 Happy man be his dole.
1 Henry IV 2.2.76, FALSTAFF; proverbial, meaning 'good luck to you', or, more literally, 'may his fortune be that of a happy man'. Also in *Taming of the Shrew* 1.1.138, HORTENSIO TO GREMIO, and *Winter's Tale* 1.2.163, LEONTES TO MAMILLIUS.

8 As merry as crickets.
1 Henry IV 2.4.88, POINS TO PRINCE HAL

1 As merry as the day is long.
   Much Ado About Nothing 2.1.45, BEATRICE TO LEONATO; *also in King John* 4.1.17, the
   boy ARTHUR, imprisoned, to HUBERT; *more at* **SINGLE LIFE, the**

2 Silence is the perfectest herald of joy; I were but little happy, if I could
   say how much.
   Much Ado About Nothing 2.1.288–9, CLAUDIO TO BEATRICE

3 There was a star danced, and under that was I born.
   Much Ado About Nothing 2.1.316, BEATRICE TO DON PEDRO

4   If it were now to die
   'Twere now to be most happy, for I fear
   My soul hath her content so absolute
   That not another comfort, like to this
   Succeeds in unknown fate.
   Othello 2.1.187–91, OTHELLO TO DESDEMONA

5 Happiness courts thee in her best array.
   Romeo and Juliet 3.3.142, FRIAR LAURENCE TO ROMEO

   See also **CONTENTMENT; HUMBLE LIFE; JOY; MERRIMENT; PRISON**

HARDSHIP

6 Plenty and peace breeds cowards: hardness ever
   Of hardiness is mother.
   Cymbeline 3.6.21–2, IMOGEN

HASTE

7 O most wicked speed! To post
   With such dexterity to incestuous sheets!
   It is not, nor it cannot come to good.
   Hamlet 1.2.156–8, HAMLET

8 Not so hot!
   King Lear 5.3.67, GONERIL to her rival REGAN

9 But yet I run before my horse to market.
   Richard III 1.1.160, RICHARD

10 It is too rash, too unadvised, too sudden,
   Too like the lightning, which doth cease to be
   Ere one can say 'It lightens'.
   Romeo and Juliet 2.2.118–20, JULIET TO ROMEO, of their love

11 Wisely and slow; they stumble that run fast.
   Romeo and Juliet 2.3.90, FRIAR LAURENCE TO ROMEO

1 Who cannot condemn rashness in cold blood?
   Timon of Athens 3.5.55, ALCIBIADES TO TWO SENATORS

   See also **MARRIAGE; SPEED**

HATRED

2 In time we hate that which we often fear.
   Antony and Cleopatra 1.3.13; CHARMIAN advises CLEOPATRA not to be too cruel to
   Antony

3 How like a fawning publican he looks!
   I hate him for he is a Christian . . .
   He hates our sacred nation, and he rails . . .
   On me, my bargains, and my well-won thrift,
   Which he calls interest: cursed be my tribe
   If I forgive him!
   Merchant of Venice 1.3.39–40, 46, 48–50, SHYLOCK

4 Deep malice makes too deep incision.
   Richard II 1.1.155, RICHARD to the bitterly quarrelling MOWBRAY and BOLINGBROKE, on
   the dangers of hatred

5 I have sworn thee fair, and thought thee bright,
   Who art as black as hell, as dark as night.
   Sonnet 147.13–14

6 Hate all, curse all, show charity to none.
   Timon of Athens 4.3.530, TIMON TO HIS STEWARD

HELEN OF TROY

7 A Grecian queen, whose youth and freshness
   Wrinkles Apollo's, and makes stale the morning.
   Troilus and Cressida 2.2.79–80, TROILUS TO HECTOR

8   Why, she is a pearl
   Whose price hath launched above a thousand ships.
   Troilus and Cressida 2.2.82–3, TROILUS TO HECTOR; Shakespeare quotes his
   contemporary, Christopher Marlowe, in *Doctor Faustus* (5.1.107): 'Was this the face
   that launched a thousand ships?'

9 For every false drop in her bawdy veins
   A Grecian's life hath sunk.
   Troilus and Cressida 4.1.70–1, DIOMEDES TO PARIS

HELL

10 The flow'ry way that leads to the broad gate and the great fire.
   All's Well That Ends Well 4.5.53–4, CLOWN

1 I had thought to have let in some of all professions, that go the
primrose way to th'everlasting bonfire.
Macbeth 2.3.17–19, PORTER

2 Whip me, ye devils,
From the possession of this heavenly sight!
Blow me about in winds, roast me in sulphur,
Wash me in steep-down gulfs of liquid fire!
Othello 5.2.277–80, OTHELLO, at Desdemona's deathbed

3 Avaunt, thou dreadful minister of hell!
Richard III 1.2.46, ANNE TO RICHARD

HENRY V

4 I know you all, and will awhile uphold
The unyoked humour of your idleness.
Yet herein will I imitate the sun,
Who doth permit the base contagious clouds
To smother up his beauty from the world,
That, when he please again to be himself,
Being wanted he may be more wondered at
By breaking through the foul and ugly mists
Of vapours that did seem to strangle him.
1 Henry IV 1.2.190–8, PRINCE HAL, speaking of his low-life companions, but looking
into the future

5 They take it already upon their salvation, that though I be but Prince
of Wales, yet I am the king of courtesy, and tell me flatly I am no
proud Jack like Falstaff, but a Corinthian, a lad of mettle, a good
boy (by the Lord, so they call me!), and when I am King of England
I shall command all the good lads in Eastcheap.
1 Henry IV 2.4.8–14, PRINCE HAL TO POINS

6 The nimble-footed madcap Prince of Wales.
1 Henry IV 4.1.95, HOTSPUR TO VERNON

7 I saw young Harry with his beaver on,
His cushes on his thighs, gallantly armed,
Rise from the ground like feathered Mercury,
And vaulted with such ease into his seat
As if an angel dropped down from the clouds
To turn and wind a fiery Pegasus,
And witch the world with noble horsemanship.
1 Henry IV 4.1.104–10, VERNON TO HOTSPUR

1 The mirror of all Christian kings.
Henry V 2.0.6, CHORUS

2 A little touch of Harry in the night.
Henry V 4.0.47, CHORUS; Henry walks amongst his troops before the battle of Agincourt

3 Henry the Fifth, too famous to live long.
1 Henry VI 1.1.6, BEDFORD TO OTHER LORDS

HISTORY

4 There is a history in all men's lives
Figuring the nature of the times deceased;
The which observed, a man may prophesy,
With a near aim, of the main chance of things
As yet not come to life.
2 Henry IV 3.1.80–4, WARWICK TO HENRY

5 The chronicle of wasted time.
Sonnet 106.1

6 ORSINO   And what's her history?
VIOLA A blank, my lord: she never told her love.
Twelfth Night 2.4.110–11; *more at* **LOVE**

HOLIDAYS

7 If all the year were playing holidays,
To sport would be as tedious as to work;
But when they seldom come, they wished-for come.
1 Henry IV 1.2.199–201, PRINCE HAL

8 Therefore are feasts so solemn and so rare,
Since seldom coming in the long year set,
Like stones of worth they thinly placed are,
Or captain jewels in the carcanet.
Sonnet 52.5–8

HONESTY

9 Speak to me home; mince not the general tongue;
Name Cleopatra as she is called in Rome.
Antony and Cleopatra 1.2.109–10, ANTONY TO A MESSENGER

10   To plainness honour's bound
When majesty falls to folly.
King Lear 1.1.149–50, KENT TO LEAR

1 I can keep honest counsel, ride, run, mar a curious tale in telling it and
   deliver a plain message bluntly.
   King Lear 1.4.32–4, KENT TO LEAR

2   Where I could not be honest
   I never yet was valiant.
   King Lear 5.1.23–4, ALBANY TO EDMUND AND REGAN

3 The weight of this sad time we must obey,
   Speak what we feel, not what we ought to say.
   King Lear 5.3.322–3, EDGAR

4 What his heart thinks his tongue speaks.
   Much Ado About Nothing 3.2.13, DON PEDRO TO CLAUDIO, of Benedick

5 Men should be what they seem.
   Othello 3.3.129, IAGO TO OTHELLO

6 To be direct and honest is not safe.
   Othello 3.3.381, IAGO TO OTHELLO, with a different view of one of his favourite topics

7 Every man has his fault, and honesty is his.
   Timon of Athens 3.1.29–30, LUCULLUS TO FLAMINIUS

8 Ha, ha! what a fool Honesty is!
   Winter's Tale 4.4.597, AUTOLYCUS, who sets no store by it himself

9 Though I am not naturally honest, I am so sometimes by chance.
   Winter's Tale 4.4.714–15, AUTOLYCUS

   See also **APPEARANCES; HYPOCRISY**

HONOUR

10   Honours thrive
   When rather from our acts we them derive
   Than our foregoers.
   All's Well That Ends Well 2.3.136–8, KING OF FRANCE TO BERTRAM; our 'foregoers' are
   our forebears

11 'Tis not my profit that does lead mine honour;
   Mine honour, it.
   Antony and Cleopatra 2.7.76–7, POMPEY TO MENAS

12   If I lose mine honour,
   I lose myself.
   Antony and Cleopatra 3.4.22–3, ANTONY TO OCTAVIA

1   Rightly to be great
Is not to stir without great argument,
But greatly to find quarrel in a straw
When honour's at the stake.
Hamlet 4.4.53–6, HAMLET

2 By heaven, methinks it were an easy leap
To pluck bright honour from the pale-faced moon.
1 Henry IV 1.3.199–200, HOTSPUR TO NORTHUMBERLAND

3 Can honour set to a leg? No. Or an arm? No. Or take away the grief of
a wound? No. Honour hath no skill in surgery then? No. What is
honour? A word. What is in that word honour? What is that honour?
Air. A trim reckoning! Who hath it? He that died a-Wednesday. Doth
he feel it? No. Doth he hear it? No. 'Tis insensible, then? Yea, to the
dead. But will it not live with the living? No. Why? Detraction will not
suffer it. Therefore I'll none of it. Honour is a mere scutcheon – and so
ends my catechism.
1 Henry IV 5.1.131–41, FALSTAFF TO PRINCE HAL

4 The fewer men, the greater share of honour.
Henry V 4.3.22, HENRY TO WESTMORLAND

5 If it be a sin to covet honour
I am the most offending soul alive.
Henry V 4.3.28–9, HENRY TO WESTMORLAND

6 A load [that] would sink a navy, too much honour.
Henry VIII 3.2.383, CARDINAL WOLSEY to his rival CROMWELL, claiming to be relieved
at his own fall

7   I love
The name of honour more than I fear death.
Julius Caesar 1.2.87–8, BRUTUS TO CASSIUS

8 Honour is the subject of my story.
Julius Caesar 1.2.91, CASSIUS TO BRUTUS

9 For Brutus is an honourable man,
So are they all, all honourable men.
Julius Caesar 3.2.83–4, MARK ANTONY's oration on the death of Julius Caesar

10 As jewels lose their glory if neglected,
So princes their renowns if not respected.
Pericles 2.2.12–13, SIMONIDES TO THAISA

1 Take honour from me, and my life is done.
   Richard II 1.1.183, MOWBRAY TO RICHARD

2 High sparks of honour in thee have I seen.
   Richard II 5.6.29, BOLINGBROKE TO PERCY

3   Take the instant way;
   For honour travels in a strait so narrow
   Where one but goes abreast.
   Troilus and Cressida 3.3.153–5, ULYSSES TO ACHILLES

   See also **EQUALITY; FAME; PERSEVERANCE; REPUTATION**

HOPE

4 The tender leaves of hopes.
   Henry VIII 3.2.353, CARDINAL WOLSEY

5 The miserable have no other medicine
   But only hope.
   Measure for Measure 3.1.2–3, CLAUDIO TO THE DUKE disguised as a friar

6 Cozening Hope – he is a flatterer,
   A parasite, a keeper-back of Death,
   Who gently would dissolve the bands of life,
   Which false Hope lingers in extremity.
   Richard II 2.2.69–72, QUEEN ISABEL TO BUSHY

HORSES

7 O happy horse, to bear the weight of Antony!
   Antony and Cleopatra 1.5.22, CLEOPATRA TO CHARMIAN; later in the scene Antony's
   horse is described as 'an arm-gaunt steed' (1.5.50)

8 For O, for O, the hobby-horse is forgot.
   Hamlet 3.2.137, HAMLET TO OPHELIA; a popular refrain expressing lament – the hobby
   horse was a figure from morris dancing. This phrase also occurs at *Love's Labour's
   Lost* 3.1.28–9.

9 Hollow pampered jades of Asia,
   Which cannot go but thirty mile a day.
   2 Henry IV 2.4.162–3, PISTOL TO HOSTESS QUICKLY AND BARDOLPH; Pistol parodies
   Christopher Marlowe's famous description of Tamburlaine urging on the captive
   kings who drag his chariot – 'Holla, ye pampered jades of Asia! / What, can ye draw
   but twenty miles a day?'

10 When I bestride him, I soar, I am a hawk. He trots the air. The earth
   sings when he touches it; . . . he is pure air and fire . . . It is the prince
   of palfreys.
   Henry V 3.7.15–16, 21, 27, DAUPHIN TO THE CONSTABLE OF FRANCE

1 I had rather have my horse to my mistress.
Henry V 3.7.58–9, DAUPHIN TO THE CONSTABLE OF FRANCE

2 Duncan's horses . . .
Beauteous and swift, the minions of their race,
Turned wild in nature, broke their stalls, flung out,
Contending 'gainst obedience, as they would make
War with mankind.
Macbeth 2.4.14–18, ROSSE TO AN OLD MAN

3 He doth nothing but talk of his horse.
Merchant of Venice 1.2.39–40, PORTIA TO NERISSA, of one of her suitors

4 Rode he on Barbary?
Richard II 5.5.81, RICHARD TO A GROOM, of his rival Bolingbroke riding his favourite horse

5 A horse! A horse! My kingdom for a horse!
Richard III 5.4.7 and 13, RICHARD at the battle of Bosworth

6 His horse hipped – with an old mothy saddle and stirrups of no kindred – besides, possessed with the glanders and like to mose in the chine, troubled with the lampass, infected with the fashions, full of windgalls, sped with spavins, rayed with the yellows, past cure of the fives, stark spoiled with the staggers, begnawn with the bots, swayed in the back and shoulder-shotten, near-legged before, and with a half-cheeked bit and a headstall of sheep's leather, which, being restrained to keep him from stumbling, hath been often burst and new-repaired with knots; one girth six times pieced, and a woman's crupper of velure, which hath two letters for her name fairly set down in studs, and here and there pieced with pack-thread.
Taming of the Shrew 3.2.48–62, BIONDELLO TO TRANIO AND BAPTISTA, describing the horse on which Petruchio arrives for his wedding

7 Round-hoofed, short-jointed, fetlocks shag and long,
Broad breast, full eye, small head, and nostril wide,
High crest, short ears, straight legs and passing strong,
Thin mane, thick tail, broad buttock, tender hide.
Venus and Adonis 295–8; a superior horse

8 The colt that's backed and burdened being young,
Loseth his pride, and never waxeth strong.
Venus and Adonis 419–20

See also **DISORDER; HENRY V**

HOSPITALITY AND PARTIES

1   Come,
Let's have one other gaudy night. Call to me
All my sad captains. Fill our bowls once more.
Let's mock the midnight bell.
Antony and Cleopatra 3.13.187–90, ANTONY TO CLEOPATRA

2 Small cheer and great welcome makes a merry feast.
Comedy of Errors 3.1.26, BALTHASAR TO ANTIPHOLUS OF EPHESUS

3 What! in our house?
Macbeth 2.3.86; LADY MACBETH expresses horror at the murder of Duncan

4 Ourself will mingle with society,
And play the humble host.
Macbeth 3.4.3–4, MACBETH TO LORDS

5 Mirth becomes a feast.
Pericles 2.3.7, SIMONIDES TO HIS KNIGHTS ('becomes' meaning 'suits' or 'graces')

6 At my poor house look to behold this night
Earth-treading stars that make dark heaven light.
Romeo and Juliet 1.2.24–5, CAPULET TO PARIS

7 Madam, the guests are come, supper served up, you called, my young
lady asked for, the Nurse cursed in the pantry, and everything in
extremity.
Romeo and Juliet 1.3.100–3, SERVINGMAN TO LADY CAPULET

8   A fashionable host
That slightly shakes his parting guest by th' hand,
And with his arms out-stretched, as he would fly,
Grasps in the comer.
Troilus and Cressida 3.3.165–8, ULYSSES TO ACHILLES, making a comparison with
Time

See also **DRINKING; FOOD; HOLIDAYS**

HUMAN FRAILTY

9 So it should be that none but Antony
Should conquer Antony.
Antony and Cleopatra 4.15.17–18, CLEOPATRA TO ANTONY

10 Frailty, thy name is woman.
Hamlet 1.2.146, HAMLET

1
>   We are all men,
> In our own natures frail, and capable
> Of our flesh; few are angels.

Henry VIII 5.2.44–6, LORD CHANCELLOR TO CRANMER AND GARDINER

2 We are all frail.

Measure for Measure 2.4.121, ANGELO TO ISABELLA

3
> Sometimes we are devils to ourselves,
> When we will tempt the frailty of our powers.

Troilus and Cressida 4.4.93–4, TROILUS TO CRESSIDA

HUMANKIND

4 What piece of work is a man, how noble in reason, how infinite in faculties, in form and moving how express and admirable, in action how like an angel, in apprehension how like a god: the beauty of the world, the paragon of animals – and yet, to me, what is this quintessence of dust? Man delights not me – nor woman neither, though by your smiling you seem to say so.

Hamlet 2.2.305–12, HAMLET TO ROSENCRANTZ AND GUILDENSTERN (the more familiar version in the First Folio begins 'What a piece of work . . .'; *more at* **DEPRESSION**)

5
>   What is a man
> If his chief good and market of his time
> Be but to sleep and feed?

Hamlet 4.4.33–5, HAMLET; *more at* **REASON AND UNREASON**

6 Is man no more than this?

King Lear 3.4.101–2, LEAR considering Edgar in his disguise as Poor Tom

7 Thou art the thing itself. Unaccommodated man is no more but such a poor, bare, forked animal as thou art.

King Lear 3.4.105–7, LEAR considering Edgar in his disguise as Poor Tom

8
>   But man, proud man,
> Dressed in a little brief authority,
> Most ignorant of what he's most assured –
> His glassy essence – like an angry ape
> Plays such fantastic tricks before high heaven
> As makes the angels weep.

Measure for Measure 2.2.118–23, ISABELLA TO ANGELO

9 But, stay, I smell a man of middle earth!

Merry Wives of Windsor 5.5.81, EVANS, disguised as a fairy, of Falstaff

1   Lord, what fools these mortals be!
    Midsummer Night's Dream 3.2.115, PUCK TO OBERON

2   NURSE What a man are you?
    ROMEO One . . . that God hath made, himself to mar.
    Romeo and Juliet 2.4.113–15

3   What have we here? a man or a fish? dead or alive?
    Tempest 2.2.24–5, TRINCULO, finding Caliban

4   O, wonder!
    How many goodly creatures are there here!
    How beauteous mankind is! O brave new world,
    That has such people in 't!
    Tempest 5.1.181–4, MIRANDA TO HER FRIENDS

5   One touch of nature makes the whole world kin.
    Troilus and Cressida 3.3.175, ULYSSES TO ACHILLES

6   As we are men,
    Thus should we do; being sensually subdued,
    We lose our human title.
    Two Noble Kinsmen 1.1.231–3, THESEUS TO THE THREE QUEENS

HUMBLE LIFE

7   Doth it not show vilely in me to desire small beer? . . . But indeed, these
    humble considerations make me out of love with greatness.
    2 Henry IV 2.2.5–6, 11–12, PRINCE HAL TO POINS

8   Gives not the hawthorn bush a sweeter shade
    To shepherds looking on their silly sheep,
    Than doth a rich embroidered canopy
    To kings that fear their subjects' treachery?
    3 Henry VI 2.5.42–5, HENRY

9   'Tis better to be lowly born,
    And range with humble livers in content,
    Than to be perked up in a glist'ring grief
    And wear a golden sorrow.
    Henry VIII 2.3.19–22, ANNE BULLEN (BOLEYN) TO HER COMPANION

10   The blessedness of being little.
    Henry VIII 4.2.66, GRIFFITH, an usher, to KATHERINE OF ARAGON

11   Home-keeping youth have ever homely wits.
    Two Gentlemen of Verona 1.1.2, VALENTINE TO PROTEUS

HUMILITY

1   She is not yet so old
But she may learn.
Merchant of Venice 3.2.160–1, PORTIA TO BASSANIO

2 Happy are they that hear their detractions and can put them to mending.
Much Ado About Nothing 2.3.220–1, BENEDICK

HUNTING

3 The game is up.
Cymbeline 3.3.107, BELARIUS; the phrase originally meant that the hunt was starting. An alternative version of this – 'The game's afoot' – occurs at *Henry V* 3.1.32, at the close of Henry's speech before Harfleur.

4 My love shall hear the music of my hounds.
Uncouple in the western valley; let them go.
Midsummer Night's Dream 4.1.105–6, THESEUS TO ATTENDANTS

5 The hunt is up, the morn is bright and grey,
The fields are fragrant and the woods are green.
Titus Andronicus 2.1.1–2, TITUS TO HIS SONS

HUSBANDS AND WIVES

6 'Tis but the shadow of a wife you see;
The name and not the thing.
All's Well That Ends Well 5.3.306–7, HELENA TO THE KING OF FRANCE

7 What, says the married woman you may go?
Antony and Cleopatra 1.3.21, CLEOPATRA railing against ANTONY's attachment to his wife

8 The third o'th' world is yours, which with a snaffle
You may pace easy, but not such a wife.
Antony and Cleopatra 2.2.68, ANTONY TO JULIUS CAESAR, referring to his own wife Fulvia

9 The fittest time to corrupt a man's wife is when she's fallen out with her husband.
Coriolanus 4.3.32–3, NICANOR TO ADRIAN (implying that the same holds for public affairs)

10   So loving to my mother
That he might not beteem the winds of heaven
Visit her face too roughly.
Hamlet 1.2.140–2, HAMLET, of his parents; *see also* SEX AND LUST

1 I would your highness would depart the field:
   The Queen hath best success when you are absent.
   3 Henry VI 2.2.73–4, A MESSENGER TO HENRY, in the presence of Queen Margaret, a
   striking example of a tyrannical wife of a man in power

2   Am I your self
   But, as it were, in sort or limitation,
   To keep with you at meals, comfort your bed,
   And talk to you sometimes? Dwell I but in the suburbs
   Of your good pleasure? If it be no more,
   Portia is Brutus' harlot, not his wife.
   Julius Caesar 2.1.282–7, PORTIA TO BRUTUS

3 You are my true and honourable wife.
   Julius Caesar 2.1.288, BRUTUS' reply

4 My dearest partner of greatness.
   Macbeth 1.5.10, MACBETH TO LADY MACBETH, in a letter

5 The Thane of Fife had a wife: where is she now?
   Macbeth 5.1.43–4, LADY MACBETH

6 I crave no other, nor no better man.
   Measure for Measure 5.1.423, MARIANA, turning down the idea of an alternative
   husband to the disgraced Angelo

7 A light wife doth make a heavy husband.
   Merchant of Venice 5.1.130, PORTIA TO BASSANIO

8 I will rather trust a Fleming with my butter, Parson Hugh the
   Welshman with my cheese, an Irishman with my aqua-vitae bottle, or
   a thief to walk my ambling gelding, than my wife with herself.
   Merry Wives of Windsor 2.2.291–5, FORD

9 Wives may be merry and yet honest too.
   Merry Wives of Windsor 4.2.99, MISTRESS PAGE TO MISTRESS FORD: the wives' reply

10 Our great captain's captain.
   Othello 2.1.74, CASSIO TO MONTANO, of Desdemona

11 Our general's wife is now the general.
   Othello 2.3.304–5, IAGO TO CASSIO

12   Let husbands know
   Their wives have sense like them: they see, and smell,
   And have their palates both for sweet and sour
   As husbands have. What is it that they do

When they change us for others? Is it sport?
I think it is. And doth affection breed it?
I think it doth. Is't frailty that thus errs?
It is so too. And have not we affections?
Desires for sport? and frailty, as men have?
Then let them use us well: else let them know,
The ills we do, their ills instruct us so.
Othello 4.3.92–102, EMILIA TO DESDEMONA

1 I am he am born to tame you, Kate,
And bring you from a wild Kate to a Kate
Conformable as other household Kates.
Taming of the Shrew 2.1.270–2, PETRUCHIO TO KATE (punning on 'cat')

2 I will be master of what is mine own.
She is my goods, my chattels, she is my house,
My household stuff, my field, my barn,
My horse, my ox, my ass, my any thing.
Taming of the Shrew 3.2.228–31, PETRUCHIO, on marriage

3 Thy husband is thy lord, thy life, thy keeper,
Thy head, thy sovereign; one that cares for thee.
Taming of the Shrew 5.2.147–8, KATHERINA to assembled HUSBANDS and WIVES

4 Such duty as the subject owes the prince
Even such a woman oweth to her husband.
Taming of the Shrew 5.2.156–7, KATHERINA to assembled HUSBANDS and WIVES

5 Fools are as like husbands as pilchards are to herrings, the husband's the bigger.
Twelfth Night 3.1.34–6, FESTE TO VIOLA

See also **MARRIAGE; MEN AND WOMEN**

HYPOCRISY

6 Do not as some ungracious pastors do,
Show me the steep and thorny way to heaven,
Whiles like a puffed and reckless libertine
Himself the primrose path of dalliance treads,
And recks not his own rede.
Hamlet 1.3.47–51, OPHELIA TO LAERTES

1   With devotion's visage
And pious action we do sugar o'er
The devil himself.
Hamlet 3.1.47–9, POLONIUS TO OPHELIA

2 Why, I can smile, and murder whiles I smile,
And cry 'Content!' to that that grieves my heart,
And wet my cheeks with artificial tears,
And frame my face to all occasions.
3 Henry VI 3.2.182–5, RICHARD OF GLOUCESTER

3 Thou, rascal beadle, hold thy bloody hand;
Why dost thou lash that whore? Strip thine own back,
Thou hotly lusts to use her in that kind
For which thou whipp'st her.
King Lear 4.6.156–9, LEAR TO GLOUCESTER

4 False face must hide what the false heart doth know.
Macbeth 1.7.83, MACBETH TO LADY MACBETH

5 To show an unfelt sorrow is an office
Which the false man does easy.
Macbeth 2.3.136–7, MALCOLM TO DONALBAIN

6 Out on thee, seeming!
Much Ado About Nothing 4.1.55, CLAUDIO TO HERO

7 Thus I clothe my naked villainy
With odd old ends stol'n forth of Holy Writ.
Richard III 1.3.336–7, RICHARD

8 Nor more can you distinguish of a man
Than of his outward show, which – God He knows –
Seldom or never jumpeth with the heart.
Richard III 3.1.9–11, RICHARD (ironically) warns his nephew PRINCE EDWARD to beware of hypocritical uncles

See also **APPEARANCES**

❧ I ❧

IDENTITY

1   Simply the thing I am
Shall make me live.
All's Well That Ends Well 4.3.327–8, PAROLLES

2   This is I,
Hamlet the Dane.
Hamlet 5.1.255–6, HAMLET, struggling with LAERTES in Ophelia's grave

3 I am myself alone.
3 Henry VI 5.6.83, RICHARD OF GLOUCESTER

4 Who is it that can tell me who I am?
King Lear 1.4.221, LEAR TO FOOL

5 Thus play I in one person many people,
And none contented.
Richard II 5.5.31–2, RICHARD

6 What do I fear? Myself?
Richard III 5.3.183, RICHARD

7 What is your substance, whereof are you made?
Sonnet 53.1

8 I am that I am.
Sonnet 121.9; near-blasphemously, Shakespeare quotes, referring to himself, God's words to Moses at Exodus 3.14. See, by contrast, Iago's 'I am not what I am', at *Othello* 1.1.64.

See also **ALIENATION; ILLEGITIMACY**

IDOLS

9   He was indeed the glass
Wherein the noble youth did dress themselves.
2 Henry IV 2.3.21–2, LADY PERCY TO THE NORTHUMBERLANDS, of her husband

1   Thy gracious self,
Which is the god of my idolatry.
Romeo and Juliet 2.2.113–14, JULIET TO ROMEO

2   'Tis mad idolatry
To make the service greater than the god.
Troilus and Cressida 2.2.57–8, HECTOR TO TROILUS

IGNORANCE

3 Ignorance is the curse of God.
2 Henry VI 4.7.70, LORD SAY TO JACK CADE

4 O! thou monster Ignorance.
Love's Labour's Lost 4.2.23, HOLOFERNES TO DULL

5 Dull unfeeling barren ignorance.
Richard II 1.3.168, MOWBRAY TO RICHARD

6 There is no darkness but ignorance.
Twelfth Night 4.2.42–3, FESTE teasing MALVOLIO

ILL TREATMENT

7   She, poor soul,
Knows not which way to stand, to look, to speak,
And sits as one new risen from a dream.
Taming of the Shrew 4.1.172–4, CURTIS TO GRUMIO, of Katherina

8 He hath been most notoriously abused.
Twelfth Night 5.1.371, OLIVIA TO ORSINO, of Malvolio

ILL WILL

9 Thy ancient malice.
Coriolanus 4.5.99, CORIOLANUS to his enemy AUFIDIUS

10 Rancour will out.
2 Henry VI 1.1.141, GLOUCESTER TO CARDINAL BEAUFORT

11 Shall I be plain? I wish the bastards dead.
Richard III 4.2.18, RICHARD, of his nephews

ILLEGITIMACY

12 I am I, howe'er I was begot.
King John 1.1.175, PHILIP THE BASTARD TO JOHN

1 Though this knave came something saucily to the world before he was sent for, yet was his mother fair, there was good sport at his making.
King Lear 1.1.20–3, GLOUCESTER TO KENT, of his son Edmund

2   Why bastard? Wherefore base?
When my dimensions are as well compact,
My mind as generous and my shape as true,
As honest madam's issue? Why brand they us
With base? With baseness, bastardy?
King Lear 1.2.6–10, EDMUND

3 Now, gods, stand up for bastards!
King Lear 1.2.22, EDMUND

4 I should have been that I am had the maidenliest star in the firmament twinkled on my bastardizing.
King Lear 1.2.131–3, EDMUND

5 I am a bastard, too: I love bastards. I am bastard begot, bastard instructed, bastard in mind, bastard in valour, in everything illegitimate.
Troilus and Cressida 5.7.16–18, THERSITES TO MARGARELON, a bastard son of Priam's

ILLNESS AND DISEASE

6 Like the owner of a foul disease
To keep it from divulging, let it feed
Even on the pith of life.
Hamlet 4.1.21–3, CLAUDIUS TO GERTRUDE

7   Diseases desperate grown
By desperate appliance are relieved,
Or not at all.
Hamlet 4.3.9–11, CLAUDIUS TO LORDS

8 In poison there is physic.
2 Henry IV 1.1.137, NORTHUMBERLAND TO MORTON

9 Abstinence engenders maladies.
Love's Labour's Lost 4.3.291, BEROWNE TO HIS FRIENDS

10 There was never yet philosopher
That could endure the toothache patiently.
Much Ado About Nothing 5.1.35–6, LEONATO TO ANTONIO

See also **DOCTORS AND MEDICINE; MADNESS**

IMAGINATION

1   Nature wants stuff
To vie strange forms with fancy.
Antony and Cleopatra 5.2.96–7, CLEOPATRA TO HER COMPANIONS

2 My imaginations are as foul
As Vulcan's stithy.
Hamlet 3.2.84–5, HAMLET TO HORATIO; Vulcan was the god of blacksmiths, a figure
of darkness, and Venus' cuckolded husband

3 Give me an ounce of civet, good apothecary, to sweeten my imagination.
King Lear 4.6.126–7, LEAR TO GLOUCESTER

4   Present fears
Are less than horrible imaginings.
Macbeth 1.3.137–8, MACBETH, unable to resist the idea of murder

5 These things seem small and undistinguishable,
Like far-off mountains turned into clouds.
Midsummer Night's Dream 4.1.186–7, DEMETRIUS TO HIS FRIENDS

6 Lovers and madmen have such seething brains,
Such shaping fantasies, that apprehend
More than cool reason ever comprehends.
Midsummer Night's Dream 5.1.4–6, THESEUS TO HIS COMPANIONS

7 The lunatic, the lover, and the poet
Are of imagination all compact.
Midsummer Night's Dream 5.1.7–8, THESEUS TO HIS COMPANIONS; *see also* **POETS**

8 O, who can hold a fire in his hand
By thinking on the frosty Caucasus?
Or cloy the hungry edge of appetite
By bare imagination of a feast?
Richard II 1.3.294–7, BOLINGBROKE TO JOHN OF GAUNT, in reply to his father's lecture
on stoicism

9 My soul's imaginary sight.
Sonnet 27.9

10   So full of shapes is fancy,
That it alone is high fantastical.
Twelfth Night 1.1.14–15, ORSINO TO CURIO

11 Prove true, imagination, O prove true.
Twelfth Night 3.4.374, VIOLA

See also **POETS**

IMPATIENCE

1 Do it, England; / . . . Till I know 'tis done,
   Howe'er my haps, my joys were ne'er begun.
   Hamlet 4.3.68, 70–1, CLAUDIUS desiring the murder of Hamlet by the English authorities

See also **ANTICIPATION**

IMPETUOSITY

2 Who can be wise, amazed, temperate and furious,
   Loyal and neutral, in a moment?
   Macbeth 2.3.106–7, MACBETH TO MACDUFF, excusing his killing the grooms who attended Duncan

INACTION

3 Thus the native hue of resolution
   Is sicklied o'er with the pale cast of thought,
   And enterprises of great pitch and moment
   With this regard their currents turn awry
   And lose the name of action.
   Hamlet 3.1.84–8, HAMLET

4   I do not know
   Why yet I live to say this thing's to do,
   Sith I have cause, and will, and strength, and means
   To do't.
   Hamlet 4.4.43–6, HAMLET

5 Nothing will come of nothing.
   King Lear 1.1.90, LEAR TO CORDELIA

See also **ACTION AND DEEDS; DELAY; INDECISION**

INADEQUACY

6   Why do you dress me
   In borrowed robes?
   Macbeth 1.3.108–9, MACBETH TO ROSSE, who has greeted him with his new title, Thane of Cawdor

7   Now does he feel his title
   Hang loose about him, like a giant's robe
   Upon a dwarfish thief.
   Macbeth 5.2.20–2, ANGUS TO COMPANIONS, of Macbeth

INDECISION

1 We would, and we would not.
Measure for Measure 4.4.35, ANGELO

INEXPERIENCE

2 He jests at scars that never felt a wound.
Romeo and Juliet 2.2.1, ROMEO

INFIDELITY

3   Take thou no scorn to wear the horn,
       It was a crest ere thou wast born.
           Thy father's father wore it,
           And thy father bore it.
As You Like It 4.2.14–17, song of the LORDS in the Forest of Arden

4 If we two be one, and thou play false,
I do digest the poison of thy flesh,
Being strumpeted by thy contagion.
Comedy of Errors 2.2.141–3, ADRIANA TO ANTIPHOLUS OF SYRACUSE, whom she imagines to be her husband

5 Alas, poor women, make us but believe
           ... that you love us;
Though others have the arm, show us the sleeve.
Comedy of Errors 3.2.21–3, Adriana's sister LUCIANA, to ANTIPHOLUS OF SYRACUSE

6   And yet within a month –
Let me not think on't – Frailty, thy name is woman –
A little month, or ere those shoes were old
With which she followed my poor father's body,
Like Niobe, all tears – why, she –
O God, a beast that wants discourse of reason
Would have mourned longer – married with my uncle,
My father's brother – but no more like my father
Than I to Hercules. Within a month,
Ere yet the salt of most unrighteous tears
Had left the flushing in her galled eyes,
She married.
Hamlet 1.2.145–56, HAMLET

7   Such an act
That blurs the grace and blush of modesty,
Calls virtue hypocrite, takes off the rose

From the fair forehead of an innocent love
And sets a blister there, makes marriage vows
As false as dicers' oaths.
Hamlet 3.4.40–5; HAMLET accuses HIS MOTHER

1 The cuckoo then, on every tree,
    Mocks married men; for thus sings he,
                Cuckoo;
    Cuckoo, cuckoo: O word of fear,
    Unpleasing to a married ear!
Love's Labour's Lost 5.2.891–5, song; *more at* **FLOWERS AND PLANTS; WINTER**

2 Sigh no more, ladies, sigh no more,
        Men were deceivers ever.
Much Ado About Nothing 2.3.61–2, BALTHASAR's song

3 It is thought abroad that 'twixt my sheets
   He's done my office.
Othello 1.3.385–6, IAGO TO RODERIGO

4 In Venice they do let God see the pranks
   They dare not show their husbands; their best conscience
   Is not to leave't undone, but keep't unknown.
Othello 3.3.205–7, IAGO TO OTHELLO

5 She's gone, I am abused, and my relief
   Must be to loathe her.
Othello 3.3.271–2, OTHELLO

6 Those pretty wrongs that liberty commits
   When I am sometime absent from thy heart,
   Thy beauty and thy years full well befits.
Sonnet 41.1–3; the poet tries to suppress his jealousy

7 For thee watch I, whilst thou dost wake elsewhere,
   From me far off, with others all too near.
Sonnet 61.13–14

8 More water glideth by the mill
   Than wots the miller of, and easy it is
   Of a cut loaf to steal a shive.
Titus Andronicus 1.1.585–7, DEMETRIUS TO AARON

9 'As false as Cressid.'
Troilus and Cressida 3.2.193, CRESSIDA TO TROILUS; this is how she swears she will be
remembered if the seemingly impossible happens and she is unfaithful to him

1 If beauty have a soul, this is not she.
  Troilus and Cressida 5.2.136, TROILUS, with Thersites

2 This is, and is not, Cressid.
  Troilus and Cressida 5.2.144, TROILUS, with Thersites

3 And many a man there is . . .
       holds his wife by th'arm,
  That little thinks she has been sluiced in's absence
  And his pond fished by his next neighbour, by
  Sir Smile, his neighbour.
  Winter's Tale 1.2.192–6, LEONTES

INGRATITUDE

4 Blow, blow, thou winter wind,
    Thou art not so unkind
     As man's ingratitude.
    Thy tooth is not so keen,
    Because thou art not seen,
     Although thy breath be rude.
    Heigh-ho, sing heigh-ho, unto the green holly
    Most friendship is feigning, most loving mere folly.
    Then heigh-ho, the holly,
     This life is most jolly.

    Freeze, freeze, thou bitter sky,
    That dost not bite so nigh
     As benefits forgot.
    Though thou the waters warp,
    Thy sting is not so sharp,
     As friend remembered not.
  As You Like It 2.7.174–89, AMIENS's song

5 Ingratitude is monstrous.
  Coriolanus 2.3.9, CITIZEN TO OTHERS

6 Ingratitude, thou marble-hearted fiend.
  King Lear 1.4.251, LEAR TO ALBANY, angered by Goneril

7 How sharper than a serpent's tooth it is
  To have a thankless child.
  King Lear 1.4.280–1, LEAR TO ALBANY, angered by Goneril

1 I hate ingratitude more in a man
   Than lying, vainness, babbling drunkenness,
   Or any taint of vice whose strong corruption
   Inhabits our frail blood.
   Twelfth Night 3.4.353–6, VIOLA TO ANTONIO

INNOCENCE

2 Some innocents 'scape not the thunderbolt.
   Antony and Cleopatra 2.5.77, CLEOPATRA TO CHARMIAN

3   I am a man
   More sinned against than sinning.
   King Lear 3.2.59–60, LEAR TO KENT

4 God and our innocence defend and guard us!
   Richard III 3.5.20, BUCKINGHAM TO RICHARD

5   What we changed
   Was innocence for innocence: we knew not
   The doctrine of ill-doing, nor dreamed
   That any did.
   Winter's Tale 1.2.68–71, POLIXENES TO HERMIONE, of his boyhood friendship with Leontes

6 The silence often of pure innocence
   Persuades, when speaking fails.
   Winter's Tale 2.2.41–2, PAULINA TO EMILIA – sadly wrong, at this point in the play

7   If powers divine
   Behold our human actions (as they do),
   I doubt not then but innocence shall make
   False accusation blush.
   Winter's Tale 3.2.27–30, HERMIONE, defending herself at her trial for infidelity

INSPIRATION

8 Or I could make a prologue to my brains,
   They had begun the play.
   Hamlet 5.2.30–1, HAMLET TO HORATIO; 'or' here means 'before'

9 O for a muse of fire!
   Henry V Prologue 1, CHORUS; *more at* **PLAYS, PLAYERS AND PLAYHOUSES**

INSULTS

10 You are not worth another word, else I'd call you knave.
   All's Well That Ends Well 2.3.262–3, LAFEW TO PAROLLES

1 I do desire we may be better strangers.
As You Like It 3.2.255, ORLANDO TO JAQUES

2 Thou clay-brained guts, thou knotty-pated fool, thou whoreson obscene greasy tallow-catch.
1 Henry IV 2.4.222–4, PRINCE HAL TO FALSTAFF; one example among many in this play

3 There's no more faith in thee than in a stewed prune.
1 Henry IV 3.3.112–13, FALSTAFF TO HOSTESS QUICKLY

4 Thou honeysuckle villain.
2 Henry IV 2.1.50–1, HOSTESS QUICKLY TO FALSTAFF

5 Heap of wrath, foul indigested lump.
As crooked in thy manners as thy shape!
2 Henry VI 5.1.157–8, CLIFFORD TO RICHARD OF YORK

6 You blocks, you stones, you worse than senseless things!
Julius Caesar 1.1.36, MARULLUS TO THE COMMONERS OF ROME

7 This is a slight unmeritable man,
Meet to be sent on errands.
Julius Caesar 4.1.12–13, MARK ANTONY TO OCTAVIUS, of Lepidus, supposed to be his ally

8 Thou whoreson zed, thou unnecessary letter!
King Lear 2.2.64, KENT TO OSWALD

9 Some carry-tale, some please-man, some slight zany,
Some mumble-news, some trencher-knight, some Dick . . .
Told our intents before.
Love's Labour's Lost 5.2.463–4, 467, BEROWNE accusing BOYET of giving the game away

10 FIRST MURDERER   We are men, my Liege.
MACBETH Ay, in the catalogue ye go for men.
Macbeth 3.1.90–1

11 Thou lily-livered boy.
Macbeth 5.3.15, MACBETH TO A SERVANT

12 You Banbury cheese!
Merry Wives of Windsor 1.1.120, BARDOLPH TO SLENDER

13 Hang off, thou cat, thou burr!
Midsummer Night's Dream 3.2.260, LYSANDER to the clinging HERMIA

1 KATHERINA Asses are made to bear, and so are you.
  PETRUCHIO Women are made to bear, and so are you.
  Taming of the Shrew 2.1.200–1

2 Such an injury would vex a saint.
  Taming of the Shrew 3.2.28, BAPTISTA; 'injury' here means 'insult'

3 A whoreson beetle-headed, flap-eared knave!
  Taming of the Shrew 4.1.145, PETRUCHIO TO KATHERINA, of a servant whom he has just struck

4 Thou flea, thou nit, thou winter-cricket thou!
  Taming of the Shrew 4.3.109, PETRUCHIO TO A TAILOR

5 Thou deboshed fish, thou.
  Tempest 3.2.26–7, TRINCULO TO CALIBAN

  See also **APPEARANCE; CURSES**

INTEGRITY

6 His nature is too noble for the world:
  He would not flatter Neptune for his trident,
  Or Jove for's power to thunder.
  Coriolanus 3.1.255–7, MENENIUS, of Coriolanus

7   Would you have me
  False to my nature? Rather say I play
  The man I am.
  Coriolanus 3.2.14–16, CORIOLANUS TO HIS MOTHER AND A NOBLEMAN

8 Not to be other than one thing.
  Coriolanus 4.7.42, AUFIDIUS TO HIS LIEUTENANT, of Coriolanus

9 This above all: to thine own self be true,
  And it must follow as the night the day
  Thou canst not then be false to any man.
  Hamlet 1.3.78–80, POLONIUS' advice to LAERTES; *more at* **ADVICE**

10 Where is truth if there be no self-trust?
  Lucrece 158

INTELLIGENCE, low

11 I am slow of study.
  Midsummer Night's Dream 1.2.64, SNUG the joiner

12 Thou sodden-witted lord, thou hast no more brain than I have in mine elbows.
  Troilus and Cressida 2.1.43–4, THERSITES TO AJAX

1 Ajax, who wears his wit in his belly and his guts in his head.
  Troilus and Cressida 2.1.74–5, THERSITES TO ACHILLES, in the presence of Ajax

2 Here's Agamemnon: an honest fellow enough, . . . but he has not so
  much brain as ear-wax.
  Troilus and Cressida 5.1.51–3, THERSITES

ITALY AND THE ITALIANS

3 Those girls of Italy, take heed of them;
  They say our French lack language to deny
  If they demand.
  All's Well That Ends Well 2.1.19–21, KING OF FRANCE

4   Proud Italy,
  Whose manners still our tardy-apish nation
  Limps after in base imitation.
  Richard II 2.1.21–3, YORK TO JOHN OF GAUNT

              Fruitful Lombardy,
5 The pleasant garden of great Italy.
  Taming of the Shrew 1.1.3–4, LUCENTIO TO TRANIO

  See also **CITIES**

JEALOUSY

6 Can Fulvia die?
  Antony and Cleopatra 1.3.59, CLEOPATRA's jealousy of Antony's wife

7 How many fond fools serve mad jealousy?
  Comedy of Errors 2.1.117, LUCIANA TO ADRIANA

8 Green-eyed jealousy.
  Merchant of Venice 3.2.110, PORTIA

9   It is my nature's plague
  To spy into abuses, and oft my jealousy
  Shapes faults that are not.
  Othello 3.3.149–51, IAGO TO OTHELLO

1   Beware . . . of jealousy!
It is the green-eyed monster, which doth mock
The meat it feeds on.
Othello 3.3.167–9, IAGO TO OTHELLO

2   Trifles light as air
Are to the jealous confirmations strong
As proofs of holy writ.
Othello 3.3.325–7, IAGO

3 Jealous souls will not be answered so:
They are not ever jealous for the cause,
But jealous for they're jealous. It is a monster
Begot upon itself, born on itself.
Othello 3.4.159–62, EMILIA TO DESDEMONA

4 One not easily jealous, but being wrought,
Perplexed in the extreme.
Othello 5.2.345–6, OTHELLO, of himself, to his colleagues before killing himself

5 Thou dost love her, because thou knowst I love her.
Sonnet 42.6

6 I must dance barefoot on her wedding-day,
And for your love to her lead apes in hell.
Taming of the Shrew 2.1.33–4, KATHERINA TO BAPTISTA, jealous of her sister; childless
women were supposed to lead apes into hell since they had no children to lead them
to heaven

7 Where love reigns, disturbing jealousy
Doth call himself affection's sentinel.
Venus and Adonis 649–50, VENUS

8   My heart dances,
But not for joy – not joy.
Winter's Tale 1.2.110–11, LEONTES

9 Inch-thick, knee-deep, o'er head and ears a forked one.
Winter's Tale 1.2.186, LEONTES, suspecting his wife Hermione of infidelity

10   Is whispering nothing?
Is leaning cheek to cheek? is meeting noses?
Kissing with inside lip? stopping the career
Of laughter with a sigh (a note infallible
Of breaking honesty)? horsing foot on foot?
Skulking in corners? wishing clocks more swift?
Winter's Tale 1.2.284–9, LEONTES TO CAMILLO

See also **ENVY; INFIDELITY**

JEWELS

1 It was my turquoise, I had it of Leah when I was a bachelor: I would
not have given it for a wilderness of monkeys.
Merchant of Venice 3.1.112–15, SHYLOCK TO TUBAL

2 Wedges of gold, great anchors, heaps of pearl,
Inestimable stones, unvalued jewels,
All scattered in the bottom of the sea.
Richard III 1.4.26–8, CLARENCE recounting his dream to the KEEPER OF THE TOWER

3 Dumb jewels often in their silent kind,
More than quick words, do move a woman's mind.
Two Gentlemen of Verona 3.1.90–1, VALENTINE TO THE DUKE

JEWS AND JEWISHNESS

4 Suff'rance is the badge of all our tribe.
Merchant of Venice 1.3.108, SHYLOCK TO ANTONIO

5 You call me misbeliever, cut-throat dog,
And spit upon my Jewish gaberdine.
Merchant of Venice 1.3.109–10, SHYLOCK TO ANTONIO

6 He hath disgraced me, and hindered me half a million, laughed at my
losses, mocked at my gains, scorned my nation, thwarted my bargains,
cooled my friends, heated mine enemies, – and what's his reason? I am
a Jew. Hath not a Jew eyes? hath not a Jew hands, organs, dimensions,
senses, affections, passions? fed with the same food, hurt with the same
weapons, subject to the same diseases, healed by the same means,
warmed and cooled by the same winter and summer as a Christian is?
– if you prick us do we not bleed? if you tickle us do we not laugh? if
you poison us do we not die? and if you wrong us shall we not revenge?
– if we are like you in the rest, we will resemble you in that.
Merchant of Venice 3.1.50–63, SHYLOCK TO SALERIO

See also **CHRISTIANS; DAUGHTERS; HATRED; RELIGION; USURY**

JOKES

7 It would be argument for a week, laughter for a month, and a good jest
forever.
1 Henry IV 2.2.94–5, PRINCE HAL TO POINS, in the middle of a youthful escapade

1 O jest unseen, inscrutable, invisible,
  As a nose on a man's face, or a weathercock on a steeple!
  Two Gentlemen of Verona 2.1.132–3, SPEED

  See also **PLOTS; WIT**

JOY

2   They threw their caps
  As they would hang them on the horns of the moon.
  Coriolanus 1.1.211–12, CORIOLANUS TO MENENIUS, of the people

3 Give me a gash, put me to present pain,
  Lest this great sea of joys rushing upon me
  O'erbear the shores of my mortality,
  And drown me with their sweetness.
  Pericles 5.1.192–5, PERICLES TO HELICANUS

4   Come what sorrow can,
  It cannot countervail the exchange of joy
  That one short minute gives me in her sight.
  Romeo and Juliet 2.6.3–5, ROMEO TO FRIAR LAURENCE

5 They seemed almost, with staring on one another, to tear the cases of
  their eyes: there was speech in their dumbness, language in their very
  gesture; they looked as they had heard of a world ransomed, or one
  destroyed.
  Winter's Tale 5.2.12–16, GENTLEMAN TO AUTOLYCUS, of Leontes and Camillo when
  Perdita is found

JUDGEMENT, good and bad

6   I'll yet follow
  The wounded chance of Antony, though my reason
  Sits in the wind against me.
  Antony and Cleopatra 3.10.35–7, ENOBARBUS

JUDGES AND JUDGEMENT

7   And then, the justice,
  In fair round belly, with good capon lined,
  With eyes severe, and beard of formal cut,
  Full of wise saws, and modern instances.
  As You Like It 2.7.153–6, from JAQUES's 'Seven Ages of Man' speech

8 See how yon justice rails upon yon simple thief. Hark in thine ear: change places
  and handy-dandy, which is the justice, which is the thief?
  King Lear 4.6.147–50, LEAR TO GLOUCESTER

1 When the judge is robbed, the prisoner dies.
Lucrece 1652

2   I not deny
The jury passing on the prisoner's life
May in the sworn twelve have a thief, or two,
Guiltier than him they try.
Measure for Measure 2.1.18–21, ANGELO TO ESCALUS

3   How would you be
If He, which is the top of judgement, should
But judge you as you are?
Measure for Measure 2.2.75–7, ISABELLA TO ANGELO

4 A Daniel come to judgement: yea a Daniel!
Merchant of Venice 4.1.221, SHYLOCK, of Portia disguised as a lawyer

5   You are a worthy judge,
You know the law, your exposition
Hath been most sound
Merchant of Venice 4.1.234–6, SHYLOCK, of Portia disguised as a lawyer

6 The court awards it, and the law doth give it.
Merchant of Venice 4.1.298, PORTIA

7 An upright judge, a learned judge!
Merchant of Venice 4.1.321, GRATIANO, mocking SHYLOCK

8 It boots thee not to be compassionate;
After our sentence plaining comes too late.
Richard II 1.3.174–5, RICHARD, turning aside MOWBRAY's 'compassionate' (passionate) pleading

JULIET *see* ROMEO AND JULIET

JULIUS CAESAR

9   Caesar's ambition,
Which swelled so much that it did almost stretch
The sides o'th' world.
Cymbeline 3.1.49–51, CYMBELINE TO CLOTEN AND HIS COURT

10 He doth bestride the narrow world
Like a Colossus, and we petty men
Walk under his huge legs, and peep about
To find ourselves dishonourable graves.
Julius Caesar 1.2.133–6, CASSIUS TO BRUTUS

1   Upon what meat doth this our Caesar feed,
    That he is grown so great?
    Julius Caesar 1.2.147–8, Cassius to Brutus

2   Caesar must bleed for it.
    Julius Caesar 2.1.171, Brutus to the conspirators

    See much more at **ELEGIES**

JUSTICE

3   Use every man after his desert, and who shall scape whipping?
    Hamlet 2.2.530–1, Hamlet to Polonius; *more at* **MANNER AND MANNERS**

4   The enginer
    Hoist with his own petard.
    Hamlet 3.4.208–9, Hamlet to Gertrude

5   Where th'offence is, let the great axe fall.
    Hamlet 4.5.215, Claudius

6   As a woodcock to mine own springe,
    I am justly killed with mine own treachery.
    Hamlet 5.2.315–16, Laertes, who dies from the poisoned foil with which he meant to
    kill Hamlet

7   Thrice is he armed that hath his quarrel just,
    And he but naked, though locked up in steel,
    Whose conscience with injustice is corrupted.
    2 Henry VI 3.2.232–4, Henry to Queen Margaret

8   Measure for measure must be answered.
    3 Henry VI 2.6.55, Warwick to the sons of Richard of York; a reference to
    Matthew 7.1–2: 'Judge not, that ye be not judged . . . With what measure ye mete, it
    shall be measured to you again.' *See also* 149.1 *below.*

9   Be just, and fear not.
    Henry VIII 3.2.446, Cardinal Wolsey to Cromwell

10 Ambition's debt is paid.
    Julius Caesar 3.1.83, Brutus, on the death of Julius Caesar

11 The gods are just and of our pleasant vices
    Make instruments to plague us.
    King Lear 5.3.168–9, Edgar to Edmund

12 Liberty plucks Justice by the nose.
    Measure for Measure 1.3.29, Duke to Friar Thomas

1 Like doth quit like, and Measure still for Measure.
   Measure for Measure 5.1.408, DUKE TO ISABELLA

2 In the course of justice, none of us
   Should see salvation.
   Merchant of Venice 4.1.197–8, PORTIA

3 Since what I am to say, must be but that
   Which contradicts my accusation, and
   The testimony on my part, no other
   But what comes from myself, it shall scarce boot me
   To say 'not guilty'.
   Winter's Tale 3.2.21–5, HERMIONE, conducting her own defence

   See also **FATE; JUDGES AND JUDGEMENT; MERCY**

JUSTIFICATION

4 I have in equal balance justly weighed
   What wrongs our arms may do, what wrongs we suffer,
   And find our griefs heavier than our offences.
   2 Henry IV 4.1.67–9, ARCHBISHOP OF YORK TO WESTMORELAND

5 To do a great right, do a little wrong.
   Merchant of Venice 4.1.214, BASSANIO TO PORTIA

K

KINGSHIP AND RULE

6   The death of Antony
   Is not a single doom; in the name lay
   A moiety of the world.
   Antony and Cleopatra 5.1.17–19, OCTAVIUS CAESAR TO DERCETUS

7   Our queen,
   Th'imperial jointress to this warlike state.
   Hamlet 1.2.8–9, CLAUDIUS, of Gertrude

8 His greatness weighed, his will is not his own.
   For he himself is subject to his birth:

He may not, as unvalued persons do,
Carve for himself, for on his choice depends
The sanity and health of this whole state.
Hamlet 1.3.17–21, LAERTES TO OPHELIA

1   The cess of majesty
Dies not alone, but like a gulf doth draw
What's near with it.
Hamlet 3.3.15–17, ROSENCRANTZ flattering CLAUDIUS

2   Never alone
Did the King sigh, but with a general groan.
Hamlet 3.3.22–3, ROSENCRANTZ, from the same speech

3 There's such divinity doth hedge a king
That treason can but peep to what it would.
Hamlet 4.5.123–4, CLAUDIUS

4 Why rather, sleep, liest thou in smoky cribs, . . .
Than in the perfumed chambers of the great.
2 Henry IV 3.1.9, 12, HENRY

5 Uneasy lies the head that wears a crown.
2 Henry IV 3.1.31, HENRY

6 But if the cause be not good, the king himself hath a heavy reckoning
to make when all those legs and arms and heads chopped off in a
battle shall join together at the latter day and cry all 'We died at such a
place'.
Henry V 4.1.132–6, MICHAEL WILLIAMS, a soldier, to HENRY incognito

7   What infinite heart's ease
Must kings neglect that private men enjoy!
Henry V 4.1.232–3, HENRY; *more at* **CEREMONY; SLEEP AND SLEEPLESSNESS**

8 Nice customs curtsey to great kings.
Henry V 5.2.266, HENRY TO KATHERINE

9 How sweet a thing it is to wear a crown,
Within whose circuit is Elysium.
3 Henry VI 1.2.29–30, RICHARD, son of Richard of York, to HIS FATHER

10   I would not be a queen
For all the world.
Henry VIII 2.3.45–6, ANNE BULLEN (BOLEYN) TO HER COMPANION

1 When beggars die there are no comets seen;
   The heavens themselves blaze forth the death of princes.
   Julius Caesar 2.2.30–1, CALPHURNIA TO JULIUS CAESAR

2 Every inch a king.
   King Lear 4.6.106, LEAR, in his madness

3 Why should the private pleasure of some one
   Become the public plague of many moe?
   Lucrece 1478–9, referring to Paris and Helen of Troy; 'moe' is 'more'

4 So doth the greater glory dim the less –
   A substitute shines as brightly as a king
   Until a king be by.
   Merchant of Venice 5.1.93–5, PORTIA TO NERISSA

5 Kings are earth's gods; in vice their law's their will;
   And if Jove stray, who dares say Jove doth ill?
   Pericles 1.1.104–5, PERICLES TO ANTIOCHUS

6 We were not born to sue, but to command.
   Richard II 1.1.196, RICHARD TO BOLINGBROKE AND MOWBRAY

7 Such is the breath of kings.
   Richard II 1.3.215, BOLINGBROKE TO RICHARD, on the power of a king's words

8 Not all the water in the rough rude sea
   Can wash the balm off from an anointed king.
   Richard II 3.2.54–5, RICHARD TO AUMERLE

9 I live with bread like you, feel want,
   Taste grief, need friends – subjected thus,
   How can you say to me, I am a king?
   Richard II 3.2.175–7, RICHARD TO AUMERLE AND SCROOPE; *more at* **DEATH**

10 What must the king do now? Must he submit?
   The king shall do it. Must he be deposed?
   The king shall be contented. Must he lose
   The name of king? a God's name, let it go.
   Richard II 3.3.143–6, RICHARD TO AUMERLE; *more at* **RENUNCIATION**

11 What subject can give sentence on his king?
   Richard II 4.1.121, BISHOP OF CARLISLE TO BOLINGBROKE

12 Give me the crown. Here, cousin, seize the crown.
   Here, cousin,

On this side my hand, and on that side thine.
Now is this golden crown like a deep well
That owes two buckets, filling one another,
The emptier ever dancing in the air,
The other down, unseen, and full of water.
That bucket down and full of tears am I,
Drinking my griefs, whilst you mount up on high.
Richard II 4.1.181–9, RICHARD TO BOLINGBROKE

1 O that I were a mockery king of snow,
Standing before the sun of Bolingbroke,
To melt myself away in water-drops!
Richard II 4.1.260–2, RICHARD TO NORTHUMBERLAND

See also **CONTENTMENT; SLEEP AND SLEEPLESSNESS**

KISSES AND KISSING

2 Nay, you were better speak first, and when you were gravelled for lack
of matter, you might take occasion to kiss.
As You Like It 4.1.69–71, ROSALIND TO ORLANDO

3 I kissed thee ere I killed thee: no way but this,
Killing myself, to die upon a kiss.
Othello 5.2.358–9, OTHELLO, dying

4 On the touching of her lips I may
Melt and no more be seen.
Pericles 5.3.42–3, PERICLES to his long-lost wife THAISA

5 Teach not thy lip such scorn; for it was made
For kissing.
Richard III 1.2.175–6, RICHARD TO ANNE

6 My lips, two blushing pilgrims, ready stand
To smooth that rough touch with a tender kiss.
Romeo and Juliet 1.5.95–6, ROMEO TO JULIET

7 Saints have hands that pilgrims' hands do touch,
And palm to palm is holy palmers' kiss.
Romeo and Juliet 1.5.99–100, JULIET's reply to ROMEO

8 You kiss by th' book.
Romeo and Juliet 1.5.110, JULIET TO ROMEO

1   Lips, O you
The doors of breath, seal with a righteous kiss
A dateless bargain to engrossing Death.
Romeo and Juliet 5.3.113–15; ROMEO kisses JULIET before dying

2   Then come kiss me, sweet and twenty:
            Youth's a stuff will not endure.
Twelfth Night 2.3.51–2, FESTE's song; *more at* **LOVE**

3 I'll smother thee with kisses.
Venus and Adonis 18

4 She murders with a kiss.
Venus and Adonis 54, of Venus

5 Incorporate then they seem, face grows to face.
Venus and Adonis 540

KNOWLEDGE

6 I know you what you are.
King Lear 1.1.271, CORDELIA TO HER SISTERS

7 Ask me not what I know.
King Lear 5.3.158, EDMUND TO ALBANY

8 Be innocent of the knowledge, dearest chuck,
Till thou applaud the deed.
Macbeth 3.2.45–6, MACBETH TO LADY MACBETH

9 Seek to know no more.
Macbeth 4.1.103, WITCHES TO MACBETH

10 Come sir, I know what I know.
Measure for Measure 3.2.146, LUCIO TO THE DUKE, disguised as a friar

L

LAW AND LAWYERS

11 The law's delay.
Hamlet 3.1.72, HAMLET

1   Why, may not that be the skull of a lawyer? Where be his quiddities
    now, his quillities, his cases, his tenures, and his tricks?
    Hamlet 5.1.98–100, HAMLET TO HORATIO, examining skulls in the graveyard

2   Old father Antic the law.
    1 Henry IV 1.2.59, FALSTAFF TO PRINCE HAL

3   An honest man, sir, is able to speak for himself, when a knave is not.
    2 Henry IV 5.1.44–5, DAVY TO SHALLOW

4   These nice sharp quillets of the law.
    1 Henry VI 2.4.17, WARWICK TO LORDS (at the scene of the affiliation to the red rose
    and the white)

5   The first thing we do, let's kill all the lawyers.
    2 Henry VI 4.2.74, BUTCHER TO JACK CADE, leader of a popular rebellion

6   What makes robbers bold but too much lenity?
    3 Henry VI 2.6.22, CLIFFORD

7   His own opinion was his law.
    Henry VIII 4.2.37, KATHERINE OF ARAGON TO GRIFFITH, the usher, of Cardinal Wolsey

8   We have strict statutes and most biting laws.
    Measure for Measure 1.3.19, DUKE TO FRIAR THOMAS

9   We must not make a scarecrow of the law,
    Setting it up to fear the birds of prey,
    And let it keep one shape till custom make it
    Their perch, and not their terror.
    Measure for Measure 2.1.1–4, ANGELO TO ESCALUS

10 The law hath not been dead, though it hath slept.
    Measure for Measure 2.2.91, ANGELO TO ISABELLA

11 In law, what plea so tainted and corrupt,
    But being seasoned with a gracious voice,
    Obscures the show of evil?
    Merchant of Venice 3.2.75–7, BASSANIO

12 I will make a Star Chamber matter of it.
    Merry Wives of Windsor 1.1.1–2, SHALLOW TO SLENDER

13 Let's choose executors and talk of wills.
    Richard II 3.2.148, RICHARD TO LORDS

1 Do as adversaries do in law,
   Strive mightily, but eat and drink as friends.
   Taming of the Shrew 1.2.274–5, TRANIO TO GRUMIO AND BIONDELLO

2 Pity is the virtue of the law.
   Timon of Athens 3.5.8, ALCIBIADES TO TWO SENATORS

3   The law, which is past depth
   To those that, without heed, do plunge into't.
   Timon of Athens 3.5.12–13, ALCIBIADES TO TWO SENATORS

4 Still you keep o'th' windy side of the law.
   Twelfth Night 3.4.163, FABIAN TO SIR TOBY BELCH

5 Let the law go whistle.
   Winter's Tale 4.4.700, SHEPHERD'S SON TO THE SHEPHERD

   See also **CONTRACTS; JUDGES AND JUDGEMENT; JUSTICE**

LAZINESS *see* EASY LIFE

LEADERSHIP

6 The choice and master spirits of this age.
   Julius Caesar 3.1.163, MARK ANTONY TO BRUTUS

7 Those he commands move only in command,
   Nothing in love.
   Macbeth 5.2.19–20, ANGUS TO COMPANIONS

8 We cannot all be masters.
   Othello 1.1.42, IAGO TO RODERIGO

LETTERS

9 There are some shrewd contents in yond same paper
   That steals the colour from Bassanio's cheek.
   Merchant of Venice 3.2.242–3, PORTIA

10 Here are a few of the unpleasant'st words
   That ever blotted paper!
   Merchant of Venice 3.2.250–1, BASSANIO TO PORTIA

11 I warrant he hath a thousand of these letters, writ with blank space for
   different names.
   Merry Wives of Windsor 2.1.68–9, MISTRESS PAGE TO MISTRESS FORD, of Falstaff and
   his love letters

LIES

1   Falsehood
Is worse in kings than beggars.
Cymbeline 3.6.13–14, IMOGEN

2 It is as easy as lying.
Hamlet 3.2.359, HAMLET TO GUILDENSTERN

3 Give me leave to tell you you lie in your throat.
2 Henry IV 1.2.84–5, SERVANT TO FALSTAFF

4 Lord, Lord, how subject we old men are to this vice of lying!
2 Henry IV 3.2.298–9, FALSTAFF; one comment on lying, amongst many from him

5 Shall Caesar send a lie?
Julius Caesar 2.2.65, JULIUS CAESAR TO CALPHURNIA

6 Detested kite, thou liest.
King Lear 1.4.254, LEAR TO GONERIL

7 She was as false as water.
Othello 5.2.134, OTHELLO TO EMILIA. Jacob (Genesis 49.4) calls his eldest son Reuben 'unstable as water', which, as here, seems to imply both general unreliability and sexual betrayal.

8 Perjury, perjury, in the highest degree.
Richard III 5.3.197, RICHARD, finally a prey to guilt

9   At lovers' perjuries,
They say, Jove laughs.
Romeo and Juliet 2.2.92–3, JULIET TO ROMEO

10   There's no trust,
No faith, no honesty in men. All perjured,
All forsworn, all naught, all dissemblers.
Romeo and Juliet 3.2.85–7, NURSE TO JULIET

11 When my love swears that she is made of truth,
I do believe her, though I know she lies.
Sonnet 138.1–2

See also **APPEARANCES; HYPOCRISY; POLICE; TALK**

LIFE

12 The web of our life is of a mingled yarn, good and ill together.
All's Well That Ends Well 4.3.68–9, ONE LORD TO ANOTHER

1   I love long life better than figs.
Antony and Cleopatra 1.2.33, CHARMIAN TO A SOOTHSAYER; 'figs' has a sexual implication

2   All the world's a stage,
And all the men and women merely players.
They have their exits and their entrances,
And one man in his time plays many parts,
His acts being seven ages. At first the infant,
Mewling and puking in the nurse's arms.
Then, the whining school-boy with his satchel
And shining morning face, creeping like snail
Unwillingly to school. And then the lover,
Sighing like furnace, with a woeful ballad
Made to his mistress' eyebrow. Then, a soldier,
Full of strange oaths, and bearded like the pard,
Jealous in honour, sudden, and quick in quarrel,
Seeking the bubble reputation
Even in the cannon's mouth. And then, the justice,
In fair round belly, with good capon lined,
With eyes severe, and beard of formal cut,
Full of wise saws, and modern instances,
And so he plays his part. The sixth age shifts
Into the lean and slippered pantaloon,
With spectacles on nose, and pouch on side,
His youthful hose well saved, a world too wide
For his shrunk shank, and his big manly voice,
Turning again toward childish treble, pipes
And whistles in his sound. Last scene of all,
That ends this strange eventful history,
Is second childishness and mere oblivion,
Sans teeth, sans eyes, sans taste, sans everything.
As You Like It 2.7.139–166, JAQUES's 'Seven Ages of Man' speech to DUKE SENIOR and HIS COMPANIONS in the Forest of Arden

3   I do not set my life at a pin's fee.
Hamlet 1.4.65, HAMLET TO HORATIO

4   POLONIUS My lord, I will take my leave of you.
HAMLET You cannot, sir, take from me anything that I will not more willingly part withal – except my life, except my life, except my life.
Hamlet 2.2.213–17

1 Lambkins, we will live.
Henry V 2.1.126, life in the face of death; PISTOL TO FALSTAFF'S OTHER COMPANIONS,
giving them heart as they go to console him on his deathbed

2 As flies to wanton boys are we to the gods,
They kill us for their sport.
King Lear 4.1.38–9, GLOUCESTER TO AN OLD MAN

3 When we are born we cry that we are come
To this great stage of fools.
King Lear 4.6.178–9, LEAR TO GLOUCESTER

4 Had I but died an hour before this chance,
I had lived a blessed time; for, from this instant,
There's nothing serious in mortality;
All is but toys: renown, and grace, is dead;
The wine of life is drawn, and the mere lees
Is left this vault to brag of.
Macbeth 2.3.89–94, MACBETH, publicly lamenting the death of Duncan

5 Tomorrow, and tomorrow, and tomorrow,
Creeps in this petty pace from day to day,
To the last syllable of recorded time;
And all our yesterdays have lighted fools
The way to dusty death. Out, out, brief candle!
Life's but a walking shadow; a poor player,
That struts and frets his hour upon the stage,
And then is heard no more: it is a tale
Told by an idiot, full of sound and fury,
Signifying nothing.
Macbeth 5.5.19–28, MACBETH TO SEYTON

6   Thou hast nor youth, nor age,
But as it were an after-dinner's sleep
Dreaming on both; for all thy blessed youth
Becomes as aged, and doth beg the alms
Of palsied eld: and when thou art old and rich,
Thou hast neither heat, affection, limb, nor beauty
To make thy riches pleasant. What's yet in this
That bears the name of life?
Measure for Measure 3.1.32–9, DUKE, disguised as a friar, to CLAUDIO

7 Put out the light, and then put out the light!
If I quench thee, thou flaming minister,

I can again thy former light restore
Should I repent me. But once put out thy light,
Thou cunning'st pattern of excelling nature,
I know not where is that Promethean heat
That can thy light relume.
Othello 5.2.7–13, OTHELLO, contemplating the sleeping Desdemona

1 The music of men's lives.
   Richard II 5.5.44, RICHARD; *more at* **MUSIC**

2 Nativity, once in the main of light,
   Crawls to maturity.
   Sonnet 60.5–6

3   We are such stuff
   As dreams are made on; and our little life
   Is rounded with a sleep.
   Tempest 4.1.156–8, PROSPERO TO MIRANDA AND FERDINAND

4 Life's uncertain voyage.
   Timon of Athens 5.1.202, TIMON TO SENATORS

   See also **BIRTH AND CHILDBEARING; EASY LIFE; FATE; FORTUNE; LIFE, making
   the most of; TRANSIENCE; WEARINESS**

LIFE, making the most of
5   The time of life is short!
   To spend that shortness basely were too long
   If life did ride upon a dial's point,
   Still ending at the arrival of an hour.
   1 Henry IV 5.2.81–4, HOTSPUR TO A MESSENGER

LOOKING
6 In silent wonder of still-gazing eyes.
   Lucrece 84; Tarquin sets eyes on Lucrece

7 Looks kill love, and love by looks reviveth.
   Venus and Adonis 464

LOSS
8   We have kissed away
   Kingdoms and provinces.
   Antony and Cleopatra 3.10.7–8, SCARUS TO ENOBARBUS

9 Othello's occupation's gone.
   Othello 3.3.360, OTHELLO, with Iago

1   O you gods!
Why do you make us love your goodly gifts,
And snatch them straight away?
Pericles 3.1.22–4, PERICLES

2 Time will come and take my love away.
This thought is as a death, which cannot choose
But weep to have that which it fears to lose.
Sonnet 64.12–14

3 VIOLA What country, friends, is this?
CAPTAIN This is Illyria, lady.
VIOLA And what should I do in Illyria?
My brother he is in Elysium.
Twelfth Night 1.2.1–4

LOVE

4   'Twere all one
That I should love a bright particular star
And think to wed it, he is so above me.
All's Well That Ends Well 1.1.86–8, HELENA

5 Love that comes too late.
All's Well That Ends Well 5.3.57, KING OF FRANCE

6 There's beggary in the love that can be reckoned.
Antony and Cleopatra 1.1.15, ANTONY TO CLEOPATRA

7 Eternity was in our lips and eyes,
Bliss in our brows' bent; none our parts so poor
But was a race of heaven.
Antony and Cleopatra 1.3.36–8, CLEOPATRA TO ANTONY

8 If thou remember'st not the slightest folly
That ever love did make thee run into,
Thou hast not loved.
As You Like It 2.4.32–4, SILVIUS TO CORIN

9 ROSALIND Not true in love?
CELIA Yes, when he is in, but I think he is not in.
As You Like It 3.4.25–6

10 The sight of lovers feedeth those in love.
As You Like It 3.4.54, ROSALIND TO CORIN AND CELIA

1 This is the very ecstasy of love,
Whose violent property fordoes itself
And leads the will to desperate undertakings.
Hamlet 2.1.102–4, POLONIUS TO OPHELIA

2 What shall Cordelia speak? Love, and be silent.
King Lear 1.1.62, CORDELIA, when she hears her sister speaking grandiloquently of her love for her father

3 Adieu, valour! rust, rapier! be still, drum! for your manager is in love.
Love's Labour's Lost 1.2.176–7, ARMADO

4 This wimpled, whining, purblind, wayward boy.
Love's Labour's Lost 3.1.180, BEROWNE TO COSTARD, of Cupid

5 Love, first learned in a lady's eyes,
Lives not alone immured in the brain,
But, with the motion of all elements,
Courses as swift as thought in every power,
And gives to every power a double power,
Above their functions and their offices.
Love's Labour's Lost 4.3.323–8, BEROWNE TO HIS FRIENDS

6 A heart to love, and in that heart
Courage, to make's love known.
Macbeth 2.3.115–16, MACBETH TO MACDUFF

7 Tell me where is Fancy bred,
Or in the heart, or in the head?
How begot, how nourished?
It is engendered in the eyes . . .
Merchant of Venice 3.2.63–5, 67, song

8 I have pursued her as love hath pursued me; which hath been on the wing of all occasions.
Merry Wives of Windsor 2.2.194–6, FORD, in disguise, to FALSTAFF, of his own wife

9 The course of true love never did run smooth.
Midsummer Night's Dream 1.1.134, LYSANDER TO HERMIA

10 Brief as the lightning in the collied night.
Midsummer Night's Dream 1.1.145, LYSANDER TO HERMIA, on love

11 Love looks not with the eyes, but with the mind,
And therefore is winged Cupid painted blind.
Midsummer Night's Dream 1.1.234–5, HELENA

1 Cupid is a knavish lad
  Thus to make poor females mad!
  Midsummer Night's Dream 3.2.440–1, PUCK

2 Speak low, if you speak love.
  Much Ado About Nothing 2.1.91, DON PEDRO TO HERO

3 Let every eye negotiate for itself,
  And trust no agent; for beauty is a witch
  Against whose charms faith melteth into blood.
  Much Ado About Nothing 2.1.169–71, CLAUDIO

4   Loving goes by haps:
  Some Cupid kills with arrows, some with traps.
  Much Ado About Nothing 3.1.105–6, HERO

5 She loved me for the dangers I had passed
  And I loved her that she did pity them.
  Othello 1.3.168–9, OTHELLO TO THE DUKE OF VENICE

6 One that loved not wisely, but too well.
  Othello 5.2.344, OTHELLO, of himself, to HIS COLLEAGUES, before killing himself

7 Love and constancy is dead;
  Phoenix and the Turtle fled
  In a mutual flame from hence.
  So they loved, as love in twain
  Had the essence but in one:
  Two distincts, division none.
  Phoenix and Turtle 22–7

8 O heavy lightness, serious vanity,
  Misshapen chaos of well-seeming forms!
  Romeo and Juliet 1.1.178–9, ROMEO TO BENVOLIO – before he has met Juliet

9 Love is a smoke made with the fume of sighs;
  Being purged, a fire sparkling in lovers' eyes;
  Being vexed, a sea nourished with lovers' tears;
  What is it else? A madness most discreet,
  A choking gall, and a preserving sweet.
  Romeo and Juliet 1.1.190–4, ROMEO TO BENVOLIO

10 Is love a tender thing? It is too rough,
   Too rude, too boisterous, and it pricks like thorn.
   Romeo and Juliet 1.4.25–6, ROMEO TO MERCUTIO

1   What love can do, that dares love attempt.
    Romeo and Juliet 2.2.68, ROMEO TO JULIET

2   This bud of love, by summer's ripening breath,
    May prove a beauteous flower when next we meet.
    Romeo and Juliet 2.2.121–2, JULIET TO ROMEO

3   It is a greater grief
    To bear love's wrong, than hate's known injury.
    Sonnet 40.11–12

4   The prize of all-too-precious you.
    Sonnet 86.2

5   Let not my love be called idolatry.
    Sonnet 105.1

6   Let me not to the marriage of true minds
    Admit impediments.
    Sonnet 116.1–2

7   Love is not love
    Which alters when it alteration finds,
    Or bends with the remover to remove.
    O no, it is an ever-fixed mark,
    That looks on tempests and is never shaken;
    It is the star to every wand'ring bark.
    Sonnet 116.2–7; *more at* **TIME**

8   Two loves I have, of comfort and despair.
    Sonnet 144.1

9   Love is too young to know what conscience is.
    Sonnet 151.1

10 Spirit of love, how quick and fresh art thou.
    Twelfth Night 1.1.9, ORSINO TO CURIO

11   O mistress mine, where are you roaming?
        O stay and hear, your true love's coming,
            That can sing both high and low.
        Trip no further, pretty sweeting:
        Journeys end in lovers meeting,
            Every wise man's son doth know.
    Twelfth Night 2.3.39–44, FESTE's song; *more at* **PRESENT, the**

1   She never told her love,
But let concealment like a worm i'th' bud
Feed on her damask cheek. She pined in thought,
And with a green and yellow melancholy
She sat like Patience on a monument,
Smiling at grief. Was not this love indeed?
Twelfth Night 2.4.111–16, VIOLA, as Cesario, to ORSINO, of herself

2 JULIA They do not love that do not show their love.
LUCETTA O, they love least that let men know their love.
Two Gentlemen of Verona 1.2.31–2; a classic dilemma

3 O, how this spring of love resembleth
The uncertain glory of an April day,
Which now shows all the beauty of the sun,
And by and by a cloud takes all away.
Two Gentlemen of Verona 1.3.84–7, PROTEUS

4 Love will not be spurred to what it loathes.
Two Gentlemen of Verona 5.2.7, JULIA

5 Love keeps his revels where there are but twain.
Venus and Adonis 123

6 Love is a spirit all compact of fire.
Venus and Adonis 149

7 Prosperity's the very bond of love,
Whose fresh complexion and whose heart together
Affliction alters.
Winter's Tale 4.4.575–7, CAMILLO TO FLORIZEL AND PERDITA

See also **FLIRTATION AND SEDUCTION; LOVE, being in; LOVE, cooling; LOVE, expressions of; LOVE, falling in; SEX AND LUST**

LOVE, being in

8 What did he when thou saw'st him? What said he? How looked he? Wherein went he? What makes he here? Did he ask for me? Where remains he? How parted he with thee? And when shalt thou see him again? Answer me in one word.
As You Like It 3.2.217–21, ROSALIND TO CELIA

9 JAQUES What stature is she of?
ORLANDO Just as high as my heart.
As You Like It 3.2.265–6

1 The worst fault you have is to be in love.
As You Like It 3.2.278, JAQUES TO ORLANDO

2 Then your hose should be ungartered, your bonnet unbanded, your sleeve unbuttoned, your shoe untied, and everything about you demonstrating a careless desolation.
As You Like It 3.2.369–72, ROSALIND TO ORLANDO

3 O coz, coz, coz, my pretty little coz, that thou didst know how many fathom deep I am in love!
As You Like It 4.1.197–8, ROSALIND TO CELIA

4 Love hath made thee a tame snake.
As You Like It 4.3.69–70, ROSALIND TO SILVIUS

5 Thinking of nothing else, putting all affairs else in oblivion, as if there were nothing else to be done but to see him.
2 Henry IV 5.5.25–7, FALSTAFF describing himself to SHALLOW and PISTOL, as he waits to greet the new King Henry V (who will reject him; *see* **BETRAYAL**)

6 My mistress with a monster is in love.
Midsummer Night's Dream 3.2.6, PUCK TO OBERON

7 My Oberon! what visions have I seen!
Methought I was enamoured of an ass.
Midsummer Night's Dream 4.1.75–6, TITANIA TO OBERON

8 Alas, poor hurt fowl, now will he creep into sedges.
Much Ado About Nothing 2.1.191–2, BENEDICK, of Claudio

9 I will not be sworn but love may transform me to an oyster.
Much Ado About Nothing 2.3.23–4, BENEDICK on the transforming powers of love

10 What a pretty thing man is when he goes in his doublet and hose and leaves off his wit!
Much Ado About Nothing 5.1.195–6, DON PEDRO TO CLAUDIO, of Benedick

11 I am to wait, though waiting so be hell.
Sonnet 58.13

LOVE, cooling

12 I did love you once.
Hamlet 3.1.115, HAMLET TO OPHELIA

13 Time qualifies the spark and fire of it.
Hamlet 4.7.113, CLAUDIUS, referring to love

1 That time . . .
  When love, converted from the thing it was,
  Shall reasons find of settled gravity.
  Sonnet 49.5, 7–8

2 Tell me thou lov'st elsewhere; but in my sight,
  Dear heart, forbear to glance thine eye aside.
  Sonnet 139.5–6

3 I was adored once too.
  Twelfth Night 2.3.178, SIR ANDREW AGUECHEEK TO SIR TOBY BELCH

LOVE, expressions of

4   Hang there like fruit, my soul,
  Till the tree die.
  Cymbeline 5.5.263–4, POSTHUMUS TO IMOGEN

5 Doubt thou the stars are fire,
  Doubt that the sun doth move,
  Doubt truth to be a liar,
  But never doubt I love.
  Hamlet 2.2.115–18, POLONIUS, reading a letter from Hamlet to Ophelia (with some scorn at his poor poetical ability)

6 I know no ways to mince it in love but directly to say 'I love you.'
  Henry V 5.2.125–6, HENRY TO KATHERINE

7 You have witchcraft in your lips.
  Henry V 5.2.273, HENRY TO KATHERINE

8 For where thou art, there is the world itself, . . .
  And where thou art not, desolation.
  2 Henry VI 3.2.361, 363, SUFFOLK TO QUEEN MARGARET

9 I do love you . . .
  Dearer than eyesight, space and liberty.
  King Lear 1.1.55–6, GONERIL TO LEAR

10 What's mine is yours, and what is yours is mine.
  Measure for Measure 5.1.533, DUKE TO ISABELLA

11 You draw me, you hard-hearted adamant.
  Midsummer Night's Dream 2.1.195, HELENA TO DEMETRIUS

12 I had rather hear my dog bark at a crow than a man swear he loves me.
  Much Ado About Nothing 1.1.126–7, BEATRICE TO BENEDICK

1 I will live in thy heart, die in thy lap, and be buried in thy eyes; and
moreover, I will go with thee to thy uncle's.
Much Ado About Nothing 5.2.95–7, BENEDICK TO BEATRICE

2 Excellent wretch! perdition catch my soul
But I do love thee! and when I love thee not
Chaos is come again.
Othello 3.3.90–2, OTHELLO, with Iago, referring to Desdemona

3 See how she leans her cheek upon her hand.
O that I were a glove upon that hand,
That I might touch that cheek.
Romeo and Juliet 2.2.23–5, ROMEO

4 You alone are you.
Sonnet 84.2

5 My five wits, nor my five senses, can
Dissuade one foolish heart from serving thee.
Sonnet 141.9–10

6 Who taught thee how to make me love thee more,
The more I hear and see just cause of hate?
Sonnet 150.9–10

7 Kiss me, Kate, we will be married o' Sunday.
Taming of the Shrew 2.1.318, PETRUCHIO TO KATHERINA

8   Hear my soul speak:
The very instant that I saw you, did
My heart fly to your service.
Tempest 3.1.63–5, FERDINAND TO MIRANDA

9 ARIEL Do you love me, master? No?
PROSPERO Dearly, my delicate Ariel.
Tempest 4.1.48–9

10 What light is light, if Silvia be not seen?
What joy is joy, if Silvia be not by? . . .
Except I be by Silvia in the night,
There is no music in the nightingale.
Two Gentlemen of Verona 3.1.174–5, 178–9, VALENTINE

See also **ROMEO AND JULIET**

LOVE, falling in

1 What think you of falling in love?
As You Like It 1.2.24, ROSALIND TO CELIA

2 Dead shepherd, now I find thy saw of might,
'Who ever loved that loved not at first sight?'
As You Like It 3.5.81–2, PHEBE TO SILVIUS; the second reference to Christopher
Marlowe – the 'dead shepherd' – Shakespeare's recently murdered contemporary, in
a short space; this is to his *Hero and Leander* (1.176). *See also* **POETRY**.

3 For your brother and my sister no sooner met, but they looked; no
sooner looked, but they loved; no sooner loved, but they sighed; no
sooner sighed, but they asked one another the reason; no sooner knew
the reason, but they sought the remedy.
As You Like It 5.2.32–7, ROSALIND TO ORLANDO

4 Are you a god? would you create me new?
Comedy of Errors 3.2.39; ANTIPHOLUS OF SYRACUSE falls in love with his twin brother's
wife's sister

5 FERDINAND   My prime request,
Which I do last pronounce, is, O you wonder!
If you be maid or no?
MIRANDA   No wonder, sir;
But certainly a maid.
Tempest 1.2.428–31

6   At the first sight
They have changed eyes.
Tempest 1.2.443–4, PROSPERO, observing the exchange above

7 The very instant that I saw you, did
My heart fly to your service.
Tempest 3.1.64–5, FERDINAND TO MIRANDA

8 I was won . . . / With the first glance.
Troilus and Cressida 3.2.115–16, CRESSIDA TO TROILUS

LOVERS

9   And then the lover,
Sighing like a furnace, with a woeful ballad
Made to his mistress' eyebrow.
As You Like It 2.7.147–9, from JAQUES's 'Seven Ages of Man' speech

10 Lovers ever run before the clock.
Merchant of Venice 2.6.4, GRATIANO TO SALERIO

1 Love is blind, and lovers cannot see
The pretty follies that themselves commit.
Merchant of Venice 2.6.36–7, JESSICA TO LORENZO

2 BOTTOM What is Pyramus? A lover, or a tyrant?
QUINCE A lover, that kills himself most gallant for love.
Midsummer Night's Dream 1.2.20–1

3 A pair of star-crossed lovers.
Romeo and Juliet Prologue 6, CHORUS

4 Lovers can see to do their amorous rites
By their own beauties.
Romeo and Juliet 3.2.8–9, JULIET

5 　　　　　　　Lovers break not hours,
Unless it be to come before their time.
Two Gentlemen of Verona 5.1.4–5, EGLAMOUR

See also **LOVE; ROMEO AND JULIET**

LOYALTY

6 Is old dog my reward? Most true, I have lost my teeth in your service.
As You Like It 1.1.80–1, old ADAM, to OLIVER who insults him

7 O! where is faith? O! where is loyalty?
2 Henry VI 5.1.166, HENRY TO LORDS

8 A jewel in a ten-times barred-up chest
Is a bold spirit in a loyal breast.
Richard II 1.1.180–1, MOWBRAY TO RICHARD

LUCK

9 The very dice obey him.
Antony and Cleopatra 2.3.32, ANTONY, of Ventidius

10 I bear a charmed life.
Macbeth 5.8.12, MACBETH TO MACDUFF

11 As good luck would have it.
Merry Wives of Windsor 3.5.79, FALSTAFF TO FORD

12 This is the third time; I hope good luck lies in odd numbers . . . They say there is divinity in odd numbers, either in nativity, chance, or death.
Merry Wives of Windsor 5.1.1–4, FALSTAFF TO MISTRESS QUICKLY

1 'Tis a lucky day, boy, and we'll do good deeds on 't.
Winter's Tale 3.3.134–5, SHEPHERD TO HIS SON

See also **CHANCE; FORTUNE**

M

MADNESS

2 An antic disposition.
Hamlet 1.5.180, HAMLET TO HORATIO; he proposes to behave strangely to confuse those around him

3 POLONIUS Do you know me, my lord?
HAMLET Excellent well. You are a fishmonger.
Hamlet 2.2.173–4

4 Though this be madness, yet there is method in't.
Hamlet 2.2.205–6, POLONIUS

5 I am but mad north-north-west. When the wind is southerly, I know a hawk from a handsaw.
Hamlet 2.2.379–80, HAMLET TO ROSENCRANTZ AND GUILDENSTERN

6 O, what a noble mind is here o'erthrown!
Hamlet 3.1.151, OPHELIA, of Hamlet

7 Now see that noble and most sovereign reason
Like sweet bells jangled out of tune and harsh,
That unmatched form and feature of blown youth
Blasted with ecstasy.
Hamlet 3.1.158–61, OPHELIA, of Hamlet

8 Madness in great ones must not unwatched go.
Hamlet 3.1.189, CLAUDIUS

9 HAMLET Do you see yonder cloud that's almost in shape of a camel?
POLONIUS By th' mass and 'tis – like a camel indeed.
HAMLET Methinks it is like a weasel.
POLONIUS It is backed like a weasel.
HAMLET Or like a whale.

POLONIUS Very like a whale . . .
HAMLET [*aside*] They fool me to the top of my bent.
Hamlet 3.2.377–84, 386

1 His madness is poor Hamlet's enemy.
   Hamlet 5.2.238, HAMLET TO LAERTES AND CLAUDIUS

2 I am not mad: I would to heaven I were!
  For then 'tis like I should forget myself.
   King John 3.3.48–9, CONSTANCE, who has lost her son, to PHILIP, KING OF FRANCE and CARDINAL PANDULPH

3 O let me not be mad, not mad, sweet heaven! I would not be mad.
   King Lear 1.5.43–4, LEAR

4 My wits begin to turn.
   King Lear 3.2.67, LEAR TO KENT

5 That way madness lies.
   King Lear 3.4.21, LEAR TO KENT, thinking about Goneril and Regan

6 Trouble him not; his wits are gone.
   King Lear 3.6.85, KENT TO GLOUCESTER, of Lear

7 Matter and impertinency mixed,
  Reason in madness.
   King Lear 4.6.170–1, EDGAR, of Lear in his madness

8   These deeds must not be thought
  After these ways: so, it will make us mad.
   Macbeth 2.2.32–3, LADY MACBETH TO MACBETH

9 Canst thou not minister to a mind diseased,
  Pluck from the memory a rooted sorrow,
  Raze out the written troubles of the brain,
  And with some sweet oblivious antidote
  Cleanse the stuffed bosom of that perilous stuff
  Which weighs upon the heart?
   Macbeth 5.3.40–5, MACBETH TO THE DOCTOR

10 As mad as a March hare.
   Two Noble Kinsmen 3.5.74, ONE COUNTRYMAN TO ANOTHER; proverbial

11 You, that are thus so tender o'er his follies,
  Will never do him good.
   Winter's Tale 2.3.127–8, PAULINA TO LEONTES' ATTENDANTS

See also **DOCTORS AND MEDICINE; ILLNESS AND DISEASE; IMAGINATION**

MAGIC

1   This rough magic
   I here abjure.
   Tempest 5.1.50–1, PROSPERO; *more at* **RETIREMENT**

2   The charm dissolves apace.
    Tempest 5.1.64, PROSPERO

See also **APPARITIONS; FAIRIES; SUPERNATURAL, the; WITCHES**

MANIPULATION

3   You would play upon me, you would seem to know my stops, you
    would pluck out the heart of my mystery, you would sound me from
    my lowest note to the top of my compass; . . . 'Sblood, do you think I
    am easier to be played on than a pipe?
    Hamlet 3.2.366–9, 371–2, HAMLET TO GUILDENSTERN

MANNER AND MANNERS

4   Be thou familiar, but by no means vulgar.
    Hamlet 1.3.61, POLONIUS' advice to LAERTES; *more at* **ADVICE**

5   Use them after your own honour and dignity: the less they deserve, the
    more merit is in your bounty.
    Hamlet 2.2.532–3, HAMLET TO POLONIUS, of the players; *more at* **JUSTICE**

6   It is certain that either wise bearing or ignorant carriage is caught, as
    men take diseases, one of another; therefore let men take heed of their
    company.
    2 Henry IV 5.1.74–7, FALSTAFF

7   We are the makers of manners, Kate, and the liberty that follows our
    places stops the mouth of all find-faults.
    Henry V 5.2.268–70, HENRY TO KATHERINE, on the benefits of high position

8   Exceeding wise, fair-spoken and persuading;
    Lofty and sour to them that loved him not,
    But to those men that sought him, sweet as summer.
    Henry VIII 4.2.52–4, GRIFFITH, an usher, to KATHERINE OF ARAGON, of Cardinal
    Wolsey

9   Civil as an orange, and something of that jealous complexion.
    Much Ado About Nothing 2.1.276–7, BEATRICE TO DON PEDRO, of Claudio

10 We must be gentle, now we are gentlemen.
    Winter's Tale 5.2.152–3, SHEPHERD TO HIS SON

MARK ANTONY

1   Our courteous Antony,
Whom ne'er the word of 'No' woman heard speak,
Being barbered ten times o'er, goes to the feast.
Antony and Cleopatra 2.2.232–4, ENOBARBUS TO AGRIPPA

2 O Antony! O thou Arabian bird!
Antony and Cleopatra 3.2.12, AGRIPPA TO ENOBARBUS

3 Not Caesar's valour hath o'erthrown Antony,
But Antony's hath triumphed on itself.
Antony and Cleopatra 4.15.15–16, ANTONY TO CLEOPATRA

4   He is given
To sports, to wildness, and much company.
Julius Caesar 2.1.188–9, BRUTUS, rejecting the idea of Mark Antony as a danger

MARRIAGE

5 Get thee a good husband, and use him as he uses thee.
All's Well That Ends Well, 1.1.214–15, PAROLLES TO HELENA

6 If men could be contented to be what they are, there were no fear in marriage.
All's Well That Ends Well 1.3.50–1, CLOWN TO COUNTESS OF ROSSILLION

7   Wars is no strife
To the dark house and the detested wife.
All's Well That Ends Well 2.3.290–1, BERTRAM TO PAROLLES; 'to' means 'in comparison with'

8 A young man married is a man that's marred.
All's Well That Ends Well 2.3.297, PAROLLES' contribution to the same debate

9 Hath homely age th'alluring beauty took
From my poor cheek? then he hath wasted it.
Comedy of Errors 2.1.90–1, ADRIANA, the married sister, to the unmarried LUCIANA

10 Thou say'st his meat was sauced with thy upbraidings;
Unquiet meals make ill digestions; . . .
Thou say'st his sports were hindered by thy brawls;
Sweet recreation barred, what doth ensue
But moody and dull melancholy?
Comedy of Errors 5.1.73–4, 77–9, ABBESS TO ADRIANA, her daughter-in-law

11 With mirth in funeral and with dirge in marriage.
Hamlet 1.2.12, CLAUDIUS excusing his marriage to Gertrude

1 The instances that second marriage move
   Are base respects of thrift, but none of love.
   Hamlet 3.2.184–5, Player Queen to Player King

2 Marriage is a matter of more worth
   Than to be dealt in by attorneyship.
   1 Henry VI 5.5.55–6, Suffolk to other lords

3 For what is wedlock forced but a hell,
   An age of discord and continual strife?
   Whereas the contrary bringeth bliss,
   And is a pattern of celestial peace.
   1 Henry VI 5.5.62–5, Suffolk to other lords

4 Hasty marriage seldom proveth well.
   3 Henry VI 4.1.18, Richard of Gloucester to King Edward IV, his brother

5   I am old, . . .
   And all the fellowship I hold now with him
   Is only my obedience.
   Henry VIII 3.1.119–21, Katherine of Aragon to Cardinal Wolsey and Cardinal Campeius

6 Hanging and wiving goes by destiny.
   Merchant of Venice 2.9.84, Nerissa to Portia

7 In love the heavens themselves do guide the state;
   Money buys lands, and wives are sold by fate.
   Merry Wives of Windsor 5.5.228–9, Ford to Fenton

8 In time the savage bull doth bear the yoke.
   Much Ado About Nothing 1.1.245–6, Don Pedro to Benedick, proverbially and prophetically

9 Time goes on crutches till love hath all his rites.
   Much Ado About Nothing 2.1.336–7, Claudio to Don Pedro, saying he plans to marry Hero on the following day

10 Thou art sad; get thee a wife, get thee a wife!
   Much Ado About Nothing 5.4.121, Benedick, the convert, to Leonato

11 A fellow almost damned in a fair wife.
   Othello 1.1.20, Iago to Roderigo

12   O curse of marriage
   That we can call these delicate creatures ours
   And not their appetites!
   Othello 3.3.272–4, Othello

1 Thinkest thou, . . . though her father be very rich, any man is so very a
   fool to be married to hell?
   Taming of the Shrew 1.1.122–4, GREMIO TO HORTENSIO

2 To wive and thrive as best I may.
   Taming of the Shrew 1.2.55, PETRUCHIO TO HORTENSIO AND GRUMIO

3 I come to wive it wealthily in Padua;
   If wealthily, then happily in Padua.
   Taming of the Shrew 1.2.74–5, PETRUCHIO TO HORTENSIO AND GRUMIO

4 Who wooed in haste and means to wed at leisure.
   Taming of the Shrew 3.2.11, KATHERINA TO BAPTISTA, of Petruchio; proverbial

5 To me she's married, not unto my clothes.
   Taming of the Shrew 3.2.116, PETRUCHIO TO BAPTISTA; for the state of the horse on
   which he rides to his wedding, *see* **HORSES**

6 This is a way to kill a wife with kindness.
   Taming of the Shrew 4.1.196, PETRUCHIO

7 Peace . . . , and love, and quiet life,
   An awful rule, and right supremacy.
   Taming of the Shrew 5.2.109–10, PETRUCHIO TO HORTENSIO AND LUCENTIO, describing
   his concept of a proper marriage; for Katherina's concurrence, *see* **HUSBANDS AND
   WIVES**

8 Honour, riches, marriage-blessing,
   Long continuance, and increasing,
   Hourly joys be still upon you!
   Tempest 4.1.106–8, JUNO (goddess of marriage) to MIRANDA and FERDINAND

   See also **AMBITION; ANTICIPATION; HUSBANDS AND WIVES; INFIDELITY; MEN
   AND WOMEN; SINGLE LIFE, the; WOMEN**

MATURITY

9 For nature crescent does not grow alone
   In thews and bulk, but as this temple waxes,
   The inward service of the mind and soul
   Grows wide withal.
   Hamlet 1.3.11–14, LAERTES TO OPHELIA

10 Consideration like an angel came
   And whipped th'offending Adam out of him.
   Henry V 1.1.28–9, ARCHBISHOP OF CANTERBURY TO THE BISHOP OF ELY, of Hal/Henry

11 Ripeness is all.
   King Lear 5.2.11, EDGAR TO GLOUCESTER

MEDICINE *see* **DOCTORS AND MEDICINE**

MELANCHOLY

1 CELIA Why cousin, why Rosalind! Cupid have mercy, not a word?
  ROSALIND Not one to throw at a dog.
  As You Like It 1.3.1–3

2 I can suck melancholy out of a song, as a weasel sucks eggs.
  As You Like It 2.5.11–12, JAQUES TO AMIENS

3 I have neither the scholar's melancholy, which is emulation; nor the
  musician's, which is fantastical; nor the courtier's, which is proud; nor
  the soldier's, which is ambitious; nor the lawyer's, which is politic; nor
  the lady's, which is nice; nor the lover's, which is all these; but it is a
  melancholy of mine own, compounded of many simples, extracted
  from many objects, and indeed the sundry contemplation of my
  travels, in which my often rumination wraps me in a most humorous
  sadness.
  As You Like It 4.1.10–19, JAQUES TO ROSALIND

4   There's something in his soul
  O'er which his melancholy sits on brood.
  Hamlet 3.1.165–6, CLAUDIUS TO POLONIUS

5 As melancholy as a lodge in a warren.
  Much Ado About Nothing 2.1.202–3, BENEDICK TO DON PEDRO, of Claudio

  See also **DEPRESSION; MUSIC**

MEMORY AND REMEMBERING

6   Praising what is lost
  Makes the remembrance dear.
  All's Well That Ends Well 5.3.19–20, KING OF FRANCE TO HIS FRIENDS

7   Heaven and earth,
  Must I remember?
  Hamlet 1.2.142–3, HAMLET

8 'Tis in my memory locked.
  Hamlet 1.3.85, OPHELIA's response to her brother's advice

9 GHOST   Remember me . . .
  HAMLET   Remember thee?
  Yea, from the table of my memory
  I'll wipe away all trivial fond records, . . .

And thy commandment all alone shall live
Within the book and volume of my brain.
Hamlet 1.5.91, 97–9, 102–3

1 There's rosemary, that's for remembrance.
Hamlet 4.5.173, OPHELIA, in her madness; *more at* **FLOWERS AND PLANTS**

2 Memory, the warder of the brain.
Macbeth 1.7.66, LADY MACBETH TO MACBETH

3 I cannot but remember such things were,
That were most precious to me.
Macbeth 4.3.222–3, MACDUFF TO MALCOLM

4 Men are men, the best sometimes forget.
Othello 2.3.233, IAGO TO MONTANO

5 That I could forget what I have been!
Or not remember what I must be now!
Richard II 3.3.138–9, RICHARD TO AUMERLE

6 ULYSSES All's done, my lord.
TROILUS   It is.
ULYSSES   Why stay we then?
TROILUS To make a recordation to my soul
Of every syllable that here was spoke.
Troilus and Cressida 5.2.113–15

See also **FORGETFULNESS; NEW BEGINNINGS; OLD AGE; PAST, the**

MEN

7 Think you there was or might be such a man
As this I dreamt of?
Antony and Cleopatra 5.2.92–3, CLEOPATRA TO DOLABELLA

8 We'll have a swashing and a martial outside,
As many other mannish cowards have
That do outface it with their semblances.
As You Like It 1.3.117–19, ROSALIND TO CELIA, deciding to adopt male disguise

9 He's proud, and yet his pride becomes him.
He'll make a proper man.
As You Like It 3.5.114–15, PHEBE TO SILVIUS

10 Men have died from time to time and worms have eaten them, but not
for love.
As You Like It 4.1.101–2, ROSALIND TO ORLANDO

1 Good sister let us dine, and never fret;
A man is master of his liberty;
Time is their master, and when they see time,
They'll go or come.
Comedy of Errors 2.1.6–9, LUCIANA TO ADRIANA

2 A was a man, take him for all in all:
I shall not look upon his like again.
Hamlet 1.2.187–8, HAMLET TO HORATIO ('a' here means 'he')

3 Percy . . . the Hotspur of the north, he that kills me some six or seven
dozen of Scots at a breakfast, washes his hands, and says to his wife,
'Fie upon this quiet life, I want work'. 'O my sweet Harry', says she,
'how many hast thou killed today?' 'Give my roan horse a drench', says
he, and answers, 'Some fourteen', an hour after; 'a trifle, a trifle'.
1 Henry IV 2.4.100–7, PRINCE HAL TO POINS, mocking his rival for manliest young
man in Britain

4 Men are merriest when they are from home.
Henry V 1.2.273, HENRY TO EXETER

5 His life was gentle, and the elements
So mixed in him, that Nature might stand up
And say to all the world, 'This was a man!'
Julius Caesar 5.5.73–5, MARK ANTONY, of Brutus

6   I am ashamed
That thou hast power to shake my manhood so.
King Lear 1.4.288–9, LEAR, brought to tears, to GONERIL

7 O, the difference of man and man!
King Lear 4.2.26; GONERIL compares her husband with Edmund

8 Lust-breathed Tarquin.
Lucrece 3

9 In men as in a rough-grown grove remain
Cave-keeping evils that obscurely sleep.
Lucrece 1249–50

10 When you durst do it, then you were a man.
Macbeth 1.7.49, LADY MACBETH TO MACBETH

11 God made him, and therefore let him pass for a man.
Merchant of Venice 1.2.54–5, PORTIA TO NERISSA on her French suitor, Monsieur Le Bon

1 A kind heart he hath: a woman would run through fire and water for such a kind heart.
Merry Wives of Windsor 3.4.100–1, MISTRESS QUICKLY

2 Manhood is melted into curtsies, valour into compliment, and men are only turned into tongue, and trim ones too: he is now as valiant as Hercules that only tells a lie and swears it.
Much Ado About Nothing 4.1.316–20, BEATRICE TO BENEDICK

3 BENVOLIO Why, what is Tybalt?
MERCUTIO More than Prince of Cats. O, he's the courageous captain of compliments: he fights as you sing pricksong, keeps time, distance and proportion. He rests his minim rests, one, two, and the third in your bosom: the very butcher of a silk button – a duellist, a duellist, a gentleman of the very first house, of the first and second cause. Ah, the immortal passado, the punto reverso, the hay!
Romeo and Juliet 2.4.19–27

4 It is a holiday to look on them. Lord, the difference of men!
Two Noble Kinsmen 2.1.55–6, JAILER'S DAUGHTER TO THE JAILER, referring to Arcite and Palamon

5 Rose-cheeked Adonis.
Venus and Adonis 3

See also **MEN AND WOMEN; YOUTH**

MEN AND WOMEN

6 ROSALIND Now tell me how long you would have her, after you have possessed her?
ORLANDO For ever, and a day.
ROSALIND Say a day, without the ever. No, no, Orlando, men are April when they woo, December when they wed. Maids are May when they are maids, but the sky changes when they are wives.
As You Like It 4.1.136–42

7 I knew what you would prove. My friends told me as much, and I thought no less.
As You Like It 4.1.174–6, ROSALIND TO ORLANDO

8 Man, more divine, the master of all these,
Lord of the wide world and wild wat'ry seas,
Indued with intellectual sense and souls,

Of more pre-eminence than fish and fowls,
Are masters to their females, and their lords.
Comedy of Errors 2.1.20–4, a conventional view expressed by LUCIANA to her sceptical married sister ADRIANA

1 Men's vows are women's traitors.
Cymbeline 3.4.53, IMOGEN TO PISANIO

2 He that hath a beard is more than a youth, and he that hath no beard is less than a man; and he that is more than a youth is not for me; and he that is less than a man I am not for him.
Much Ado About Nothing 2.1.32–5, BEATRICE TO LEONATO

3 Would it not grieve a woman to be over-mastered with a piece of valiant dust, to make an account of her life to a clod of wayward marl?
Much Ado About Nothing 2.1.55–7, BEATRICE TO LEONATO

4 Rich she shall be, that's certain; wise, or I'll none; virtuous, or I'll never cheapen her; fair, or I'll never look on her; mild, or come not near me; noble, or not I for an angel; of good discourse, an excellent musician, and her hair shall be – of what colour it please God.
Much Ado About Nothing 2.3.29–34, BENEDICK, on the only kind of woman he would submit to marrying

5 They are all but stomachs, and we all but food:
They eat us hungerly, and when they are full
They belch us.
Othello 3.4.105–7, EMILIA TO DESDEMONA, of men

6 Men prize the thing ungained more than it is.
Troilus and Cressida 1.2.289, CRESSIDA TO PANDARUS

7   Prithee, tarry.
You men will never tarry.
O foolish Cressid, I might have still held off,
And then you would have tarried.
Troilus and Cressida 4.2.15–18, CRESSIDA TO TROILUS, on playing hard-to-get

8 We men may say more, swear more, but indeed
Our shows are more than will: for still we prove
Much in our vows, but little in our love.
Twelfth Night 2.4.117–19, VIOLA, as Cesario, to ORSINO

9 That man that hath a tongue, I say is no man,
If with his tongue he cannot win a woman.
Two Gentlemen of Verona 3.1.104–5, VALENTINE TO THE DUKE

See also **GENDER; HUSBANDS AND WIVES; INFIDELITY; MARRIAGE; MEN; WOMEN**

MENDING AND IMPROVING

1 Patches set upon a little breach
   Discredit more in hiding of the fault
   Than did the fault before it was so patched.
   King John 4.2.32–4, PEMBROKE TO SALISBURY

2 Striving to better, oft we mar what's well.
   King Lear 1.4.342, ALBANY TO GONERIL

3 This is like the mending of highways
   In summer, where the ways are fair enough!
   Merchant of Venice 5.1.263–4, GRATIANO TO NERISSA AND PORTIA, describing an
   unnecessary action (in this case taking a lover when your husband is still young and
   amorous)

4 Why so large cost, having so short a lease,
   Dost thou upon thy fading mansion spend?
   Sonnet 146.5–6; Shakespeare addresses his soul; the fading mansion is the body

MERCY

5 No ceremony that to great ones longs,
   Not the king's crown, nor the deputed sword,
   The marshal's truncheon, nor the judge's robe,
   Become them with one half so good a grace
   As mercy does.
   Measure for Measure 2.2.59–63, ISABELLA TO ANGELO

6   Lawful mercy
   Is nothing kin to foul redemption.
   Measure for Measure 2.4.112–13, ISABELLA TO ANGELO; by 'foul redemption' she means
   a corrupt or cruel bargain

7 How shalt thou hope for mercy, rendering none?
   Merchant of Venice 4.1.88, DUKE OF VENICE TO SHYLOCK

8 The quality of mercy is not strained,
   It droppeth as the gentle rain from heaven
   Upon the place beneath: it is twice blest,
   It blesseth him that gives, and him that takes,
   'Tis mightiest in the mightiest, it becomes
   The throned monarch better than his crown.
   His sceptre shows the force of temporal power,
   The attribute to awe and majesty,
   Wherein doth sit the dread and fear of kings:

But mercy is above this sceptred sway,
It is enthroned in the hearts of kings,
It is an attribute to God himself;
And earthly power doth then show likest God's
When mercy seasons justice.
Merchant of Venice 4.1.182–95, PORTIA's celebrated speech on mercy

1 Sweet mercy is nobility's true badge.
Titus Andronicus 1.1.122, TAMORA TO TITUS; perhaps the formality of phrasing here indicates that this does not come from the heart

See also **JUSTICE; PITY**

MERIT

2   Let none presume
To wear an undeserved dignity:
O that estates, degrees, and offices,
Were not derived corruptly, and that clear honour
Were purchased by the merit of the wearer!
Merchant of Venice 2.9.39–43, PRINCE OF ARRAGON

MERRIMENT

3 I shall never laugh but in that maid's company.
Merry Wives of Windsor 1.4.143, MISTRESS QUICKLY TO FENTON, of Anne Page

4 There is either liquor in his pate or money in his purse when he looks so merrily.
Merry Wives of Windsor 2.1.178–9, PAGE TO FORD, of the host of the Garter

5 From the crown of his head to the sole of his foot he is all mirth.
Much Ado About Nothing 3.2.8–9, DON PEDRO TO CLAUDIO, of Benedick

6 I am not merry, but I do beguile
The thing I am by seeming otherwise.
Othello 2.1.122–3, DESDEMONA TO IAGO

7 If you will . . . laugh yourselves into stitches, follow me.
Twelfth Night 3.2.66–7, MARIA TO SIR TOBY BELCH AND FABIAN

See also **HAPPINESS; JOY**

MIDDLE AGE

8   At your age
The heyday in the blood is tame, it's humble,
And waits upon the judgement.
Hamlet 3.4.68–70, HAMLET TO GERTRUDE; a case of wishful thinking

1 Your lordship, though not clean past your youth, have yet some smack of age in you, some relish of the saltness of time.
2 Henry IV 1.2.96–8, FALSTAFF making fun of the LORD CHIEF JUSTICE

2 Not so young to love a woman for singing, nor so old to dote on her for anything. I have years on my back forty-eight.
King Lear 1.4.37–9, KENT TO LEAR

3 Though we are justices, and doctors, and churchmen, Master Page, we have some salt of our youth in us.
Merry Wives of Windsor 2.3.42–4, SHALLOW TO PAGE

4 Our loves and comforts should increase
Even as our days do grow.
Othello 2.1.192–3, DESDEMONA TO OTHELLO

5   I am declined
Into the vale of years.
Othello 3.3.269–70, OTHELLO, desperately jealous

6 When forty winters shall besiege thy brow,
And dig deep trenches in thy beauty's field,
Thy youth's proud livery, so gazed on now,
Will be a tattered weed of small worth held.
Sonnet 2.1–4

MIND, the

7 A mote it is to trouble the mind's eye.
Hamlet 1.1.115, HORATIO TO BARNARDO

8   Methinks I see my father . . .
In my mind's eye.
Hamlet 1.2.183, 185, HAMLET TO HORATIO

9 All things are ready, if our minds be so.
Henry V 4.3.71, HENRY TO LORDS

10 'Tis the mind that makes the body rich.
Taming of the Shrew 4.3.170, PETRUCHIO TO KATE

See also BODY, the; MADNESS

MISANTHROPY

11   Live loathed, and long,
Most smiling, smooth, detested parasites,
Courteous destroyers, affable wolves, meek bears,

You fools of fortune, trencher-friends, time's flies,
Cap-and-knee slaves, vapours, and minute-jacks!
Timon of Athens 3.6.90–4, TIMON TO FORMER FRIENDS

1 I am *Misanthropos*, and hate mankind.
Timon of Athens 4.3.54, TIMON TO ALCIBIADES

MISCHIEF

2 Marry, this is miching malicho. It means mischief.
Hamlet 3.2.139–40, HAMLET TO OPHELIA, of the dumb show play

3 Mischief, thou art afoot.
Julius Caesar 3.2.261; MARK ANTONY, gratified, surveys the effect of his speeches on the plebeians

4 You have beaten my men, killed my deer, and broke open my lodge.
Merry Wives of Windsor 1.1.106–7, SHALLOW TO FALSTAFF

5 My thoughts are ripe in mischief.
Twelfth Night 5.1.126, ORSINO TO VIOLA as Cesario

See also **TROUBLE; WILD BEHAVIOUR**

MISFORTUNE

6 One woe doth tread upon another's heel.
Hamlet 4.7.163, GERTRUDE TO LAERTES

7 Death and destruction dogs thee at thy heels.
Richard III 4.1.39, QUEEN ELIZABETH TO DORSET

8 Thou art wedded to calamity.
Romeo and Juliet 3.3.3, FRIAR LAURENCE TO ROMEO

9 When in disgrace with fortune and men's eyes . . .
Sonnet 29.1

MISGIVINGS

10 Thou wouldst not think how ill all's here about my heart; but it is no matter.
Hamlet 5.2.211–12, HAMLET TO HORATIO

11 My mind misgives
Some consequence yet hanging in the stars.
Romeo and Juliet 1.4.106–7, ROMEO TO BENVOLIO AND MERCUTIO

See also **ANXIETY; CARES; FEAR; FOREBODING; FORTUNE**

MISTAKES

1 I have shot my arrow o'er the house
   And hurt my brother.
   Hamlet 5.2.242–3, HAMLET TO LAERTES

2   O negligence!
   Fit for a fool to fall by.
   Henry VIII 3.2.213–14, CARDINAL WOLSEY, foreseeing his ruin

3 I stumbled when I saw.
   King Lear 4.1.21, GLOUCESTER, blinded, to an OLD MAN

MODERATION

4 Like to the time o'th' year between the extremes
   Of hot and cold, he was nor sad nor merry.
   Antony and Cleopatra 1.5.54–5, ALEXAS TO CLEOPATRA

5 Though you can guess what temperance should be,
   You know not what it is.
   Antony and Cleopatra 3.13.126–7, ANTONY TO CLEOPATRA

6 Rather rejoicing to see another merry, than merry at anything which
   professed to make him rejoice.
   Measure for Measure 3.2.229–31, ESCALUS TO THE DUKE, disguised as a friar

7 Why tell you me of moderation?
   Troilus and Cressida 4.4.2, CRESSIDA TO PANDARUS, who tries to persuade her to
   moderate her grief at the loss of Troilus

MODESTY

8 An ill-favoured thing sir, but mine own.
   As You Like It 5.4.56–7, TOUCHSTONE TO DUKE SENIOR

9   'Twere a concealment
   Worse than a theft, no less than a traducement,
   To hide your doings, and to silence that
   Which, to the spire and top of praises vouched,
   Would seem but modest.
   Coriolanus 1.9.21–5, COMINIUS TO CORIOLANUS

10 You see me Lord Bassanio where I stand,
   Such as I am.
   Merchant of Venice 3.2.149–50, PORTIA

11 I will not praise, that purpose not to sell.
   Sonnet 21.14

1 A thing slipped idly from me.
Timon of Athens 1.1.20, POET TO OTHERS, describing his work

MONEY

2   'Tis gold
Which buys admittance.
Cymbeline 2.3.68–9, CLOTEN

3 Neither a borrower nor a lender be.
Hamlet 1.3.75, POLONIUS TO LAERTES; *more at* **ADVICE**

4 Bell, book and candle shall not drive me back
When gold and silver becks me to come on.
King John 3.2.22–3, PHILIP THE BASTARD TO JOHN; 'bell, book and candle' was a form of words for excommunication

5 Remuneration! O that's the Latin word for three farthings.
Love's Labour's Lost 3.1.137–8, MOTH

6   You take my life
When you do take the means whereby I live.
Merchant of Venice 4.1.374–5, SHYLOCK TO PORTIA

7 If money go before, all ways do lie open.
Merry Wives of Windsor 2.2.163–4, FORD TO FALSTAFF

8 O, what a world of vile ill-favoured faults
Looks handsome in three hundred pounds a year!
Merry Wives of Windsor 3.4.32–3, ANNE PAGE

9 Put money in thy purse.
Othello 1.3.343; IAGO urges RODERIGO to get his priorities right

10 Saint-seducing gold.
Romeo and Juliet 1.1.214, ROMEO TO BENVOLIO

11 This yellow slave
Will knit and break religions, bless th'accursed,
Make the hoar leprosy adored, place thieves,
And give them title, knee and approbation
With senators on the bench.
Timon of Athens 4.3.34–8, TIMON

See also **DAUGHTERS; GREED; POVERTY; RICHES**

MOON, the

12 How sweet the moonlight sleeps upon this bank!
Merchant of Venice 5.1.54, LORENZO TO JESSICA

1 Peace! – how the moon sleeps with Endymion!
   Merchant of Venice 5.1.109, PORTIA TO NERISSA

2 Ill met by moonlight, proud Titania.
   Midsummer Night's Dream 2.1.60, OBERON TO TITANIA

3 A calendar, a calendar! Look in the almanac; find out moonshine, find
   out moonshine!
   Midsummer Night's Dream 3.1.49–50, BOTTOM TO HIS COMPANIONS

4 All that I have to say is, to tell you that the lantern is the moon; I the
   Man i'th' Moon; this thorn-bush my thorn-bush; and this dog my dog.
   Midsummer Night's Dream 5.1.251–3, ROBIN STARVELING as Moonshine, getting
   irritated at audience interruptions

5 It is the very error of the moon,
   She comes more nearer earth than she was wont
   And makes men mad.
   Othello 5.2.109–11, OTHELLO TO EMILIA

   See also **MUSIC; NIGHT; VOWS**

MORNING

6   Hark, hark, the lark at heaven's gate sings,
              And Phoebus gins arise,
           His steeds to water at those springs
              On chaliced flowers that lies;
        And winking Mary-buds begin to ope their golden eyes;
        With every thing that pretty is, my lady sweet arise:
              Arise, arise!
   Cymbeline 2.3.20–6, song

7 But look, the morn in russet mantle clad
   Walks o'er the dew of yon high eastward hill.
   Hamlet 1.1.171–2, HORATIO TO MARCELLUS

8 But soft, methinks I scent the morning air.
   Hamlet 1.5.58, GHOST TO HAMLET

9 The glow-worm shows the matin to be near
   And gins to pale his uneffectual fire.
   Hamlet 1.5.89–90, GHOST TO HAMLET

10 The country cocks do crow, the clocks do toll.
   Henry V 4.0.15, CHORUS, describing the morning of the battle of Agincourt

1   The morning's war,
When dying clouds contend with growing light,
What time the shepherd, blowing of his nails,
Can neither call it perfect day nor night.
3 Henry VI 2.5.1–4, HENRY

2 MACBETH   What is the night?
LADY MACBETH Almost at odds with morning, which is which.
Macbeth 3.4.125–6

3 Fairy king, attend and mark:
I do hear the morning lark.
Midsummer Night's Dream 4.1.92–3, PUCK TO OBERON

4 The grey-eyed morn smiles on the frowning night,
Chequering the eastern clouds with streaks of light;
And darkness fleckled like a drunkard reels
From forth day's pathway, made by Titan's wheels.
Romeo and Juliet 2.2.188–91, ROMEO

5 JULIET Wilt thou be gone? It is not yet near day.
It was the nightingale and not the lark
That pierced the fearful hollow of thine ear.
Nightly she sings on yond pomegranate tree.
Believe me, love, it was the nightingale.
ROMEO It was the lark, the herald of the morn,
No nightingale. Look, love, what envious streaks
Do lace the severing clouds in yonder east.
Night's candles are burnt out, and jocund day
Stands tiptoe on the misty mountain tops.
Romeo and Juliet 3.5.1–10

6 Full many a glorious morning have I seen
Flatter the mountain tops with sovereign eye,
Kissing with golden face the meadows green,
Gilding pale streams with heavenly alchemy;
Anon permit the basest clouds to ride
With ugly rack on his celestial face.
Sonnet 33.1–6

7 The golden sun salutes the morn,
And, having gilt the ocean with his beams,
Gallops the zodiac in his glistering coach,
And overlooks the highest-peering hills.
Titus Andronicus 1.1.504–7, AARON

1 Like a red morn that ever yet betokened
   Wrack to the seaman, tempest to the field,
   Sorrow to shepherds, woe unto the birds,
   Gusts and foul flaws to herdmen and to herds.
   Venus and Adonis 453–6

2 The morning, from whose silver breast
   The sun ariseth in his majesty;
   Who doth the world so gloriously behold
   That cedar tops and hills seem burnished gold.
   Venus and Adonis 855–8

MORTALITY

3   Fear no more the heat o'th' sun,
         Nor the furious winter's rages,
       Thou thy worldly task has done,
         Home art gone and ta'en thy wages.
       Golden lads and girls all must,
       As chimney-sweepers, come to dust . . .
       The sceptre, learning, physic, must
       All follow this and come to dust.
   Cymbeline 4.2.258–63, 268–9, GUIDERIUS' AND ARVIRAGUS' song; *more at* DEATH

4   All that lives must die,
   Passing through nature to eternity.
   Hamlet 1.2.72–3, GERTRUDE TO HAMLET

5 Get you to my lady's chamber and tell her, let her paint an inch thick,
   to this favour she must come.
   Hamlet 5.1.190–2, HAMLET TO HORATIO, examining skulls in the graveyard

6 To what base uses we may return, Horatio! Why, may not imagination
   trace the noble dust of Alexander till a find it stopping a bung-hole?
   Hamlet 5.1.200–2, HAMLET TO HORATIO in the graveyard

7 Imperious Caesar, dead and turned to clay,
   Might stop a hole to keep the wind away.
   Hamlet 5.1.211–12, HAMLET TO HORATIO

8 When wilt thou leave fighting a-days, and foining a-nights, and begin
   to patch up thine old body for heaven?
   2 Henry IV 2.4.231–3, DOLL TEARSHEET TO FALSTAFF

1   Methinks it were a happy life
   To be no better than a homely swain;
   To sit upon a hill, as I do now,
   To carve out dials quaintly, point by point,
   Thereby to see the minutes how they run –
   How many makes the hour full complete,
   How many hours brings about the day,
   How many days will finish up the year,
   How many years a mortal man may live.
   3 Henry VI 2.5.21–9, HENRY, during a battle in which he takes no part

2 But yesterday the word of Caesar might
   Have stood against the world; now he lies there,
   And none so poor to do him reverence.
   Julius Caesar 3.2.119–21, MARK ANTONY TO PLEBEIANS

3 We cannot hold mortality's strong hand.
   King John 4.2.82, JOHN TO PEMBROKE

4 What surety of the world, what hope, what stay,
   When this was now a king, and now is clay?
   King John 5.7.68–9, PRINCE HENRY, after his father's death, to COMPANIONS

5 GLOUCESTER O, let me kiss that hand!
   LEAR Let me wipe it first, it smells of mortality.
   King Lear 4.6.128–9

6 A man that apprehends death no more dreadfully but as a drunken
   sleep; careless, reckless, and fearless of what's past, present, or to come:
   insensible of mortality, and desperately mortal.
   Measure for Measure 4.2.142–5, PROVOST's description, to the DUKE disguised as a
   friar, of Barnadine

7 Since brass, nor stone, nor earth, nor boundless sea,
   But sad mortality o'er-sways their power,
   How with this rage shall beauty hold a plea
   Whose action is no stronger than a flower?
   Sonnet 65.1–4

8 Is this thy body's end?
   Sonnet 146.8

9 The vine shall grow but we shall never see it.
   Two Noble Kinsmen 2.2.43, ARCITE TO PALAMON

See also **DEATH; TIME; TRANSIENCE**

MOTHERS

1 My mother told me just how he would woo
As if she sat in's heart.
All's Well That Ends Well 4.2.69–70, DIANA, of Bertram

2 He did it to please his mother.
Coriolanus 1.1.37–8, TWO CITIZENS discussing Coriolanus

3 Nature makes them partial.
Hamlet 3.3.32, POLONIUS TO CLAUDIUS, of mothers

4   Bring forth men-children only!
For thy undaunted mettle should compose
Nothing but males.
Macbeth 1.7.73–5, MACBETH TO LADY MACBETH

5   My heart
Leaps to be gone into my mother's bosom.
Pericles 5.3.44–5, MARINA to her long-lost mother THAISA

MURDER

6 Murder most foul.
Hamlet 1.5.27, GHOST TO HAMLET

7 How now? A rat! Dead for a ducat, dead.
Hamlet 3.4.23, HAMLET, on murdering an unknown person, who might be Claudius

8 No place indeed should murder sanctuarize.
Hamlet 4.7.127, CLAUDIUS TO LAERTES

9 Let's carve him as a dish fit for the gods,
Not hew him as a carcass fit for hounds.
Julius Caesar 2.1.173–4, BRUTUS; *see also* **SACRIFICES AND SCAPEGOATS**

10 There is no sure foundation set on blood,
No certain life achieved by others' death.
King John 4.2.104–5, JOHN, repenting his crimes

11 Most sacrilegious Murther hath broke ope
The Lord's anointed Temple, and stole thence
The life o'th' building!
Macbeth 2.3.67–9, MACDUFF TO MACBETH AND LENOX, at the discovery of Duncan's murder

12 Truth will come to light, murder cannot be hid long.
Merchant of Venice 2.2.76, LAUNCELOT GOBBO TO OLD GOBBO

1   O ill-starred wench,
Pale as thy smock. When we shall meet at compt
This look of thine will hurl my soul from heaven
And fiends will snatch at it.
Othello 5.2.272–5, OTHELLO, of the dead Desdemona

2   The object poisons sight,
Let it be hid.
Othello 5.2.364–5, LODOVICO, of the corpses at the end of the play

3 Murder's as near to lust as flame to smoke.
Pericles 1.1.139, PERICLES

4 Go, tread the path that thou shalt ne'er return.
Richard III 1.1.117, RICHARD, seeing off Clarence

5   I do love thee so
That I will shortly send thy soul to Heaven –
If Heaven will take the present at our hands.
Richard III 1.1.118–20, RICHARD, of Clarence

6 Murder, stern murder, in the direst degree.
Richard III 5.3.198, RICHARD, finally a prey to guilt

7 I do begin to have bloody thoughts.
Tempest 4.1.220–1, STEPHANO, with Caliban and Trinculo

8 A deed of death done on the innocent.
Titus Andronicus 3.2.56, TITUS TO MARCUS

See also **BLOOD; CRIMES; GUILT**

MUSIC

9 Give me some music – music, moody food
Of us that trade in love.
Antony and Cleopatra 2.5.1–2, CLEOPATRA TO HER COMPANIONS

10 For my voice, I have lost it with hallooing, and singing of anthems.
2 Henry IV 1.2.188–9, FALSTAFF TO THE LORD CHIEF JUSTICE; hallooing refers to hunting

11 Sneak's noise.
2 Henry IV 2.4.10, FRANCIS TO A DRAWER, referring to a company of musicians

12 A French song and a fiddle has no fellow.
Henry VIII 1.3.41, LOVEL TO SANDS

1   Orpheus with his lute made trees,
       And the mountain tops that freeze,
         Bow themselves when he did sing . . .
       In sweet music is such art,
       Killing care and grief of heart.
Henry VIII 3.1.3–5, 12–13, song

2   As sweet and musical
   As bright Apollo's lute, strung with his hair.
Love's Labour's Lost 4.3.338–9, BEROWNE TO HIS FRIENDS

3 The words of Mercury are harsh after the songs of Apollo.
Love's Labour's Lost 5.2.923, the closing words of the play

4 Let music sound while he doth make his choice,
   Then if he lose he makes a swan-like end,
   Fading in music.
Merchant of Venice 3.2.43–5, PORTIA, while Bassanio chooses a casket that will win or lose him her hand in marriage

5 How sweet the moonlight sleeps upon this bank!
   Here will we sit, and let the sounds of music
   Creep in our ears – soft stillness and the night
   Become the touches of sweet harmony:
   Sit Jessica, – look how the floor of heaven
   Is thick inlaid with patens of bright gold,
   There's not the smallest orb which thou behold'st
   But in his motion like an angel sings,
   Still quiring to the young-eyed cherubins;
   Such harmony is in immortal souls,
   But whilst this muddy vesture of decay
   Doth grossly close it in, we cannot hear it.
Merchant of Venice 5.1.54–65, LORENZO TO JESSICA

6 I am never merry when I hear sweet music.
Merchant of Venice 5.1.69, JESSICA TO LORENZO

7 The man that hath no music in himself,
   Nor is not moved with concord of sweet sounds,
   Is fit for treasons, stratagems, and spoils,
   The motions of his spirit are dull as night,
   And his affections dark as Erebus:
   Let no such man be trusted.
Merchant of Venice 5.1.83–8, LORENZO TO JESSICA

1 Once I sat upon a promontory,
  And heard a mermaid on a dolphin's back
  Uttering such dulcet and harmonious breath
  That the rude sea grew civil at her song
  And certain stars shot madly from their spheres
  To hear the sea-maid's music.
  Midsummer Night's Dream 2.1.149–54, OBERON TO PUCK

2 I have a reasonable good ear in music. Let's have the tongs and the bones.
  Midsummer Night's Dream 4.1.28–9, BOTTOM TO TITANIA

3 Music ho, music, such as charmeth sleep!
  Midsummer Night's Dream 4.1.82, TITANIA, with Oberon

4 Now, divine air! Now is his soul ravished! Is it not strange that sheep's guts should hale souls out of men's bodies?
  Much Ado About Nothing 2.3.57–9, BENEDICK

5   She had a song of 'willow',
  An old thing 'twas, but it expressed her fortune
  And she died singing it. That song tonight
  Will not go from my mind.
  Othello 4.3.26–9, DESDEMONA TO EMILIA; for the song, *see* **SORROW**

6   I will play the swan
  And die in music.
  Othello 5.2.247–8, EMILIA, stabbed by Iago, singing to the dead DESDEMONA

7   How sour sweet music is
  When time is broke and no proportion kept!
  So is it in the music of men's lives.
  Richard II 5.5.42–4, RICHARD

8 This music mads me. Let it sound no more.
  Richard II 5.5.61, RICHARD

9 The true concord of well-tuned sounds.
  Sonnet 8.5

10 Mark how one string, sweet husband to another,
  Strikes each in each by mutual ordering.
  Sonnet 8.9–10

11 Where should this music be? i'th' air or the 'arth?
  It sounds no more: and, sure, it waits upon

Some god o'th' island. Sitting on a bank,
Weeping again the King my father's wrack,
This music crept by me upon the waters,
Allaying both their fury and my passion
With its sweet air.
Tempest 1.2.390–6, FERDINAND, listening to Ariel's song; for the song, *see* **SEA, the**

1   Be not afeard; the isle is full of noises,
Sounds and sweet airs, that give delight, and hurt not.
Sometimes a thousand twangling instruments
Will hum about mine ears; and sometime voices.
Tempest 3.2.137–40, CALIBAN TO STEPHANO AND TRINCULO

2   If music be the food of love, play on,
Give me excess of it, that, surfeiting,
The appetite may sicken, and so die.
That strain again, it had a dying fall:
O, it came o'er my ear like the sweet sound
That breathes upon a bank of violets,
Stealing and giving odour.
Twelfth Night 1.1.1–7, ORSINO TO CURIO

See also **DEATH; MELANCHOLY**

MYSTERY

3   I cannot delve him to the root.
Cymbeline 1.1.28, TWO GENTLEMEN discussing Posthumus

4   [We'll] take upon's the mystery of things
As if we were God's spies.
King Lear 5.3.16–17, LEAR TO CORDELIA

N

NAMES

5   There was no thought of pleasing you when she was christened.
As You Like It 3.2.263–4, ORLANDO TO JAQUES, of Rosalind

1 I cannot tell what the dickens his name is.
   Merry Wives of Windsor 3.2.17–18, MISTRESS PAGE TO FORD; the origin of this phrase is certainly long-lived

2 What's in a name? That which we call a rose
   By any other word would smell as sweet;
   So Romeo would, were he not Romeo called,
   Retain that dear perfection which he owes
   Without that title.
   Romeo and Juliet 2.2.43–7, JULIET

3 Make but my name thy love, and love that still;
   And then thou lov'st me, for my name is Will.
   Sonnet 136.13–14

4 Kate of Kate Hall, my super-dainty Kate.
   Taming of the Shrew 2.1.189, PETRUCHIO TO KATHERINA

NATURE

5 In nature's infinite book of secrecy
   A little I can read.
   Antony and Cleopatra 1.2.9–10, SOOTHSAYER TO CHARMIAN

6 This most excellent canopy the air, look you, this brave o'erhanging firmament, this majestical roof fretted with golden fire.
   Hamlet 2.2.301–3, HAMLET TO ROSENCRANTZ AND GUILDENSTERN

7 Thou, Nature, art my goddess.
   King Lear 1.2.1, EDMUND, a 'natural' son; *see also* **ILLEGITIMACY**

8 The earth that's nature's mother is her tomb.
   Romeo and Juliet 2.3.5, FRIAR LAURENCE

9 Mickle is the powerful grace that lies
   In plants, herbs, stones, and their true qualities.
   Romeo and Juliet 2.3.11–12, FRIAR LAURENCE

10   What fine chisel
    Could ever yet cut breath?
    Winter's Tale 5.3.78–9, LEONTES TO PAULINA

NECESSITY

11 Necessity so bowed the state
   That I and greatness were compelled to kiss.
   2 Henry IV 3.1.73–4, HENRY TO WARWICK AND SURREY

1   Are these things then necessities?
Then let us meet them like necessities.
2 Henry IV 3.1.92–3, HENRY TO WARWICK AND SURREY

2   Necessity's sharp pinch.
King Lear 2.2.403, LEAR TO REGAN

3   The art of our necessities is strange,
And can make vile things precious.
King Lear 3.2.70–1, LEAR TO KENT, looking for straw to sleep on

4   There is no virtue like necessity.
Richard II 1.3.278, JOHN OF GAUNT TO BOLINGBROKE, who has just been sentenced to exile

5   For do we must what force will have us do.
Richard II 3.3.207, RICHARD TO BOLINGBROKE

6   I am sworn brother . . .
To grim Necessity, and he and I
Will keep a league till death.
Richard II 5.1.20–2, RICHARD TO QUEEN ISABEL

7   Are you content . . .
To make a virtue of necessity?
Two Gentlemen of Verona 4.1.61–2, OUTLAW TO VALENTINE

NEW BEGINNINGS

8   There is a world elsewhere!
Coriolanus 3.3.135, CORIOLANUS' farewell to the people, who have rejected him

9   O brave new world,
That has such people in 't!
Tempest 5.1.183–4, MIRANDA TO HER FRIENDS

10 Let us not burthen our remembrance with
A heaviness that's gone.
Tempest 5.1.199–200, PROSPERO TO HIS FRIENDS

11 Thou met'st with things dying, I with things new-born.
Winter's Tale 3.3.111–12, SHEPHERD, who has discovered the abandoned infant Perdita, to HIS SON, who has just witnessed Antigonus being killed by a bear

NEWNESS

1   New honours come upon him,
   Like our strange garments, cleave not to their mould,
   But with the aid of use.
   Macbeth 1.3.145–7, Banquo, of Macbeth

2 The fault and glimpse of newness.
   Measure for Measure 1.2.155, Claudio to Lucio

NEWS

3 What's the news in Rome?
   Coriolanus 4.3.9–10, Volsce to a Roman

4   Horatio, I am dead,
   Thou livest. Report me and my cause aright
   To the unsatisfied.
   Hamlet 5.2.345–7, Hamlet to Horatio

5 Absent thee from felicity awhile,
   And in this harsh world draw thy breath in pain
   To tell my story.
   Hamlet 5.2.354–6, Hamlet to Horatio

6 Let me tell the world.
   1 Henry IV 5.2.65, Vernon to Hotspur

7 What news on the Rialto?
   Merchant of Venice 1.3.37, Shylock to Bassanio

NEWS, bad

8 The nature of bad news infects the teller.
   Antony and Cleopatra 1.2.99, messenger to Antony

9 Though it be honest, it is never good
   To bring bad news.
   Antony and Cleopatra 2.5.85–6, Cleopatra to a messenger

10 The first bringer of unwelcome news
   Hath but a losing office, and his tongue
   Sounds ever after as a sullen bell,
   Remembered tolling a departing friend.
   2 Henry IV 1.1.100–3, Northumberland to Morton and Lord Bardolph

11 Let the Angel, whom thou still hast served,
   Tell thee, Macduff was from his mother's womb

Untimely ripped.

Macbeth 5.8.14–16; MACDUFF tells MACBETH that he was not 'of woman born' (he was delivered by Caesarian section), and that the safety the witches promised means nothing.

See also **LETTERS**

NEWS, good

1 Thou still hast been the father of good news.
Hamlet 2.2.42, CLAUDIUS TO POLONIUS

NIGHT

2 Swift, swift, you dragons of the night.
Cymbeline 2.2.48, IACHIMO

3 In the dead waste and middle of the night.
Hamlet 1.2.198, HORATIO TO HAMLET

4 'Tis now the very witching time of night.
When churchyards yawn and hell itself breathes out
Contagion to this world.
Hamlet 3.2.389–91, HAMLET

5 Let us be Diana's foresters, gentlemen of the shade, minions of the moon.
1 Henry IV 1.2.25–6, FALSTAFF TO PRINCE HAL

6 Now entertain conjecture of a time
When creeping murmur and the poring dark
Fills the wide vessel of the universe.
Henry V 4.0.1–3, CHORUS

7 Deep night, dark night, the silent of the night, . . .
The time when screech-owls cry, and ban-dogs howl,
And spirits walk, and ghosts break up their graves.
2 Henry VI 1.4.18, 20–1, BOLINGBROKE TO THE DUCHESS OF GLOUCESTER

8 The gaudy, blabbing, and remorseful day
Is crept into the bosom of the sea,
And now loud-howling wolves arouse the jades
That drag the tragic melancholy night;
Who with their drowsy, slow, and flagging wings
Clip dead men's graves, and from their misty jaws
Breathe foul contagious darkness in the air.
2 Henry VI 4.1.1–7, LIEUTENANT TO SAILORS AND OTHERS

1   Things that love night
Love not such nights as these. The wrathful skies
Gallow the very wanderers of the dark,
And make them keep their caves.
King Lear 3.2.42–5, LEAR in the storm

2 O comfort-killing night, image of hell,
Dim register and notary of shame,
Black stage for tragedies and murders fell,
Vast sin-concealing Chaos, nurse of blame!
Blind muffled bawd, dark harbour for defame,
Grim cave of death, whisp'ring conspirator
With close-tongued treason and the ravisher!
Lucrece 764–70

3   There's husbandry in heaven;
Their candles are all out.
Macbeth 2.1.4–5, BANQUO TO FLEANCE

4   Come, seeling Night,
Scarf up the tender eye of pitiful Day,
And, with thy bloody and invisible hand,
Cancel, and tear to pieces, that great bond
Which keeps me pale! – Light thickens; and the crow
Makes wing to th' rooky wood;
Good things of Day begin to droop and drowse,
Whiles Night's black agents to their preys do rouse.
Macbeth 3.2.46–53, MACBETH TO LADY MACBETH

5 The west yet glimmers with some streaks of day;
Now spurs the lated traveller apace,
To gain the timely inn.
Macbeth 3.3.5–7, MURDERER TO HIS COMPANIONS

6 This will last out a night in Russia
When nights are longest there.
Measure for Measure 2.1.132–3, ANGELO TO ESCALUS, POMPEY AND FROTH

7 The moon shines bright. In such a night as this,
When the sweet wind did gently kiss the trees,
And they did make no noise, in such a night
Troilus methinks mounted the Trojan walls,

And sighed his soul toward the Grecian tents
Where Cressid lay that night.
Merchant of Venice 5.1.1–6, LORENZO TO JESSICA

1 Night and silence – Who is here?
Midsummer Night's Dream 2.2.69, PUCK

2 The iron tongue of midnight hath told twelve.
Lovers, to bed; 'tis almost fairy time.
Midsummer Night's Dream 5.1.357–8, THESEUS TO HIS FRIENDS

3 Now the hungry lion roars,
And the wolf behowls the moon;
Whilst the heavy ploughman snores,
All with weary task fordone.
Now the wasted brands do glow,
Whilst the screech-owl, screeching loud,
Puts the wretch that lies in woe
In remembrance of a shroud.
Now it is the time of night
That the graves, all gaping wide,
Every one lets forth his sprite
In the church-way paths to glide.
Midsummer Night's Dream 5.1.365–76, PUCK; *see also* **FAIRIES**

4 How silver-sweet sound lovers' tongues by night,
Like softest music to attending ears.
Romeo and Juliet 2.2.165–6, ROMEO TO JULIET

5 Spread thy close curtain, love-performing night,
That runaway's eyes may wink, and Romeo
Leap to these arms untalked-of and unseen.
Romeo and Juliet 3.2.5–7, JULIET

6   Come, civil night,
Thou sober-suited matron, all in black,
And learn me how to lose a winning match
Played for a pair of stainless maidenhoods.
Romeo and Juliet 3.2.10–13, JULIET; *see also* **LOVERS; ROMEO AND JULIET**

7   [Night] flies the grasps of love
With wings more momentary-swift than thought.
Troilus and Cressida 4.2.13–14, TROILUS

1 'In night', quoth she, 'desire sees best of all.'
Venus and Adonis 720, VENUS

NOBILITY

2 His nature is too noble for the world.
Coriolanus 3.1.255, MENENIUS TO A PATRICIAN, of Coriolanus

3 This was the noblest Roman of them all.
Julius Caesar 5.5.68, MARK ANTONY, of Brutus

4 For he was great of heart.
Othello 5.2.361, CASSIO TO OTHERS at Othello's death

OATHS

5 When a gentleman is disposed to swear, it is not for any standers-by to curtail his oaths.
Cymbeline 2.1.11–12, CLOTEN TO TWO LORDS

6 Swear me, Kate, like a lady as thou art,
A good mouth-filling oath, and leave 'In sooth',
And such protest of pepper-gingerbread,
To velvet-guards, and Sunday citizens.
1 Henry IV 3.1.247–50, HOTSPUR TO HIS WIFE

ODDS

7 Hercules himself must yield to odds;
And many strokes, though with a little axe,
Hews down and fells the hardest-timbered oak.
3 Henry VI 2.1.53–5, A MESSENGER TO EDWARD AND RICHARD, sons of Richard of York, telling them of their father's death

OLD AGE

8 For we are old, and on our quick'st decrees
Th'inaudible and noiseless foot of time
Steals ere we can effect them.
All's Well That Ends Well 5.3.40–2, KING OF FRANCE TO BERTRAM

1 Unregarded age in corners thrown.
As You Like It 2.3.42, ADAM TO ORLANDO

2   He that doth the ravens feed,
Yea providently caters for the sparrow,
Be comfort to my age.
As You Like It 2.3.43–5, ADAM TO ORLANDO

3 My age is as a lusty winter,
Frosty but kindly.
As You Like It 2.3.52–3, ADAM TO ORLANDO

4   The sixth age shifts
Into the lean and slippered pantaloon,
With spectacles on nose, and pouch on side,
His youthful hose well saved, a world too wide
For his shrunk shank, and his big manly voice,
Turning again toward childish treble, pipes
And whistles in his sound.
As You Like It 2.7.157-63, from JAQUES's 'Seven Ages of Man' speech

5   Last scene of all,
That ends this strange eventful history,
Is second childishness and mere oblivion,
Sans teeth, sans eyes, sans taste, sans everything.
As You Like It 2.7.163-66, from JAQUES's 'Seven Ages of Man' speech

6 These tedious old fools.
Hamlet 2.2.219, HAMLET, referring to Polonius

7 What doth gravity out of his bed at midnight?
1 Henry IV 2.4.290–1, FALSTAFF TO HOSTESS QUICKLY

8 If to be old and merry be a sin, then many an old host that I know is damned.
1 Henry IV 2.4.465–6, FALSTAFF TO PRINCE HAL

9 Have you not a moist eye, a dry hand, a yellow cheek, a white beard, a decreasing leg, an increasing belly? Is not your voice broken, your wind short, your chin double, your wit single, and every part about you blasted with antiquity?
2 Henry IV 1.2.180–4, LORD CHIEF JUSTICE TO FALSTAFF

10 I am old, I am old.
2 Henry IV 2.4.271, FALSTAFF TO DOLL TEARSHEET

1 How ill white hairs becomes a fool and jester!
2 Henry IV 5.5.48, the new KING HENRY V in his rejection of FALSTAFF

2 Old men forget.
Henry V 4.3.49, HENRY TO WESTMORLAND; *see* **WAR** for more of this speech

3   His silver hairs
Will purchase us a good opinion.
Julius Caesar 2.1.144–5; METELLUS proposes approaching Cicero to join the
conspiracy

4 'Tis the infirmity of his age.
King Lear 1.1.294, REGAN TO GONERIL, of Lear

5 I am too old to learn.
King Lear 2.2.128, KENT TO CORNWALL, scornfully ironic, on being threatened with
the stocks

6   You are old:
Nature in you stands on the very verge
Of her confine. You should be ruled and led
By some discretion that discerns your state
Better than you yourself.
King Lear 2.2.338–42; REGAN insults her father LEAR

7 Age is unnecessary.
King Lear 2.2.347; LEAR's humbled reply

8   Here I stand your slave,
A poor, infirm, weak and despised old man.
King Lear 3.2.19–20, LEAR to the elements

9   Pray do not mock me.
I am a very foolish, fond old man,
Fourscore and upward, not an hour more nor less;
And to deal plainly,
I fear I am not in my perfect mind.
King Lear 4.7.59–63, LEAR TO CORDELIA

10 Ripeness is all.
King Lear 5.2.11, EDGAR TO GLOUCESTER; *more at* **DEATH**

11 Why art thou old and not yet wise?
Lucrece 1550, addressed to PRIAM

12 I have lived long enough: my way of life
Is fall'n into the sere, the yellow leaf.
Macbeth 5.3.22–3, MACBETH

1 That which should accompany old age,
As honour, love, obedience, troops of friends.
Macbeth 5.3.24–5, MACBETH, regretting what he foresees he will not have

2 With mirth and laughter let old wrinkles come.
Merchant of Venice 1.1.80, GRATIANO TO ANTONIO

3 A good old man, sir, he will be talking; as they say, 'When the age is in,
the wit is out.'
Much Ado About Nothing 3.5.32–3, DOGBERRY TO LEONATO, of his colleague Verges

4 You shall more command with years
Than with your weapons.
Othello 1.2.60–1, OTHELLO TO BRABANTIO

5 Crabbed age and youth cannot live together.
Passionate Pilgrim 12.1

6 Old John of Gaunt, time-honoured Lancaster.
Richard II 1.1.1, RICHARD TO JOHN OF GAUNT

7 Thou canst help time to furrow me with age,
But stop no wrinkle in his pilgrimage.
Richard II 1.3.229–30, JOHN OF GAUNT TO RICHARD, who has just banished his son

8 Old folks . . .
Unwieldy, slow, heavy, and pale as lead.
Romeo and Juliet 2.5.16–17, JULIET

9 That time of year thou mayst in me behold,
When yellow leaves, or none, or few do hang
Upon those boughs which shake against the cold,
Bare ruined choirs where late the sweet birds sang;
In me thou seest the twilight of such day
As after sunset fadeth in the west,
Which by and by black night doth take away,
Death's second self that seals up all in rest.
Sonnet 73.1–8

10 In me thou seest the glowing of such fire
That on the ashes of his youth doth lie.
Sonnet 73.9–10

11 To me, fair friend, you never can be old;
For as you were when first your eye I eyed,
Such seems your beauty still.
Sonnet 104.1–3

1 Eternal love . . .
Weighs not the dust and injury of age.
Sonnet 108.9–10

2 My old bones ache.
Tempest 3.3.2, Gonzalo to his companions

3   Sir, I am vexed;
Bear with my weakness; my old brain is troubled:
Be not disturbed with my infirmity.
Tempest 4.1.158–60, Prospero to Ferdinand

4 Give me a staff of honour for mine age,
But not a sceptre to control the world.
Titus Andronicus 1.1.201–2, Titus to the tribunes

See also **LOYALTY; MIDDLE AGE; POVERTY; TIME; YOUTH**

OLD TIMES

5 Jesu, Jesu, the mad days that I have spent! And to see how many of my
old acquaintance are dead!
2 Henry IV 3.2.33–5, Shallow to Silence

6 We have heard the chimes at midnight, Master Shallow.
2 Henry IV 3.2.214–15, Falstaff to Shallow

7 Where is the life that late I led?
2 Henry IV 5.3.141, a song quoted by Pistol

8 This is enough to be the decay of lust and late-walking through the
realm.
Merry Wives of Windsor 5.5.144–6, Falstaff, in disgust at his humiliation

9   Hear this, thou age unbred.
Ere you were born was beauty's summer dead.
Sonnet 104.13–14

See also **BETTER DAYS; GOOD TIMES**

OMENS AND PORTENTS

10 This bodes some strange eruption to our state.
Hamlet 1.1.72, Horatio to Marcellus on the appearance of the ghost

11 In the most high and palmy state of Rome,
A little ere the mightiest Julius fell,
The graves stood tenantless and the sheeted dead
Did squeak and gibber in the Roman streets;

As stars with trains of fire and dews of blood,
Disasters in the sun; and the moist star,
Upon whose influence Neptune's empire stands,
Was sick almost to doomsday with eclipse.
Hamlet 1.1.116–23, HORATIO TO BARNARDO

1 GLENDOWER   At my nativity
The front of heaven was full of fiery shapes,
Of burning cressets, and at my birth
The frame and huge foundation of the earth
Shaked like a coward.
HOTSPUR   Why, so it would have done
At the same season if your mother's cat
Had but kittened, though yourself had never been born.
1 Henry IV 3.1.11–17; for more mockery of Glendower *see* **SUPERNATURAL, the**

2 Yesterday the bird of night did sit,
Even at noon-day, upon the market-place,
Hooting and shrieking.
Julius Caesar 1.3.26–8, CASCA TO CICERO

3 The noise of battle hurtled in the air,
Horses did neigh, and dying men did groan,
And ghosts did shriek and squeal about the streets.
Julius Caesar 2.2.22–4, CALPHURNIA warning JULIUS CAESAR

4 These late eclipses in the sun and moon portend no good to us.
King Lear 1.2.103–4, GLOUCESTER TO EDMUND

5   The raven himself is hoarse
That croaks the fatal entrance of Duncan
Under my battlements.
Macbeth 1.5.37–9, LADY MACBETH

6 The night has been unruly: where we lay,
Our chimneys were blown down; and, as they say,
Lamentings heard i'th' air; strange screams of death,
And, prophesying with accents terrible
Of dire combustion, and confused events,
New hatched to th' woeful time, the obscure bird
Clamoured the livelong night: some say, the earth
Was feverous, and did shake.
Macbeth 2.3.54–61, LENOX TO MACBETH; this was the night of Duncan's murder

1 By the pricking of my thumbs,
 Something wicked this way comes.
 Macbeth 4.1.44–5, SECOND WITCH

2 The bay-trees in our country are all withered,
 And meteors fright the fixed stars of heaven,
 The pale-faced moon looks bloody on the earth.
 Richard II 2.4.8–10, CAPTAIN TO SALISBURY

 See also **BIRDS; SUPERNATURAL, the; WITCHES**

OPHELIA

3   Soft you now,
 The fair Ophelia! Nymph, in thy orisons
 Be all my sins remembered.
 Hamlet 3.1.88–90, HAMLET

4   O rose of May!
 Dear maid – kind sister – sweet Ophelia.
 Hamlet 4.5.157–8, LAERTES, of the mad Ophelia

OPPORTUNITY

5 Who seeks and will not take, when once 'tis offered,
 Shall never find it more.
 Antony and Cleopatra 2.7.83–4, MENAS

6 Now might I do it pat.
 Hamlet 3.3.73, HAMLET finding Claudius at prayer, and seeing a chance to kill him

7 There is a tide in the affairs of men,
 Which, taken at the flood, leads on to fortune;
 Omitted, all the voyage of their life
 Is bound in shallows and in miseries.
 Julius Caesar 4.3.217–20, BRUTUS TO CASSIUS

8 How oft the sight of means to do ill deeds
 Makes deeds ill done!
 King John 4.2.219–20, JOHN TO HUBERT

9 O opportunity, thy guilt is great!
 Lucrece 876

10 On the wing of all occasions.
 Merry Wives of Windsor 2.2.195–6, FORD, in disguise, to FALSTAFF

ORDER

1   The heavens themselves, the planets, and this centre
    Observe degree, priority, and place,
    Insisture, course, proportion, season, form,
    Office, and custom, in all line of order.
    Troilus and Cressida 1.3.85–8, ULYSSES TO THE GREEK PRINCES

2   O, when degree is shaked,
    Which is the ladder of all high designs,
    The enterprise is sick.
    Troilus and Cressida 1.3.101–3, ULYSSES TO THE GREEK PRINCES

3   Take but degree away, untune that string,
    And hark what discord follows.
    Troilus and Cressida 1.3.109–10, ULYSSES TO THE GREEK PRINCES

OUTRAGE

4   They durst not do't:
    They could not, would not do't.
    King Lear 2.2.215–16, LEAR TO KENT, whom Regan has had put in the stocks

PARENTS AND CHILDREN

5   PRINCE HAL I never thought to hear you speak again.
    KING HENRY Thy wish was father, Harry, to that thought.
    2 Henry IV 4.5.91–2

6   How sharper than a serpent's tooth it is
    To have a thankless child.
    King Lear 1.4.280–1, LEAR TO ALBANY, angered by Goneril

7   I have another daughter.
    King Lear 1.4.297, LEAR TO GONERIL, misguidedly hoping for better from Regan

8   I prithee, daughter, do not make me mad.
    King Lear 2.2.410, LEAR TO GONERIL

1   O dear father,
It is thy business that I go about.
King Lear 4.4.23–4, CORDELIA; an echo of Jesus' words in Luke 2.49: 'Knew ye not that I must be about my father's business?'

2 Had doting Priam checked his son's desire,
Troy had been bright with fame and not with fire.
Lucrece 1490–1

3 The boy was the very staff of my age, my very prop.
Merchant of Venice 2.2.63–4, LAUNCELOT GOBBO TO OLD GOBBO

4 It is a wise father that knows his own child.
Merchant of Venice 2.2.73–4, LAUNCELOT GOBBO TO OLD GOBBO; proverbial, though usually the other way round

5 Alack, what heinous sin is it in me
To be ashamed to be my father's child!
Merchant of Venice 2.3.16–17, JESSICA

6 The sins of the father are to be laid upon the children.
Merchant of Venice 3.5.1–2, LAUNCELOT GOBBO TO JESSICA, quoting the law of Moses

7 I would my father looked but with my eyes.
Midsummer Night's Dream 1.1.56, HERMIA TO THESEUS; *more at* **FATHERS**

8 DON PEDRO I think this is your daughter.
LEONATO Her mother hath many times told me so.
Much Ado About Nothing 1.1.99–101

9 Hang! Beg! Starve! Die in the streets!
For by my soul I'll ne'er acknowledge thee.
Romeo and Juliet 3.5.192–3, CAPULET TO JULIET

10 I have done nothing but in care of thee.
Tempest 1.2.16, PROSPERO TO MIRANDA

11 Good wombs have borne bad sons.
Tempest 1.2.119, MIRANDA TO PROSPERO

See also **CHILDREN; DAUGHTERS; FAMILY; FATHERS; MOTHERS**

PARTINGS

12 There cannot be a pinch in death
More sharp than this is.
Cymbeline 1.2.61–2, IMOGEN TO CYMBELINE

1 Good night, good night. Parting is such sweet sorrow
That I shall say good night till it be morrow.
Romeo and Juliet 2.2.184–5, JULIET TO ROMEO

See also **FAREWELLS**

PAST, the

2 Things that are past are done with me.
Antony and Cleopatra 1.2.101, ANTONY

3 When to the sessions of sweet silent thought
I summon up remembrance of things past . . .
Sonnet 30.1–2

See also **BETTER DAYS; DECLINE AND FALL; OLD TIMES**

PATIENCE

4 Patience is for poltroons.
3 Henry VI 1.1.62, CLIFFORD TO HENRY

5   To climb steep hills
Requires slow pace at first.
Henry VIII 1.1.131–2, NORFOLK TO BUCKINGHAM

6 Some time I shall sleep out, the rest I'll whistle.
King Lear 2.2.157, KENT TO GLOUCESTER

7 Like Patience gazing on kings' graves, and smiling
Extremity out of act.
Pericles 5.1.139–40, PERICLES TO MARINA

8 That which in mean men we intitle patience
Is pale cold cowardice in noble breasts.
Richard II 1.2.33–4, DUCHESS OF GLOUCESTER TO JOHN OF GAUNT

9 Patience is stale, and I am weary of it.
Richard II 5.5.103, RICHARD TO THE KEEPER OF HIS PRISON

10 Be patient, for the world is broad and wide.
Romeo and Juliet 3.3.16, FRIAR LAURENCE TO ROMEO

11 She sat like Patience on a monument,
Smiling at grief.
Twelfth Night 2.4.115–16, VIOLA, as Cesario, to ORSINO

See also **DESPAIR; STOICISM**

PATRIOTISM

1 Not that I loved Caesar less, but that I loved Rome more.
Julius Caesar 3.2.21–2, BRUTUS' answer to the hypothesised question as to why he had conspired against Julius Caesar

2 Bleed, bleed, poor country!
Macbeth 4.3.31, MACDUFF TO MALCOLM; *see also* **SCOTLAND AND THE SCOTS**

3 Dear earth, I do salute thee with my hand.
Richard II 3.2.6, RICHARD

PEACE

4 The time of universal peace is near.
Antony and Cleopatra 4.6.5, OCTAVIUS CAESAR TO AGRIPPA

5 Why, then we shall have a stirring world again. This peace is nothing but to rust iron, increase tailors, and breed ballad-makers.
Coriolanus 4.5.225–7, ONE SERVANT TO ANOTHER

6   We have made peace
With no less honour to the Antiates
Than shame to th' Romans.
Coriolanus 5.6.79–81, CORIOLANUS TO LORDS

7 The naked, poor, and mangled peace,
Dear nurse of arts, plenties and joyful births.
Henry V 5.2.34–5, BURGUNDY TO THE FRENCH KING AND QUEEN

8 Expect Saint Martin's summer, halcyon's days.
1 Henry VI 1.2.131, PUCELLE (JOAN OF ARC) TO CHARLES, DAUPHIN OF FRANCE

9 Blessed are the peacemakers on earth.
2 Henry VI 2.1.34, HENRY TO HIS COURT; a reference to *Matthew* 5.9

10 In her days every man shall eat in safety
Under his own vine what he plants, and sing
The merry songs of peace to all his neighbours.
Henry VIII 5.4.33–5, CRANMER TO HENRY, of the future reign of the infant Elizabeth

11 The grappling vigour and rough frown of war
Is cold in amity, and painted peace.
King John 3.1.30–1, CONSTANCE TO PHILIP, KING OF FRANCE, AND THE DUKE OF AUSTRIA

12 Keep up your bright swords, for the dew will rust them.
Othello 1.2.59, OTHELLO TO IAGO AND BRABANTIO

1 Now is the winter of our discontent
  Made glorious summer by this son of York.
  Richard III 1.1.1–2, RICHARD

2 Grim-visaged War hath smoothed his wrinkled front.
  Richard III 1.1.9, RICHARD

3 This weak piping time of peace.
  Richard III 1.1.24, RICHARD

4 To reap the harvest of perpetual peace.
  Richard III 5.2.15, RICHMOND TO COMPANIONS IN ARMS

5 Now civil wounds are stopped; peace lives again.
  Richard III 5.5.40, RICHMOND TO LORDS

6 Uncertainties now crown themselves assured,
  And peace proclaims olives of endless age.
  Sonnet 107.7–8

PEOPLE, the

7 The many-headed multitude.
  Coriolanus 2.3.16–17, ONE CITIZEN TO ANOTHER

8 STAFFORD Villain! thy father was a plasterer;
  And thou thyself a shearman, art thou not?
  JACK CADE And Adam was a gardener.
  2 Henry VI 4.2.128–30

9 The common people swarm like summer flies.
  3 Henry VI 2.6.8, CLIFFORD

10   The body public [is]
   A horse whereon the governor doth ride.
   Measure for Measure 1.2.156–7, CLAUDIO TO LUCIO

   See also **CLASS, social; DEMOCRACY; EQUALITY; POLITICS AND POLITICIANS;
   PUBLIC OPINION; WORKING PEOPLE**

PERCEPTION

11 That which is now a horse, even with a thought
   The rack dislimns and makes it indistinct
   As water is in water.
   Antony and Cleopatra 4.14.9–11, ANTONY TO EROS, in defeat

   See also **MADNESS** (170.9)

PERMISSION

1 He hath, my lord, wrung from me my slow leave
By laboursome petition.
Hamlet 1.2.58–9, POLONIUS TO CLAUDIUS

PERSEVERANCE

2   Stand fast.
We have as many friends as enemies.
Coriolanus 3.1.231–2, CORIOLANUS TO HIS ALLIES

3 Fight till the last gasp.
1 Henry VI 1.2.127, PUCELLE (JOAN OF ARC) TO REIGNIER AND THE BASTARD OF ORLEANS

4 Much rain wears the marble.
3 Henry VI 3.2.50, RICHARD, commenting on his brother King Edward IV's wooing
of Lady Grey; a commonplace, with a number of variations through Shakespeare's
work

5 I am a kind of burr, I shall stick.
Measure for Measure 4.3.176, LUCIO TO THE FRIAR

6   Perseverance, dear my lord,
Keeps honour bright.
Troilus and Cressida 3.3.150–1, ULYSSES TO ACHILLES

PERSUASION

7   Three parts of him
Is ours already, and the man entire
Upon the next encounter yields him ours.
Julius Caesar 1.3.154–6, CASSIUS TO CASCA

8 A still soliciting eye.
King Lear 1.1.233, CORDELIA describing to LEAR what she does not have

PHILOSOPHY

9 There are more things in heaven and earth, Horatio,
Than are dreamt of in your philosophy.
Hamlet 1.5.174–5, HAMLET TO HORATIO

10 Preach some philosophy to make me mad.
King John 3.3.51, CONSTANCE TO CARDINAL PANDULPH

11 Adversity's sweet milk, philosophy.
Romeo and Juliet 3.3.55, FRIAR LAURENCE TO ROMEO

1 Young men, whom Aristotle thought
  Unfit to hear moral philosophy.
  Troilus and Cressida 2.2.167–8, HECTOR TO TROJAN PRINCES

2 FESTE What is the opinion of Pythagoras concerning wildfowl?
  MALVOLIO That the soul of our grandam might haply inhabit a bird.
  Twelfth Night 4.2.49–52; Feste is pretending to ascertain whether Malvolio is mad.
  For more on this concept *see* **ANIMALS**.

PITY

3   As small a drop of pity
  As a wren's eye.
  Cymbeline 4.2.304–5, IMOGEN

4 He hath a tear for pity, and a hand
  Open as day for melting charity.
  2 Henry IV 4.4.31–2, HENRY to his son THOMAS, DUKE OF CLARENCE, of Prince Hal; he
  adds, 'Notwithstanding, being incensed, he's flint.'

5   Mine enemy's dog
  Though he had bit me should have stood that night
  Against my fire.
  King Lear 4.7.36–8, CORDELIA TO A GENTLEMAN

6   Yet do I fear thy nature:
  It is too full o'th' milk of human kindness,
  To catch the nearest way.
  Macbeth 1.5.15–17, LADY MACBETH, of Macbeth; *more at* **AMBITION**

7 Pity, like a naked new-born babe,
  Striding the blast.
  Macbeth 1.7.21–2, MACBETH

8 A stony adversary, an inhuman wretch,
  Uncapable of pity, void, and empty
  From any dram of mercy.
  Merchant of Venice 4.1.4–6, DUKE OF VENICE TO ANTONIO, of Shylock

9 But yet the pity of it, Iago – O, Iago, the pity of it, Iago!
  Othello 4.1.192–3, OTHELLO TO IAGO

PLACES

10 This castle hath a pleasant seat; the air
  Nimbly and sweetly recommends itself
  Unto our gentle senses.
  Macbeth 1.6.1–3, DUNCAN, misjudging as usual, to BANQUO

PLANNING

1   When we mean to build,
We first survey the plot, then draw the model,
And when we see the figure of the house,
Then must we rate the cost of the erection,
Which if we find outweighs ability,
What do we then but draw anew the model
In fewer offices, or at least desist
To build at all?
2 Henry IV 1.3.41–8, LORD BARDOLPH TO HASTINGS

PLAYS, PLAYERS AND PLAYHOUSES

2 The king's a beggar, now the play is done.
   All's Well That Ends Well Epilogue 1, KING OF FRANCE

3   Saucy lictors
Will catch at us like strumpets, and scald rhymers
Ballad us out o' tune. The quick comedians
Extemporally will stage us, and present
Our Alexandrian revels: Antony
Shall be brought drunken forth, and I shall see
Some squeaking Cleopatra boy my greatness
I'th' posture of a whore.
Antony and Cleopatra 5.2.213–20, CLEOPATRA, before her suicide

4   All the world's a stage,
And all the men and women merely players.
As You Like It 2.7.139–40, from JAQUES's 'Seven Ages of Man' speech; *more at* **LIFE**

5   Like a dull actor now
I have forgot my part.
Coriolanus 5.3.40–1, CORIOLANUS TO HIS WIFE AND MOTHER

6 Let them be well used, for they are the abstract and brief chronicles of
   the time.
   Hamlet 2.2.524–5, HAMLET TO POLONIUS, of the players

7   And all for nothing!
For Hecuba!
What's Hecuba to him, or he to her,
That he should weep for her?
Hamlet 2.2.557–60, HAMLET, of a player

1   The play's the thing
Wherein I'll catch the conscience of the King.
Hamlet 2.2.606–7, HAMLET

2 He would drown the stage with tears,
And cleave the general ear with horrid speech,
Make mad the guilty and appal the free,
Confound the ignorant, and amaze indeed
The very faculties of eyes and ears.
Hamlet 2.2.562–6, HAMLET, of a player

3 Speak the speech, I pray you, as I pronounced it to you, trippingly on the tongue; but if you mouth it as many of your players do, I had as lief the town-crier spoke my lines. Nor do not saw the air too much with your hand, thus, but use all gently; for in the very torrent, tempest, and, as I may say, whirlwind of your passion, you must acquire and beget a temperance that may give it smoothness. O, it offends me to the soul to hear a robustious periwig-pated fellow tear a passion to tatters, to very rags, to split the ears of the groundlings, who for the most part are capable of nothing but inexplicable dumb-shows and noise. I would have such a fellow whipped for o'erdoing Termagant. It out-Herods Herod. Pray you avoid it . . .

Be not too tame neither, but let your own discretion be your tutor. Suit the action to the word, the word to the action, with this special observance, that you o'erstep not the modesty of nature. For anything so o'erdone is from the purpose of playing, whose end, both at the first and now, was and is to hold as 'twere the mirror up to nature; to show virtue her feature, scorn her own image, and the very age and body of the time his form and pressure. Now this overdone or come tardy off, though it makes the unskilful laugh, cannot but make the judicious grieve, the censure of the which one must in your allowance o'erweigh a whole theatre of others . . .

And let those that play your clowns speak no more than is set down for them – for there be of them that will themselves laugh, to set on some quantity of barren spectators to laugh too, though in the meantime some necessary question of the play be then to be considered.
Hamlet 3.2.1–15, 17–29, 39–44, HAMLET TO THE FIRST PLAYER

1 O, for a muse of fire, that would ascend
   The brightest heaven of invention,
   A kingdom for a stage, princes to act,
   And monarchs to behold the swelling scene!
   Henry V Prologue 1–4, CHORUS

2 Within this wooden O.
   Henry V Prologue 13, CHORUS; the 'wooden O' refers to the shape of the Elizabethan
   theatre

3   The scene
   Is now transported, gentles, to Southampton.
   There is the playhouse now, there must you sit,
   And thence to France shall we convey you safe
   And bring you back, charming the narrow seas
   To give you gentle pass.
   Henry V 2.0.34–9, CHORUS

4 Thus with imagined wing our swift scene flies
   In motion of no less celerity
   Than that of thought.
   Henry V 3.0.1–3, CHORUS

5 'Tis ten to one this play can never please
   All that are here.
   Henry VIII Epilogue 1–2

6   How many ages hence
   Shall this our lofty scene be acted over,
   In states unborn, and accents yet unknown?
   Julius Caesar 3.1.111–3, CASSIUS TO BRUTUS

7   Two truths are told
   As happy prologues to the swelling act
   Of the imperial theme.
   Macbeth 1.3.127–9, MACBETH; two of the witches' prophecies have been fulfilled,
   which promises well for the third – his kingship

8 Life's but a walking shadow; a poor player,
   That struts and frets his hour upon the stage,
   And then is heard no more.
   Macbeth 5.5.24–6, MACBETH TO SEYTON

9 QUINCE Marry, our play is 'The most lamentable comedy, and most
   cruel death of Pyramus and Thisbe'.
   BOTTOM A very good piece of work, I assure you, and a merry.
   Midsummer Night's Dream 1.2.11–15

1 I could play Ercles rarely, or a part to tear a cat in, to make all split
... This is Ercles' vein, a tyrant's vein: a lover is more condoling.
Midsummer Night's Dream 1.2.26–7, 37–8, BOTTOM TO PETER QUINCE, showing off his
acting skills; 'Ercles' is Hercules

2 Let me play the lion too. I will roar, that I will do any man's heart good
to hear me ... I will aggravate my voice so, that I will roar you as gently
as any sucking dove; I will roar you and 'twere any nightingale.
Midsummer Night's Dream 1.2.67–8, 77–9, BOTTOM, longing to play the lion full
throttle, and then dealing with objections from his fellow players

3 We will meet, and there we may rehearse most obscenely and
courageously. Take pains, be perfect: adieu.
Midsummer Night's Dream 1.2.101–3, PETER QUINCE addressing his cast

4 You can never bring in a wall.
Midsummer Night's Dream 3.1.61, the pragmatic TOM SNOUT

5 What hempen homespuns have we swaggering here?
Midsummer Night's Dream 3.1.72, PUCK

6 And most dear actors, eat no onions nor garlic, for we are to utter
sweet breath.
Midsummer Night's Dream 4.2.39–41, BOTTOM TO HIS FRIENDS

7 Come now; what masques, what dances shall we have,
To wear away this long age of three hours
Between our after-supper and bed-time?
Where is our usual manager of mirth?
What revels are in hand? Is there no play
To ease the anguish of a torturing hour?
Midsummer Night's Dream 5.1.32–7, THESEUS TO HIS COMPANIONS

8 Merry and tragical? Tedious and brief?
That is hot ice, and wondrous strange snow!
Midsummer Night's Dream 5.1.58–9, THESEUS, commenting on the mechanicals'
description of their play

9 HIPPOLYTA This is the silliest stuff that ever I heard.
THESEUS The best in this kind are but shadows; and the worst are no
worse, if imagination amend them.
Midsummer Night's Dream 5.1.208–10

10 This passion, and the death of a dear friend, would go near to make a
man look sad.
Midsummer Night's Dream 5.1.282–3; THESEUS comments with sophisticated
cynicism on Bottom's performance as Pyramus

1 Here she comes, and her passion ends the play.
   Midsummer Night's Dream 5.1.310, THESEUS, commenting on the return to the stage of Thisbe

2 No epilogue, I pray you; for your play needs no excuse.
   Midsummer Night's Dream 5.1.350–1, THESEUS TO BOTTOM

3 If we shadows have offended,
   Think but this, and all is mended,
   That you have but slumbered here
   While these visions did appear.
   Midsummer Night's Dream 5.1.417–20; PUCK addresses the audience

4   The eyes of men,
   After a well-graced actor leaves the stage,
   Are idly bent on him that enters next,
   Thinking his prattle to be tedious.
   Richard II 5.2.23–6, YORK TO THE DUCHESS OF YORK, comparing Bolingbroke's reception to Richard's

5 I can counterfeit the deep tragedian,
   Speak, and look back, and pry on every side.
   Richard III 3.5.5–6, BUCKINGHAM TO RICHARD

6 The two hours' traffic of our stage.
   Romeo and Juliet Prologue 12, CHORUS

7 Our revels now are ended. These our actors,
   As I foretold you, were all spirits, and
   Are melted into air, into thin air:
   And, like the baseless fabric of this vision,
   The cloud-capped towers, the gorgeous palaces,
   The solemn temples, the great globe itself,
   Yea, all which it inherit, shall dissolve,
   And, like this insubstantial pageant faded,
   Leave not a rack behind.
   Tempest 4.1.148–56, PROSPERO TO MIRANDA AND FERDINAND; *see also* LIFE

8 Like a strutting player, whose conceit
   Lies in his hamstring and doth think it rich
   To hear the wooden dialogue and sound
   'Twixt his stretched footing and the scaffoldage.
   Troilus and Cressida 1.3.153–6, ULYSSES TO THE GREEK PRINCES, describing Achilles

See also SPECTATORS

PLEASURE

1 There's not a minute of our lives should stretch
   Without some pleasure now.
   Antony and Cleopatra 1.1.47–8, ANTONY TO CLEOPATRA; *see also* **EAST, the**

2 No profit grows where is no pleasure ta'en.
   Taming of the Shrew 1.1.39, TRANIO TO LUCENTIO

PLOTS

3   That's the way
   To fool their preparation and to conquer
   Their most absurd intents.
   Antony and Cleopatra 5.2.223–5, CLEOPATRA, at her suicide

4 The plot is laid.
   1 Henry VI 2.3.4, COUNTESS OF AUVERGNE TO HER PORTER

5 My brain, more busy than the labouring spider,
   Weaves tedious snares to trap mine enemies.
   2 Henry VI 3.1.339–40, RICHARD OF YORK

6 Their hats are plucked about their ears,
   And half their faces buried in their cloaks.
   Julius Caesar 2.1.73–4, LUCIUS describing the conspirators

7 Work on,
   My medicine, work!
   Othello 4.1.44–5, IAGO, witnessing the effects on Othello of his scheming

8 I have a young conception in my brain.
   Troilus and Cressida 1.3.311, ULYSSES TO NESTOR

9 Excellent, I smell a device.
   Twelfth Night 2.3.159; SIR TOBY BELCH TO SIR ANDREW AGUECHEEK, who replies, 'I have't in my nose too.'

   See also **TRAPS AND TRICKS**

POETRY

10 When a man's verses cannot be understood, nor a man's good wit seconded with the forward child, understanding, it strikes a man more dead than a great reckoning in a little room.
   As You Like It 3.3.11–14, TOUCHSTONE TO AUDREY; the last phrase in this passage may reflect Shakespeare's feelings about the violent early death of his admired contemporary, the poet and playwright Christopher Marlowe

1 Truly, I would the gods had made thee poetical.
As You Like It 3.3.14–15, TOUCHSTONE TO AUDREY

2 Assist me some extemporal god of rhyme, for I am sure I shall turn sonnet.
Love's Labour's Lost 1.2.178–9, ARMADO

3 By heaven, I do love, and it hath taught me to rhyme, and to be melancholy.
Love's Labour's Lost 4.3.11–13, BEROWNE

4 I was not born under a rhyming planet.
Much Ado About Nothing 5.2.39–40, BENEDICK TO MARGARET

5 Nor shall death brag thou wander'st in his shade
When in eternal lines to time thou grow'st.
    So long as men can breathe or eyes can see,
    So long lives this, and this gives life to thee.
Sonnet 18.11–14

6 Not marble, nor the gilded monuments
Of princes, shall outlive this powerful rhyme.
Sonnet 55.1–2

7 When wasteful war shall statues overturn
And broils root out the work of masonry,
Nor Mars his sword, nor war's quick fire, shall burn
The living record of your memory.
Sonnet 55.5–8

POETS

8 The poet's eye, in a fine frenzy rolling,
Doth glance from heaven to earth, from earth to heaven;
And as imagination bodies forth
The forms of things unknown, the poet's pen
Turns them to shapes, and gives to airy nothing
A local habitation and a name.
Midsummer Night's Dream 5.1.12–17, THESEUS TO COMPANIONS

POISON

9 The leperous distilment, whose effect
Holds such an enmity with blood of man
That swift as quicksilver it courses through
The natural gates and alleys of the body,

And with a sudden vigour it doth posset
And curd, like eager droppings into milk,
The thin and wholesome blood. So did it mine,
And a most instant tetter barked about,
Most lazar-like, with vile and loathsome crust
All my smooth body.

Hamlet 1.5.64–73, GHOST TO HAMLET

POLICE

1 One whose hard heart is buttoned up with steel;
   A fiend, a fury, pitiless and rough,
   A wolf, nay worse, a fellow all in buff.
   Comedy of Errors 4.2.34–6, DROMIO OF SYRACUSE TO ADRIANA, of the policeman who
   has just arrested his master

2 You filthy famished correctioner.
   2 Henry IV 5.4.21, DOLL TEARSHEET TO A BEADLE

3 CONRADE Away! You are an ass, you are an ass.
   DOGBERRY Dost thou not suspect my place? Dost thou not suspect my
   years? O that he were here to write me down an ass! But masters,
   remember that I am an ass: though it be not written down, yet forget
   not that I am an ass. No, thou villain, thou art full of piety, as shall be
   proved upon thee by good witness. I am a wise fellow, and which is
   more, an officer, and which is more, a householder, and . . . one that
   knows the law.
   Much Ado About Nothing 4.2.72–82

4 Marry, sir, they have committed false report, moreover they have
   spoken untruths, secondarily they are slanders, sixth and lastly they
   have belied a lady, thirdly they have verified unjust things, and to
   conclude, they are lying knaves.
   Much Ado About Nothing 5.1.208–12, DOGBERRY's report on the reasons for
   apprehending two suspects

POLITENESS

5 The price is, to ask it kindly.
   Coriolanus 2.3.74, A CITIZEN TO CORIOLANUS

6 The very pink of courtesy.
   Romeo and Juliet 2.4.57, MERCUTIO's description of himself, to ROMEO

POLITICS AND POLITICIANS

1   Your dishonour
   Mangles true judgement, and bereaves the state
   Of that integrity which should become it.
   Coriolanus 3.1.157–9, CORIOLANUS TO BRUTUS AND MENENIUS

2 Your bait of falsehood takes this carp of truth;
   And thus do we of wisdom and of reach, . . .
   By indirections find directions out.
   Hamlet 2.1.64–5, 67, POLONIUS TO REYNALDO

3 I do think – or else this brain of mine
   Hunts not the trail of policy so sure
   As it hath used to do – that I have found
   The very cause.
   Hamlet 2.2.46–9, POLONIUS TO CLAUDIUS

4   This counsellor
   Is now most still, most secret, and most grave,
   Who was in life a foolish prating knave.
   Hamlet 3.4.215–17, HAMLET TO GERTRUDE, of Polonius

5 This might be the pate of a politician . . . , one that would circumvent
   God, might it not?
   Hamlet 5.1.77–9, HAMLET TO HORATIO, examining skulls in the graveyard

6 This vile politician.
   1 Henry IV 1.3.238, HOTSPUR TO NORTHUMBERLAND, of Bolingbroke (Henry IV)

7 I stole all courtesy from heaven,
   And dressed myself in such humility
   That I did pluck allegiance from men's hearts . . .
   Even in the presence of the crowned King . . .
   The skipping King, . . .
                    being daily swallowed by men's eyes,
   They surfeited with honey, and began
   To loathe the taste of sweetness, whereof a little
   More than a little is by much too much.
   So, when he had occasion to be seen,
   He was but as the cuckoo is in June,
   Heard, not regarded.
   1 Henry IV 3.2.50–2, 54, 60, 70–6; HENRY describes to his son PRINCE HAL his tactics
   for winning popularity during the reign of his predecessor, Richard II

1 Be it thy course to busy giddy minds
   With foreign quarrels.
   2 Henry IV 4.5.213–14, HENRY TO PRINCE HAL

2 With silence . . . be thou politic.
   1 Henry VI 2.5.101, MORTIMER TO RICHARD PLANTAGENET

3 The commons, like an angry hive of bees
   That want their leader, scatter up and down,
   And care not who they sting in his revenge.
   2 Henry VI 3.2.124–6, WARWICK TO HENRY AND LORDS

4 Thou setter up and plucker down of kings.
   3 Henry VI 2.3.37, EDWARD, son of Richard of York, to WARWICK 'the Kingmaker'

5   I know his sword
   Hath a sharp edge: it's long, and't may be said
   It reaches far, and where 'twill not extend,
   Thither he darts it.
   Henry VIII 1.1.109–12, NORFOLK TO BUCKINGHAM, of Cardinal Wolsey

6 Those that with haste will make a mighty fire
   Begin it with weak straws.
   Julius Caesar 1.3.107–8, CASSIUS TO CASCA

7 Like a scurvy politician seem
   To see the things thou dost not.
   King Lear 4.6.167–8, LEAR TO GLOUCESTER

8 Who loses and who wins, who's in, who's out.
   King Lear 5.3.15, LEAR TO CORDELIA

9 The caterpillars of the commonwealth,
   Which I have sworn to weed and pluck away.
   Richard II 2.3.165–6, BOLINGBROKE TO LORDS, of 'Bushy, Bagot, and their complices'

10   Policy, . . .
   Which works on leases of short-numbered hours.
   Sonnet 124.9–10

11 Troy in our weakness stands, not in her strength.
   Troilus and Cressida 1.3.137, ULYSSES TO THE GREEK PRINCES

12 They tax our policy and call it cowardice.
   Troilus and Cressida 1.3.197, ULYSSES TO THE GREEK PRINCES

1 Let thy tongue tang arguments of state.
Twelfth Night 2.5.145–6, MALVOLIO reads the anonymous letter which he believes is
from Olivia

POSSESSION

2 Have is have, however men do catch.
King John 1.1.173, PHILIP THE BASTARD TO JOHN

POVERTY

3 Oppressed with two weak evils, age and hunger.
As You Like It 2.7.132, ORLANDO TO DUKE SENIOR, of Adam

4 I am as poor as Job, my lord, but not so patient.
2 Henry IV 1.2.126–7, FALSTAFF TO THE LORD CHIEF JUSTICE

5 LORD CHIEF JUSTICE Your means are very slender, and your waste is
    great.
FALSTAFF I would it were otherwise, I would my means were greater
    and my waist slenderer.
2 Henry IV 1.2.140–3

6 I can get no remedy against this consumption of the purse; borrowing
only lingers and lingers it out, but the disease is incurable.
2 Henry IV 1.2.236–8, FALSTAFF TO THE LORD CHIEF JUSTICE

7   Prayers and wishes
Are all I can return.
Henry VIII 2.3.69–70, ANNE BULLEN (BOLEYN) TO THE LORD CHAMBERLAIN, who has
just detailed the gifts Henry proposes to give her

8 Whiles I am a beggar, I will rail
And say there is no sin but to be rich;
And being rich, my virtue then shall be
To say there is no vice but beggary.
King John 2.1.593–6, PHILIP THE BASTARD

9 O, reason not the need! Our basest beggars
Are in the poorest thing superfluous;
Allow not nature more than nature needs,
Man's life is cheap as beast's.
King Lear 2.2.456–9, LEAR TO REGAN

10 A most poor man, made tame to fortune's blows.
King Lear 4.6.217, EDGAR, of himself, to GLOUCESTER

1 The naked truth of it is, I have no shirt.
Love's Labour's Lost 5.2.703, ARMADO TO BEROWNE

2   Famine is in thy cheeks,
Need and oppression starveth in thy eyes,
Contempt and beggary hangs upon thy back.
Romeo and Juliet 5.1.69–71, ROMEO TO THE APOTHECARY

3 What an alteration of honour has desp'rate want made!
Timon of Athens 4.3.464, STEWARD, of Timon

See also BEGGARS; THRIFT; WORLD, the

POWER

4 Let Rome in Tiber melt, and the wide arch
Of the ranged empire fall! Here is my space!
Kingdoms are clay!
Antony and Cleopatra 1.1.34–6, ANTONY TO CLEOPATRA

5   [I] who
With half the bulk o'th' world played as I pleased,
Making and marring fortunes.
Antony and Cleopatra 3.11.63–5, ANTONY TO CLEOPATRA

6 Great men tremble when the lion roars.
2 Henry VI 3.1.19, QUEEN MARGARET TO HENRY – the lion she has in mind is
Humphrey, Duke of Gloucester

7 Great men have reaching hands.
2 Henry VI 4.7.77, LORD SAY TO JACK CADE; he says that he has been responsible for
the deaths of people he has never met, without having struck a blow himself

8 A sceptre snatched with an unruly hand
Must be as boisterously maintained as gained.
King John 3.3.135–6, CARDINAL PANDULPH TO LEWIS, DAUPHIN OF FRANCE

9 When Caesar says, 'Do this,' it is performed.
Julius Caesar 1.2.10, MARK ANTONY TO JULIUS CAESAR

10   Ye gods, it doth amaze me
A man of such a feeble temper should . . .
. . . bear the palm alone.
Julius Caesar 1.2.127–8, 130, CASSIUS' description of Julius Caesar's power

11   We shall see
If power change purpose, what our seemers be.
Measure for Measure 1.3.53–4, DUKE TO FRIAR THOMAS; he means to test whether his
deputy Angelo is as virtuous as he seems by giving him greater power

1   It is excellent
To have a giant's strength, but it is tyrannous
To use it like a giant.
Measure for Measure 2.2.108–10, ISABELLA TO ANGELO

See also **SELF-CONTROL**

PRAYER

2 My words fly up, my thoughts remain below.
Words without thoughts never to heaven go.
Hamlet 3.3.97–8, CLAUDIUS

3 But wherefore could not I pronounce 'Amen'?
I had most need of blessing, and 'Amen'
Stuck in my throat.
Macbeth 2.2.30–2, MACBETH TO LADY MACBETH

4 When I would pray and think, I think and pray
To several subjects: Heaven hath my empty words,
Whilst my invention, hearing not my tongue,
Anchors on Isabel.
Measure for Measure 2.4.1–4, ANGELO

5 His worst fault is that he is given to prayer; he is something peevish
that way.
Merry Wives of Windsor 1.4.11–12, MISTRESS QUICKLY TO SIMPLE, of a servant

6   Now I want
Spirits to enforce, Art to enchant;
And my ending is despair,
Unless I be relieved by prayer,
Which pierces so, that it assaults
Mercy itself, and frees all faults.
Tempest Epilogue 13–18, PROSPERO

PREPAREDNESS

7 The readiness is all.
Hamlet 5.2.221, HAMLET TO HORATIO

8 Our legions are brim-full, our cause is ripe.
Julius Caesar 4.3.214, BRUTUS TO CASSIUS

PRESENT, the

9 Past and to come seems best; things present, worst.
2 Henry IV 1.3.108, ARCHBISHOP OF YORK TO HASTINGS AND LORD BARDOLPH

1   What is love? 'Tis not hereafter,
      Present mirth hath present laughter:
         What's to come is still unsure.
      In delay there lies no plenty,
      Then come kiss me, sweet and twenty:
         Youth's a stuff will not endure.
Twelfth Night 2.3.47–52, FESTE's song; *more at* **LOVE**

PRIDE

2 My pride fell with my fortunes.
As You Like It 1.2.242, ROSALIND TO ORLANDO

3   You speak o'th' people
As if you were a god to punish, not
A man of their infirmity.
Coriolanus 3.1.80–2, BRUTUS TO CORIOLANUS

4   I can see his pride
Peep through each part of him.
Henry VIII 1.1.68–9, ABERGAVENNY TO BUCKINGHAM, of Cardinal Wolsey

5 You sign your place and calling, in full seeming,
With meekness and humility: but your heart
Is crammed with arrogancy, spleen and pride.
Henry VIII 2.4.107–9, KATHERINE OF ARAGON TO CARDINAL WOLSEY

6 New-made honour doth forget men's names.
King John 1.1.187; PHILIP THE BASTARD

7   Take physic, pomp
Expose thyself to feel what wretches feel.
King Lear 3.4.33–4, LEAR, in the storm

8 I will not jump with common spirits,
And rank me with the barbarous multitudes.
Merchant of Venice 2.9.32–3, PRINCE OF ARRAGON

9 Being so great, I have no need to beg.
Richard II 4.1.309, RICHARD TO BOLINGBROKE

10 I have a touch of your condition,
That cannot brook the accent of reproof.
Richard III 4.4.158–9, RICHARD TO THE DUCHESS OF YORK, his mother

11 Some glory in their birth, some in their skill,
Some in their wealth, some in their body's force,

Some in their garments, though new-fangled ill,
Some in their hawks and hounds, some in their horse.
Sonnet 91.1–4

1 He that is proud eats up himself: pride is his own glass, his own trumpet, his own chronicle.
Troilus and Cressida 2.3.156–8, AGAMEMNON TO AJAX

2 I do hate a proud man as I do hate the engendering of toads.
Troilus and Cressida 2.3.160–1, AJAX's contribution to the discussion of pride

3 Things small as nothing, for request's sake only,
He makes important; possessed he is with greatness.
Troilus and Cressida 2.3.170–1, ULYSSES TO AJAX, of Achilles

4 He'll answer nobody: he professes not answering; speaking is for beggars, he wears his tongue in's arms.
Troilus and Cressida 3.3.266–8, THERSITES TO ACHILLES, of Ajax

5 Be opposite with a kinsman, surly with servants.
Twelfth Night 2.5.144–5, MALVOLIO reads the anonymous letter which he believes is from Olivia

See also **SCORN**

PRIESTS

6 Out, scarlet hypocrite!
1 Henry VI 1.3.56, GLOUCESTER TO THE BISHOP OF WINCHESTER

7 This meddling priest.
King John 3.1.89, JOHN TO PHILIP, KING OF FRANCE, of Cardinal Pandulph

See also **RELIGION**

PRISON

8   Come, let's away to prison;
We two alone will sing like birds i'the cage.
When thou dost ask me blessing I'll kneel down
And ask of thee forgiveness. So we'll live
And pray, and sing, and tell old tales, and laugh
At gilded butterflies.
King Lear 5.3.8–13, LEAR TO CORDELIA

9 I have been studying how I may compare
This prison where I live unto the world.
Richard II 5.5.1–2, RICHARD

PROMISES

1 'Tis not the many oaths that makes the truth,
But the plain single vow that is vowed true.
All's Well That Ends Well 4.2.21–2, DIANA TO BERTRAM

2 I have not kept my square, but that to come
Shall all be done by th' rule.
Antony and Cleopatra 2.3.6–7, MARK ANTONY TO OCTAVIA

3 His promises were as he then was, mighty,
But his performance, as he is now, nothing.
Henry VIII 4.2.41–2, KATHERINE OF ARAGON TO GRIFFITH, an usher, of Cardinal Wolsey

4   If thou swear'st,
Thou mayst prove false.
Romeo and Juliet 2.2.91–2, JULIET TO ROMEO

5 To promise is most courtly and fashionable; performance is a kind of will or testament which argues a great sickness in his judgment that makes it.
Timon of Athens 5.1.27–9, PAINTER TO A POET

6 It is the purpose that makes strong the vow.
Troilus and Cressida 5.3.23, CASSANDRA TO HECTOR

7   Stuffed with protestations,
And full of new-found oaths.
Two Gentlemen of Verona 4.4.126–7, JULIA TO SILVIA

PROPHECIES

8 The time will come that foul sin, gathering head,
Shall break into corruption.
2 Henry IV 3.1.76–7, HENRY TO WARWICK AND SURREY, quoting Richard II

9 Beware the ides of March.
Julius Caesar 1.2.19, SOOTHSAYER TO JULIUS CAESAR

10   Be Kent unmannerly
When Lear is mad.
King Lear 1.1.146–7, KENT TO LEAR

11 Jesters do oft prove prophets.
King Lear 5.3.72, REGAN TO ALBANY AND GONERIL

1 If you can look into the seeds of time,
   And say which grain will grow, and which will not,
   Speak then to me.
   Macbeth 1.3.58–60, BANQUO TO THE WITCHES

2 Macbeth! Macbeth! Macbeth! beware Macduff;
   Beware the Thane of Fife . . .
                      None of woman born
   Shall harm Macbeth . . .
   Macbeth shall never vanquished be, until
   Great Birnam wood to high Dunsinane hill
   Shall come against him.
   Macbeth 4.1.71–2, 80–1, 92–4, THREE APPARITIONS TO MACBETH

3 I see, as in a map, the end of all.
   Richard III 2.4.54, QUEEN ELIZABETH TO THE DUCHESS OF YORK

4 Bloody thou art; bloody will be thy end.
   Richard III 4.4.195, DUCHESS OF YORK TO RICHARD, her son

5 Cry, Trojans, cry.
   Troilus and Cressida 2.2.98, CASSANDRA, foreseeing Troy's fate

   See also **OMENS AND PORTENTS**

PROSPERITY

6 No day without a deed to crown it.
   Henry VIII 5.4.58, CRANMER TO HENRY, foreseeing the reign of Elizabeth I

PROVIDENCE

7 There is special providence in the fall of a sparrow.
   Hamlet 5.2.218–19, HAMLET TO HORATIO; *more at* **FATE**

PRUDENCE

8   His noble hand
   Did win what he did spend, and spent not that
   Which his triumphant father's hand had won.
   Richard II 2.1.179–80, YORK TO RICHARD, of Edward, Richard's grandfather

PUBLIC OPINION

9   This common body,
   Like to a vagabond flag upon the stream,
   Goes to, and back, lackeying the varying tide,
   To rot itself with motion.
   Antony and Cleopatra 1.4.44–7, OCTAVIUS CAESAR

1 There hath been many great men that have flattered the people, who
ne'er loved them; and there be many that they have loved, they know
not wherefore.
Coriolanus 2.2.7–10, ONE OFFICER TO ANOTHER

2 The play, I remember, pleased not the million, 'twas caviare to the
general.
Hamlet 2.2.436–8, HAMLET TO THE PLAYERS

3 He's loved of the distracted multitude,
Who like not in their judgment but their eyes.
Hamlet 4.3.4–5, CLAUDIUS TO LORDS

4 An habitation giddy and unsure
Hath he that buildeth on the vulgar heart.
2 Henry IV 1.3.89–90, ARCHBISHOP OF YORK TO HASTINGS AND LORD BARDOLPH

5   I love the people,
But do not like to stage me to their eyes:
Though it do well, I do not relish well
Their loud applause and *Aves* vehement;
Nor do I think the man of safe discretion
That does affect it.
Measure for Measure 1.1.67–72, DUKE TO ANGELO

6 The fool multitude that choose by show.
Merchant of Venice 2.9.26, PRINCE OF ARRAGON TO PORTIA

PUNISHMENT

7 Where th'offence is, let the great axe fall.
Hamlet 4.5.215, CLAUDIUS TO LAERTES

8   It was a grievous fault,
And grievously hath Caesar answered it.
Julius Caesar 3.2.80–1, MARK ANTONY's oration on the death of Julius Caesar

9 All sects, all ages smack of this vice, and he
To die for't!
Measure for Measure 2.2.5–6, PROVOST TO A SERVANT; the vice is sex outside marriage

10 He who the sword of heaven will bear
Should be as holy as severe.
Measure for Measure 3.2.254–5, DUKE

1 You must prepare your bosom for his knife.
   Merchant of Venice 4.1.243, PORTIA TO ANTONIO

2 A punishment more in policy than in malice.
   Othello 2.3.265, IAGO TO CASSIO

3 Off with his head!
   Richard III 3.4.76, RICHARD TO HASTINGS

   See also **DEATH; GUILT; JUDGES AND JUDGEMENT; JUSTICE**

QUARRELS

4 To be put to the arbitrement of swords.
   Cymbeline 1.5.49–50, A FRENCHMAN TO IACHIMO

5 Gentlemen, enough of this, it came in too suddenly, let it die as it was
   born, and I pray you be better acquainted.
   Cymbeline 1.5.121–3, PHILARIO TO POSTHUMUS AND IACHIMO

6   Beware
   Of entrance to a quarrel, but being in,
   Bear't that th'opposed may beware of thee.
   Hamlet 1.3.65–7, POLONIUS TO LAERTES *more at* **ADVICE**

7 In a false quarrel there is no true valour.
   Much Ado About Nothing 5.1.121, BENEDICK TO DON PEDRO

8 Thou? Why, thou wilt quarrel with a man that hath a hair more or a
   hair less in his beard than thou hast. Thou wilt quarrel with a man for
   cracking nuts, having no other reason but because thou hast hazel eyes.
   What eye but such an eye would spy out such a quarrel? Thy head is as
   full of quarrels as an egg is full of meat, and yet thy head hath been
   beaten as addle as an egg for quarrelling.
   Romeo and Juliet 3.1.16–24, MERCUTIO TO BENVOLIO

QUESTIONS

9 To be, or not to be, that is the question.
   Hamlet 3.1.56, HAMLET; for the rest of this speech *see* **SUICIDE**

1 Ask me what question thou canst possible,
And I will answer unpremeditated.
1 Henry VI 1.2.87–8, PUCELLE (JOAN OF ARC) TO CHARLES, DAUPHIN OF FRANCE, AND
REIGNIER

2 Demand me nothing. What you know, you know.
Othello 5.2.302, IAGO, to those assembled round the body of Desdemona

QUIET

3 Not a mouse stirring.
Hamlet 1.1.11, FRANCISCO TO BARNARDO, on the night watch

4 No tongue! all eyes! be silent.
Tempest 4.1.59, PROSPERO, introducing a masque

5 Pray you, tread softly, that the blind mole may not
Hear a foot fall.
Tempest 4.1.194–5, CALIBAN TO STEPHANO AND TRINCULO

R

READING

6 POLONIUS What do you read, my lord?
HAMLET Words, words, words.
Hamlet 2.2.191–2

See also **BOOKS; EDUCATION; WORDS**

REASON AND UNREASON

7 You cannot speak of reason to the Dane
And lose your voice.
Hamlet 1.2.44–5, CLAUDIUS claims his accessibility

8 He that made us with such large discourse,
Looking before and after, gave us not
That capability and godlike reason
To fust in us unused.
Hamlet 4.4.36–9, HAMLET

1 O judgment, thou art fled to brutish beasts,
And men have lost their reason.
Julius Caesar 3.2.105–6, MARK ANTONY's oration on the death of Julius Caesar

2 The will of man is by his reason swayed.
Midsummer Night's Dream 2.2.114, LYSANDER TO HELENA

3 We have reason to cool our raging motions, our carnal stings, our unbitted lusts.
Othello 1.3.331–3, IAGO TO RODERIGO

4 My reason, the physician to my love,
Angry that his prescriptions are not kept,
Hath left me.
Sonnet 147.5–7

5 Past cure I am, now reason is past care.
Sonnet 147.9

6   Pleasure and revenge
Have ears more deaf than adders to the voice
Of any true decision.
Troilus and Cressida 2.2.172–4, HECTOR TO TROJAN PRINCES

REASONS

7 Every why hath a wherefore.
Comedy of Errors 2.2.43–4, DROMIO OF SYRACUSE TO ANTIPHOLUS OF SYRACUSE

8 If reasons were as plentiful as blackberries, I would give no man a reason upon compulsion.
1 Henry IV 2.4.235–7, FALSTAFF TO POINS; this joke puns on 'reasons' and the similarly pronounced 'raisins'

9 It is the cause, it is the cause, my soul!
Othello 5.2.1, OTHELLO contemplating the sleeping Desdemona

10 My reasons are too deep and dead:
Too deep and dead, poor infants, in their graves.
Richard III 4.4.362–3, QUEEN ELIZABETH TO RICHARD

11 I have no other but a woman's reason:
I think him so, because I think him so.
Two Gentlemen of Verona 1.2.23–4, LUCETTA TO JULIA

REBELLION AND REVOLUTION

1 There was a time, when all the body's members
Rebelled against the belly; thus accused it:
That only like a gulf it did remain
I'th' midst o'th' body, idle and unactive,
Still cupboarding the viand.

Coriolanus 1.1.95–9, MENENIUS TO CITIZENS; a well-known fable about the role of the governing class; the body replies to its critics (129–38):

'True is it, my incorporate friends,' quoth he,
'That I receive the general food at first
Which you do live upon; and fit it is,
Because I am the store-house and the shop
Of the whole body. But, if you do remember,
I send it through the rivers of your blood
Even to the court, the heart, to th' seat o'th' brain;
And through the cranks and offices of man,
The strongest nerves and small inferior veins
From me receive that natural competency
Whereby they live.'

2 WORCESTER   I protest
I have not sought the day of this dislike.
HENRY You have not sought it? How comes it, then?
FALSTAFF Rebellion lay in his way, and he found it.
1 Henry IV 5.1.25–8

3 The first thing we do, let's kill all the lawyers.
2 Henry VI 4.2.74, BUTCHER TO JACK CADE, leader of a popular rebellion

4 The smallest worm will turn being trodden on.
3 Henry VI 2.2.17, CLIFFORD TO HENRY AND QUEEN MARGARET

5 We shall be called purgers, not murderers.
Julius Caesar 2.1.180, BRUTUS TO CASSIUS

6 Liberty! Freedom! Tyranny is dead!
Julius Caesar 3.1.78, CINNA's cry on the death of Julius Caesar

7 Rebellion, flat rebellion!
King John 3.1.224, DUKE OF AUSTRIA to assembled nobility

1   Flout 'em and cout 'em,
        And scout 'em and flout 'em;
          Thought is free.
Tempest 3.2.123–5, STEPHANO, singing

REGRET

2 What our contempts doth often hurl from us
    We wish it ours again.
    Antony and Cleopatra 1.2.128–9, ANTONY

3 Let him have time to mark how slow time goes
    In time of sorrow, and how swift and short
    His time of folly and his time of sport.
    Lucrece 990–2

4 Wake Duncan with thy knocking: I would thou couldst!
    Macbeth 2.2.73, MACBETH

5   Things without all remedy
    Should be without regard: what's done is done.
    Macbeth 3.2.11–12, LADY MACBETH TO MACBETH

6 What's done cannot be undone.
    Macbeth 5.1.69, LADY MACBETH, mad

7 Things past redress are now with me past care.
    Richard II 2.3.170, YORK TO BOLINGBROKE

8 After-hours gives leisure to repent.
    Richard III 4.4.293, RICHARD TO QUEEN ELIZABETH

9 Th'offender's sorrow lends but weak relief
    To him that bears the strong offence's loss.
    Sonnet 34.11–12

REJECTION

10 Am I so round with you, as you with me,
    That like a football you do spurn me thus?
    Comedy of Errors 2.1.83–4, DROMIO OF EPHESUS TO ADRIANA, who thinks he is her servant

11 Get thee to a nunnery.
    Hamlet 3.1.121, HAMLET TO OPHELIA; for fuller context *see* **CHILDREN, having or not having**

1 Stand not upon the order of your going,
But go at once.
Macbeth 3.4.118–19, LADY MACBETH TO HER GUESTS

2 She sent him away as cold as a snowball.
Pericles 4.6.137–8, BOULT TO THE BAWD

3 The door is open, sir, there lies your way.
Taming of the Shrew 3.2.208, KATHERINA TO PETRUCHIO

RELIGION

4 Am I Rome's slave?
King John 5.2.97, LEWIS, DAUPHIN OF FRANCE, TO CARDINAL PANDULPH, the papal legate

5 I will buy with you, sell with you, talk with you, walk with you, and so following: but I will not eat with you, drink with you, nor pray with you.
Merchant of Venice 1.3.34–6, SHYLOCK TO BASSANIO

6   In religion,
What damned error but some sober brow
Will bless it, and approve it with a text?
Merchant of Venice, 3.2.77–9, BASSANIO

7 For aye to be in shady cloister mewed,
To live a barren sister all your life,
Chanting faint hymns to the cold fruitless moon.
Midsummer Night's Dream 1.1.71–3, THESEUS TO HERMIA, threatening her with the prospect of being a nun

8   'Tis mad idolatry
To make the service greater than the god.
Troilus and Cressida 2.2.57–8, HECTOR TO TROILUS

9 It is an heretic that makes the fire,
Not she which burns in 't.
Winter's Tale 2.3.114–15, PAULINA TO LEONTES

See also **CHRISTIANS; GOD; JEWS AND JEWISHNESS; PRIESTS**

RENUNCIATION

10 I'll give my jewels for a set of beads;
My gorgeous palace for a hermitage;
My gay apparel for an almsman's gown;
My figured goblets for a dish of wood;

My sceptre for a palmer's walking staff;
My subjects for a pair of carved saints,
And my large kingdom for a little grave,
A little little grave, an obscure grave.
Richard II 3.3.147–54, RICHARD TO AUMERLE

1 With mine own tears I wash away my balm,
With mine own hands I give away my crown,
With mine own tongue deny my sacred state,
With mine own breath release all duteous oaths;
All pomp and majesty I do forswear.
Richard II 4.1.207–11, RICHARD TO BOLINGBROKE

REPUTATION

2 The bubble reputation
As You Like It 2.7.152, from JAQUES's 'Seven Ages of Man' speech

3   I have bought
Golden opinions from all sorts of people
Which would be worn now in their newest gloss.
Macbeth 1.7.32–4, MACBETH TO LADY MACBETH

4 The purest treasure mortal times afford
Is spotless reputation.
Richard II 1.1.177–8, MOWBRAY TO RICHARD

5 Reputation, reputation, reputation! O, I have lost my reputation, I
have lost the immortal part of myself.
Othello 2.3.254–6, CASSIO TO IAGO

6 Reputation is an idle and most false imposition, oft got without merit
and lost without deserving.
Othello 2.3.260–2, IAGO TO CASSIO, in reply to the above

7 Good name in man and woman, dear my lord,
Is the immediate jewel of their souls: . . .
He that filches from me my good name
Robs me of that which not enriches him
And makes me poor indeed.
Othello 3.3.158–9, 162–4, IAGO TO OTHELLO

8 The painful warrior famoused for worth,
After a thousand victories once foiled,
Is from the book of honour razed quite.
Sonnet 25.9–11

1 I see my reputation is at stake.
Troilus and Cressida 3.3.226, ACHILLES TO PATROCLUS

2 Never dream on infamy, but go.
Two Gentlemen of Verona 2.7.64, LUCETTA TO JULIA, 'infamy' meaning getting a bad name

RESENTMENT

3   Under him
My Genius is rebuked; as, it is said,
Mark Antony's was by Caesar.
Macbeth 3.1.54–6, MACBETH, of Banquo

4 They hailed him father to a line of kings:
Upon my head they placed a fruitless crown,
And put a barren sceptre in my gripe.
Macbeth 3.1.59–61, MACBETH, of Banquo

5 I had rather be a canker in a hedge than a rose in his grace.
Much Ado About Nothing 1.3.25–6, DON JOHN TO CONRADE, of his brother Don Pedro

6 He hath a daily beauty in his life
That makes me ugly.
Othello 5.1.19–20, IAGO TO RODERIGO, of Cassio

RESIGNATION

7 We lose it not so long as we can smile.
Othello 1.3.212, BRABANTIO TO THE DUKE OF VENICE

RESOLVE

8 My resolution's placed, and I have nothing
Of woman in me. Now from head to foot
I am marble-constant. Now the fleeting moon
No planet is of mine.
Antony and Cleopatra 5.2.237–40, CLEOPATRA

9 I will set this foot of mine as far
As who goes furthest.
Julius Caesar 1.3.119–20, CASCA TO CASSIUS; *see also* **STARS**

10 How high a pitch his resolution soars!
Richard II 1.1.109, RICHARD, of Bolingbroke

11 [We are] metal, . . . steel to the very back.
Titus Andronicus 4.3.48, TITUS TO MARCUS

RESPECT

1 I hold you as a thing enskied and sainted.
   Measure for Measure 1.4.34, LUCIO TO ISABELLA

RESPONSIBILITY

2 Our remedies oft in ourselves do lie
   Which we ascribe to heaven.
   All's Well That Ends Well 1.1.216–17, HELENA TO PAROLLES

3 The fault, dear Brutus, is not in our stars,
   But in ourselves, that we are underlings.
   Julius Caesar 1.2.138–9, CASSIUS TO BRUTUS

4 When we are sick in fortune, often the surfeits of our own behaviour,
   we make guilty of our disasters the sun, the moon and the stars, as if
   we were villains on necessity, fools by heavenly compulsion.
   King Lear 1.2.120–3, EDMUND

5   Ebbing men . . .
   Most often do so near the bottom run
   By their own fear or sloth.
   Tempest 2.1.227–9, ANTONIO TO SEBASTIAN

   See also **FATE; FORTUNE**

RETIREMENT

6   'Tis our fast intent
   To shake all cares and business from our age,
   Conferring them on younger strengths, while we
   Unburdened crawl toward death.
   King Lear 1.1.37–40, LEAR TO GLOUCESTER

7 The life removed.
   Measure for Measure 1.3.8, DUKE TO FRIAR THOMAS, expressing his preference for a
   quiet life

8   This rough magic
   I here abjure; and, when I have required
   Some heavenly music, – which even now I do, –
   To work mine end upon their senses, that
   This airy charm is for, I'll break my staff,
   Bury it certain fadoms in the earth,

And deeper than did ever plummet sound
I'll drown my book.

Tempest 5.1.50–7, PROSPERO TO ARIEL, a great gesture of renunciation near the end of the last play Shakespeare wrote single-handedly; also, probably, a recollection of Christopher Marlowe's Doctor Faustus, vowing at the close of the play to burn his books

REVENGE

1 He was a kind of nothing, titleless,
Till he had forged himself a name o'th' fire
Of burning Rome.
Coriolanus 5.1.13–15, COMINIUS TO MENENIUS, of Coriolanus

2 The croaking raven doth bellow for revenge.
Hamlet 3.2.256, HAMLET, encouraging the dumb show

3 How all occasions do inform against me,
And spur my dull revenge.
Hamlet 4.4.32–3, HAMLET

4   O, from this time forth
My thoughts be bloody or be nothing worth.
Hamlet 4.4.65–6, HAMLET

5 Revenge should have no bounds.
Hamlet 4.7.128, CLAUDIUS TO LAERTES (with unknowing irony)

6 If I digged up thy forefathers' graves
And hung their rotten coffins up in chains,
It could not slake mine ire nor ease my heart.
3 Henry VI 1.3.27–9, CLIFFORD TO EDMUND, EARL OF RUTLAND, whom he is about to murder

7 Thy father slew my father; therefore die.
3 Henry VI 1.3.46, CLIFFORD's farewell to EDMUND, EARL OF RUTLAND – *see previous entry*

8   Caesar, thou art revenged
Even with the sword that killed thee.
Julius Caesar 5.2.45–6; CASSIUS kills himself with the sword with which he struck Julius Caesar

9 I will have such revenges on you both
That all the world shall – I will do such things –
What they are yet I know not, but they shall be
The terrors of the earth!
King Lear 2.2.471–4, LEAR TO GONERIL AND REGAN

1 Then kill, kill, kill, kill, kill, kill!
King Lear 4.6.183, LEAR expressing his hatred of his son-in-laws to GLOUCESTER

2 Blood will have blood.
Macbeth 3.4.121, MACBETH TO LADY MACBETH

3 Kill Claudio!
Much Ado About Nothing 4.1.287, BEATRICE TO BENEDICK

4 O God that I were a man! I would eat his heart in the market-place.
Much Ado About Nothing 4.1.304–5, BEATRICE TO BENEDICK, of Claudio

5   Like to the Pontic sea
Whose icy current and compulsive course
Ne'er keeps retiring ebb but keeps due on
To the Propontic and the Hellespont:
Even so my bloody thoughts with violent pace
Shall ne'er look back, ne'er ebb to humble love
Till that a capable and wide revenge
Swallow them up.
Othello 3.3.456–63, OTHELLO TO IAGO

6 For those that were, it is not square to take
On those that are, revenge: crimes, like lands,
Are not inherited.
Timon of Athens 5.4.36–8, ONE SENATOR TO ANOTHER

7 Vengeance is in my heart, death in my hand,
Blood and revenge are hammering in my head.
Titus Andronicus 2.2.38–9, AARON TO TAMORA

8 I'll be revenged on the whole pack of you.
Twelfth Night 5.1.370, MALVOLIO

RICHARD III

9 Sin, death, and hell have set their marks on him.
Richard III 1.3.293, QUEEN MARGARET TO BUCKINGHAM

10 A cockatrice hast thou hatched to the world
Whose unavoided eye is murderous.
Richard III 4.1.54–5, DUCHESS OF YORK, Richard's mother, blaming herself

11 From forth the kennel of thy womb hath crept
A hell-hound that doth hunt us all to death.
Richard III 4.4.47–8, QUEEN MARGARET TO THE DUCHESS OF YORK

1 Hell's black intelligencer.
Richard III 4.4.71, QUEEN MARGARET TO THE DUCHESS OF YORK AND QUEEN ELIZABETH

2 That bottled spider, that foul bunch-backed toad.
Richard III 4.4.81, QUEEN ELIZABETH TO QUEEN MARGARET; these epithets appear in an earlier conversation between the two women, at 1.3.242 and 246

RICHES

3 She bears a duke's revenues on her back,
And in her heart she scorns our poverty.
2 Henry VI 1.3.80–1, QUEEN MARGARET, of the Duchess of Gloucester

4   How i'th' name of thrift
Does he rake this together?
Henry VIII 3.2.108–9, HENRY TO LORDS, of Cardinal Wolsey

5 Through tattered clothes great vices do appear;
Robes and furred gowns hide all.
King Lear 4.6.160–1, LEAR TO GLOUCESTER

6 Honour for wealth; and oft that wealth doth cost
The death of all, and all together lost.
Lucrece 146–7

See also **MONEY**

RISK

7   Men that hazard all
Do it in hope of fair advantages.
Merchant of Venice 2.7.18–19, PRINCE OF MOROCCO

8 I have set my life upon a cast,
And I will stand the hazard of the die.
Richard III 5.4.9–10, RICHARD TO CATESBY AND NORFOLK, at the battle of Bosworth

RIVALRY

9 Two stars keep not their motion in one sphere.
1 Henry IV 5.4.64, PRINCE HAL TO HOTSPUR

10 Such men as he be never at heart's ease
Whiles they behold a greater than themselves,
And therefore are they very dangerous.
Julius Caesar 1.2.205–7, JULIUS CAESAR TO MARK ANTONY, of Cassius; *more at* **DANGEROUS PEOPLE**

1 Nay, I'll go with thee, cheek by jowl.
   Midsummer Night's Dream 3.2.338, DEMETRIUS TO LYSANDER

2 Ajax employed plucks down Achilles' plumes.
   Troilus and Cressida 1.3.385, ULYSSES TO NESTOR

3 Emulation hath a thousand sons
   That one by one pursue; if you give way,
   Or hedge aside from the direct forthright,
   Like to an entered tide they all rush by
   And leave you hindmost.
   Troilus and Cressida 3.3.156–60, ULYSSES TO ACHILLES

4 I saw her first.
   Two Noble Kinsmen 2.2.160, PALAMON TO ARCITE

ROME AND THE ROMANS

5 He was disposed to mirth, but on the sudden
   A Roman thought hath struck him.
   Antony and Cleopatra 1.2.85–6, CLEOPATRA TO HER COMPANIONS

6 I am more an antique Roman than a Dane.
   Hamlet 5.2.348, HORATIO TO HAMLET

7 The sun of Rome is set. Our day is gone.
   Julius Caesar 5.3.63, TITINIUS TO MESSALA

8 Rome is but a wilderness of tigers.
   Titus Andronicus 3.1.54, TITUS TO LUCIUS

   See also **NOBILITY; SERIOUSNESS**

ROMEO AND JULIET

9 My only love sprung from my only hate.
   Too early seen unknown, and known too late.
   Romeo and Juliet 1.5.138–9, JULIET TO HER NURSE

10 Romeo! Humours! Madman! Passion! Lover!
   Appear thou in the likeness of a sigh.
   Romeo and Juliet 2.1.7–8, MERCUTIO, with Benvolio

11 But soft, what light through yonder window breaks?
   It is the east and Juliet is the sun!
   Romeo and Juliet 2.2.2–3, ROMEO

12 O Romeo, Romeo, wherefore art thou Romeo?
   Romeo and Juliet 2.2.33, JULIET TO ROMEO; *more at* **NAMES**

1 My bounty is as boundless as the sea,
   My love as deep: the more I give to thee
   The more I have, for both are infinite.
   Romeo and Juliet 2.2.133–5, JULIET TO ROMEO

2 Come night, come Romeo, come thou day in night, . . .
   Come gentle night, come loving black-browed night,
   Give me my Romeo; and when I shall die
   Take him and cut him out in little stars,
   And he will make the face of heaven so fine
   That all the world will be in love with night,
   And pay no worship to the garish sun.
   Romeo and Juliet 3.2.17, 20–5, JULIET

3   Heaven is here
   Where Juliet lives.
   Romeo and Juliet 3.3.29–30, ROMEO TO FRIAR LAURENCE

4   O my love, my wife,
   Death that hath sucked the honey of thy breath
   Hath had no power yet upon thy beauty.
   Thou art not conquered. Beauty's ensign yet
   Is crimson in thy lips and in thy cheeks,
   And Death's pale flag is not advanced there.
   Romeo and Juliet 5.3.91–6, ROMEO

5 Never was a story of more woe
   Than this of Juliet and her Romeo.
   Romeo and Juliet 5.3.310–11, PRINCE OF VERONA, closing the play

RUMOUR

6   They say!
   They'll sit by th' fire, and presume to know
   What's done i'th' Capitol: who's like to rise,
   Who thrives, and who declines; side factions, and give out
   Conjectural marriages; making parties strong,
   And feebling such as stand not in their liking.
   Coriolanus 1.1.189–94, CAIUS MARTIUS TO MENENIUS

7 Open your ears; for which of you will stop
   The vent of hearing when loud Rumour speaks?
   2 Henry IV Induction 1–2, RUMOUR

1   Rumour is a pipe
Blown by surmises, jealousies, conjectures,
And of so easy and so plain a stop
That the blunt monster with uncounted heads,
The still-discordant wav'ring multitude,
Can play upon it.
2 Henry IV Induction 15–20, RUMOUR

2 Rumour doth double, like the voice and echo,
The numbers of the feared.
2 Henry IV 3.1.97–8, WARWICK TO HENRY

3 I find the people strangely fantasied;
Possessed with rumours, full of idle dreams,
Not knowing what they fear, but full of fear.
King John 4.2.144–6, PHILIP THE BASTARD TO JOHN

4 Foul whisp'rings are abroad. Unnatural deeds
Do breed unnatural troubles.
Macbeth 5.1.73–4, LADY MACBETH'S DOCTOR TO HER GENTLEWOMAN

5 Pitchers have ears.
Taming of the Shrew 4.4.52, BAPTISTA TO TRANIO, referring to servants; *see also*
CHILDREN

SACRIFICES AND SCAPEGOATS

6 Let's be sacrificers, but not butchers.
Julius Caesar 2.1.166, BRUTUS TO THE CONSPIRATORS

7 Upon such sacrifices . . .
The gods themselves throw incense.
King Lear 5.3.20–1, LEAR TO CORDELIA

8 I am a tainted wether of the flock,
Meetest for death.
Merchant of Venice 4.1.114–15, ANTONIO TO BASSANIO AND THE DUKE

SADNESS

1 In sooth I know not why I am so sad.
Merchant of Venice 1.1.1, ANTONIO TO SALERIO

See also **GRIEF; SORROW**

SCORN

2 What, my dear Lady Disdain! Are you yet living?
Much Ado About Nothing 1.1.113–14, BENEDICK TO BEATRICE

3 Disdain and scorn ride sparkling in her eyes.
Much Ado About Nothing 3.1.51, HERO TO URSULA, of Beatrice

4   If I should speak,
She would mock me into air. O, she would laugh me
Out of myself, press me to death with wit!
Much Ado About Nothing 3.1.74–6, HERO TO URSULA, of Beatrice

5 What a deal of scorn looks beautiful
In the contempt and anger of his lip!
Twelfth Night 3.1.146–7, OLIVIA, of Viola as Cesario

SCOTLAND AND THE SCOTS

6 That sprightly Scot of Scots, Douglas, that runs a-horseback up a hill perpendicular.
1 Henry IV 2.4.338–40, FALSTAFF TO PRINCE HAL AND POINS

7 Alas, poor country! / . . . It cannot
Be called our mother, but our grave.
Macbeth 4.3.164–6, ROSSE TO MACDUFF; *see also* **PATRIOTISM**

SEA, the

8   How fearful
And dizzy 'tis to cast one's eyes so low.
The crows and choughs that wing the midway air
Show scarce so gross as beetles. Half way down
Hangs one that gathers samphire, dreadful trade;
Methinks he seems no bigger than his head.
The fishermen that walk upon the beach
Appear like mice, and yon tall anchoring barque
Diminished to her cock, her cock a buoy
Almost too small for sight. The murmuring surge
That on th'unnumbered idle pebble chafes,
Cannot be heard so high. I'll look no more,

Lest my brain turn and the deficient sight
Topple down headlong.
King Lear 4.6.11–24, EDGAR to the blind GLOUCESTER, standing on an imaginary clifftop

1 If after every tempest come such calms
May the winds blow till they have wakened death,
And let the labouring bark climb hills of seas,
Olympus-high, and duck again as low
As hell's from heaven.
Othello 2.1.183–7, OTHELLO TO DESDEMONA

2   The belching whale
And humming water must o'erwhelm thy corpse,
Lying with simple shells.
Pericles 3.1.62–4, PERICLES, committing his wife's corpse to the waves

3   What pain it was to drown:
What dreadful noise of waters in my ears;
What sights of ugly death within my eyes!
Richard III 1.4.21–3, CLARENCE recounting his dream to the KEEPER OF THE TOWER

4 What cares these roarers for the name of King?
Tempest 1.1.16–17, BOATSWAIN TO GONZALO, of the waves

5   Come unto these yellow sands,
           And then take hands.
Tempest 1.2.377–8, ARIEL's song

6   Full fadom five thy father lies;
           Of his bones are coral made;
     Those are pearls that were his eyes:
           Nothing of him that doth fade,
     But doth suffer a sea-change
     Into something rich and strange.
     Sea-nymphs hourly ring his knell:
           Burthen: Ding-dong.
ARIEL Hark! now I hear them, – Ding-dong, bell.
Tempest 1.2.399–407, ARIEL's song

See also **SHIPS; SWIMMING**

SEASONS, the

7 [The labourer] follows so the ever-running year
With profitable labour to his grave.
Henry V 4.1.272–3, HENRY

1 At Christmas I no more desire a rose
    Than wish a snow in May's new-fangled shows;
    But like of each thing that in season grows.
    Love's Labour's Lost 1.1.105–7, BEROWNE TO THE KING OF NAVARRE

2 How many things by season, seasoned are
    To their right praise, and true perfection.
    Merchant of Venice 5.1.107–8, PORTIA TO NERISSA

3 The seasons alter: hoary-headed frosts
    Fall in the fresh lap of the crimson rose;
    And on old Hiems' thin and icy crown,
    An odorous chaplet of sweet summer buds
    Is, as in mockery, set; the spring, the summer,
    The childing autumn, angry winter, change
    Their wonted liveries.
    Midsummer Night's Dream 2.1.107–13, TITANIA TO OBERON, describing the effects of
    their quarrel; *see also* **DISORDER; FAIRIES**

4   Three winters cold
    Have from the forests shook three summers' pride;
    Three beauteous springs to yellow autumn turned
    In process of the seasons have I seen;
    Three April perfumes in three hot Junes burned,
    Since first I saw you.
    Sonnet 104.3–8

SECRECY

5   We have done but greenly
    In hugger-mugger to inter him.
    Hamlet 4.5.83–4, CLAUDIUS TO GERTRUDE

6 Here walk I in the black brow of night
    To find you out.
    King John 5.6.17–18, HUBERT TO PHILIP THE BASTARD

7 He, his own affections' counsellor,
    Is to himself . . . / so secret and so close,
    So far from sounding and discovery,
    As is the bud bit with an envious worm
    Ere he can spread his sweet leaves to the air
    Or dedicate his beauty to the sun.
    Romeo and Juliet 1.1.147–53, MONTAGUE TO BENVOLIO, of Romeo

1 I see thou wilt not trust the air
  With secrets.
  Titus Andronicus 4.2.171–2, CHIRON TO AARON

2 What I am, and what I would, are as secret as maidenhead.
  Twelfth Night 1.5.209–10, VIOLA, as Cesario, to OLIVIA

SECURITY

3 Fast bind, fast find. –
  A proverb never stale in thrifty mind.
  Merchant of Venice 2.5.53–4, SHYLOCK TO JESSICA

SELF-CONTROL

4   Lord Angelo is precise;
  Stands at a guard with Envy; scarce confesses
  That his blood flows; or that his appetite
  Is more to bread than stone.
  Measure for Measure 1.3.50–3, DUKE TO FRIAR THOMAS

5 They that have power to hurt, and will do none,
  That do not do the thing they most do show,
  Who, moving others, are themselves as stone,
  Unmoved, cold and to temptation slow:
  They rightly do inherit heaven's graces,
  And husband nature's riches from expense;
  They are the lords and owners of their faces.
  Sonnet 94.1–7

SELF-DOUBT

6   Our doubts are traitors,
  And makes us lose the good we oft might win
  By fearing to attempt.
  Measure for Measure 1.4.77–9, LUCIO TO ISABELLA

SELF-INTEREST

7 In following him, I follow but myself.
  Othello 1.1.57, IAGO TO RODERIGO, speaking of why he follows Othello

SELF-KNOWLEDGE

8 The knowledge of mine own desert.
  Sonnet 49.10

9 With mine own weakness being best acquainted.
  Sonnet 88.5

1 Be that thou know'st thou art, and then thou art
  As great as that thou fear'st.
  Twelfth Night 5.1.146–7, OLIVIA TO VIOLA, as Cesario

SELF-LOATHING

2 O what a rogue and peasant slave am I!
  Hamlet 2.2.550, HAMLET

3 I am very proud, revengeful, ambitious, with more offences at my beck
  than I have thoughts to put them in, imagination to give them shape,
  or time to act them in.
  Hamlet 3.1.124–8, HAMLET TO OPHELIA

4 Thou turn'st my eyes into my very soul,
  And there I see such black and grained spots
  As will not leave their tint.
  Hamlet 3.4.89–91, GERTRUDE TO HAMLET

5 Self-love, my liege, is not so vile a sin
  As self-neglecting.
  Henry V 2.4.74–5, DAUPHIN OF FRANCE TO THE KING OF FRANCE

SELF-PROTECTION

6 The single and peculiar life is bound
  With all the strength and armour of the mind
  To keep itself from noyance.
  Hamlet 3.3.11–13, ROSENCRANTZ TO CLAUDIUS

SERIOUSNESS

7 He was disposed to mirth, but on the sudden
  A Roman thought hath struck him.
  Antony and Cleopatra 1.2.85–6, CLEOPATRA TO HER COMPANIONS, of Antony

8 Octavia is of a holy, cold and still conversation.
  Antony and Cleopatra 2.6.122–3, ENOBARBUS TO MENAS

SEX AND LUST

9 COUNTESS Tell me the reason why thou wilt marry.
  CLOWN My poor body, madam, requires it; I am driven on by the flesh,
  and he must needs go that the devil drives.
  All's Well That Ends Well 1.3.27–30

10 The triple pillar of the world transformed
  Into a strumpet's fool.
  Antony and Cleopatra 1.1.12–13, PHILO TO DEMETRIUS, of Antony

1   The nobleness of life
Is to do thus, when such a mutual pair
And such a twain can do't.
Antony and Cleopatra 1.1.37–9, Antony embracing Cleopatra

2   Cleopatra hath
Nodded him to her.
Antony and Cleopatra 3.6.66–7, Octavius Caesar to Octavia, his sister and Antony's wife

3   The stroke of death is as a lover's pinch
Which hurts and is desired.
Antony and Cleopatra 5.2.293–4, Cleopatra

4   They are in the very wrath of love, and they will together. Clubs cannot part them.
As You Like It 5.2.40–1, Rosalind to Orlando

5   She would hang on him
As if increase of appetite had grown
By what it fed on.
Hamlet 1.2.143–5, Hamlet, of his parents; *see also* **HUSBANDS AND WIVES**

6   The primrose path of dalliance.
Hamlet 1.3.50, Hamlet; *more at* **HYPOCRISY**

7   So lust, though to a radiant angel linked,
Will sate itself in a celestial bed
And prey on garbage.
Hamlet 1.5.55–7, Ghost to Hamlet

8   Here's metal more attractive.
Hamlet 3.2.111, Hamlet to Gertrude, of Ophelia

9   Do you think I meant country matters?
Hamlet 3.2.118, Hamlet to Ophelia (country meaning rural and basic, but with an additional sexual pun)

10   O shame, where is thy blush?
Rebellious hell,
If thou canst mutine in a matron's bones,
To flaming youth let virtue be as wax
And melt in her own fire; proclaim no shame
When the compulsive ardour gives the charge,
Since frost itself as actively doth burn
And reason panders will.
Hamlet 3.4.81–8, Hamlet to Gertrude

1   To live
In the rank sweat of an enseamed bed,
Stewed in corruption, honeying and making love
Over the nasty sty!
Hamlet 3.4.91–4, HAMLET, overwhelmed by disgust at his mother's infidelity

2   Is it not strange that desire should so many years outlive performance?
2 Henry IV 2.4.260–1, POINS TO PRINCE HAL, of Falstaff

3   [I] did the act of darkness with her.
King Lear 3.4.86–7, EDGAR, disguised as Poor Tom, to LEAR

4   The wren goes to't and the small gilded fly
Does lecher in my sight. Let copulation thrive.
King Lear 4.6.111–12, LEAR TO GLOUCESTER

5   Thou, rascal beadle, hold thy bloody hand;
Why dost thou lash that whore? Strip thine own back,
Thou hotly lusts to use her in that kind
For which thou whipp'st her.
King Lear 4.6.156–9, LEAR TO GLOUCESTER

6   Desire my pilot is, beauty my prize.
Lucrece 279, TARQUIN

7   This momentary joy breeds months of pain;
This hot desire converts to cold disdain.
Lucrece 690–1

8   There's no bottom, none,
In my voluptuousness: your wives, your daughters,
Your matrons, and your maids, could not fill up
The cistern of my lust.
Macbeth 4.3.60–3, MALCOLM, feigning a bad character to MACDUFF to test him

9   Groping for trouts in a peculiar river.
Measure for Measure 1.2.89, POMPEY explains to MISTRESS OVERDONE the offence for which Claudio is being imprisoned.

10   Even now, now, very now, an old black ram
Is tupping your white ewe.
Othello 1.1.87–8, IAGO TO BRABANTIO, speaking of Othello and Desdemona, expert as always in goading

11   The beast with two backs.
Othello 1.1.115, IAGO TO BRABANTIO

1 She is sport for Jove.
Othello 2.3.16–17, IAGO TO CASSIO, of Desdemona

2 I know a lady in Venice would have walked barefoot to Palestine for a touch of his nether lip.
Othello 4.3.37–8, EMILIA TO DESDEMONA, of Lodovico

3 Will you not go the way of womenkind?
Pericles 4.6.147–8, BAWD TO MARINA

4 Th'expense of spirit in a waste of shame
Is lust in action; and till action, lust
Is perjured, murd'rous, bloody, full of blame,
Savage, extreme, rude, cruel, not to trust;
Enjoyed no sooner but despised straight;
Past reason hunted, and no sooner had,
Past reason hated as a swallowed bait,
On purpose laid to make the taker mad;
Mad in pursuit, and in possession so,
Had, having, and in quest to have, extreme;
A bliss in proof, and proved, a very woe;
Before, a joy proposed; behind, a dream.
    All this the world well knows, yet none knows well
      To shun the heaven that leads men to this hell.
Sonnet 129

5   Do not give dalliance
Too much the rein. The strongest oaths are straw
To th' fire in th' blood.
Tempest 4.1.51–3, PROSPERO TO FERDINAND

6 Worse-than-killing lust.
Titus Andronicus 2.2.175, LAVINIA TO TAMORA

7 Is this the generation of love? Hot blood, hot thoughts, and hot deeds? Why, they are vipers. Is love a generation of vipers?
Troilus and Cressida 3.1.127–9, PANDARUS TO PARIS AND HELEN

8 This is the monstruosity in love . . . : that the will is infinite, and the execution confined: that the desire is boundless, and the act a slave to limit.
Troilus and Cressida 3.2.78–81, TROILUS TO CRESSIDA

1 They say all lovers swear more performance than they are able, and yet reserve an ability that they never perform.
Troilus and Cressida 3.2.82–4, CRESSIDA TO TROILUS

2 How now, how go maidenheads?
Troilus and Cressida 4.2.23, PANDARUS TO CRESSIDA AND TROILUS

3 The devil Luxury, with his fat rump and potato finger.
Troilus and Cressida 5.2.55–6, THERSITES TO CRESSIDA, TROILUS, DIOMEDES AND OTHERS

4 Fry, lechery, fry.
Troilus and Cressida 5.2.56, THERSITES TO DIOMEDES

5 Lechery, lechery, still wars and lechery!
Troilus and Cressida 5.2.192–3, THERSITES

6 An oven that is stopped, or river stayed
Burneth more hotly, swelleth with more rage.
Venus and Adonis 331–2

7 The sea hath bounds, but deep desire hath none.
Venus and Adonis 389, VENUS

8 Careless lust stirs up a desperate courage,
Planting oblivion, beating reason back.
Venus and Adonis 556–7

9 Now is she in the very lists of love,
Her champion mounted for the hot encounter.
Venus and Adonis 595–6, of Venus

10 Love comforteth like sunshine after rain,
But lust's effect is tempest after sun;
Love's gentle spring doth always fresh remain,
Lust's winter comes ere summer half be done;
Love surfeits not, lust like a glutton dies;
Love is all truth, lust full of forged lies.
Venus and Adonis 799–804, ADONIS

11 Paddling palms, and pinching fingers, . . .
And making practised smiles.
Winter's Tale 1.2.115–16, LEONTES, suspecting Hermione and Polixenes

12 It is a bawdy planet.
Winter's Tale 1.2.201, LEONTES

1 No barricado for a belly . . .
It will let in and out the enemy,
With bag and baggage.
Winter's Tale 1.2.204–6, LEONTES

2 He . . . wears her like her medal, hanging
About his neck.
Winter's Tale 1.2.307–8, LEONTES TO CAMILLO

3 This has been some stair-work, some trunk-work, some behind-door-
work.
Winter's Tale 3.3.73–4, SHEPHERD

SEXUAL ABUSE

4   The fault is thine, . . .
Thy beauty hath ensnared thee to this night.
Lucrece 482, 485, TARQUIN TO LUCRECE

5 Tears harden lust.
Lucrece 560

6 O unseen shame, invisible disgrace!
Lucrece 827

7 You are a fair viol, and your sense the strings,
Who, fingered to make man his lawful music,
Would draw heaven down and all the gods to hearken;
But being played upon before your time,
Hell only danceth at so harsh a chime.
Pericles 1.1.82–6, PERICLES TO ANTIOCHUS' DAUGHTER

8 Crack the glass of her virginity, and make the rest malleable.
Pericles 4.6.140–1, BAWD TO BOULT, of Marina

SHAME

9 What, must I hold a candle to my shames?
Merchant of Venice 2.6.41, JESSICA TO LORENZO

SHIPS

10   Behold
Upon the hempen tackle ship-boys climbing;
Hear the shrill whistle which doth order give
To sounds confused; behold the threaden sails,
Borne with th'invisible and creeping wind,
Draw the huge bottoms through the furrowed sea,

Breasting the lofty surge. O, do but think
You stand upon the rivage and behold
A city on th'inconstant billows dancing;
For so appears this fleet majestical,
Holding due course to Harfleur.
Henry V 3.0.8–18, CHORUS

1 Ships are but boards, sailors but men, there be land-rats, and water-rats, water-thieves, and land-thieves, and then there is the peril of waters, winds and rocks.
Merchant of Venice 1.3.21–4, SHYLOCK TO BASSANIO

2 How like a younger or a prodigal
The scarfed bark puts from her native bay –
Hugged and embraced by the strumpet wind!
How like the prodigal doth she return
With over-weathered ribs and ragged sails –
Lean, rent, and beggared by the strumpet wind!
Merchant of Venice 2.6.14–19, GRATIANO TO SALERIO

3   The seaman's whistle
Is as a whisper in the ears of death,
Unheard.
Pericles 3.1.8–10, PERICLES, on board ship

4 The sea works high, the wind is loud, and will not lie till the ship be cleared of the dead.
Pericles 3.1.47–9, SAILOR TO PERICLES

5 A rotten carcass of a butt, not rigged,
Nor tackle, sail, nor mast; the very rats
Instinctively have quit it.
Tempest 1.2.146–8, PROSPERO TO MIRANDA

6 O, the most piteous cry of the poor souls! sometimes to see 'em, and not to see 'em: now the ship boring the moon with her main-mast, and anon swallowed with yest and froth, as you'd thrust a cork into a hogs-head.
Winter's Tale 3.3.89–93, SHEPHERD'S SON TO THE SHEPHERD

SIDEKICKS

7   Thou ladder wherewithal
The mounting Bolingbroke ascends my throne.
Richard II 5.1.55–6, RICHARD TO NORTHUMBERLAND

SIN

1 No reck'ning made, but sent to my account
  With all my imperfections on my head.
  Hamlet 1.5.78–9, GHOST TO HAMLET

2   Commit
  The oldest sins the newest kind of ways.
  2 Henry IV 4.5.125–6, HENRY TO PRINCE HAL, inveighing against his companions

3 I am stifled with this smell of sin.
  King John 4.3.113, SALISBURY TO HUBERT AND OTHERS

4 Few love to hear the sins they love to act.
  Pericles 1.1.93, PERICLES TO ANTIOCHUS

5 The time shall not be many hours of age
  More than it is, ere foul sin gathering head
  Shall break into corruption.
  Richard II 5.1.57–9, RICHARD TO NORTHUMBERLAND

SINGLE LIFE, the

6 Shall I never see a bachelor of threescore again?
  Much Ado about Nothing 1.1.189–90, BENEDICK TO CLAUDIO; *see also* ENNUI

7 Saint Peter . . . shows me where the bachelors sit, and there live we as merry as the day is long.
  Much Ado About Nothing 2.1.43–5, BEATRICE's view of heaven

8 I may sit in a corner and cry 'Heigh-ho for a husband!'
  Much Ado About Nothing 2.1.300–1, BEATRICE TO CLAUDIO

9 When I said I would die a bachelor, I did not think I should live till I were married.
  Much Ado About Nothing 2.3.233–4, BENEDICK

10 Contempt, farewell, and maiden pride, adieu!
  Much Ado About Nothing 3.1.109, BEATRICE

11 Where is the life that late I led?
  Taming of the Shrew 4.1.128, PETRUCHIO singing to KATHERINA

SLANDER

12 Slander lives upon succession,
  For e'er housed where it gets possession.
  Comedy of Errors 3.1.105–6, BALTHASAR TO ANTIPHOLUS OF EPHESUS

1   Slander,
Whose edge is sharper than the sword, whose tongue
Outvenoms all the worms of Nile, whose breath
Rides on the posting winds, and doth belie
All corners of the world.
Cymbeline 3.4.32–6, Pisanio to Imogen

2 Be thou as chaste as ice, as pure as snow, thou shalt not escape
calumny.
Hamlet 3.1.137–8, Hamlet to Ophelia

3   Back-wounding calumny
The whitest virtue strikes.
Measure for Measure 3.2.179–80, Duke, disguised as a friar, to Lucio

4 Done to death by slanderous tongues.
Much Ado About Nothing 5.3.3, Claudio, of Hero

5 Slander's mark was ever yet the fair.
Sonnet 70.2

6 He's truly valiant that can wisely suffer
The worst that man can breathe.
Timon of Athens 3.5.31–2, Senator to Alcibiades

7   Slander,
Whose sting is sharper than the sword's.
Winter's Tale 2.3.85–6, Paulina to Antigonus and Leontes

See also **REPUTATION**

SLAVERY

8 For I am all the subjects that you have,
Which first was mine own King: and here you sty me
In this hard rock, whiles you do keep from me
The rest o'th' island.
Tempest 1.2.343–6, Caliban to Prospero

9 A plague upon the tyrant that I serve!
Tempest 2.2.160; Caliban to Trinculo and Stephano

SLEEP AND SLEEPLESSNESS

10 O sleep, thou ape of death.
Cymbeline 2.2.31, Iachimo

1 Since I received command to do this business
  I have not slept one wink.
  Cymbeline 3.4.99–100, PISANIO TO IMOGEN

2   Weariness
  Can snore upon the flint, when resty sloth
  Finds the down-pillow hard.
  Cymbeline 3.7.6–8, BELARIUS TO GUIDERIUS AND ARVIRAGUS

3   O sleep, O gentle sleep,
  Nature's soft nurse, how have I frighted thee,
  That thou no more wilt weigh my eyelids down,
  And steep my senses in forgetfulness?
  2 Henry IV 3.1.5–8, HENRY

4 Not all these, thrice-gorgeous ceremony,
  Not all these, laid in bed majestical,
  Can sleep so soundly as the wretched slave,
  Who with a body filled and vacant mind
  Gets him to rest, crammed with distressful bread:
  Never sees horrid night, the child of hell,
  But like a lackey from the rise to set
  Sweats in the eye of Phoebus, and all night
  Sleeps in Elysium.
  Henry V 4.1.262–70, HENRY; *more at* **CEREMONY**

5 Enjoy the honey-heavy dew of slumber:
  Thou hast no figures nor no fantasies
  Which busy care draws in the brains of men.
  Julius Caesar 2.1.230–2, BRUTUS

6 Nature must obey necessity.
  Julius Caesar 4.3.226, BRUTUS TO CASSIUS, advising sleep

7 Methought, I heard a voice cry, 'Sleep no more!
  Macbeth does murther Sleep.'
  Macbeth 2.2.34–5, MACBETH TO LADY MACBETH

8 Sleep, that knits up the ravelled sleave of care,
  The death of each day's life, sore labour's bath,
  Balm of hurt minds, great Nature's second course,
  Chief nourisher in life's feast.
  Macbeth 2.2.36–9, MACBETH TO LADY MACBETH

1 'Glamis hath murthered Sleep, and therefore Cawdor
Shall sleep no more, Macbeth shall sleep no more!'
Macbeth 2.2.41–2, MACBETH TO LADY MACBETH, continuing the passage above

2 You lack the season of all natures, sleep.
Macbeth 3.4.140, LADY MACBETH TO MACBETH

3 I have an exposition of sleep come upon me.
Midsummer Night's Dream 4.1.38, BOTTOM TO TITANIA

4   Are you sure
That we are awake? It seems to me
That yet we sleep, we dream.
Midsummer Night's Dream 4.1.191–3, DEMETRIUS TO HIS FRIENDS

5 Care keeps his watch in every old man's eye,
And where care lodges sleep will never lie,
But where unbruised youth with unstuffed brain
Doth couch his limbs, there golden sleep doth reign.
Romeo and Juliet 2.3.31–4, FRIAR LAURENCE TO ROMEO

6 Weary with toil, I haste me to my bed,
The dear repose for limbs with travail tired;
But then begins a journey in my head
To work my mind, when body's work's expired.
Sonnet 27.1–4

7 How can I then return in happy plight
That am debarred the benefit of rest?
When day's oppression is not eased by night
But day by night and night by day oppressed.
Sonnet 28.1–4

See also **DREAMS**

SOLDIERS

8 Thou, the greatest soldier of the world.
Antony and Cleopatra 1.3.39, CLEOPATRA TO ANTONY

9 ANTONY Thou art a soldier only. Speak no more.
ENOBARBUS That truth should be silent, I had almost forgot.
Antony and Cleopatra 2.2.113–14

10   Then, a soldier,
Full of strange oaths, and bearded like the pard,

Jealous in honour, sudden, and quick in quarrel,
Seeking the bubble reputation
Even in the cannon's mouth.
As You Like It 2.7.149–53, from JAQUES's 'Seven Ages of Man' speech

1 Before him he carries noise, and behind him he leaves tears: Death,
that dark spirit, in's nervy arm doth lie.
Coriolanus 2.1.158–60, VOLUMNIA TO MENENIUS, of Coriolanus

2   From face to foot
He was a thing of blood, whose every motion
Was timed with dying cries.
Coriolanus 2.2.108–10, COMINIUS TO MENENIUS, of Coriolanus

3 Not to be other than one thing, not moving
From th' casque to th' cushion, but commanding peace
Even with the same austerity and garb
As he controlled the war.
Coriolanus 4.7.42–5, AUFIDIUS TO HIS LIEUTENANT, of Coriolanus

4   All furnished, all in arms;
All plumed like estridges that with the wind
Bated, like eagles having lately bathed,
Glittering in golden coats like images,
As full of spirit as the month of May,
And gorgeous as the sun at midsummer.
1 Henry IV 4.1.97–102, VERNON TO HOTSPUR, of Prince Hal and his companions in
arms

5 They come like sacrifices in their trim
And to the fire-eyed maid of smoky war
All hot and bleeding will we offer them.
1 Henry IV 4.1.113–15, HOTSPUR TO VERNON

6 My whole charge consists of ancients, corporals, lieutenants,
gentlemen of companies – slaves as ragged as Lazarus: and such as
indeed were never soldiers, but discarded unjust servingmen, younger
sons to younger brothers, revolted tapsters, and ostlers trade-fallen,
the cankers of a calm world and a long peace.
1 Henry IV 4.2.23–30, FALSTAFF's contrasting unheroic view of his soldiery

7 O God of battles, steel my soldiers' hearts;
Possess them not with fear.
Henry V 4.1.285–6, HENRY before the battle of Agincourt

1 They have said their prayers, and they stay for death.
   Henry V 4.2.55, CONSTABLE OF FRANCE TO GRANDPRÉ

2 What bloody man is this?
   Macbeth 1.2.1, DUNCAN TO MALCOLM, of a captain coming from battle

3 Fie, my lord, fie! a soldier, and afeard?
   Macbeth 5.1.37–8, LADY MACBETH, mad

4 Your son, my Lord, has paid a soldier's debt.
   Macbeth 5.9.5, ROSSE TO OLD SIWARD; he has paid with his life

5   Rude am I in my speech,
   And little blest with the set phrase of peace, . . .
   And little of this great world can I speak,
   More than pertains to feats of broil, and battle.
   Othello 1.3.82–3, 87–8, OTHELLO TO BRABANTIO

6 Soft you, a word or two before you go.
   I have done the state some service, and they know't:
   No more of that.
   Othello 5.2.338–40, OTHELLO TO HIS COLLEAGUES, before killing himself

7 Sleep in peace, slain in your country's wars.
   Titus Andronicus 1.1.94, TITUS over the coffin of his sons

8 Th'unconsidered soldier.
   Two Noble Kinsmen 1.2.31, ARCITE TO PALAMON

   See also **ARMIES; FIGHTING; WAR**

SOLITUDE AND SOLITARINESS

9   Antony,
   Enthroned i'th' market-place, did sit alone,
   Whistling to th'air, which, but for vacancy,
   Had gone to gaze on Cleopatra, too,
   And made a gap in nature.
   Antony and Cleopatra 2.2.224–8, ENOBARBUS describing Antony while Cleopatra triumphs on her golden barge

10   Society is no comfort
   To one not sociable.
   Cymbeline 4.2.12–13, IMOGEN TO GUIDERIUS AND ARVIRAGUS at a low point in her fortunes

11 A poor lone woman.
   2 Henry IV 2.1.31, HOSTESS QUICKLY TO FANG, referring to herself

1 Who alone suffers, suffers most i'the mind.
    King Lear 3.6.102, EDGAR

2   I myself am best
    When least in company.
    Twelfth Night 1.4.37–8, ORSINO TO VIOLA, as Cesario

3 I am all the daughters of my father's house,
    And all the brothers too.
    Twelfth Night 2.4.121–2, VIOLA, as Cesario, to ORSINO, thinking about the loss of her brother as well as riddling about herself

SORROW

4 More in sorrow than in anger.
    Hamlet 1.2.231, HORATIO TO HAMLET, describing the ghost's expression

5 When sorrows come, they come not single spies,
    But in battalions.
    Hamlet 4.5.78–9, CLAUDIUS TO GERTRUDE

6 A plague of sighing and grief, it blows a man up like a bladder.
    1 Henry IV 2.4.327–8, FALSTAFF TO PRINCE HAL AND POINS

7 What private griefs they have, alas, I know not.
    Julius Caesar 3.2.214, MARK ANTONY TO PLEBEIANS, of the conspirators

8 It easeth some, though none it ever cured,
    To think their dolour others have endured.
    Lucrece 1581–2

9 Give sorrow words; the grief, that does not speak,
    Whispers the o'er-fraught heart, and bids it break.
    Macbeth 4.3.209–10, MALCOLM TO MACDUFF

10 What a sigh is there! The heart is sorely charged.
    Macbeth 5.1.54–5, LADY MACBETH'S DOCTOR TO HER GENTLEWOMAN

11   The poor soul sat sighing by a sycamore tree,
              Sing all a green willow:
         Her hand on her bosom, her head on her knee,
              Sing willow, willow, willow. . .
         Sing all a green willow must be my garland.
    Othello 4.3.39–42, 50, DESDEMONA, singing Barbary's song

12 Gnarling sorrow hath less power to bite
    The man that mocks at it.
    Richard II 1.3.292–3, JOHN OF GAUNT TO BOLINGBROKE

1   Hath sorrow struck
So many blows upon this face of mine
And made no deeper wounds?
Richard II 4.1.277–9, RICHARD TO NORTHUMBERLAND AND BOLINGBROKE

2 How soon my sorrow hath destroyed my face.
Richard II 4.1.291, RICHARD TO NORTHUMBERLAND

3 Sorrow breaks seasons and reposing hours,
Makes the night morning, and the noontide night.
Richard III 1.4.76–7, BRAKENBURY

4 My grief lies onward and my joy behind.
Sonnet 50.14

5 To weep with them that weep doth ease some deal,
But sorrow flouted at is double death.
Titus Andronicus 3.1.245–6, MARCUS TO LUCIUS AND TITUS

SOUL, the

6 I do not set my life at a pin's fee,
And for my soul, what can it do to that,
Being a thing immortal as itself?
Hamlet 1.4.65–7, HAMLET TO HORATIO

7 O my prophetic soul! My uncle!
Hamlet 1.5.41, HAMLET TO THE GHOST, who has revealed that he was murdered

8 Poor soul, the centre of my sinful earth.
Sonnet 146.1; the soul struggles within while trying to keep up bodily appearances in
time of trouble

SPECTATORS

9 These are the youths that thunder at a playhouse, and fight for bitten
apples.
Henry VIII 5.3.58–9, PORTER TO HIS MAN

10 These scroyles of Angiers flout you, kings,
And stand securely on their battlements,
As in a theatre, whence they gape and point
At your industrious scenes and acts of death.
King John 2.1.373–6, PHILIP THE BASTARD TO JOHN

SPEECHES

11 I am no orator, as Brutus is,
But (as you know me all) a plain blunt man . . .

For I have neither wit, nor words, nor worth
Action, nor utterance, nor the power of speech
To stir men's blood.

Julius Caesar 3.2.218–19, 222–4, MARK ANTONY on the death of Julius Caesar; an overwhelming piece of false modesty, coming from a man who has just made a sequence of some of the most highly rhetorical speeches in Shakespeare

1 I would be loath to cast away my speech: for besides that it is excellently well penned, I have taken great pains to con it.

Twelfth Night 1.5.167–9, VIOLA, as Cesario, to OLIVIA

SPEED

2 Celerity is never more admired
Than by the negligent.

Antony and Cleopatra 3.7.24–5, CLEOPATRA TO ANTONY

3 O, for a horse with wings!

Cymbeline 3.2.47, IMOGEN, on receiving a letter from her husband asking her to come to him

4   That I with wings as swift
As meditation or the thoughts of love
May sweep to my revenge.

Hamlet 1.5.29–31, HAMLET TO THE GHOST

5 The rogue fled from me like quicksilver.

2 Henry IV 2.4.227–8, FALSTAFF TO DOLL TEARSHEET

6 OBERON   Be thou here again
Ere the leviathan can swim a league.
PUCK I'll put a girdle round about the earth
In forty minutes.

Midsummer Night's Dream 2.1.173–6

7 I go, I go, look how I go!
Swifter than arrow from the Tartar's bow.

Midsummer Night's Dream 3.2.100–1, PUCK TO OBERON

8 Be swift like lightning in the execution.

Richard II 1.3.79, JOHN OF GAUNT TO BOLINGBROKE

See also **HASTE**

SPIRITS

9 How now, mad spirit?

Midsummer Night's Dream 3.2.4, OBERON TO PUCK

1 Approach, my Ariel, come.
   Tempest 1.2.188, PROSPERO, calling ARIEL

2   To fly,
   To swim, to dive into the fire, to ride
   On the curled clouds.
   Tempest 1.2.190–2, ARIEL TO PROSPERO

3 My brave spirit!
   Tempest 1.2.206, PROSPERO TO ARIEL

SPORT

4 HENRY   What treasure, uncle?
   EXETER   Tennis-balls, my liege.
   Henry V 1.2.259

5 When we have matched our rackets to these balls,
   We will in France, by God's grace, play a set
   Shall strike his father's crown into the hazard.
   Henry V 1.2.262–4, HENRY TO EXETER

6 You base football player.
   King Lear 1.4.84–5, KENT TO OSWALD, Goneril's steward

   See also **SWIMMING**

SPRING

7   It was a lover and his lass,
             With a hey and a ho and a hey nonino,
         That o'er the green corn-field did pass,
             In spring-time, the only pretty ring-time,
         When birds do sing, hey ding a ding, ding,
         Sweet lovers love the spring.
   As You Like It 5.3.15–20, song for TWO PAGES

8 Love, whose month is ever May.
   Love's Labour's Lost 4.3.99, DUMAIN, reading his sonnet

9 From you have I been absent in the spring,
   When proud pied April, dressed in all his trim,
   Hath put a spirit of youth in every thing.
   Sonnet 98.1–3

10   When daffodils begin to peer,
             With heigh! the doxy over the dale,

> Why then comes in the sweet o'the year,
> > For the red blood reigns in the winter's pale.

> The white sheet bleaching on the hedge,
> > With hey! the sweet birds, O how they sing!

Winter's Tale 4.3.1–6, AUTOLYCUS' song

See also **FLOWERS AND PLANTS**

STARS

1 I am constant as the northern star,
Of whose true-fixed and resting quality
There is no fellow in the firmament.
The skies are painted with unnumbered sparks,
They are all fire, and every one doth shine;
But there's but one in all doth hold his place.
Julius Caesar 3.1.60–5, JULIUS CAESAR TO CASSIUS

2 > > There's husbandry in heaven;
Their candles are all out.
Macbeth 2.1.4–5, BANQUO TO FLEANCE

3 > > Look how the floor of heaven
Is thick inlaid with patens of bright gold.
Merchant of Venice 5.1.58–9, LORENZO TO JESSICA

4 These blessed candles of the night.
Merchant of Venice 5.1.220, BASSANIO TO PORTIA

5 Take him and cut him out in little stars,
And he will make the face of heaven so fine
That all the world will be in love with night.
Romeo and Juliet 3.2.22–4, JULIET; *more at* **LOVERS; ROMEO AND JULIET**

6 Night's candles are burnt out.
Romeo and Juliet 3.5.9, ROMEO; *more at* **MORNING**

See also **FATE** *for stars that govern our lives*

STOICISM

7 BRUTUS With meditating that she must die once,
I have the patience to endure it now.
MESSALA Even so great men great losses should endure.
Julius Caesar 4.3.190–2; Brutus' reaction to the death of his wife

1 Let's reason with the worst that may befall.
   Julius Caesar 5.1.97, CASSIUS TO BRUTUS

2   Henceforth I'll bear
   Affliction till it do cry out itself
   'Enough, enough' and die.
   King Lear 4.6.75–7, GLOUCESTER TO LEAR

3 Have patience and endure.
   Much Ado About Nothing 4.1.253, FRIAR TO LEONATO

STORIES

4 Thereby hangs a tale.
   As You Like It 2.7.28, JAQUES; and a number of other locations through Shakespeare's plays

5 I could a tale unfold whose lightest word
   Would harrow up thy soul, freeze thy young blood,
   Make thy two eyes like stars start from their spheres,
   Thy knotted and combined locks to part,
   And each particular hair to stand an end
   Like quills upon the fretful porpentine.
   Hamlet 1.5.15–20, GHOST TO HAMLET

6 Childe Rowland to the dark tower came,
   His word was still 'Fie, foh and fum,
   I smell the blood of a British man.'
   King Lear 3.4.178–80, EDGAR, disguised as Poor Tom, to GLOUCESTER; this is probably gleaned from a lost ballad

7   A tale
   Told by an idiot, full of sound and fury,
   Signifying nothing.
   Macbeth 5.5.26–8, MACBETH TO SEYTON; *more at* **LIFE**

8 I spake of most disastrous chances,
   Of moving accidents by flood and field,
   Of hair-breadth scapes i'th' imminent deadly breach,
   Of being taken by the insolent foe
   And sold to slavery; and my redemption thence
   And portance in my travailous history;
   Wherein of antres vast and deserts idle,
   Rough quarries, rocks and hills whose heads touch heaven
   It was my hint to speak – such was my process –

And of the cannibals that each other eat,
The Anthropophagi, and men whose heads
Do grow beneath their shoulders.
Othello 1.3.135–46, OTHELLO TO THE DUKE OF VENICE, describing how he wooed
Desdemona

1   My story being done,
She gave me for my pains a world of sighs.
Othello 1.3.159–60, OTHELLO TO THE DUKE OF VENICE, describing Desdemona's
response

2   'Tis a chronicle of day by day.
Tempest 5.1.163, PROSPERO TO ALONSO

3   If this were played upon a stage now, I could condemn it as an
improbable fiction.
Twelfth Night 3.4.127–8, FABIAN TO SIR TOBY BELCH AND MARIA

4   A sad tale's best for winter. I have one
Of sprites and goblins.
Winter's Tale 2.1.25–6, MAMILLIUS, a little boy, to his mother HERMIONE

STRATEGY

5   In cases of defence 'tis best to weigh
The enemy more mighty than he seems.
Henry V 2.4.43–4, DAUPHIN OF FRANCE TO FRENCH LORDS

6   Advantage is a better soldier than rashness.
Henry V 3.6.120, MONTJOY TO HENRY

SUCCESS

7   Upon your sword
Sit laurel victory, and smooth success
Be strewed before your feet.
Antony and Cleopatra 1.3.101–3, CLEOPATRA TO ANTONY

8   I have lived
To see inherited my very wishes,
And the buildings of my fancy.
Coriolanus 2.1.198–200, VOLUMNIA TO CORIOLANUS

9   A hit, a very palpable hit.
Hamlet 5.2.285, OSRIC commenting on the duel between Hamlet and Laertes

10   They well deserve to have
That know the strong'st and surest way to get.
Richard II 3.3.200–1, RICHARD TO BOLINGBROKE

1 Now does my project gather to a head:
My charms crack not; my spirits obey; and time
Goes upright with his carriage.
Tempest 5.1.1–3, PROSPERO TO ARIEL

2 You're a made old man.
Winter's Tale 3.3.117, SHEPHERD'S SON TO THE SHEPHERD, on the finding of the infant
Perdita, obviously the child of rich parents

See also **AMBITION; VICTORY**

SUFFERING

3 O ye gods, ye gods! Must I endure all this?
Julius Caesar 4.3.41, CASSIUS TO BRUTUS

4 You do me wrong to take me out o'the grave.
Thou art a soul in bliss, but I am bound
Upon a wheel of fire that mine own tears
Do scald like molten lead.
King Lear 4.7.45–8, LEAR TO CORDELIA

SUICIDE

5   Then is it sin
To rush into the secret house of death
Ere death dare come to us?
Antony and Cleopatra 4.15.84–6, CLEOPATRA

6 Let's do't after the high Roman fashion
And make death proud to take us.
Antony and Cleopatra 4.15.91–2, CLEOPATRA

7   We have no friend
But resolution and the briefest end.
Antony and Cleopatra 4.15.94–5, CLEOPATRA

8 I am fire and air; my other elements
I give to baser life.
Antony and Cleopatra 5.2.287–8, CLEOPATRA

9 She hath pursued conclusions infinite
Of easy ways to die.
Antony and Cleopatra 5.2.353–4, OCTAVIUS CAESAR, of Cleopatra

10 O that this too too sullied flesh would melt,
Thaw and resolve itself into a dew,

Or that the Everlasting had not fixed
His canon 'gainst self-slaughter.
Hamlet 1.2.129–32, HAMLET

1   To be, or not to be, that is the question:
    Whether 'tis nobler in the mind to suffer
    The slings and arrows of outrageous fortune,
    Or to take arms against a sea of troubles
    And by opposing end them. To die – to sleep,
    No more; and by a sleep to say we end
    The heart-ache and the thousand natural shocks
    That flesh is heir to: 'tis a consummation
    Devoutly to be wished. To die, to sleep;
    To sleep, perchance to dream – ay, there's the rub:
    For in that sleep of death what dreams may come,
    When we have shuffled off this mortal coil,
    Must give us pause – there's the respect
    That makes calamity of so long life.
    For who would bear the whips and scorns of time,
    Th'oppressor's wrong, the proud man's contumely,
    The pangs of disprized love, the law's delay,
    The insolence of office, and the spurns
    That patient merit of th'unworthy takes,
    When he himself might his quietus make
    With a bare bodkin? Who would fardels bear,
    To grunt and sweat under a weary life,
    But that the dread of something after death,
    The undiscovered country, from whose bourn
    No traveller returns, puzzles the will,
    And makes us rather bear those ills we have
    Than fly to others that we know not of?
    Thus conscience does make cowards of us all.
    Hamlet 3.1.56–83, HAMLET

2   Life, being weary of these worldly bars,
    Never lacks power to dismiss itself.
    Julius Caesar 1.3.96–7, CASSIUS TO CASCA

3   Every bondman in his own hand bears
    The power to cancel his captivity.
    Julius Caesar 1.3.101–2, CASCA TO CASSIUS

1 Brutus only overcame himself,
   And no man else hath honour by his death.
   Julius Caesar 5.5.56–7, STRATO TO MESSALA AND OCTAVIUS

2 Why should I play the Roman fool, and die
   On mine own sword?
   Macbeth 5.8.1, MACBETH

SUMMER

3 Now these hot days is the mad blood stirring.
   Romeo and Juliet 3.1.4, BENVOLIO TO MERCUTIO

4 Shall I compare thee to a summer's day?
   Thou art more lovely and more temperate:
   Rough winds do shake the darling buds of May,
   And summer's lease hath all too short a date:
   Sometime too hot the eye of heaven shines,
   And often is his gold complexion dimmed;
   And every fair from fair sometime declines,
   By chance or nature's changing course untrimmed:
   But thy eternal summer shall not fade.
   Sonnet 18.1–9; *more at* **POETRY**

5 This is very midsummer madness.
   Twelfth Night 3.4.56, OLIVIA TO MALVOLIO

6 More matter for a May morning!
   Twelfth Night 3.4.142, FABIAN TO SIR ANDREW AGUECHEEK AND SIR TOBY BELCH; May
   is definitely summer here

SUPERNATURAL, the

7 They say miracles are past; and we have our philosophical persons to
   make modern and familiar, things supernatural and causeless.
   All's Well That Ends Well 2.3.1–3, LAFEW TO PAROLLES

8 In nature's infinite book of secrecy
   A little I can read.
   Antony and Cleopatra 1.2.10–11, SOOTHSAYER

9 GLENDOWER I can call spirits from the vasty deep.
   HOTSPUR Why, so can I, or so can any man,
   But will they come when you do call for them?
   1 Henry IV 3.1.50–2; for more mockery of Glendower *see* **OMENS AND PORTENTS**

1   Miracles are ceased,
And therefore we must needs admit the means
How things are perfected.
Henry V 1.1.67–9, ARCHBISHOP OF CANTERBURY TO THE BISHOP OF ELY

2   Descend to darkness and the burning lake:
False fiend, avoid!
2 Henry VI 1.4.40–1, BOLINGBROKE TO A SPIRIT

3   The foul fiend bites my back.
King Lear 3.6.17, EDGAR, disguised as Poor Tom, to LEAR

4   Night's swift dragons cut the clouds full fast;
And yonder shines Aurora's harbinger,
At whose approach, ghosts wandering here and there
Troop home to churchyards. Damned spirits all,
That in cross-ways and floods have burial,
Already to their wormy beds are gone.
Midsummer Night's Dream 3.2.379–84, PUCK TO OBERON

See also **APPARITIONS; FAIRIES; OMENS AND PORTENTS; SPIRITS; WITCHES**

SUPERSTITION *see* LUCK

SUSPICION

5   See what a ready tongue suspicion hath!
He that but fears the thing he would not know
Hath by instinct knowledge from others' eyes
That what he feared is chanced.
2 Henry IV 1.1.84–7, NORTHUMBERLAND TO MORTON

6   Thou echo'st me
As if there were some monster in thy thought
Too hideous to be shown.
Othello 3.3.109–11, OTHELLO TO IAGO

7   You smell this business with a sense as cold
As is a dead man's nose.
Winter's Tale 2.1.151–2, the suspicious LEONTES accusing ANTIGONUS of being unobservant

SWIMMING

8   I saw him beat the surges under him,
And ride upon their backs; he trod the water,
Whose enmity he flung aside, and breasted

The surge most swoln that met him; his bold head
'Bove the contentious waves he kept, and oared
Himself with his good arms in lusty stroke
To th' shore.
Tempest 2.1.116–22, FRANCISCO TO ALONSO, of Ferdinand

1 Swum ashore, man, like a duck.
Tempest 2.2.126, TRINCULO, in reply to STEPHANO who asked him how he escaped the shipwreck

2 Like Arion on the dolphin's back.
I saw him hold acquaintance with the waves.
Twelfth Night 1.2.15–16, CAPTAIN TO VIOLA, describing her brother after a shipwreck

T

TALK

3 He words me, girls, he words me, that I should not
Be noble to myself.
Antony and Cleopatra 5.2.190–1, CLEOPATRA TO HER COMPANIONS

4 What I think, I utter, and spend my malice in my breath.
Coriolanus 2.1.53–4, MENENIUS TO SICINIUS

5 QUEEN   More matter with less art.
POLONIUS Madam, I swear I use no art at all.
That he is mad, 'tis true; 'tis true 'tis pity;
And pity 'tis 'tis true. A foolish figure –
But farewell it, for I will use no art.
Hamlet 2.2.95–9

6 GUILDENSTERN Good my lord, vouchsafe me a word with you.
HAMLET Sir, a whole history.
Hamlet 3.2.297–9

7 HAMLET Who is to be buried in't?
GRAVEDIGGER One that was a woman, sir; but rest her soul, she's dead.
HAMLET How absolute the knave is. We must speak by the card or equivocation will undo us.
Hamlet 5.1.133–7

1 His sweet and honeyed sentences.
   Henry V 1.1.50, ARCHBISHOP OF CANTERBURY TO THE BISHOP OF ELY, of Henry

2 Men of few words are the best men.
   Henry V 3.2.37–8, BOY

3   I cannot heave
   My heart into my mouth.
   King Lear 1.1.92–3, CORDELIA TO LEAR

4   Mend your speech a little,
   Lest you may mar your fortunes.
   King Lear 1.1.94–5, LEAR's reply

5 Your large speeches may your deeds approve.
   King Lear 1.1.185, KENT TO GONERIL AND REGAN; the implication is of doubt that they
   will live up to their professions of love for their father. (The phrase is more easily
   understood if the two halves are reversed.)

6   That glib and oily art
   To speak and purpose not.
   King Lear 1.1.226–7, CORDELIA TO LEAR

7 A man . . .
   That hath a mint of phrases in his brain.
   Love's Labour's Lost 1.1.164–5, KING OF NAVARRE TO BEROWNE, of Armado

8 I praise God for you, sir: your reasons at dinner have been sharp and
   sententious; pleasant without scurrility, witty without affection,
   audacious without impudency, learned without opinion, and strange
   without heresy.
   Love's Labour's Lost 5.1.2–6, NATHANIEL TO HOLOFERNES

9 They have been at a great feast of languages, and stolen the scraps.
   Love's Labour's Lost 5.1.35–6, MOTH TO HIS COMPANIONS

10 Gratiano speaks an infinite deal of nothing.
   Merchant of Venice 1.1.114, BASSANIO TO ANTONIO

11 Have I lived to stand at the taunt of one that makes fritters of English?
   Merry Wives of Windsor 5.5.143–4, FALSTAFF, in disgust at Evans's mangling of the
   language

12 I wonder that you will still be talking, Signior Benedick: nobody
   marks you.
   Much Ado About Nothing 1.1.111–12, BEATRICE TO BENEDICK

1   She speaks poniards, and every word stabs.
    Much Ado About Nothing 2.1.232–3, BENEDICK TO DON PEDRO, of Beatrice

2   O God, sir, here's a dish I love not! I cannot endure my Lady Tongue.
    Much Ado About Nothing 2.1.257–8, BENEDICK TO DON PEDRO, on the arrival of Beatrice

3   His words are a very fantastical banquet, just so many strange dishes.
    Much Ado About Nothing 2.3.20–1, BENEDICK, of Claudio in love

4   Demand me nothing. What you know, you know.
    From this time forth I never will speak word.
    Othello 5.2.302–3, IAGO, to those assembled round the body of Desdemona

5   Talkers are no good doers.
    Richard III 1.3.351, MURDERER TO RICHARD

6   A gentleman that loves to hear himself talk, and will speak more in a minute than he will stand to in a month.
    Romeo and Juliet 2.4.146–8, ROMEO TO JULIET'S NURSE, of Mercutio

    See also **WORDS**

TAXATION

7   That's the wavering commons, for their love
    Lies in their purses, and whoso empties them,
    By so much fills their hearts with deadly hate.
    Richard II 2.2.128–30, BAGOT TO GREENE

TEARS AND WEEPING

8   Mine eyes smell onions; I shall weep anon.
    All's Well That Ends Well, 5.3.319, LAFEW

9   Fall not a tear, I say, one of them rates
    All that is won and lost.
    Antony and Cleopatra 3.11.69–70, ANTONY TO CLEOPATRA

10 Like Niobe, all tears.
    Hamlet 1.2.149, HAMLET's description of his mother at his father's funeral

11   He has strangled
    His language in his tears.
    Henry VIII 5.1.156–7, HENRY, of Cranmer

12 If you have tears, prepare to shed them now.
    Julius Caesar 3.2.170, MARK ANTONY's oration on the death of Julius Caesar

1 Let not women's weapons, water-drops,
  Stain my man's cheeks.
  King Lear 2.2.469–70, LEAR TO REGAN

2 No, I'll not weep.
  I have full cause of weeping, but this heart
  Shall break into a hundred thousand flaws
  Or e'er I'll weep.
  King Lear 2.2.475–8, LEAR TO REGAN AND GONERIL

3   Mine eyes do itch,
  Doth that bode weeping?
  Othello 4.3.57–8, DESDEMONA TO EMILIA

4 What store of parting tears were shed?
  Richard II 1.4.5, RICHARD TO AUMERLE

5 I am not prone to weeping, as our sex
  Commonly are: . . . / but I have
  That honourable grief lodged here which burns
  Worse than tears drown.
  Winter's Tale 2.1.108–12, HERMIONE TO LEONTES

TEMPTATION

6 Thou . . . art indeed able to corrupt a saint.
  1 Henry IV 1.2.89–90, FALSTAFF TO PRINCE HAL

7 Why do I yield to that suggestion
  Whose horrid image doth unfix my hair,
  And make my seated heart knock at my ribs,
  Against the use of nature?
  Macbeth 1.3.134–7, MACBETH, tempted to murder

8 'Tis one thing to be tempted, . . .
  Another thing to fall.
  Measure for Measure 2.1.17–18, ANGELO TO ESCALUS

9   Can it be
  That modesty may more betray our sense
  Than woman's lightness? Having waste ground enough,
  Shall we desire to raze the sanctuary
  And pitch our evils there?
  Measure for Measure 2.2.168–72, ANGELO

1 O cunning enemy, that, to catch a saint,
With saints dost bait thy hook!
Measure for Measure 2.2.180–1, ANGELO

2 Tempt not a desperate man.
Romeo and Juliet 5.3.59, ROMEO TO PARIS

THANKS

3 For this relief much thanks.
Hamlet 1.1.8, FRANCISCO TO BARNARDO

THIEVES

4 These pickers and stealers.
Hamlet 3.2.337, HAMLET TO ROSENCRANTZ (refers to the Church catechism: 'To keep
my hands from picking and stealing')

5 Who, I rob? I a thief? Not I, by my faith.
1 Henry IV 1.2.135, FALSTAFF TO PRINCE HAL

6 I'll starve ere I'll rob a foot further.
1 Henry IV 2.2.21, FALSTAFF

7 A plague upon it when thieves cannot be true to one another.
1 Henry IV 2.2.26–7, FALSTAFF

8 Flat burglary as ever was committed.
Much Ado About Nothing 4.2.49, DOGBERRY TO HIS COLLEAGUES

9 We are not thieves, but men that much do want.
Timon of Athens 4.3.417, BANDIT TO TIMON

10 Every lane's end, every shop, church, session, hanging, yields a careful
man work.
Winter's Tale 4.4.687–8, AUTOLYCUS

See also **CRIMES; TRIFLES**

THOUGHTS

11 ROSALIND A woman's thought runs before her actions.
ORLANDO So do all thoughts, they are winged.
As You Like It 4.1.133–5

12 There is nothing either good or bad but thinking makes it so.
Hamlet 2.2.250–1, HAMLET TO ROSENCRANTZ AND GUILDENSTERN

13 Our thoughts are ours, their ends none of our own.
Hamlet 3.2.215, PLAYER KING

1 Cudgel thy brains no more about it.
   Hamlet 5.1.56, GRAVEDIGGER TO HIS MATE

2 Faster than spring-time showers comes thought on thought.
   2 Henry VI 3.1.337, RICHARD OF YORK, the schemer

3 Thoughts of great value, worthy cogitations.
   Julius Caesar 1.2.49, CASSIUS TO BRUTUS

4 Dive, thoughts, down to my soul.
   Richard III 1.1.41, RICHARD

5   Love's heralds should be thoughts
   Which ten times faster glides than the sun's beams
   Driving back shadows over lowering hills.
   Romeo and Juliet 2.5.4–6, JULIET

6   Slight air, and purging fire, . . .
   The first my thought, the other my desire.
   Sonnet 45.1, 3

7 I think good thoughts, whilst other write good words.
   Sonnet 85.5

THREATS

8 There is no terror, Cassius, in your threats;
   For I am armed so strong in honesty
   That they pass by me as the idle wind,
   Which I respect not.
   Julius Caesar 4.3.66–9, BRUTUS TO CASSIUS

THRIFT

9 Thrift, thrift, Horatio. The funeral baked meats
   Did coldly furnish forth the marriage tables.
   Hamlet 1.2.180–1, HAMLET TO HORATIO

10   How i'th' name of thrift
   Does he rake this together?
   Henry VIII 3.2.108–9, HENRY TO LORDS, of Cardinal Wolsey

11 Our purses shall be proud, our garments poor.
   Taming of the Shrew 4.3.169, PETRUCHIO TO KATHERINA, frightening her with the prospect of a poor but honest future; the phrase 'poor but honest' is itself used by Helena in *All's Well That Ends Well* (1.3.192), to describe her friends and family

TIME

1 Th'inaudible and noiseless foot of time.
   All's Well That Ends Well 5.3.41, KING OF FRANCE TO BERTRAM

2   Every time
   Serves for the matter that is then born in't.
   Antony and Cleopatra 2.2.9–10, ENOBARBUS TO LEPIDUS

3 'Thus we may see', quoth he, 'how the world wags:
   'Tis but an hour ago since it was nine,
   And after one hour more 'twill be eleven;
   And so from hour to hour, we ripe, and ripe,
   And then from hour to hour, we rot, and rot,
   And thereby hangs a tale.'
   As You Like It 2.7.23–8, JAQUES reports his conversation with a fool in the Forest of
   Arden

4 Time travels in divers paces with divers persons. I'll tell you who Time
   ambles withal, who Time trots withal, who Time gallops withal, and
   who he stands still withal.
   As You Like It 3.2.303–6, ROSALIND TO ORLANDO

5   Let the time run on,
   To good or bad.
   Cymbeline 5.5.128–9, PISANIO

6 Take thy fair hour, Laertes, time be thine,
   And thy best graces spend it at thy will.
   Hamlet 1.2.62–3, CLAUDIUS TO LAERTES

7 What a devil hast thou to do with the time of the day? Unless hours
   were cups of sack, and minutes capons, and clocks the tongues of
   bawds, and dials the signs of leaping-houses, and the blessed sun
   himself a fair hot wench in flame-coloured taffeta, I see no reason why
   thou shouldst be so superfluous to demand the time of the day.
   1 Henry IV 1.2.6–12, PRINCE HAL TO FALSTAFF

8 The dust of old oblivion.
   Henry V 2.4.88, EXETER TO THE KING OF FRANCE

9   He weighs time
   Even to the utmost grain.
   Henry V 2.4.138–9, EXETER TO THE DAUPHIN AND THE KING OF FRANCE, of Henry

10 Cormorant devouring Time.
   Love's Labour's Lost 1.1.4, KING OF NAVARRE TO HIS FRIENDS

1 The seeds of time.
   Macbeth 1.3.58, BANQUO TO THE WITCHES

2   Come what come may,
   Time and the hour runs through the roughest day.
   Macbeth 1.3.147–8, MACBETH

3 This bank and shoal of time.
   Macbeth 1.7.6, MACBETH

4 Pleasure and action make the hours seem short.
   Othello 2.3.367, IAGO TO RODERIGO

5   Time's the king of men;
   He's both their parent, and he is their grave,
   And gives them what he will, not what they crave.
   Pericles 2.3.45–7, PERICLES

6 Devouring time.
   Sonnet 19.1

7 Do thy worst, old Time.
   Sonnet 19.13

8 My glass shall not persuade me I am old
   So long as youth and thou are of one date;
   But when in thee time's furrows I behold,
   Then look I death my days should expiate.
   Sonnet 22.1–4

9 Like as the waves make towards the pebbled shore,
   So do our minutes hasten to their end.
   Sonnet 60.1–2

10 Time, that gave, doth now his gift confound.
   Sonnet 60.8

11 Time doth transfix the flourish set on youth
   And delves the parallels in beauty's brow,
   Feeds on the rarities of nature's truth,
   And nothing stands but for his scythe to mow.
   Sonnet 60.9–12

12 Time's injurious hand.
   Sonnet 63.2

1   Time decays.
O fearful meditation!
Sonnet 65.8–9

2   Time's thievish progress to eternity.
Sonnet 77.8

3   Love's not Time's fool, though rosy lips and cheeks
Within his bending sickle's compass come;
Love alters not with his brief hours and weeks,
But bears it out even to the edge of doom.
Sonnet 116.9–12

4   When time is old and hath forgot itself,
When water-drops have worn the stones of Troy,
And blind oblivion swallowed cities up.
Troilus and Cressida 3.2.182–4, CRESSIDA TO TROILUS

5   Time hath, my lord, a wallet at his back
Wherein he puts alms for oblivion,
A great-sized monster of ingratitudes.
Those scraps are good deeds past, which are devoured
As fast as they are made, forgot as soon
As done.
Troilus and Cressida 3.3.145–50, ULYSSES TO ACHILLES

6   Time is like a fashionable host
That slightly shakes his parting guest by th' hand,
And with his arms out-stretched, as he would fly,
Grasps in the comer. Welcome ever smiles,
And farewell goes out sighing. O let not virtue seek
Remuneration for the thing it was;
For beauty, wit,
High birth, vigour of bone, desert in service,
Love, friendship, charity, are subjects all
To envious and calumniating Time.
Troilus and Cressida 3.3.165–74, ULYSSES; *more at* **HONOUR; PERSEVERANCE; RIVALRY**

7   Injurious Time now with a robber's haste
Crams his rich thiev'ry up, he knows not how.
Troilus and Cressida 4.4.41–2, TROILUS TO CRESSIDA

1 What's past and what's to come is strewed with husks
   And formless ruin of oblivion.
   Troilus and Cressida 4.5.165–6, AGAMEMNON TO THE GREEK PRINCES

2 And thus the whirligig of time brings in his revenges.
   Twelfth Night 5.1.368–9, FESTE TO OLIVIA

   See also **FUTURE, the; TIME, wasting; TIMELINESS; TOMORROW; TRANSIENCE**

TIME, wasting

3 By heaven, Poins, I feel me much to blame,
   So idly to profane the precious time.
   2 Henry IV 2.4.361–2, PRINCE HAL

4 We burn daylight.
   Merry Wives of Windsor 2.1.49, MISTRESS FORD TO MISTRESS PAGE; also in *Romeo and Juliet* 1.4.43, MERCUTIO TO ROMEO

5 I wasted time, and now doth time waste me.
   Richard II 5.5.49, RICHARD, in prison

6 I would I had bestowed that time in the tongues that I have in fencing, dancing, and bear-baiting. O, had I but followed the arts!
   Twelfth Night 1.3.90–3, SIR ANDREW AGUECHEEK TO SIR TOBY BELCH

   See also **DELAY; TIME**

TIMELINESS

7 You come most carefully upon your hour.
   Hamlet 1.1.6, FRANCISCO TO BARNARDO

8 Think him as a serpent's egg,
   Which, hatched, would, as his kind, grow mischievous,
   And kill him in the shell.
   Julius Caesar 2.1.32–4, BRUTUS TO LUCIUS, of Julius Caesar

9 Make use of time, let not advantage slip.
   Venus and Adonis 129; *more at* **FLOWERS AND PLANTS**

   See also **ACTION, immediate; TIME**

TOMORROW

10 Tomorrow is a busy day!
   Richard III 5.3.18, RICHARD before the battle of Bosworth

11 Stir with the lark tomorrow.
   Richard III 5.3.57, RICHARD before the battle of Bosworth

TRANSIENCE

1   Packs and sects of great ones
That ebb and flow by the moon.
King Lear 5.3.18–19, LEAR TO CORDELIA, in prison

2   Everything that grows
Holds in perfection but a little moment.
Sonnet 15.1–2

3 The summer's flower is to the summer sweet,
Though to itself it only live and die.
Sonnet 94.9–10

4 Yet doth beauty, like a dial hand,
Steal from his figure, and no pace perceived.
Sonnet 104.9–10

5   Youth's a stuff will not endure.
Twelfth Night 2.3.52, FESTE's song

6 Women are as roses, whose fair flower
Being once displayed, doth fall that very hour.
Twelfth Night 2.4.38–9, ORSINO TO VIOLA, rather conventionally

TRAPS AND TRICKS

7 Ay, springes to catch woodcocks.
Hamlet 1.3.115, POLONIUS TO OPHELIA, describing young men's seduction techniques

8 *The Mousetrap.*
Hamlet 3.2.239; HAMLET names the dumb show which mirrors the crimes of Claudius and Gertrude

9 I know a trick worth two of that.
1 Henry IV 2.1.35–6, CARRIER TO GADSHILL

10 My purpose is indeed a horse of that colour.
Twelfth Night 2.3.164, MARIA TO SIR TOBY BELCH AND SIR ANDREW AGUECHEEK, planning a trick on Malvolio

11 Here comes the trout that must be caught with tickling.
Twelfth Night 2.5.21–2, MARIA TO SIR TOBY BELCH, of Malvolio

12 Remember who commended thy yellow stockings, and wished to see thee ever cross-gartered.
Twelfth Night 2.5.148–9, MALVOLIO reads the anonymous letter which he believes is from Olivia

See also **PLOTS; POLITICS AND POLITICIANS**

TRAVEL

1 Ay, now am I in Arden, the more fool I; when I was at home I was in a better place, but travellers must be content.
As You Like It 2.4.14–16, TOUCHSTONE TO ROSALIND

2 I had rather have a fool to make me merry than experience to make me sad, and to travel for it too!
As You Like It 4.1.25–7, ROSALIND TO JAQUES

3 Farewell Monsieur Traveller. Look you lisp, and wear strange suits; disable all the benefits of your own country; be out of love with your nativity, and almost chide God for making you that countenance you are; or I will scarce think you have swam in a gondola.
As You Like It 4.1.31–6, ROSALIND TO JAQUES

4 Five summers have I spent in farthest Greece,
Roaming clean through the bounds of Asia.
Comedy of Errors 1.1.132–3, EGEON TO THE DUKE OF EPHESUS

5 Till that I'll view the manners of the town,
Peruse the traders, gaze upon the buildings.
Comedy of Errors 1.2.12–13, ANTIPHOLUS OF SYRACUSE TO A MERCHANT

6 I hope to see London once ere I die.
2 Henry IV 5.3.60, DAVY TO FALSTAFF AND COMPANIONS

7 Now spurs the lated traveller apace,
To gain the timely inn.
Macbeth 3.3.6–7, ONE MURDERER TO ANOTHER

8 I will fetch you a toothpicker now from the furthest inch of Asia; bring you the length of Prester John's foot; fetch you a hair off the great Cham's beard.
Much Ado About Nothing 2.1.249–52, BENEDICK TO DON PEDRO, asking for any challenge rather than having to talk to Beatrice

9 I am a stranger here in Gloucestershire.
These high wild hills and rough uneven ways
Draws out our miles and makes them wearisome.
Richard II 2.3.3–5, NORTHUMBERLAND TO BOLINGBROKE

10 Journeys end in lovers meeting.
Twelfth Night 2.3.43, FESTE's song

1 Then westward ho!
   Twelfth Night 3.1.135, VIOLA TO OLIVIA

2 [He] did request me to importune you
   To let him spend his time no more at home;
   Which would be great impeachment to his age,
   Having known no travel in his youth.
   Two Gentlemen of Verona 1.3.13–16, PANTHINO TO ANTONIO; the young man is Antonio's son Proteus.

3 Thou art perfect, then, our ship hath touched upon
   The deserts of Bohemia?
   Winter's Tale 3.3.1–2, ANTIGONUS TO A MARINER; an unlikely landing, unless they have arrived by river

4   Jog on, jog on, the foot-path way,
         And merrily hent the stile-a:
      A merry heart goes all the day,
         Your sad tires in a mile-a.
   Winter's Tale 4.3.121–4, AUTOLYCUS' song

TREASON AND TREACHERY

5 Treachery! Seek it out.
   Hamlet 5.2.321, HAMLET

6 What a brood of traitors have we here!
   2 Henry VI 5.1.141, CLIFFORD TO RICHARD OF YORK

7 When the fox hath once got in his nose,
   He'll soon find means to make the body follow.
   3 Henry VI 4.7.25, RICHARD OF GLOUCESTER

8 A nest of traitors!
   Winter's Tale 2.3.81, LEONTES TO PAULINA; he is referring to his children, since he believes his wife to be unfaithful

See also **MUSIC** (193.7)

TRIFLES

9 Small things make base men proud.
   2 Henry VI 4.1.105, SUFFOLK TO HIS MURDERERS

10 Dispense with trifles.
   Merry Wives of Windsor 2.1.43, MISTRESS PAGE TO MISTRESS FORD

11 Small winds shake him.
   Two Noble Kinsmen 1.2.88, PALAMON TO VALERIUS, of Theseus

1 A snapper-up of unconsidered trifles.
   Winter's Tale 4.3.25–6, light-fingered AUTOLYCUS' description of his father, and himself

TROJAN WAR, the

2 All the argument is a whore and a cuckold.
   Troilus and Cressida 2.3.74–5, THERSITES TO ACHILLES; the unheroic view

TROUBLE

3 There is strange things toward . . . pray you, be careful.
   King Lear 3.3.19–20, GLOUCESTER TO EDMUND

4 How cam'st thou in this pickle?
   Tempest 5.1.281, ALONSO TO SEBASTIAN AND TRINCULO

5 O time, thou must untangle this, not I,
   It is too hard a knot for me to untie.
   Twelfth Night 2.2.40–1, VIOLA

TRUANCY

6 A truant disposition.
   Hamlet 1.2.169, HORATIO TO HAMLET, describing his own character

TRUST

7 Love all, trust a few
   All's Well That Ends Well 1.1.63, COUNTESS OF ROSSILLION TO BERTRAM; *more at* **ADVICE**

8 What trust is in these times?
   2 Henry IV 1.3.100, ARCHBISHOP OF YORK TO HASTINGS AND LORD BARDOLPH

9 He's mad that trusts in the tameness of a wolf, a horse's health, a boy's love or a whore's oath.
   King Lear 3.6.18–19, FOOL TO EDGAR AND LEAR

10 He was a gentleman on whom I built
   An absolute trust.
   Macbeth 1.4.13–14, DUNCAN TO MALCOLM, of the Thane of Cawdor – a title which ironically will now be given to Macbeth

TRUTH

11 Tell truth, and shame the devil.
   1 Henry IV 3.1.55, HOTSPUR TO GLENDOWER

12 Truth's a dog that must to kennel; he must be whipped out, when the Lady Brach may stand by the fire and stink.
   King Lear 1.4.109–11, FOOL TO LEAR

1   Truth is truth
To th'end of reck'ning.
Measure for Measure 5.1.48–9, Isabella to the Duke

2 Truth will come to light . . . in the end truth will out.
Merchant of Venice 2.2.76, 77, Launcelot Gobbo to Old Gobbo

3 I will a round unvarnished tale deliver.
Othello 1.3.91, Othello to Brabantio and the Duke of Venice

4 Speak of me as I am. Nothing extenuate,
Nor set down aught in malice
Othello 5.2.342–3, Othello to his colleagues, before killing himself

5 Truth hath a quiet breast.
Richard II 1.3.96, Mowbray to Bolingbroke and Richard

6 An honest tale speeds best being plainly told.
Richard III 4.4.358, Queen Elizabeth to Richard

7 Simple truth miscalled simplicity.
Sonnet 66.11

TYRANNY

8 Th'abuse of greatness is when it disjoins
Remorse from power.
Julius Caesar 2.1.18–19, Brutus to Lucius

9   The foot
That leaves the print of blood where'er it walks.
King John 4.3.25–6, Salisbury to Philip the Bastard and Pembroke

10   The laws are mine, not thine.
Who can arraign me for't?
King Lear 5.3.156–7, Goneril to Albany

11 'Tis safer to be that which we destroy,
Than by destruction dwell in doubtful joy.
Macbeth 3.2.6–7, Lady Macbeth to a servant

12   Each new morn,
New widows howl, new orphans cry; new sorrows
Strike heaven on the face.
Macbeth 4.3.4–6, Macduff to Malcolm

13 Our country sinks beneath the yoke;
It weeps, it bleeds; and each new day a gash

Is added to her wounds.
Macbeth 4.3.39–41, MALCOLM TO MACDUFF

1 There is pretty orders beginning, I can tell you. It is but heading and hanging.
Measure for Measure 2.1.232–3, ESCALUS TO POMPEY

2 'Tis time to fear when tyrants seem to kiss.
Pericles 1.2.79, PERICLES TO HELICANUS

3 Think what you will, we seize into our hands
His plate, his goods, his money and his lands.
Richard II 2.1.209–10, RICHARD TO YORK

4   They that set you on
To do this deed will hate you for the deed.
Richard III 1.4.251–2, CLARENCE tries to dissuade his MURDERERS from their task

5 I will converse with iron-witted fools
And unrespective boys; none are for me
That look into me with considerate eyes.
Richard III 4.2.28–30, RICHARD, describing appropriate companions for a tyrant

6 Mine eyes are cloyed with view of tyranny.
Titus Andronicus 3.2.55, TITUS TO MARCUS, who has just killed a fly

7 Power into will, will into appetite,
And appetite, an universal wolf.
Troilus and Cressida 1.3.120–1, ULYSSES TO THE GREEK PRINCES

🦋 U 🦋

UNCERTAINTY

8   O, that a man might know
The end of this day's business ere it come!
Julius Caesar 5.1.123–4, BRUTUS TO CASSIUS

USURY

9 Neither a borrower nor a lender be.
Hamlet 1.3.75, POLONIUS TO LAERTES; *more at* **ADVICE**

1 'Twas never merry world since, of two usuries, the merriest was put
down, and the worser allowed by order of law.
Measure for Measure 3.2.5–7, POMPEY TO THE DUKE, disguised as a friar; the first
'usury' is sex

2   In low simplicity
He lends out money gratis.
Merchant of Venice 1.3.41–2, SHYLOCK, of Antonio

3 This is the fool that lent out money gratis.
Merchant of Venice 3.3.2, SHYLOCK, of Antonio on his imprisonment

VALUE

4 All that glisters is not gold.
Merchant of Venice 2.7.65, PRINCE OF MOROCCO

5 What we have we prize not to the worth
Whiles we enjoy it, but being lacked and lost,
Why then we rack the value, then we find
The virtue that possession would not show us
Whiles it was ours.
Much Ado About Nothing 4.1.217–21, FRIAR TO HERO AND LEONATO

6 What's aught but as 'tis valued?
Troilus and Cressida 2.2.53, TROILUS TO HECTOR

7 Value dwells not in particular will:
It holds his estimate and dignity
As well wherein 'tis precious of itself
As in the prizer.
Troilus and Cressida 2.2.54–7, HECTOR's reply

See also **WORTH**

VANITY

8 God hath given you one face and you make yourselves another.
Hamlet 3.1.144–5, HAMLET TO OPHELIA, inveighing against make-up

1 There was never yet fair woman but she made mouths in a glass.
   King Lear 3.2.35–6, Fool to Lear

2 What a sweep of vanity comes this way.
   Timon of Athens 1.2.133, Apemantus watching a masque of ladies dressed as Amazons

   See also **PRIDE**

VICTORY

3 'I came, saw, and overcame.'
   2 Henry IV 4.3.41–2, Falstaff quoting Julius Caesar to Prince John of Lancaster

4 A victory is twice itself when the achiever brings home full numbers.
   Much Ado About Nothing 1.1.8–9, Leonato to a messenger

5 They laugh that win.
   Othello 4.1.123, Othello to Cassio and Iago

   See also **SUCCESS**

VIOLENCE

6 Let's beat him before his whore.
   2 Henry IV 2.4.257, Poins to Prince Hal, of Falstaff

7 All pity choked with custom of fell deeds.
   Julius Caesar 3.1.269, Mark Antony

8 It is a damned and a bloody work;
   The graceless action of a heavy hand.
   King John 4.3.57–8, Philip the Bastard to lords

9 He unseamed him from the nave to th' chops,
   And fixed his head upon our battlements.
   Macbeth 1.2.22–3, Captain to Duncan and Malcolm, describing Macbeth's desperate energy in battle

10   O horror! horror! horror!
   Tongue nor heart cannot conceive, nor name thee!
   Macbeth 2.3.63–4, Macduff, at the discovery of Duncan's murder

11 Bloody thou art; bloody will be thy end.
   Richard III 4.4.195, Duchess of York to Richard, her son

VIRTUE

12 O infinite virtue! Com'st thou smiling from
   The world's great snare uncaught?
   Antony and Cleopatra 4.8.17–18, Cleopatra to Antony

1 If she be furnished with a mind so rare,
  She is alone th'Arabian bird.
  Cymbeline 1.7.16–17, IACHIMO, of Imogen

2 Virtue itself scapes not calumnious strokes.
  Hamlet 1.3.38, LAERTES TO OPHELIA

3 Assume a virtue if you have it not.
  Hamlet 3.4.162, HAMLET TO GERTRUDE, suggesting that assuming a virtue is the first step towards possessing it

4 There lives not three good men unhanged in England, and one of them is fat, and grows old.
  1 Henry IV 2.4.128–9, FALSTAFF TO PRINCE HAL AND POINS; the old, fat one is, of course, himself

5 Virtue finds no friends.
  Henry VIII 3.1.125, KATHERINE OF ARAGON TO CARDINALS CAMPEIUS AND WOLSEY

6   His virtues
  Will plead like angels, trumpet-tongued.
  Macbeth 1.7.18–19, MACBETH, of Duncan

7 Never anything can be amiss
  When simpleness and duty tender it.
  Midsummer Night's Dream 5.1.82–3, THESEUS TO PHILOSTRATE AND HIS COMPANIONS

8 Are you good men and true?
  Much Ado About Nothing 3.3.1, DOGBERRY TO THE WATCH

9   While we do admire
  This virtue and this moral discipline,
  Let's be no stoics nor no stocks, I pray.
  Taming of the Shrew 1.1.29–31, TRANIO TO LUCENTIO

10 'Tis the mind that makes the body rich,
   And as the sun breaks through the darkest clouds,
   So honour peereth in the meanest habit.
   Taming of the Shrew 4.3.170–2, PETRUCHIO TO KATE

11 Dost thou think because thou art virtuous, there shall be no more cakes and ale?
   Twelfth Night 2.3.113–14, SIR TOBY BELCH TO FESTE

12 In nature there's no blemish but the mind:
   None can be called deformed but the unkind.
   Virtue is beauty.
   Twelfth Night 3.4.366–8, ANTONIO TO SEBASTIAN

See also **COMMUNICATION; ELEGIES; GOOD AND GOODNESS; HONESTY; HONOUR; TIME**

VOWS

1   Yours in the ranks of death.
    King Lear 4.2.24, EDMUND TO GONERIL

2   I swear to thee by Cupid's strongest bow,
    By his best arrow with the golden head,
    By the simplicity of Venus' doves,
    By that which knitteth souls and prospers loves, . . .
    By all the vows that ever men have broke
    (In number more than ever women spoke).
    Midsummer Night's Dream 1.1.169–72, 175–6, HERMIA TO LYSANDER

3   I am your own for ever.
    Othello 3.3.482, IAGO TO OTHELLO

4   Swear not by the moon, th'inconstant moon,
    That monthly changes in her circled orb,
    Lest that thy love prove likewise variable.
    Romeo and Juliet 2.2.109–11, JULIET TO ROMEO

WAITING

5   I am to wait, though waiting so be hell.
    Sonnet 58.13

WALES AND THE WELSH

6   I think there's no man speaks better Welsh.
    1 Henry IV 3.1.47, HOTSPUR's ironic compliment to his ally GLENDOWER, who has just been boasting

7   Thy tongue
    Makes Welsh as sweet as ditties highly penned,
    Sung by a fair queen in a summer's bow'r
    With ravishing division to her lute.
    1 Henry IV 3.1.201–4, MORTIMER TO HIS WIFE

1   The devil understands Welsh.
    1 Henry IV 3.1.224, HOTSPUR TO HIS WIFE

2   LADY PERCY Lie still, ye thief, and hear the lady sing in Welsh.
    HOTSPUR I had rather hear Lady my brach howl in Irish.
    1 Henry IV 3.1.229–30

3   I tell you, Captain, if you look in the maps of the world, I warrant you
    shall find, in the comparisons between Macedon and Monmouth, that
    the situations, look you, is both alike. There is a river in Macedon, and
    there is also moreover a river at Monmouth.
    Henry V 4.7.23–8, FLUELLEN TO GOWER

4   FLUELLEN I do believe your majesty takes no scorn to wear the leek
    upon Saint Tavy's day.
    KING HENRY I wear it for a memorable honour,
    For I am Welsh, you know, good countryman.
    Henry V 4.7.100–4

5   If you can mock a leek you can eat a leek.
    Henry V 5.1.37, FLUELLEN gets his revenge on PISTOL

6   Heavens defend me from that Welsh fairy!
    Merry Wives of Windsor 5.5.82, FALSTAFF, of Evans disguised as a fairy

WAR

7   The end of war's uncertain.
    Coriolanus 5.3.143, VOLUMNIA TO HER FAMILY

8   We go to gain a little patch of ground
    That hath in it no profit but the name.
    Hamlet 4.4.18–19, CAPTAIN in Fortinbras's army, to HAMLET

9   I see
    The imminent death of twenty thousand men
    That, for a fantasy and trick of fame,
    Go to their graves like beds, fight for a plot
    Whereon the numbers cannot try the cause,
    Which is not tomb enough and continent
    To hide the slain.
    Hamlet 4.4.59–65, HAMLET

10 We must all to the wars.
    1 Henry IV 2.4.536–7, PRINCE HAL TO PETO

1 FALSTAFF I would 'twere bedtime, Hal, and all well.
PRINCE Why, thou owest God a death.
1 Henry IV 5.1.125–6

2   Full bravely hast thou fleshed
Thy maiden sword.
1 Henry IV 5.4.128–9, PRINCE HAL to his brother LORD JOHN OF LANCASTER

3 For God's sake, go not to these wars!
2 Henry IV 2.3.9, LADY PERCY TO THE NORTHUMBERLANDS

4 I have in equal balance justly weighed
What wrongs our arms may do, what wrongs we suffer,
And find our griefs heavier than our offences.
2 Henry IV 4.1.67–9, ARCHBISHOP OF YORK TO WESTMORELAND

5 God, and not we, hath safely fought today.
2 Henry IV 4.2.121, PRINCE JOHN OF LANCASTER TO HIS COMPANIONS

6 Now all the youth of England are on fire,
And silken dalliance in the wardrobe lies.
Henry V 2.0.1–2, CHORUS

7 Once more unto the breach, dear friends, once more,
Or close the wall up with our English dead.
In peace there's nothing so becomes a man
As modest stillness and humility;
But when the blast of war blows in our ears,
Then imitate the action of the tiger:
Stiffen the sinews, conjure up the blood,
Disguise fair nature with hard-favoured rage.
Henry V 3.1.1–8, HENRY TO HIS FORCES

8 I see you stand like greyhounds in the slips,
Straining upon the start. The game's afoot.
Follow your spirit, and upon this charge
Cry 'God for Harry! England and Saint George!'
Henry V 3.1.32–5, HENRY TO HIS FORCES

9 Would I were in an alehouse in London! I would give all my fame for
a pot of ale and safety.
Henry V 3.2.14–15, BOY TO PISTOL, on the battlefields of France

10 I know the disciplines of war.
Henry V 3.2.141, FLUELLEN TO MACMORRIS

1 The gates of mercy shall be all shut up,
   And the fleshed soldier, rough and hard of heart,
   In liberty of bloody hand shall range
   With conscience wide as hell.
   Henry V 3.3.10–13, HENRY TO HIS COMPANIONS IN WAR

2 We see yonder the beginning of the day, but I think we shall never see
   the end of it.
   Henry V 4.1.89–90, MICHAEL WILLIAMS, a soldier, to HENRY incognito

3 There are few die well that die in a battle.
   Henry V 4.1.139–40, MICHAEL WILLIAMS, a soldier, to HENRY incognito

4 This day is called the feast of Crispian.
   He that outlives this day and comes safe home
   Will stand a-tiptoe when this day is named
   And rouse him at the name of Crispian.
   He that shall see this day and live old age
   Will yearly on the vigil feast his neighbours,
   And say 'Tomorrow is Saint Crispian.'
   Then will he strip his sleeve and show his scars,
   And say 'These wounds I had on Crispin's day.'
   Old men forget; yet all shall be forgot
   But he'll remember, with advantages
   What feats he did that day . . .
   We few, we happy few, we band of brothers.
   For he today that sheds his blood with me
   Shall be my brother; . . .
   And gentlemen in England now abed
   Shall think themselves accursed they were not here,
   And hold their manhoods cheap whiles any speaks
   That fought with us upon Saint Crispin's day.
   Henry V 4.3.40–51, 60–2, 64–7, HENRY TO WESTMORLAND

5 Lean Famine, quartering Steel, and climbing Fire.
   1 Henry VI 4.2.11, TALBOT parlaying with the GENERAL OF BORDEAUX

6 Now thou art come unto a feast of death.
   1 Henry VI 4.5.7, TALBOT TO HIS SON

7 Cry havoc and let slip the dogs of war.
   Julius Caesar 3.1.273, MARK ANTONY; *more at* **WAR, civil**

1 The storm is up, and all is on the hazard.
Julius Caesar 5.1.68, CASSIUS TO BRUTUS

2 Now doth death line his dead chaps with steel;
The swords of soldiers are his teeth, his fangs;
And now he feasts, mousing the flesh of men.
King John 2.1.352–4, PHILIP THE BASTARD TO PHILIP, KING OF FRANCE

3 War! war! no peace! peace is to me a war.
King John 3.1.39, CONSTANCE TO PHILIP, KING OF FRANCE, AND THE DUKE OF AUSTRIA

4 Now for the bare-picked bone of majesty
Doth dogged war bristle his angry crest
And snarleth in the gentle eye of peace.
King John 4.3.148–50, PHILIP THE BASTARD TO HUBERT

5 Farewell the plumed troops and the big wars
That makes ambition virtue! O farewell,
Farewell the neighing steed and the shrill trump,
The spirit-stirring drum, th'ear-piercing fife,
The royal banner, and all quality,
Pride, pomp and circumstance of glorious war!
And, O you mortal engines whose rude throats
Th'immortal Jove's dread clamours counterfeit,
Farewell: Othello's occupation's gone.
Othello 3.3.352–60, OTHELLO, with Iago

6 What would you have me do? go to the wars, would you? where a man
may serve seven years for the loss of a leg, and have not money enough
in the end to buy him a wooden one?
Pericles 4.6.167–70, BOULT TO MARINA

7   He is come to open
The purple testament of bleeding war.
Richard II 3.3.93–4, RICHARD TO NORTHUMBERLAND, of Bolingbroke

8 Religious canons, civil laws are cruel;
Then what should war be?
Timon of Athens 4.3.60–1, TIMON TO ALCIBIADES

9 The ministers and instruments
Of cruel war.
Troilus and Cressida Prologue 4–5

10 War and lechery confound all!
Troilus and Cressida 2.3.77, THERSITES TO ACHILLES

See also **FIGHTING; PEACE; SOLDIERS; STRATEGY; WAR, civil; WEAPONS**

WAR, civil

1 All of one nature, of one substance bred,
  Did lately meet in the intestine shock
  And furious close of civil butchery.
  1 Henry IV 1.1.11–13, HENRY to assembled LORDS

2 Let one spirit of the first-born Cain
  Reign in all bosoms, that, each heart being set
  On bloody courses, the rude scene may end,
  And darkness be the burier of the dead!
  2 Henry IV 1.1.157–60, NORTHUMBERLAND to LORD BARDOLPH AND MORTON

3 Over thy wounds now do I prophesy . . .
  A curse shall light upon the limbs of men;
  Domestic fury and fierce civil strife
  Shall cumber all the parts of Italy;
  Blood and destruction shall be so in use,
  And dreadful objects so familiar,
  That mothers shall but smile when they behold
  Their infants quartered with the hands of war,
  All pity choked with custom of fell deeds;
  And Caesar's spirit, ranging for revenge,
  With Ate by his side come hot from hell,
  Shall in these confines with a monarch's voice
  Cry havoc and let slip the dogs of war.
  Julius Caesar 3.1.259, 262–73, MARK ANTONY, on the death of Julius Caesar

4 [I'll] lay the summer's dust with showers of blood
  Rained from the wounds of slaughtered Englishmen.
  Richard II 3.3.43–4, BOLINGBROKE TO NORTHUMBERLAND

5   Tumultuous wars
  Shall kin with kin, and kind with kind, confound.
  Disorder, horror, fear, and mutiny,
  Shall here inhabit, and this land be called
  The field of Golgotha and dead men's skulls.
  Richard II 4.1.140–4, BISHOP OF CARLISLE TO YORK AND BOLINGBROKE

6 England hath long been mad, and scarred herself:
  The brother blindly shed the brother's blood;

The father rashly slaughtered his own son;
The son, compelled, been butcher to the sire.
Richard III 5.5.23–6, RICHMOND to other LORDS

WEAKNESS

1 The weakest goes to the wall.
Romeo and Juliet 1.1.14–15, GREGORY TO SAMPSON; proverbial

2 I may be negligent, foolish, and fearful;
In every one of these no man is free.
Winter's Tale 1.2.250–1, CAMILLO TO LEONTES

3 I am a feather for each wind that blows.
Winter's Tale 2.3.153, LEONTES TO ANTIGONUS AND LORDS

WEAPONS

4 His sword Philippan.
Antony and Cleopatra 2.5.23, CLEOPATRA's description of Antony's sword

5 We measured swords and parted.
As You Like It 5.4.85, TOUCHSTONE TO JAQUES

6 It is a simple one, but what though? It will toast cheese, and it will
endure cold as another man's sword will, and there's an end.
Henry V 2.1.7–9, NYM TO BARDOLPH; part of the unheroic counterpoint to the play's
official heroics

7   The sword is out
That must destroy thee.
King Lear 4.6.225–6, OSWALD TO GLOUCESTER

WEARINESS

8 I 'gin to be aweary of the sun,
And wish th'estate o'th' world were now undone.
Macbeth 5.5.49–50, MACBETH TO SEYTON AND A MESSENGER

9 By my troth Nerissa, my little body is aweary of this great world.
Merchant of Venice 1.2.1–2, PORTIA TO NERISSA

10 Things past redress are now with me past care.
Richard II 2.3.170, YORK TO BOLINGBROKE

11 Tired with all these, from these would I be gone.
Sonnet 66.13

See also **WORLD, the**

WEATHER

1 The storm is up, and all is on the hazard.
   Julius Caesar 5.1.68, CASSIUS TO BRUTUS

2 Blow winds and crack your cheeks! Rage, blow!
   You cataracts and hurricanoes, spout
   Till you have drenched our steeples, drowned the cocks!
   You sulphurous and thought-executing fires,
   Vaunt-couriers of oak-cleaving thunderbolts,
   Singe my white head! And thou, all-shaking thunder,
   Strike flat the thick rotundity o'the world!
   Crack nature's moulds, all germens spill at once
   That make ingrateful man!
   King Lear 3.2.1–9, LEAR, in the storm

3 I tax you not, you elements, with unkindness.
   King Lear 3.2.16, LEAR; it is his daughters who are unkind

4 This is a brave night to cool a courtesan.
   King Lear 3.2.78, FOOL, in the storm

5 So foul and fair a day I have not seen.
   Macbeth 1.3.38, MACBETH TO BANQUO

6   When that I was and a little tiny boy,
           With hey, ho, the wind and the rain,
       A foolish thing was but a toy,
           For the rain it raineth every day.
   Twelfth Night 5.1.381–4, FESTE's song; the last line is also sung by the Fool in *King Lear* at 3.2.76

See also **COLD; MORNING; NIGHT; OMENS AND PORTENTS; WINTER**

WEEPING *see* **TEARS AND WEEPING**

WILD BEHAVIOUR

7 Once in my days I'll be a madcap.
   1 Henry IV 1.2.139, PRINCE HAL TO FALSTAFF

8   He is given
   To sports, to wildness, and much company.
   Julius Caesar 2.1.188–9, BRUTUS, of Mark Antony

9 My masters, are you mad? Or what are you? Have you no wit,
   manners, nor honesty, but to gabble like tinkers at this time of night?

. . . Is there no respect of place, persons, nor time in you?
Twelfth Night 2.3.86–8, 90–1, MALVOLIO TO SIR TOBY BELCH AND SIR ANDREW AGUECHEEK

See also **MISCHIEF**

WILFULNESS

1 Antony . . . that would make his will
   Lord of his reason.
   Antony and Cleopatra 3.13.3–4, ENOBARBUS TO CLEOPATRA

WINTER

2 After summer evermore succeeds
   Barren winter, with his wrathful nipping cold.
   2 Henry VI 2.4.2–3, GLOUCESTER TO HIS SERVANTS

3 A killing frost.
   Henry VIII 3.2.355, WOLSEY

4 Winter's not gone yet, if the wild geese fly that way.
   King Lear 2.2.239–40, FOOL TO LEAR AND KENT

5   When icicles hang by the wall,
           And Dick the shepherd blows his nail,
       And Tom bears logs into the hall,
           And milk comes frozen home in pail,
       When blood is nipped, and ways be foul,
       Then nightly sings the staring owl,
                   Tu-whit;
       Tu-who, a merry note,
       While greasy Joan doth keel the pot.

       When all aloud the wind doth blow,
           And coughing drowns the parson's saw,
       And birds sit brooding in the snow,
           And Marian's nose looks red and raw,
       When roasted crabs hiss in the bowl,
       Then nightly sings the staring owl,
                   Tu-whit;
       Tu-who, a merry note,
       While greasy Joan doth keel the pot.
   Love's Labour's Lost 5.2.905–22, song

1 Sap checked with frost and lusty leaves quite gone,
  Beauty o'er-snowed and bareness everywhere.
  Sonnet 5.7–8

2 What freezings have I felt, what dark days seen,
  What old December's bareness everywhere!
  Sonnet 97.3–4

3 Winter tames man, woman, and beast.
  Taming of the Shrew 4.1.21, GRUMIO TO CURTIS

  See also **COLD; OLD AGE**

WISDOM

4 The fool doth think he is wise, but the wiseman knows himself to be a fool.
  As You Like It 5.1.30–1, TOUCHSTONE TO WILLIAM

5 Wisdom cries out in the streets and no man regards it.
  1 Henry IV 1.2.87–8, PRINCE HAL TO FALSTAFF

6 To that dauntless temper of his mind,
  He hath a wisdom that doth guide his valour
  To act in safety.
  Macbeth 3.1.51–3, MACBETH, of Banquo

7 Young in limbs, in judgement old.
  Merchant of Venice 2.7.71, PRINCE OF MOROCCO, reading from a scroll

WISE SAYINGS

8 Full of wise saws, and modern instances.
  As You Like It 2.7.156, from JAQUES's 'Seven Ages of Man' speech

9 Ill will never said well.
  Henry V 3.7.115, ORLEANS; this is the first in an exchange of maxims between Orleans and the Constable of France, which also includes: 'There is flattery in friendship'; 'Give the devil his due'; and 'A fool's bolt is soon shot'

WISHING

10 Wishers were ever fools.
  Antony and Cleopatra 4.15.38, CLEOPATRA to the dying ANTONY

11 Thy wish was father . . . to that thought.
  2 Henry IV 4.5.92, HENRY TO PRINCE HAL; *more at* **PARENTS AND CHILDREN**

WIT

1 The dullness of the fool is the whetstone of the wits.
As You Like It 1.2.52–3, CELIA TO TOUCHSTONE

2 He uses his folly like a stalking-horse, and under the presentation of that he shoots his wit.
As You Like It 5.4.104–5, DUKE SENIOR TO JAQUES, of Touchstone

3 Since brevity is the soul of wit,
And tediousness the limbs and outward flourishes,
I will be brief.
Hamlet 2.2.90–2, POLONIUS TO GERTRUDE; he is indeed unaccustomedly brief, continuing 'Your noble son is mad.'

4 I am not only witty in myself, but the cause that wit is in other men.
2 Henry IV 1.2.9–10, FALSTAFF TO HIS PAGE

5 Your wit's too hot, it speeds too fast, 'twill tire.
Love's Labour's Lost 2.1.119, BEROWNE TO ROSALINE

6 This is a gift that I have, simple, simple; a foolish extravagant spirit, full of forms, figures, shapes, objects, ideas, apprehensions, motions, revolutions: these are begot in the ventricle of memory, nourished in the womb of pia mater, and delivered upon the mellowing of occasion. But the gift is good in those in whom it is acute, and I am thankful for it.
Love's Labour's Lost 4.2.66–73. HOLOFERNES TO DULL AND NATHANIEL

7 A jest's prosperity lies in the ear
Of him that hears it, never in the tongue
Of him that makes it.
Love's Labour's Lost 5.2.854–6, ROSALINE TO BEROWNE

8 How every fool can play upon the word!
Merchant of Venice 3.5.42, LORENZO TO LAUNCELOT GOBBO

9 They never meet but there's a skirmish of wit between them.
Much Ado About Nothing 1.1.60–1, LEONATO TO A MESSENGER, of Beatrice and Benedick

10 He doth indeed show some sparks that are like wit.
Much Ado About Nothing 2.3.181–2, DON PEDRO TO CLAUDIO, grudgingly, of Benedick

11   Her wit
Values itself so highly that to her
All matter else seems weak.
Much Ado About Nothing 3.1.52–4, HERO TO URSULA, of Beatrice

1 She would . . . press me to death with wit!
Much Ado About Nothing 3.1.75–6, HERO TO URSULA, of Beatrice

2 These are old fond paradoxes to make fools laugh i'th' alehouse.
Othello 2.1.138–9, DESDEMONA TO IAGO AND EMILIA

3 KATHERINA Where did you study all this goodly speech?
PETRUCHIO It is extempore, from my mother-wit.
Taming of the Shrew 2.1.257–8

4 Look, he's winding up the watch of his wit; by and by it will strike.
Tempest 2.1.14–15, SEBASTIAN TO ANTONIO, of Gonzalo

5 It lies as coldly in him as fire in a flint, which will not show without
knocking.
Troilus and Cressida 3.3.254–5, THERSITES TO ACHILLES, of Ajax

WITCHES

6 FIRST WITCH When shall we three meet again?
In thunder, lightning, or in rain?
SECOND WITCH When the hurlyburly's done,
When the battle's lost and won.
THIRD WITCH That will be ere the set of sun.
FIRST WITCH Where the place?
SECOND WITCH   Upon the heath.
THIRD WITCH There to meet with Macbeth.
FIRST WITCH I come, Graymalkin!
SECOND WITCH Paddock calls.
THIRD WITCH Anon!
ALL Fair is foul, and foul is fair:
Hover through the fog and filthy air.
Macbeth 1.1.1–12

7 'Aroynt thee, witch!' the rump-fed ronyon cries.
Macbeth 1.3.6, FIRST WITCH

8 THIRD WITCH A drum! a drum!
Macbeth doth come.
ALL The Weïrd Sisters, hand in hand,
Posters of the sea and land,
Thus do go about, about:
Thrice to thine, and thrice to mine,
And thrice again, to make up nine.
Macbeth 1.3.30–6

1 Each at once her choppy finger laying
 Upon her skinny lips.
 Macbeth 1.3.44–5, BANQUO TO THE WITCHES

2 FIRST WITCH Round about the cauldron go;
 In the poisoned entrails throw. –
 Toad, that under cold stone
 Days and nights has thirty-one
 Sweltered venom, sleeping got,
 Boil thou first i'th' charmed pot.
 ALL Double, double toil and trouble:
 Fire, burn; and, cauldron, bubble.
 SECOND WITCH Fillet of a fenny snake,
 In the cauldron boil and bake;
 Eye of newt, and toe of frog,
 Wool of bat, and tongue of dog,
 Adder's fork, and blind-worm's sting,
 Lizard's leg, and howlet's wing, . . .
 THIRD WITCH Scale of dragon, tooth of wolf;
 Witches' mummy; maw, and gulf,
 Of the ravined salt-sea shark;
 Root of hemlock, digged i'th' dark;
 Liver of blaspheming Jew;
 Gall of goat, and slips of yew,
 Slivered in the moon's eclipse;
 Nose of Turk, and Tartar's lips;
 Finger of birth-strangled babe,
 Ditch-delivered by a drab,
 Make the gruel thick and slab.
 Macbeth 4.1.4–17, 22–32

3 Show his eyes, and grieve his heart;
 Come like shadows, so depart.
 Macbeth 4.1.110–11, WITCHES

 See also **APPARITIONS; GREETINGS; OMENS AND PORTENTS; SUPERNATURAL, the**

WIVES *see* HUSBANDS AND WIVES

WOMEN

4 No more but e'en a woman, and commanded
 By such poor passion as the maid that milks,

And does the meanest chares.
Antony and Cleopatra 4.15.77–9, CLEOPATRA, at the death of Antony

1 A woman is a dish for the gods.
Antony and Cleopatra 5.2.271–2, CLOWN TO CLEOPATRA, continuing, 'if the devil dress her not.'

2 Heavenly Rosalind!
As You Like It 1.2.279, ORLANDO, after his first meeting with her

3 If ladies be but young and fair
They have the gift to know it.
As You Like It 2.7.37–8, JAQUES TO DUKE SENIOR

4 The fair, the chaste, and unexpressive she.
As You Like It 3.2.10, ORLANDO, of Rosalind

5 Do you not know I am a woman? When I think I must speak.
As You Like It 3.2.246–7, ROSALIND TO CELIA

6 Mistress, know yourself. Down on your knees
And thank heaven, fasting, for a good man's love;
For I must tell you friendly in your ear,
Sell when you can, you are not for all markets.
As You Like It 3.5.57–60, ROSALIND TO PHEBE

7 Make the doors upon a woman's wit, and it will out at the casement.
As You Like It 4.1.154–5, ROSALIND TO ORLANDO

8 I know a wench of excellent discourse,
Pretty and witty; wild and yet, too, gentle.
Comedy of Errors 3.1.109–10, ANTIPHOLUS OF EPHESUS recommends to BALTHASAR a woman of easy virtue

9 Who is't can read a woman?
Cymbeline 5.5.48, CYMBELINE, who has been unaware of his wife's true character

10 Frailty, thy name is woman.
Hamlet 1.2.146, HAMLET

11 A poor lone woman.
2 Henry IV 2.1.31, HOSTESS QUICKLY TO FANG, referring to herself

12 You are the weaker vessel, as they say, the emptier vessel.
2 Henry IV 2.4.58–9, HOSTESS QUICKLY TO DOLL TEARSHEET

13 A woman's general; what should we fear?
3 Henry VI 1.2.68, RICHARD, son of Richard of York, to HIS FATHER, of Queen Margaret, who is far more belligerent than King Henry

1 O tiger's heart wrapped in a woman's hide!
   3 Henry VI 1.4.137, RICHARD OF YORK TO QUEEN MARGARET; this line was parodied by
   Robert Greene in a dying attack on Shakespeare, whom he saw as an uneducated
   upstart aping his betters

2 I have a man's mind, but a woman's might.
   Julius Caesar 2.4.8, PORTIA TO LUCIUS

3 How hard it is for women to keep counsel!
   Julius Caesar 2.4.9, PORTIA TO LUCIUS

4 A woman, naturally born to fears.
   King John 2.2.15, CONSTANCE TO SALISBURY, of herself

5 Down from the waist they are centaurs, though women all above. But
   to the girdle do the gods inherit, beneath is all the fiend's: there's hell,
   there's darkness, there is the sulphurous pit, burning, scalding, stench,
   consumption!
   King Lear 4.6.121–5, LEAR TO GLOUCESTER

6 O indistinguished space of woman's will!
   King Lear 4.6.265, EDGAR, of Goneril; 'indistinguished' here means 'limitless', and
   'will', 'lust'

7   Her voice was ever soft,
   Gentle and low, an excellent thing in woman.
   King Lear 5.3.270–1, LEAR, of Cordelia

8 A child of our grandmother Eve, a female; or, for thy more sweet
   understanding, a woman.
   Love's Labour's Lost 1.1.256–7, KING OF NAVARRE, reading a letter from Armado

9 For when would you, my lord, or you, or you,
   Have found the ground of study's excellence
   Without the beauty of a woman's face?
   From women's eyes this doctrine I derive:
   They are the ground, the books, the academes,
   From whence doth spring the true Promethean fire.
   Love's Labour's Lost 4.3.295–300, BEROWNE TO HIS FRIENDS; *see also* **BOOKS**

10 From women's eyes this doctrine I derive:
   They sparkle still the right Promethean fire;
   They are the books, the arts, the academes,
   That show, contain, and nourish all the world.
   Love's Labour's Lost 4.3.346–9, BEROWNE TO HIS FRIENDS, in an alternative version of
   his remark above

1 Look to the Lady!
Macbeth 2.3.117, MACDUFF, as Lady Macbeth collapses after the discovery of Duncan's murder

2 She has brown hair, and speaks small like a woman.
Merry Wives of Windsor 1.1.44–5, SLENDER's description to EVANS of Anne Page

3 She is a region in Guiana, all gold and bounty.
Merry Wives of Windsor 1.3.65–6, FALSTAFF TO PISTOL AND NYM

4 Nature never framed a woman's heart
Of prouder stuff than that of Beatrice.
Much Ado About Nothing 3.1.49–50, HERO TO URSULA

5   A maid
That paragons description and wild fame;
One that excels the quirks of blazoning pens.
Othello 2.1.61–3, CASSIO TO MONTANO, of Desdemona

6   You are pictures out of doors;
Bells in your parlours, wild-cats in your kitchens,
Saints in your injuries, devils being offended,
Players in your housewifery, and housewives in . . .
Your beds!
Othello 2.1.109–113, IAGO to his wife EMILIA

7 To suckle fools, and chronicle small beer.
Othello 2.1.160, IAGO TO DESDEMONA, giving his view of all that a virtuous woman is good for

8 My mother had a maid called Barbary.
Othello 4.3.24, DESDEMONA TO EMILIA

9 Faith, she would serve after a long voyage at sea.
Pericles 4.6.42–3, LYSIMACHUS TO THE BAWD, of Marina

10 My mistress when she walks treads on the ground.
Sonnet 130.12; i.e. she is a real woman, not an idealized figure of the lover's imagination

11 A woman moved is like a fountain troubled,
Muddy, ill-seeming, thick, bereft of beauty.
Taming of the Shrew 5.2.143–4, KATHERINA to assembled HUSBANDS and WIVES

12 Admired Miranda!
Tempest 3.1.37, FERDINAND TO MIRANDA

1   For several virtues
   Have I liked several women.
   Tempest 3.1.42–3, FERDINAND TO MIRANDA; fortunately, he likes her best

2 Thou shalt find she will outstrip all praise.
   Tempest 4.1.10, PROSPERO TO FERDINAND, of Miranda

3 The spinsters and the knitters in the sun.
   Twelfth Night 2.4.44, ORSINO TO VIOLA as Cesario

4   Who is Silvia? What is she
       That all our swains commend her?
       Holy, fair, and wise is she,
       The heaven such grace did lend her,
          That she might admired be.

       Is she kind as she is fair?
       For beauty lives with kindness.
       Love doth to her eyes repair,
       To help him of his blindness;
          And, being helped, inhabits there.

       Then to Silvia let us sing,
       That Silvia is excelling;
       She excels each mortal thing
       Upon the dull earth dwelling.
          To her let us garlands bring.
   Two Gentlemen of Verona 4.2.38–52, song

5 That fortunate bright star, the fair Emilia.
   Two Noble Kinsmen 3.6.146, PALAMON TO THESEUS

6   A lady's Verily's
   As potent as a lord's.
   Winter's Tale 1.2.50–1, HERMIONE TO POLIXENES

7 Women will love her, that she is a woman
   More worth than any man; men, that she is
   The rarest of all women.
   Winter's Tale 5.1.110–12, SERVANT TO PAULINA, of Perdita

See also **HUSBANDS AND WIVES; MARRIAGE; MEN AND WOMEN; VANITY; WOOING**

WOMEN, loose

1 They appear to men like angels of light; light is an effect of fire, and fire
will burn; ergo, light wenches will burn.
Comedy of Errors 4.3.54–6, DROMIO OF SYRACUSE TO ANTIPHOLUS OF SYRACUSE AND A
COURTESAN

2 The harlot's cheek, beautied with plast'ring art.
Hamlet 3.1.51, CLAUDIUS, with an image of his own hypocrisy

3   'Tis the strumpet's plague
To beguile many and be beguiled by one.
Othello 4.1.97–8, IAGO

4 O, these encounterers, so glib of tongue,
That give accosting welcome ere it comes,
And wide unclasp the tables of their thoughts
To every ticklish reader: set them down
For sluttish spoils of opportunity
And daughters of the game.
Troilus and Cressida 4.5.58–63, ULYSSES TO THE GREEK PRINCES, reacting to Cressida

WOOING

5 We cannot fight for love as men may do;
We should be wooed, and were not made to woo.
Midsummer Night's Dream 2.1.241–2, HELENA TO DEMETRIUS

6 Was ever woman in this humour wooed?
Was ever woman in this humour won?
Richard III 1.2.232–3, RICHARD

7 Gentle thou art, and therefore to be won;
Beauteous thou art, therefore to be assailed.
Sonnet 41.5–6

8 She is a woman, therefore may be wooed;
She is a woman, therefore may be won.
Titus Andronicus 1.1.582–3, DEMETRIUS TO AARON, of Lavinia

9   Women are angels, wooing:
Things won are done.
Troilus and Cressida 1.2.286, CRESSIDA TO PANDARUS

10 Whoe'er I woo, myself would be his wife.
Twelfth Night 1.4.42, VIOLA

1 Make me a willow cabin at your gate,
   And call upon my soul within the house;
   Write loyal cantons of contemnèd love,
   And sing them loud even in the dead of night;
   Halloo your name to the reverberate hills,
   And make the babbling gossip of the air
   Cry out 'Olivia!'
   Twelfth Night 1.5.262–8, VIOLA, as Cesario, to OLIVIA, answering the question as to
   what she would do if she loved as Orsino loves

WORDS

2 Not to crack the wind of the poor phrase,
   Running it thus.
   Hamlet 1.3.108–9, POLONIUS TO OPHELIA

3 These are but wild and whirling words.
   Hamlet 1.5.139, HORATIO TO HAMLET

4   This is most brave,
   That I, the son of a dear father murdered,
   Prompted to my revenge by heaven and hell,
   Must like a whore unpack my heart with words
   And fall a-cursing like a very drab.
   Hamlet 2.2.584–8, HAMLET

5 Why should she live to fill the world with words?
   3 Henry VI 5.5.43, RICHARD OF GLOUCESTER TO EDWARD IV, urging the death of the
   termagant Queen Margaret

6 Words are no deeds.
   Henry VIII 3.2.154, HENRY TO CARDINAL WOLSEY

7 CASSIUS Did Cicero say anything?
   CASCA Ay, he spoke Greek.
   CASSIUS To what effect?
   CASCA Nay, and I tell you that, I'll ne'er look you i'th' face again. But
   those that understood him smiled at one another, and shook their
   heads; but for mine own part, it was Greek to me.
   Julius Caesar 1.2.274–80

8 A man of fire-new words.
   Love's Labour's Lost 1.1.176, BEROWNE TO THE KING OF NAVARRE, of Armado

9 In the posteriors of this day, which the rude multitude call the
   afternoon.
   Love's Labour's Lost 5.1.83–5, ARMADO TO HOLOFERNES

1 Taffeta phrases, silken terms precise,
Three-piled hyperboles, spruce affection,
Figures pedantical.
Love's Labour's Lost 5.2.406–8, BEROWNE TO HIS FRIENDS, renouncing rhetoric

2 Out idle words, servants to shallow fools,
Unprofitable sounds, weak arbitrators!
Busy yourselves in skill-contending schools,
Debate where leisure serves with dull debaters.
Lucrece 1016–19

3 Whereat with blade, with bloody blameful blade,
He bravely broached his boiling bloody breast.
Midsummer Night's Dream 5.1.145–6, PETER QUINCE as the Prologue; Shakespeare
makes fun of less talented contemporary dramatists

4 Shall quips and sentences and these paper bullets of the brain awe a
man from the career of his humour?
Much Ado About Nothing 2.3.230–2, BENEDICK

5 How long a time lies in one little word!
Richard II 1.3.213, BOLINGBROKE TO RICHARD, who has just reduced the term of his
banishment

6 Where words are scarce they are seldom spent in vain.
Richard II 2.1.7, JOHN OF GAUNT, on his deathbed, to YORK

7   Though what they will impart
Help nothing else, yet do they ease the heart.
Richard III 4.4.129–30, QUEEN ELIZABETH TO THE DUCHESS OF YORK

8 You taught me language; and my profit on't
Is, I know how to curse.
Tempest 1.2.365–6, CALIBAN TO PROSPERO

9 Words pay no debts.
Troilus and Cressida 3.2.53, PANDARUS TO TROILUS

10 Words, words, mere words, no matter from the heart.
Troilus and Cressida 5.3.108, TROILUS TO PANDARUS

11 Who you are and what you would are out of my welkin. I might say
'element', but the word is overworn.
Twelfth Night 3.1.57–8, FESTE TO VIOLA

See also **BOOKS; CRITICISM; NAMES; TALK; WRITING**

WORK

1 To business that we love we rise betime
   And go to't with delight.
   Antony and Cleopatra 4.4.20–1, ANTONY TO A SOLDIER

2 Thou art not for the fashion of these times,
   Where none will sweat but for promotion.
   As You Like It 2.3.59–60, ORLANDO to the faithful retainer ADAM

3 Why such impress of shipwrights, whose sore task
   Does not divide the Sunday from the week . . .
                     This sweaty haste
   Doth make the night joint-labourer with the day.
   Hamlet 1.1.78–81, MARCELLUS TO HORATIO

4 That which ordinary men are fit for I am qualified in, and the best of
   me is diligence.
   King Lear 1.4.34–5, KENT, disguised, to LEAR

5 If it be man's work, I'll do it.
   King Lear 5.3.40, CAPTAIN TO EDMUND (agreeing to murder Cordelia)

6 The labour we delight in physics pain.
   Macbeth 2.3.50, MACBETH TO MACDUFF, discussing the work involved in playing host
   to a king

7 Weary with toil, I haste me to my bed
   Sonnet 27.1

8   My nature is subdued
   To what it works in, like the dyer's hand.
   Sonnet 111.6–7

   See also **BUSINESS; EXPERIENCE**

WORKING PEOPLE

9 Sir, I am a true labourer: I earn that I eat, get that I wear; owe no man
   hate, envy no man's happiness; glad of other men's good, content with
   my harm.
   As You Like It 3.2.70–3, CORIN TO TOUCHSTONE

10 There is no ancient gentlemen but gardeners, ditchers, and grave-
   makers – they hold up Adam's profession.
   Hamlet 5.1.29–31, GRAVEDIGGER TO HIS MATE

1 You that have worn your eyes almost out in the service, you will be considered.
Measure for Measure 1.2.109–11, POMPEY TO MISTRESS OVERDONE; her trade is brothel-keeping

2 Hard-handed men that work in Athens here,
Which never laboured in their minds till now.
Midsummer Night's Dream 5.1.72–3, PHILOSTRATE's description to THESEUS of Peter Quince and his cast

WORLD, the

3 O how full of briars is this working-day world!
As You Like It 1.3.11–12, ROSALIND TO CELIA

4 'Thus we may see', quoth he, 'how the world wags.'
As You Like It 2.7.23, JAQUES TO DUKE SENIOR; *more at* **TIME**

5 This wide and universal theatre
Presents more woeful pageants than the scene
Wherein we play in.
As You Like It 2.7.137–9, DUKE SENIOR TO ORLANDO, immediately before Jaques's 'Seven Ages of Man' speech, for which *see* **LIFE**

6   O God! God!
How weary, stale, flat, and unprofitable
Seem to me all the uses of this world!
Fie on't, ah fie, 'tis an unweeded garden
That grows to seed; things rank and gross in nature
Possess it merely.
Hamlet 1.2.132–7, HAMLET

7 Mad world! mad kings! mad composition!
King John 2.1.561, PHILIP THE BASTARD

8 There's nothing in this world can make me joy:
Life is as tedious as a twice-told tale
Vexing the dull ear of a drowsy man.
King John 3.3.107–9, LEWIS, DAUPHIN, TO PHILIP, KING OF FRANCE

9 I am amazed, methinks and lose my way
Among the thorns and dangers of this world.
King John 4.3.140–1, PHILIP THE BASTARD TO HUBERT

10 This earthly world, where, to do harm
Is often laudable; to do good, sometime
Accounted dangerous folly.
Macbeth 4.2.74–6, LADY MACDUFF

1 GRATIANO You have too much respect upon the world:
They lose it that do buy it with much care . . .
ANTONIO I hold the world but as the world Gratiano,
A stage, where every man must play a part,
And mine a sad one.
Merchant of Venice 1.1.74–5, 77–9

2 O wicked, wicked world.
Merry Wives of Windsor 2.1.18–19, MISTRESS PAGE

3 The world's mine oyster.
Merry Wives of Windsor 2.2.2, PISTOL TO FALSTAFF, continuing, 'which I with sword
will open.'

4 This world to me is as a lasting storm.
Pericles 4.1.19, MARINA

5 Comfort's in heaven, and we are on the earth,
Where nothing lives but crosses, cares, and grief.
Richard II 2.2.78–9, YORK TO QUEEN ISABEL

6 The world is not thy friend, nor the world's law;
The world affords no law to make thee rich.
Romeo and Juliet 5.1.72–3, ROMEO TO THE APOTHECARY

7 POET   How goes the world?
PAINTER It wears, sir, as it grows.
Timon of Athens 1.1.2–3

8 I am sick of this false world.
Timon of Athens 4.3.378, TIMON TO APEMANTUS

9 This world's a city full of straying streets,
And death's the market-place where each one meets.
Two Noble Kinsmen 1.5.15–16, THIRD QUEEN TO TWO OTHERS

See also **ADVERSITY; LIFE; PLAYS, PLAYERS AND PLAYHOUSES**

WORLDLINESS

10 A serving-man, proud in heart and mind, that curled my hair, wore
gloves in my cap, served the lust of my mistress' heart and did the act
of darkness with her; swore as many oaths as I spake words and broke
them in the sweet face of heaven. One that slept in the contriving of
lust and waked to do it. Wine loved I deeply, dice dearly; and, in
woman, out-paramoured the Turk: false of heart, light of ear, bloody

of hand; hog in sloth, fox in stealth, wolf in greediness, dog in madness,
lion in prey.

King Lear 3.4.84–93, EDGAR, disguised as Poor Tom, in answer to LEAR's question
'What hast thou been?'

1 Alas, 'tis true, I have gone here and there,
And made myself a motley to the view,
Gored mine own thoughts, sold cheap what is most dear,
Made old offences of affections new.
Most true it is that I have looked on truth
Askance and strangely.
Sonnet 110.1–6

See also **COURTIERS**

WORST, the

2   To be worst.
The lowest and most dejected thing of fortune,
Stands still in esperance, lives not in fear.
The lamentable change is from the best,
The worst returns to laughter.
King Lear 4.1.2–6, EDGAR

3 O gods! Who is't can say 'I am at the worst'?
King Lear 4.1.27, EDGAR

4   The worst is not
So long as we can say 'This is the worst.'
King Lear 4.1.29–30, EDGAR

5 To fear the worst oft cures the worse.
Troilus and Cressida 3.2.70, CRESSIDA TO TROILUS

WORTH

6 GONERIL I have been worth the whistling.
ALBANY You are not worth the dust which the rude wind
Blows in your face.
King Lear 4.2.30–2

7 Things of like value, differing in the owners,
Are prized by their masters. Believe't, dear lord,
You mend the jewel by the wearing it.
Timon of Athens 1.1.173–5

8 Distinction, with a broad and powerful fan
Puffing at all, winnows the light away,

And what hath mass or matter by itself
Lies rich in virtue and unmingled.
Troilus and Cressida 1.3.27–30, AGAMEMNON TO THE GREEK PRINCES

1   To her own worth
She shall be prized.
Troilus and Cressida 4.4.131–2, DIOMEDES, speaking with some irony, to TROILUS

See also **VALUE**

WORTHLESS PEOPLE

2 A barren-spirited fellow; one that feeds
On objects, arts, and imitations,
Which, out of use and staled by other men,
Begin his fashion.
Julius Caesar 4.1.36–9, MARK ANTONY TO OCTAVIUS, of Lepidus

WOUNDS

3 'Tis not so deep as a well, nor so wide as a church door, but 'tis enough,
'twill serve. Ask for me tomorrow and you shall find me a grave man.
Romeo and Juliet 3.1.97–9, MERCUTIO TO ROMEO, on his death wound

WRITING

4 I once did hold it, as our statists do,
A baseness to write fair, and laboured much
How to forget that learning, but, sir, now
It did me yeoman's service.
Hamlet 5.2.33–6, HAMLET TO HORATIO

5 Devise, wit; write pen, for I am for whole volumes in folio.
Love's Labour's Lost 1.2.178–9, ARMADO

6 Ware pencils, ho!
Love's Labour's Lost 5.2.43, ROSALINE TO HER FRIENDS

7 O let my books be then the eloquence
And dumb presagers of my speaking breast.
Sonnet 23.9–10

8 Let there be gall enough in thy ink, though thou write with a goose-
pen.
Twelfth Night 3.2.47–9, SIR TOBY BELCH TO SIR ANDREW AGUECHEEK, who proposes to
write a challenge.

See also **BOOKS; LETTERS; POETRY; POETS; WORDS**

WRONGS

1 Think'st thou it honourable for a noble man
   Still to remember wrongs?
   Coriolanus 5.3.156–7, VOLUMNIA to her son CORIOLANUS

 Y

YOUTH

2   My salad days,
   When I was green in judgement.
   Antony and Cleopatra 1.5.76–7, CLEOPATRA TO CHARMIAN

3   He wears the rose
   Of youth upon him.
   Antony and Cleopatra 3.13.20–1, ANTONY TO CLEOPATRA, of Octavius Caesar

4   Briefly die their joys
   That place them on the truth of girls and boys.
   Cymbeline 5.5.106–7, LUCIUS TO IMOGEN

5 For Hamlet, and the trifling of his favour,
   Hold it a fashion and a toy in blood,
   A violet in the youth of primy nature.
   Hamlet 1.3.5–7, LAERTES' warning to OPHELIA

6 The canker galls the infants of the spring
   Too oft before their buttons be disclosed,
   And in the morn and liquid dew of youth
   Contagious blastments are most imminent.
   Hamlet 1.3.39–42, LAERTES, from the same speech

7 Youth to itself rebels, though none else near.
   Hamlet 1.3.44, LAERTES again

8 You speak like a green girl.
   Hamlet 1.3.101, POLONIUS TO OPHELIA

9 A very ribbon in the cap of youth.
   Hamlet 4.7.77, CLAUDIUS, of Laertes

1 Though the camomile, the more it is trodden on the faster it grows, yet youth, the more it is wasted the sooner it wears.
   1 Henry IV 2.4.396–8, FALSTAFF TO HOSTESS QUICKLY AND PRINCE HAL

2 As full of spirit as the month of May,
   And gorgeous as the sun at midsummer.
   1 Henry IV 4.1.101–2, VERNON TO HOTSPUR, describing Prince Hal and his companions in arms

3 What! A young knave, and begging! Is there not wars? Is there not employment? Doth not the King lack subjects? Do not the rebels need soldiers?
   2 Henry IV 1.2.72–4, FALSTAFF putting down the LORD CHIEF JUSTICE

4 A man can no more separate age and covetousness than a can part young limbs and lechery.
   2 Henry IV 1.2.228–30, FALSTAFF TO THE LORD CHIEF JUSTICE

5 In the very May-morn of his youth,
   Ripe for exploits.
   Henry V 1.2.120–1, BISHOP OF ELY TO HENRY, of Henry himself (in the third person)

6 How green you are and fresh in this old world!
   King John 3.3.145, CARDINAL PANDULPH TO LEWIS, DAUPHIN OF FRANCE

7 LEAR So young and so untender?
   CORDELIA So young, my lord, and true.
   King Lear 1.1.107–8

8 The younger rises when the old doth fall.
   King Lear 3.3.25, EDMUND

9 The oldest hath borne most; we that are young
   Shall never see so much, nor live so long.
   King Lear 5.3.324–5, EDGAR

10 Why should a man whose blood is warm within,
   Sit like his grandsire, cut in alabaster?
   Merchant of Venice 1.1.83–4, GRATIANO TO ANTONIO

11 I never knew so young a body with so old a head.
   Merchant of Venice 4.1.161–2, DUKE OF VENICE, reading a letter describing Portia as a supposed young (male) lawyer; *see also* **WISDOM**

1   A youth,
A kind of boy, a little scrubbed boy,
No higher than thyself.
Merchant of Venice 5.1.161–3, GRATIANO TO NERISSA (Nerissa, in disguise, was herself the boy)

2 In the holiday-time of my beauty.
Merry Wives of Windsor 2.1.1–2, MISTRESS PAGE, of her youth

3 He capers, he dances, he has eyes of youth; he writes verses, he speaks holiday, he smells April and May.
Merry Wives of Windsor 3.2.61–3, HOST OF THE GARTER TO CAIUS AND PAGE, of Fenton

4 These lisping hawthorn-buds that come like women in men's apparel, and smell like Bucklersbury in simple time.
Merry Wives of Windsor 3.3.68–70, FALSTAFF wooing MISTRESS FORD; 'simples' are herbs

5 So wise so young, they say, do never live long.
Richard III 3.1.79, RICHARD, aside, villainously, referring to his nephew Prince Edward

6   Young men's love then lies
Not truly in their hearts but in their eyes.
Romeo and Juliet 2.3.63–4, FRIAR LAURENCE TO ROMEO

7 Not yet old enough for a man, nor young enough for a boy: as a squash is before 'tis a peascod, or a codling when 'tis almost an apple. 'Tis with him in standing water, between boy and man.
Twelfth Night 1.5.153–6, MALVOLIO TO OLIVIA, describing Viola disguised as Cesario

8   Then come kiss me, sweet and twenty:
        Youth's a stuff will not endure.
Twelfth Night 2.3.51–2, FESTE's song; *more at* **LOVE**

9 Young, and so unkind!
Venus and Adonis 187, VENUS, of Adonis

10 Would there were no age between ten and three-and-twenty, or that youth would sleep out the rest; for there is nothing in the between but getting wenches with child, wronging the ancientry, stealing, fighting.
Winter's Tale 3.3.59–63, SHEPHERD

See also **CHILDHOOD; EXPERIENCE; GIRLS; LOVE; OLD AGE**

❧ Life of Shakespeare ❧

William Shakespeare was christened on 26 April 1564 in Stratford-upon-Avon, in the centre of England. The exact date of his birth is unknown, but is conventionally assumed to be 23 April, St George's Day, which was also the day of his death, fifty-two years later, in 1616. His father, John Shakespeare, was a tradesman – first a glover and later a wool-merchant – and also, possibly, a covert Catholic; and his mother Mary Arden, from slightly higher up the social scale, was the daughter of a yeoman farmer. By the end of his life, after a very successful career as actor, 'sharer' (part-owner) in an acting company, and playwright, he had retired back to Stratford, where he had bought the second largest house in the town and some farming land. The scale of his success was all the more remarkable in comparison with the fate of a number of his contemporary playwrights, of whom several, after initial fame and success, died in poverty, and at least one, Christopher Marlowe, in suspicious circumstances. Shakespeare seems to have been competent at handling practical affairs and business relationships, as well as being an extremely successful playwright. He also had the good fortune to have the qualities which enabled him to become a playwright at a moment when English society, the English language and the theatre were in a ferment of creation, growth and change.

Popular wisdom has it that we know almost nothing about Shakespeare except that there is no proof that he wrote the plays to which his name is attached. Neither of these beliefs is in fact true. We now know more about the outline of his life than might normally be expected for someone from his time, although much of what we know relates, inevitably, to the kind of transaction that is noted in official records, which tends to give a dry, legalistic feel to the story. At the age of eighteen, on 28 November 1582, he married Anne Hathaway, eight years his senior. Their daughter Susanna was born on 26 May 1583, and on 2 February 1585 their twins Hamnet and Judith followed; Hamnet died at the age of eleven, though both daughters survived to adulthood and married. Anne Hathaway died in 1623, shortly before the publication of the First Folio, the collected edition of Shakespeare's plays published in honour of his memory.

History is tantalizingly silent as to how Shakespeare entered the theatrical world. The first reference to a play which is probably his is to 'harey the vj' (probably *1 Henry VI*), which was performed by Lord Strange's Men at the Rose playhouse on 3 March 1592. By this point Shakespeare was evidently established in London as an actor and playwright, and references begin to appear both in the writings of contemporaries and in Court records, where in 1594 are noted payments to him as a sharer in the newly formed players' company, the Lord Chamberlain's Men. This company played first at the Theatre in Finsbury, then, from 1599, at the newly built Globe in Southwark, to which they added, in 1608, winter quarters at the private indoor theatre at Blackfriars, where they continued to play during the rebuilding of the Globe after it burned down in 1613. They became the most successful company of their day, thanks both to their leading playwright and to their actors. Chief amongst these was Richard Burbage, co-sharer with his father James in the company, the creator of many of Shakespeare's greatest roles, and evidently a compelling performer. Shakespeare himself seems to have continued to take part as an actor, though perhaps only in minor roles – traditionally the Ghost in *Hamlet* and old Adam in *As You Like It*. His main tasks would have been to write, either single-handedly or in collaboration, and probably to some extent to direct the actors. After a twenty-year career with the company, interrupted only when the theatres were closed as a measure against plague, and including collaboration on three plays with his successor as house playwright, John Fletcher, Shakespeare retired to Stratford, where he lived till his death.

What we do not know, at least for certain, about Shakespeare's life, includes questions such as where he was educated, how he was occupied in the 'lost years' of his early adulthood, and the identities of the man to whom he dedicated his sonnets and the woman to whom he may have addressed the latter part of them. These have provided endless matter for speculation, and inspired assiduous search for evidence from within his work and outside it.

William would almost certainly have been educated at the King's Free Grammar School at Stratford-upon-Avon, and what he would have learned there would have had a crucial bearing upon his work as a playwright. His education would have included the study of the major Latin authors from Roman times, of Christian works such as the Catechism, of grammar, and of the works – in Latin – of the early sixteenth-century scholar Erasmus, who taught Christian principles and the arts of rhetoric and embellishment. A grammar-school boy would have spent many hours construing, translating and enlarging upon the works of the great authors, writing compositions on themes, and ultimately composing formal orations, all in Latin. Many of the proverbial sayings and wise *sententiae* which appear through his work would have been acquired in this way, and so would the techniques of working from and embellishing source material. Almost all his plays were based on earlier sources – classical texts, English chronicles, English or continental prose romances and plays in Latin, Italian or English – which they often followed very closely. The art he learned at school was to make them his own.

There is no similar probability about how he spent the years between 1585 and the early 1590s when he surfaced in London. We have no substantial evidence as to where he was or what he was doing. Possibilities include working as a schoolmaster or tutor in a well-to-do family, where he may have taken part in private theatricals; or, as some suggest because of the frequent references in his plays to the law, as a lawyer's clerk; or he may have remained in Stratford.

The identity of 'Mr W.H.', the dedicatee of his sonnets, is not certain, but the chief candidates are Henry Wriothesley, Earl of Southampton, and William Herbert, Earl of Pembroke; somebody, at any rate, who would have been an invaluable patron at times when the theatres were closed, but who also appears to have been admired by Shakespeare and to have become a close friend. Who the 'dark lady' addressed in the later sonnets may have been is completely open to speculation (if, indeed, she is more than a composite or fictional figure). There is no firm evidence of any kind. She is, at any rate, represented as compelling – unconventionally beautiful, strong-minded, unfaithful, and the source of both bitterness and self-knowledge in the poet. The intense pain and lack of distance of the later sonnets, and many moments in the plays which are reminiscent of them, suggest a major figure in Shakespeare's life.

With the probable exception of an addition of 147 lines to the *Book of Sir Thomas More*, no dramatic manuscript in Shakespeare's hand is known to have survived. Plays appeared in print after performance (sometimes long after) in quarto format (pocket-sized); nearly half of his plays survive in Quarto and the earliest of these Quartos, published between 1594 and 1597, named no author, as was usual. The remaining Quartos, published from 1598 to 1622, did name Shakespeare as author, attesting to his growing reputation. After his death his plays were collected, as a commercial venture and as a memorial, in a single large-format volume, the First Folio. In some cases the differences between Quarto and Folio versions are quite considerable, suggesting perhaps revision for later performance, impecunious printers, or changes made by publishers' editors in one version or another. Until the late eighteenth century, however, Shakespeare's authorship of the plays attributed to him was not questioned, and it was only at this later date, when he was elevated by the Romantic age to the role of genius, that social and intellectual snobbery led to the suggestion that without a university education and courtly experience he could not have written them.

Ironically, the very fact that he had been so successful without a university education had been noted, with jealousy or with admiration, by his contemporaries. The envious Robert Greene, Master of Arts of both Oxford and Cambridge, who died in poverty, described him as 'an upstart Crow, beautified with our feathers, that with his *Tiger's heart wrapped in a Player's hide* [see p. 310], supposes he is as well able to bombast out a blank verse as the best of you'. Ben Jonson, also someone without the benefit of a university education, but who valued classical knowledge highly, said that Shakespeare had 'small Latin and less Greek' (which he meant as a compliment to his achievement), and remarked that 'the Players have often mentioned it as an honour to Shakespeare that in his writing, whatsoever he penned, he never blotted out line' (which he didn't). What is apparent, however, from the quite numerous contemporary references, was that he was a man of breadth – who was much envied, much admired, and much loved. Jonson suggested that 'He was not of an age, but for all time'; and many others since then from other times and other cultures have agreed.

❧ Glossary ❧

Abbreviations
(?)	possible meaning
adj.	adjective
adv.	adverb
cf.	compare
esp.	especially
Fr.	French
Gr.	Greek
Ital.	Italian
Lat.	Latin
prep.	preposition
sb.	substantive
v.	verb

'a, a he
abhor reject
abroad on the move; apart
absolute perfect, complete, without limitation; determined
abuse *sb.* deception; *v.* deceive
accident incident
achieve win
Adam fallen man, wickedness
adamant exceedingly hard metal; magnet
admiral flagship
admire wonder
advantage *sb.* addition; interest; *v.* help, benefit
Aeneas Trojan prince who carried his father, Anchises, out of burning Troy and became the lover of Dido before abandoning her to found the Roman state
affect *sb.* passion, appetite; affection; *v.* admire, have affection for, favour; impersonate, put on
affection feeling, disposition, propensity; passion; affectation
after in the manner of
again back, reciprocally
agate jewel sometimes carved with a small figure
aidance help
aim conjecture, idea

Ajax Greek hero in the Trojan war
alter exchange
amain aloud; at speed
an *see* **and**
ancient standard-bearer
and if
angel spirit
anon in a moment
Anthropophagi cannibals
antic *sb.* grotesque figure, fool; *adj.* in grotesque disguise, masked
antre cave
Apollo god of song and music, of the sun, of healing and of the oracle at Delphi; he fell in love with Daphne who was transformed into a laurel as he chased her
appliance treatment
apprehensive possessing reason
approve prove; put to proof
apt ready, inclined; probable, likely
aqua-vitae strong spirits
Arabian bird the phoenix, a mythical bird supposed to be unique
arbitrement arbitration, decision
argument theme, subject of controversy; proof, demonstration
Arion poet who charmed a dolphin into carrying him over the waves
arm-gaunt lean from bearing arms
aroynt thee be off with you
Ate goddess of confusion and strife
aught anything
avoid leave, begone

back saddle or ride (a horse)
ban *sb.* curse; *v.* curse
Banbury cheese proverbially thin cheese
bank shore
banquet light refreshment
Barbary breed of horse
bark ship
base-court lower courtyard
bastinado cudgelling, hefty wallop
bated let off

bawd pimp
bay chase with barking
beached of the beach
beadle parish constable
beaver helmet's visor
beck *sb.* beckoning; *v.* beckon
become be appropriate for, suit
bedlam insane
bend turn
bent limit, disposition
beteem grant, allow
bide endure
bite the thumb make an insulting gesture
blastment blight
blazon *sb.* coat of arms; proclamation; description; *v.* proclaim; describe
blind-worm slow-worm
block mould for shaping a hat; mounting-block (for mounting horses)
blood character, disposition; appetite, passion
blow swell; (of plants) blossom
bodkin short dagger; hair-pin
bolt arrow
bolting-hutch sifting-bin
bombard wine vessel
bones rustic musical instrument accompanied by bells or tongs
boot *sb.* booty; advantage, help; *v.* help
borrowed taken, feigned, not genuine
bots maggot infection in horses
bottom ship's hold, ship
bounce bang
bourn limit; burn, brook
boy endow with the characteristics of a boy
brach bitch-hound
brave fine, admirable; fearless, insolent
brinded patterned with streaks
broach pierce
broken fragmented
Bucklersbury London street known for its apothecaries
buff hard-wearing leather worn by constables
burgonet close-fitting helmet
burn heat up; light up; **burn daylight** = waste time
burthen burden; refrain (of song)
by and by immediately; in due course

cabin hut
Cain son of Adam and Eve, who murdered his brother Abel

candied frosted, as if with sugar
canker sore; wild rose; parasitic caterpillar
canon Church law, *hence* law, edict
canton song
capable responsive, appreciative; capacious; qualified to inherit
Capitol temple of Jupiter in Rome
carcanet jewelled necklace
card, by the correctly
carriage carrying; ability to carry
carry-tale spy
carve *v.* compliment; **carve for oneself** = be independent
case question; body, skin or clothes; **in case** = in a position or mood
cashiered discarded
cast vomit; discharge
caterpillar parasite
censure judgement; opinion
centre the earth's mid-point
century one hundred
cess ceasing, decease
chaps chops, jaws
character write
charactery writing
chare chore
chase hunt
cheapen bargain for
check rebuke
cherubin cherub
childe title used by young nobles aspiring to knighthood
childing generative, fertile
choler one of the four humours (*see* **humour**); anger
chough jackdaw
civet perfume derived from a civet cat's anal glands
civil of citizens, urban; well-behaved
clip encircle, embrace
close *sb.* encounter; (in music) cadence; *adj.* secret; secretive
cloth-of-gold sumptuous, top-quality cloth
clown person from the country
cock rowing boat towed behind a larger ship; weathercock
cockatrice legendary creature with a fatal stare
cockle cockleshell; weed; **cockle hat** = pilgrim's hat
cod husk
coil commotion, fuss
collied darkened

colour *sb.* appearance; pretext; sort, type; *v.* disguise
commeddled mingled
commodity supply of merchandise
complain bewail
complexion constitution, nature; face
compt account, reckoning; the Day of Judgement
con study, memorize
conclusion experiment
condition disposition; compact, contract
condolement grieving
conscience matter of conscience; mind, thoughts
consign subscribe, endorse
continent container, vessel
conversation social conduct
converse associate, be in company (with)
convert change
cope encounter; have dealings
Corinthian one from Corinth, ancient city known for its licentiousness and partying
corporal of the body, physical
correctioner one from the 'House of Correction'
costard large apple; the head
cote *sb.* cottage; *v.* overtake
couch lie hidden
counsel secrets
countenance face, outward appearance, demeanour; approval, patronage
countervail counterbalance, be equal to
course sail of a ship
cousin any near relation
coz cousin (*see* **cousin**)
cozen cheat
crab crab apple
crank *sb.* winding passage; *v.* twist and turn
cressets fire-baskets, beacons
cross-gartered wearing garters above and below the knee (and so crossed behind)
crow-flower the ragged robin flower
crown imperial the fritillary plant
crudy thick
crupper strap fixing the saddle to the horse's back end
cry *sb.* barking pack of hounds; rumour; *v.* proclaim
cunning skilful; ingenious
Cupid son of Venus, a winged boy, sometimes thought of as blind, whose arrows caused people to fall in (and out of) love
curious elaborate
cushes thigh-armour
cypress cypress wood; crape, linen
Cytherea the goddess Venus

dainty particular, finicky
dam mother
darkling in the dark
date fixed term or limit
dear important; intense, ardent
debate contend about
deboshed debauched
deed performance, doing
deep-fet fetched from deep down
deer animals
demi-cannon large gun
derogate degenerate, debased
design purpose, enterprise
dial clock; sundial
Diana goddess of chastity, hunting and the moon
diet prescribed course; food
difference distinguishing mark in heraldry
Dis Pluto, god of the underworld
disable disparage
disaster sign of ill-omen, as seen in the stars
discandy melt, thaw
discourse *sb.* talk, conversation; process or faculty of reasoning; *v.* talk
discovery revelation
diseased made uneasy, troubled
dispark put (parkland) to other uses
distance (in fencing) correct space between the opponents
distaste make distasteful
distract *adj.* deranged, confused; *v.* divide; confuse
distressful gained by misery and toil
divers several, various, different;
division musical notes that elaborate upon a basic melody; military arrangement
doctrine lesson
dogged dog-like, cruel
dole grief; share; **happy man be his dole** = may his lot be that of a happy man (*i.e.* good luck to him)
doom *sb.* judgement; day of judgement; *v.* judge, sentence
doublet and hose vest and breeches (basic Elizabethan male dress)

doubt *sb.* suspicion; fear; *v.* suspect; fear

doxy female beggar

drab strumpet

draw drain

drawer tapster, waiter

dress adorn

ducat gold coin

eager sharp, bitter

easy easily won over; small; light

ecstasy deranged mental state; unconsciousness

eld old age; people of a previous time

element one of the four universal substances (earth, water, air, fire)

elf fairy, spirit

elf-locks hair tangled or matted together

Elysium abode of the virtuous after death in the ancient world

elm tree used to train vines

eminence superiority, high rank

emulation envious rivalry

engine plot, device; instrument; military machine

enginer contriver, plotter, creator; maker of military works or machines

engross fatten; amass, gather; monopolize

enskied placed in heaven

enseamed greasy

entertain employ; maintain

entertainment treatment; employment

envy malice, spite

Ercles Hercules

Erebus place of darkness on the way to the underworld

ergo therefore (*Lat.*)

event outcome

ever always; **not ever** = not always

exempt separated, far away

exercise devotional exercise

exhalation meteor, falling star

expectancy expectation, hope

expense expenditure

express *adj.* well formed, well executed; *v.* show forth, make known

extemporal extempore

extenuate mitigate, weaken the force of

extravagant straying beyond its proper bounds, vagrant

faculty power; quality, nature

fain gladly

fall *sb.* cadence in music; *v.* let fall, bring

down; befall; happen, turn out; waste away; **fall off** = revolt

fame public image or opinion

familiar *sb.* close friend; *adj.* native, accustomed

fan sift (*e.g.* grain) by means of an air current

fancy love

fancy-free free from love

fangled pretentiously fashionable

fantastic *sb.* person given to flights of fancy; fop, gallant; *adj.* of the mind; given to or produced by extravagant flights of fancy, crazy

fantastical *see* **fantastic** (*adj.*)

fantasy imagination; imagining, fancy; self-delusion

farced stuffed

fardel pack

fashions farcy, a disease in horses

fat stuffy; (?) sweating

fault sin; misfortune

favour appearance, face, feature; charm; token of good will

feature appearance of the body

fell terrible, savage

fico fig (*Ital.*); contemptuous exclamation; obscene gesture sometimes called the 'fig of Spain'

figure numeral or letter; esoteric diagram; rhetorical device; imagining

film gossamer

find find out

fine *sb.* end; *adj.* refined

fire-new brand-new, as if fresh from the forge

firstling first offspring

fit be appropriate (for)

fives avives, a disease in horses

flaw fragment; gust or blast of wind; outburst

fleckled spotted, blotchy

flesh (in hunting) awaken an appetite for bloodshed

flourish fanfare; decoration

flower-de-luce *fleur-de-lis* (iris), French heraldic device also used later by English kings

flush ripe, full of vigour

flushing redness caused by weeping

foil defeat, overthrow

foin thrust or parry with a sword

fond foolish

fool jester

for for lack of; for fear of
fordo ruin, destroy
fordone tired out
fork snake's tongue; arrow's head; leg or legs (where the body forks)
forked barbed; horned, cuckolded (*cf.* **horn**)
formal conventional, regular
frame *sb.* systematic form; design; *v.* form, contrive, execute
fraught laden
fresh freshwater spring
fret adorn, ornament
friend family member; lover
front forehead, face
fumiter the fumitory plant, a weed
fury transcendental state; poetic inspiration
fust become musty
fustian *sb.* coarse cloth; nonsense; *adj.* bombastic, highflown

gaberdine cloak
gage pledge, engage, bind
gall suffering; indignation
gallow scare
garland crown; hero
garnish clothe, decorate
generous of noble birth
genius spirit, especially a person's guardian spirit
gentle *sb.* gentleman or gentlewoman; *adj.* noble, well bred
germen seed
get beget, sire
ghost corpse
gillyvors gillyflowers
glass mirror
globe name of Shakespeare's theatre
gloss attractive external appearance
goodly handsome
gossip godparent; merry, talkative woman
government self-discipline, self-control
grained ingrained
groundlings theatregoers who stood in front of the stage

habit clothing, garments; bearing, disposition
habited dressed
halcyon kingfisher; **halcyon's days** = period of calm
half-cheeked (of a horse's bit) giving insufficient control

halloo call, shout
handsaw small saw; (?) heron
handy-dandy take your choice (from a children's game)
haply by chance
harbinger one who runs on ahead
hardness difficulty
havoc signal for indiscriminate slaughter
hay (in fencing) thrust reaching the antagonist
hazard *sb.* dice game; risk; stake; *v.* risk
head headland, promontory
headstall part of the bridle that fits round the head
heavy serious, grievous, sad; tiresome
Hecate goddess of witchcraft
Hector Trojan hero
Hecuba Queen of Troy
hedge-pig hedgehog
hent reach
herb of grace rue
Hercules legendary hero, supposedly a kinsman of Theseus
Herod biblical tyrant
Hiems Winter
high-day exclamation of joy
hint occasion, opportunity
hipped having a dislocated hip-bone
hit agree
hoar mouldy; whitish
home thoroughly
honest worthy, decent; truthful; chaste
honesty uprightness, decency; chastity; generosity
horn deer; sign of a cuckold
hose breeches
housewife hussy, prostitute
howlet owlet or owl
hugger-mugger secrecy
humorous temperamental, capricious, whimsical (*see* **humour**)
humour one of the four physiological 'elements' (melancholy, blood, choler, phlegm) governing disposition, *hence* temperament, mood, inclination
hurricano waterspout
husband cultivate, manage
husbandry management (*cf.* **husband**), thrift; farming, cultivation
hyperbole figure of speech used for exaggeration
Hyperion Phoebus, the sun god

idea image
ides of March 15 March in the Roman dating system
Ilion Troy; palace of Priam in Troy
ill-favoured ugly, unpleasant (*cf.* **favour**)
illness evil nature
image archetypal image, perfect example
imaginary imagining, imaginative
immediate direct; next in succession
impart say, reveal
impeachment charge; impediment, hindrance
impertinency irrelevance, nonsense.
imposition accusation; penalty,
imposture abscess
impress conscription
impudency immodesty
incorporate united in one body
incorrect uncorrected, incorrigible
indifferent moderately
indigested crude, amorphous
indirection oblique method
influence planetary emanation supposed to exert a determining effect upon men
inform take on a form; direct; report
infuse pour into or onto
injurious abusive, offensive
insensible unable to be sensed
insisture (?) persistence; (?) moment of stasis
instance proof, sign, evidence; motive
intelligencer messenger; spy
intrinsicate intricate

Jack, jack term of contempt, meaning fool or knave; mechanized human figure that strikes a clock bell
jade mangy or difficult horse
jealous anxious; suspicious, doubtful
jealousy anxiety; suspicion
jointress widow who inherits her husband's estate
Jove Jupiter, principal god in classical mythology, brother and husband of Juno but given to affairs with mortals
Jovial of Jupiter, *hence* kingly, liberal, *etc.*
jump coincide, agree
Juno sister and wife of Jupiter, sometimes associated with marriage, otherwise imagined as formidably jealous and prone to anger
just precisely, indeed

keel cool
kind *sb.* nature; lineage, family; way, manner; *adj.* natural; gracious
kindless unnatural
kindly *adj.* natural, in accordance with one's nature; *adv.* naturally; graciously; exactly
kite bird of prey; whore
knoll toll
knot flower-bed
knotted laid with flower-beds (*cf.* **knot**)
knotty-pated block-headed

laboursome finely worked; persistent
lace interlace, embroider
lackey page, footman
lady-smock (?) cuckoo-flower
lampass a disease in horses
large liberal, unrestrained
lark's-heels larkspur
laud hymn, song of praise
lay song
lazar leper
leaping-house brothel
learn teach
leer cheek, complexion
lees sediment
let *sb.* hindrance; *v.* hinder; forbear; (of blood) drain off; **let slip** = let (hounds) loose
level line of fire, range; **level with** = equal
liberal unrestrained
liberty right, prerogative; licence, licentiousness
lie live, lodge
lief dear; **have as lief** = hold as dear, be as willing
liege lord
light alight, descend, fall
lighten flash, as lightning
like *adj.* likely; *adv.* alike, identically; *v.* please; liken; thrive
lime birdlime, a kind of glue used to trap small birds
limitation time allotted
line category
lined padded
linger protract
lists arena for a contest
little, in in miniature
little, in a in brief
liver dweller; organ supposedly responsible for intense feeling, especially love
lodge flatten, beat down

long purples kind of wild orchis
look upon stand by and watch
loon rogue, low-bred person
looped full of holes
lop cut back or down a tree
lose cause to lose; bring to ruin; waste
love-in-idleness pansy
Lupercal = Lupercalia, an ancient Roman festival at which participants ran around striking the citizens with animal skins
lusty vigorous
luxurious lecherous
luxury lechery

main *sb.* main part; sea; *adj.* important
malicho iniquity
malkin wench
manage management; (of a horse) training, exercise
manhood manliness, masculinity
map image
margent margin
mark (in archery) something aimed at
market profit
marry a mild oath, from the name of the Virgin Mary
Mars god of war and lover of Venus
Martin's summer, Saint good weather late in the year (St Martin's day = 11 November)
martlet swift or house-martin
Mary-buds marigolds
measure dance or piece of music; punishment
mechanic, mechanical *sb.* manual labourer, artisan; *adj.* performing manual labour, common
medicinable medicinal, curative
melancholy depression, associated with a thickening of the blood
memorize make memorable
Mercury the messenger god, associated with eloquence; he was depicted with winged sandals
mere utter, total
merit reward, desert
mew confine (a bird) in a cage
miching lurking, stealthy
mince trivialize; walk or talk in an affected manner
minim basic short note-value in Tudor music
minion favourite or mistress; slut

minute-jacks clock figures (*cf.* **Jack**)
mirror pattern, example
Misanthropos man-hater (*Gr.*)
mischief evil; misfortune
mobbled with face muffled
mockery semblance, imitation
model pattern; mould
modern trite, commonplace
modest moderate, sober
moe more
moiety portion, sometimes a half
monstruosity monstrosity
mortified insensate, subdued
mose in the chine (?) display the symptoms of glanders (a disease in horses) in its final stages
mote speck, mentioned by Christ as a metaphor for trivial sinfulness
motion impulse, feeling
motive mover, cause or instrument
motley pied garments of a jester
mountebank pedlar of quack medicines
murrion infected (of animals)
mutine mutiny
mutiny riot
mutual shared, common; intimate
mystery art or craft, calling

naked unarmed
native innate, natural
naturalize familiarize
naught bad, worthless
naughty bad, worthless
nave navel
near-legged knock-kneed
Neptune god of the sea
nerve nerve or sinew
nervy courageous; sinewy
Nestor Hellenic king famed for his advanced age and wisdom
next closest
nice delicate; particular; refined
nine-men's-morris rustic game played on a diagram cut in turf
Niobe mother of fourteen children slain by Apollo and Diana, transformed into stone as she wept
noise concert or small company of musicians
note mark, characteristic; notice, apprehension
noyance annoyance, harm

O the Globe theatre

oblivious causing oblivion or forgetfulness
observance observation
observation respectful attention
observe pay due respect to
obstruction lack of movement
occasion need; opportunity
occupation labour, trade
o'erpeer look down upon
o'erpicturing outdoing in pictorial
    qualities
offend trouble, injure
offer attempt
office duty
offices servants' quarters, pantry, *etc.*
omit neglect, disregard
ope open
opinion reputation; general opinion;
    (high) opinion of oneself
opposite antagonistic
oppress distress
oppression distress
or ere, before; **or ... or** = either ... or
orb ring; earth; *see* **sphere**
ostler groom, stable-boy
owe bear

pace *sb.* horse's trained walk; way, passage;
    v. train or exercise (a horse) in walking
paddock toad
pageant spectacular show or float
pain labour, pains
painful involving labour; undergoing
    labour
painted hollow, false
pale fence, rail; enclosure
palfrey small horse
pall wrap
palmer pilgrim
palmy flourishing, victorious
pandar, pander *sb.* pimp, go-between; *v.*
    serve, as a pandar
pantaloon stock figure of the foolish old
    man in Italian comedy
paradox improbable or unusual
    proposition
paragon surpass
part *sb.* ability, accomplishment; quality;
    action; *v.* depart
passado forward lunge with a sword
passion strong emotion; suffering;
    passionate speech
patch jester, clown
paten shallow metal dish, as used in Holy
    Communion

patience sufferance
pattern example, model
peculiar own, personal, private
pedant schoolmaster
Pegasus winged horse associated with the
    hero Perseus
pelican bird supposed to feed its young
    with its own blood
pelting trivial, petty, worthless
pencil paintbrush
pensioner royal attendant
perdition loss; ruin
perfect *adj.* matured; ripe, prepared;
    learned; certain; *v.* finish; enlighten
perfection fulfilment
petard bomb
Phaeton son of Phoebus (*see* **Phoebus**) and
    stepson of Merops; attempting to drive
    Phoebus' sun chariot, he failed to
    control its horses and almost crashed
    into the earth, whereupon Jupiter
    killed him with a lightning bolt
phantasma nightmare
Philippan from the Battle of Philippi,
    where Antony and Octavius defeated
    the republicans
Philomel daughter of King Pandion, she
    was raped and mutilated by her
    brother-in-law Tereus but revealed her
    ordeal by depicting it in a tapestry; she
    was subsequently transformed into a
    nightingale
Phoebus the god Apollo in his role as sun
    god and father of Phaeton
    (*see* **Phaeton**)
phoenix fabulous bird supposed to be one
    of a kind and to rise again from its
    ashes
physic *sb.* medicine; *v.* mend,
    heal
pia mater membrane in the brain, *hence*
    brain
pickers and stealers hands
piece masterpiece, paragon
pieced supplemented
pigeon-livered incapable of anger
pitch height
place (in falconry) a hawk's highest pitch;
    high position
placket skirt or slit in a skirt
plate coin
plausive approved, worthy of applause;
    plausible
pleasant jesting

point sword
pole standard
policy politics; wisdom; strategy; stratagem
politician plotter, schemer
porpentine porcupine
porridge soup, broth
port portal, gate
portance attitude, behaviour
posset *sb.* drink made by curdling hot milk
with wine; *v.* curdle
post hurry
poster one who travels quickly
potato supposed to be an aphrodisiac
power military force; person in authority;
faculty
praise virtue, merit
prank offensive act
precise morally scrupulous, puritanical
pregnant skilful; ready
preposterous topsy-turvy, perverse
presage prediction, omen
presence presence chamber, where royalty
entertains visitors
present *sb.* present moment; *adj.* sudden,
immediate; ready; *v.* act
presentation representation, image
pressure image, as if impressed on wax
Prester John legendary ruler of a medieval
Eastern kingdom
price value
prick urge
pricksong singing from printed music
pride highest pitch; splendour
prime *sb.* spring; *adj.* first, principal
prithee '(I) pray thee', please
prize *sb.* privilege; *v.* esteem, care for
process sequence of events; relation, story
profit learning, advancement
project thought, anticipation
Promethean of Prometheus, legendary
figure who stole fire from the gods to
give to man and was punished by being
shackled to a mountain where an eagle
pecked at his liver
proper decent, fine
property individual quality
proportion number, magnitude
Proserpina maiden abducted by Pluto
while she gathered flowers and then
imprisoned in the underworld
proud resplendent, luxurious
provender food, fodder
pudding stuffed intestine,
sausage

punto (in fencing) thrust (*Ital.*); *punto
reverso* = back-handed thrust
(*Ital.*)
purblind blind or weak-sighted
purpose proposal
push crisis; action
pyramid obelisk, pillar

quail overpower
quaint ingenious, artful; pretty
quality nature; accomplishment; rank;
company
question *sb.* examination, consideration; *v.*
talk (to), discuss
questionable which invites questioning
quick living; lively; fresh
quiddities quibbles
quietus clearing of accounts
quillets, quillities quibbles
quit acquit; reward, requite

race hereditary nature; (of horses) stud; (of
ginger) root
rack cloud or bank of clouds; instrument
of torture
raisins o'th' sun grapes dried naturally in
the open air
rank excessively grown or swollen, bloated;
sexually excited
rankle make sore, aggravate
rash sudden, hasty, violent
rate estimate, evaluate; be valued at
ravined (?) ravenous; (?) having gorged
itself
ravish violate; enthral
rayed soiled
reach range of understanding
reason *sb.* something reasonable; talk,
discourse; way of thinking; *v.* ask;
argue rationally about; explain
reck take account of
reckless thoughtless, having no care for
recommend commend
recordation record, memorial
rede guidance, instruction
reek *sb.* fumes; *v.* be exhaled in the form of
smoke or fumes
regard *sb.* consideration; heed; *v.* respect,
pay attention to; tend
region stratum of the atmosphere, sky
relish taste, quality
relume reignite
remember commemorate; remind;
mention

remorse compassion, sensitivity; (?) obligation

remorseful sensitive, compassionate

remover person who changes or withdraws

repair make one's way

reproof condemnation; disproof

resolve dissolve

respect *sb.* consideration; respectability, worth; *v.* consider; value

rest remain; pause in music

resting changeless

restrained tightly drawn

resty lethargic, idle

return reply

reverberate reverberating, echoing

reverso see punto

revolt change or transfer (of allegiance); disgust; rebellion

revolution turn, as of Fortune's or time's wheel; turning of the thoughts

ripe *adj.* ready; urgent; *v.* ripen

rivage shore

rivelled wrinkled

robustious turbulent

ronyon mangy animal; term of abuse for a woman

round direct

rub (in bowls) something that impedes or deflects the bowl from its course

rude rough, unskilled, unsophisticated

rue pity; a herbal plant

rugged bristling

rug-headed having long, wild hair

ruinous in ruins, damaged

rump-fed (?) fed on choice cuts; (?) having fat buttocks

russet reddish-brown, the colour of a coarse cloth worn by peasants

sack white wine, often sherry

sad serious, solemn; dark-coloured

sadly seriously, soberly

sadness seriousness

safe well, sound

saffron a dye used in both clothing and food

salad days youth

salute cheer

sanctuarize provide with sanctuary or immunity from punishment

sans without (*Fr.*)

sauce season, spice, make hot

saucy impudent; sexually bold or carefree

savour smell; nature

saw wise saying

say speak

'Sblood (by God)'s blood (an oath)

scaffoldage stage

scald scabby, scurvy

'scape, scape *sb.* escapade, transgression; *v.* escape

scarf sling; sash used to indicate rank in the army

school *sb.* university; *v.* teach (a lesson); govern, control

scope purpose, aim; opportunity

scorch cut, gash

scorn, take scorn

scotch gash

scour clean out (a pistol) with a ramrod

scroyles scabby scoundrels

scrubbed dwarfish

scruple doubt

scullion kitchen servant of either sex

scutcheon cheap coat of arms used at funerals

sea-coal superior type of coal transported to London by sea

sea-maid mermaid

sect class, profession; political faction; sex

securely with (false) confidence

seel sew up (the eyelids of a hawk in training)

seeming *sb.* appearance; deception, falseness; *adj.* apparent

sense senses; sexual awareness; mind

senseless insensate, unresponsive

sensible able to sense, having sensation; able to be sensed, material, evident

sentence opinion; decision, ruling; memorable saying

sententious memorable, using choice words

sere *sb.* dried-up condition; *adj.* dry

sergeant arresting officer

several different, various; individual, distinct

shadow illusory image, picture; actor; spirit; ghost

shag rough, untrimmed

shame natural modesty

shamefaced shy; full of shame

shard cow-pat

shark up snatch indiscriminately, as a shark its food

shearman one involved in the manufacture of cloth

sherris sherry

shive slice
shoal area of shallow water
shoon shoes
shoulder-shotten having dislocated shoulders
shrewd sharp
shrewdly sharply; sorely
siege seat, *esp.* of office or high rank
sightless invisible; unpleasant to look at
silly simple; defenceless
simple *sb.* herb used as a medicine; ingredient; *adj.* unadulterated, pure
simpleness plain honesty
simplicity stupidity
single alone, unaided; honest, direct
singularity unusual behaviour
sith since
skill reason
slab thick and slimy
slander accusation; disgrace; disgraceful person
slanderous of accusation; bringing disgrace
sleave a coarse silk
slip *sb.* cutting or graft from a plant; leash; *v.* unleash (a greyhound)
sliver split off
smock petticoat
smoke fog
smooth *sb.* flatter, indulge; gloss over; *adj.* flattering
solicit urge, excite; make petition
sooth truth
sort rank; lot; way; keeping company (with)
sound fathom
spavin tumour on a horse's leg-joint
sped ruined
speed fare; meet with success
spend speak; use up
sphere (in Ptolomaic astronomy) one of the massive crystalline spheres around the earth in which the planets, stars, *etc.* were believed fixed; they revolved, generating harmonious music, inaudible on earth
spill destroy
spinners (?) spiders; (?) craneflies
spinster woman spinning flax or wool
spleen organ supposedly responsible for fierce passion, laughter and melancholy, *hence* the abstract condition or a fit or bout of any of these moods
spoil sacking, carrying off booty; booty

spot blemish
springe snare for catching birds
spurn *sb.* blow, rude rejection; *v.* kick fiercely
square *sb.* measuring rule; *adj.* just, fair
squash unripe pea-pod
staff quarterstaff, spear or lance
staggers disease in horses causing staggering
stain *sb.* blemish; *v.* eclipse
stair-work furtive business on the back stairs
stale make stale; cheapen, debase
stamp *sb.* seal, official mark; *v.* create, manufacture, (of coins) mint
stand stand about; stand still; stand up to
staple texture of wool
start frighten
starve destroy, *esp.* with cold, freeze; suffer or perish with cold
state property, condition or social position; throne; court
station stance, posture
statist politician, man of affairs
stay *sb.* support; *v.* check, interrupt; support, hold (up); wait
stew brothel
stick pierce, kill
still *adj.* constant; *adv.* always, constantly;
stilly quietly
stint stop
stithy smithy, forge
stock family
stomach part of the body supposedly the seat of pride, ambition and courage; appetite; inclination
stoop bow, bend over
stop (in horseriding) rapid switch from a gallop to a halt; point where the finger determines a note on a musical instrument
strain force; transgress; pervert; **strain courtesy** = be unceremonious; hang back
strait narrow passage
strange alien, foreign, unfamiliar; remarkable
strangely like a foreigner or stranger; remarkably
stratagem trick, plot; violent act
strength body of soldiers
strike (of a planet) ruin with evil influence; resound
stubborn hard, rigid

stuffed congested; full (of qualities or accomplishments)
succeed follow; pass by succession
succession that which follows
sue make a petition, ask
sufferance, suff'rance suffering; patience, endurance
suggestion prompting; temptation
suppose estimate
surcease end, *hence* death
sure safe
swagger act like a bragging ruffian
swashing swashbuckling, rough
sway *sb.* rule, authority, control; *v.* rule, exert influence
swayed broken, deformed
sweat plague
sweet *sb.* scent; flower; *adj.* scented
sweeting sweet apple, used as a term of affection

table writing-tablet
taffeta type of silk
taint fault
take encounter; enchant, possess
tang clang forth, as a bell
tardy off, come executed inadequately
tarry await
Tartar Mongol, an archer warrior from the East
tax charge, reproach, condemn
teem breed, *esp.* abundantly
temper character as defined by the humours (*see* humour); stability of character, as from a balance of the humours
temperate well-tempered, balanced, modest
tempt make trial of
tender *sb.* offer, token; *v.* attend to; offer, lay (down); cherish
Termagant a blustering, villainous role in the Mystery plays
tetchy touchy, irritable
tetter disfiguring skin complaint
text motto; sermon
Thane Scottish nobleman of middling rank
thews sinews, strength
thick *adj.* dull; numerous; *adv.* in a hectic manner, hurriedly
thing, a something
think be gloomily introspective
thought melancholy contemplation; **with a thought** = quick as a thought

three-piled of thick, costly velvet
thrift profit
thwart cross
tickle flatter; entertain
tide full flood, chance for action
tinct colouring
title entitlement, claim
to cry of encouragement
toil hunter's snare or net
touch brushstroke; facial feature
toy something trivial or imaginary
trade traffic, business
trade-fallen out of work
trammel up entangle, as in a net
transfix pierce, impale
translate metamorphose
travail *sb.* labour; journey; *v.* labour
trencher wooden plate
trencher-friends friends won by feeding
trencher-knight one who is brave only at the dinner table
tribune Roman magistrate representing the interests of ordinary citizens
trick trifle; knack; distinctive feature
triple third
triumph pageant of processions and tournaments
truncheon baton, symbol of military command
try test, prove
tup (of a ram) mount, penetrate
tyranny violence, fierceness

umber brown earth
unaccommodated not provided with the usual clothes or comforts
unadvised unintentional
unavoided unable to be avoided, inevitable
unbitted unrestrained
unclasp open up, reveal
unction ointment
undergo go under, bear
unexpressive unable to be expressed
unfold open up, expose, reveal
unhandsome unskilful
unhappy unlucky, cursed
unimproved unchecked, unrestrained
unjust false
unkind acting against one's family or the natural order
unproportioned unruly, unrestrained
unrespective heedless
untrimmed stripped; set off balance

unvalued of no value; of inestimable value
unyoked unbridled
use custom, habit, way; interest; profit

vacancy spare time; air; the vacuum created by a removal of air
vain foolish
value evaluate, consider
vaunt-couriers forerunners
vein spirit, style
velure velvet
velvet-guards those wearing fine clothes; **guards** = trimmings of a garment
vent *sb.* venting; *v.* discharge
ventricle chamber in the brain
Venus goddess of love and lover of Mars
Ver Spring
verge rim
vice a comic villain in sixteenth-century moral interludes
vicious wicked
vie vie with, rival
vigil evening before a feast-day
villain person of low birth, servant
viol stringed instrument, a predecessor of the violin family
virtue masculine virtue, courage; power; essence
vizarded masked
voice determining say, vote
vouch testify
voyage enterprise
Vulcan god of fire and cuckolded husband of Venus, represented as a smith
vulgar of or among the ordinary people, common

wag go, move
wake not sleep, stay up
want lack; feel the lack of
wanton vibrant, skittish; delicate
warden type of pear or apple
ware beware
warp turn; change
war-proof, of experienced in war
warrant guarantee
warren enclosure for rabbits and other game
waste consume, destroy
watch *sb.* fixed period of time; *v.* catch by lying in wait for

watchful sleepless, of sleeplessness
wealth prosperity
wear wear out
weed piece of clothing
welkin sky
westward ho! Thames watermen's call for passengers heading west
whirligig spinning-top
whoreson bastard, used technically, offensively or affectionately
wild deserted, wasteland; headstrong, unthinking
wilderness wildness, wild stock
will sexual organ
wimpled muffled, blindfolded
wind *sb.* breath; (in hunting) direction of the wind and thus of scent; *v.* wheedle
windgalls tumours on the legs of horses
wink shut the eyes
winking with closed eyes
winnow sift, refine
wit *sb.* mind, intelligence, cleverness; *v.* know; **five wits** = five mental faculties
withal *prep.* with; *adv.* therewith, with (something specified)
without outside, beyond
witty intelligent, clever
woodbine honeysuckle or similar plant
woodcock a stupid, easily trapped bird
woollen, in the in scratchy blankets
world body
worm snake
worn worn out
worship dignity
worshipped dignified
wot know (*cf.* wit)
wrack wrecking, wreck
wrath raging passion
writ Holy writ, scripture

yea-forsooth given to using mild oaths in a servile manner
yellows jaundice in horses
yest yeast, foam
younger younger son, prodigal

zany clown's assistant
zounds (by God)'s wounds (an oath)

✨ Topic Index ✨

absence 1
action and deeds 1
action, immediate 2
adversity 2
advice 3
alienation 4
alliance 5
ambition 5
anger 7
animals 8
anticipation 9
anxiety 10
apparitions 10
appearance 11
appearances 13
argument 14
armies 14
art 15
authority 15
autumn 16

babies 16
bad behaviour 16
bad people 16
bad times 17
beards 17
beauty 18
beggars 18
betrayal 19
better days 20
birds 20
birth and childbearing 21
blood 22
body, the 22
boldness 23
books 24
braggadocio 24
bravado 24
bravery 25
Britain 26
brothers 26
business 26

cares 27
cats 27
causes 28
caution 28
ceremony 28
certainty 28
chance 29
change 29

chastity 29
childhood 30
children 30
children, having or not having 31
choice 31
Christians 32
Christmas 32
cities 32
class, social 33
cleanliness 33
Cleopatra 33
cold 34
comfort 35
communication 35
comparisons 35
compassion 36
compromise 36
comradeship 36
confusion 36
conscience 36
contentment 37
contracts 38
corruption 38
counsel, keeping your own 40
country life 40
courage 41
courtiers 42
cowardice 42
crimes 43
criticism 45
cruelty 45
curses 46
custom 47

dancing 48
danger 48
dangerous people 49
darkness 50
daughters 50
death 50
deceptiveness 58
decline and fall 58
dedications 60
delay 60
delusion 60
democracy 60
depression 61
desires 61
despair 62
Devil, the 63
discretion 63

disorder 63
divinity 64
doctors and medicine 64
dogs 65
dreams 66
drinking 67
duty 68
dying words 69

East, the 70
easy life 70
eccentricity 71
ecology 71
education 71
elegies 73
Elizabeth I 74
emotion 75
ends and endings 75
enemies 76
England and the English 76
ennui 78
enthusiasm 78
envy 78
equality 79
events 79
evil 80
evil deeds 80
evil people 80
excess 81
excuses 82
exile 82
expectation 83
experience 83

faction 83
failure 84
fairies 84
faithfulness 87
Falstaff 87
fame 88
familiarity 88
family 88
farewells 88
fashion 89
fate 90
fathers 91
faults 93
fear 93
fighting 94
flattery 94
flirtation and seduction 95
flowers and plants 96
food 98
fools and foolishness 100
foreboding 100
forgetfulness 100
forgiveness 101
fortitude 101
fortune 101
France and the French 102
freedom 103

friends and friendship 103
friends, false 104
future, the 104

gardens and gardening 105
gender 106
genetics 106
gifts and giving 107
girls 107
God 108
good and goodness 108
good intentions 108
good times 109
graffiti 109
graves 109
greatness 110
greed 111
greetings 111
grief 112
grief, expressions of 113
guilt 114
gullibility 115

habit 116
hair 116
happiness 116
hardship 117
haste 117
hatred 118
Helen of Troy 118
hell 118
Henry V 119
history 120
holidays 120
honesty 120
honour 121
hope 123
horses 123
hospitality and parties 125
human frailty 125
humankind 126
humble life 127
humility 128
hunting 128
husbands and wives 128
hypocrisy 130

identity 132
idols 132
ignorance 133
ill treatment 133
ill will 133
illegitimacy 133
illness and disease 134
imagination 135
impatience 136
impetuosity 136
inaction 136
inadequacy 136
indecision 137
inexperience 137

infidelity 137
ingratitude 139
innocence 140
inspiration 140
insults 140
integrity 142
intelligence, low 142
Italy and the Italians 143

jealousy 143
jewels 145
Jews and Jewishness 145
jokes 145
joy 146
judgement, good and bad 146
judges and judgement 146
Julius Caesar 147
justice 148
justification 149

kingship and rule 149
kisses and kissing 152
knowledge 153

law and lawyers 153
leadership 155
letters 155
lies 156
life 156
life, making the most of 159
looking 159
loss 159
love 160
love, being in 164
love, cooling 165
love, expressions of 166
love, falling in 168
lovers 168
loyalty 169
luck 168

madness 170
magic 172
manipulation 172
manner and manners 172
Mark Antony 173
marriage 173
maturity 175
melancholy 176
memory and remembering 176
men 177
men and women 179
mending and improving 181
mercy 181
merit 182
merriment 182
middle age 182
mind, the 183
misanthropy 183
mischief 184
misfortune 184

misgivings 184
mistakes 185
moderation 185
modesty 185
money 186
moon, the 186
morning 187
mortality 189
mothers 191
murder 191
music 192
mystery 195

names 195
nature 196
necessity 196
new beginnings 197
newness 198
news 198
news, bad 198
news, good 199
night 199
nobility 202

oaths 202
odds 202
old age 202
old times 206
omens and portents 206
Ophelia 208
opportunity 208
order 209
outrage 209

parents and children 209
partings 210
past, the 211
patience 211
patriotism 212
peace 212
people, the 213
perception 213
permission 214
perseverance 214
persuasion 214
philosophy 214
pity 215
places 215
planning 216
plays, players and playhouses 216
pleasure 221
plots 221
poetry 221
poets 222
poison 222
police 223
politeness 223
politics and politicians 224
possession 226
poverty 226
power 227

prayer 228
preparedness 228
present, the 228
pride 229
priests 230
prison 230
promises 231
prophecies 231
prosperity 232
providence 232
prudence 232
public opinion 232
punishment 233

quarrels 234
questions 234
quiet 235

reading 235
reason and unreason 235
reasons 236
rebellion and revolution 237
regret 238
rejection 238
religion 239
renunciation 239
reputation 240
resentment 241
resignation 241
resolve 241
respect 242
responsibility 242
retirement 242
revenge 243
Richard III 244
riches 245
risk 245
rivalry 245
Rome and the Romans 246
Romeo and Juliet 246
rumour 247

sacrifices and scapegoats 248
sadness 249
scorn 249
Scotland and the Scots 249
sea, the 249
seasons, the 250
secrecy 251
security 252
self-control 252
self-doubt 252
self-interest 252
self-knowledge 252
self-loathing 253
self-protection 253
seriousness 253
sex and lust 253
sexual abuse 258
shame 258
ships 258

sidekicks 259
sin 260
single life, the 260
slander 260
slavery 261
sleep and sleeplessness 261
soldiers 263
solitude and solitariness 265
sorrow 266
soul, the 267
spectators 267
speeches 267
speed 268
spirits 268
sport 269
spring 269
stars 270
stoicism 270
stories 271
strategy 272
success 272
suffering 273
suicide 273
summer 275
supernatural, the 275
suspicion 276
swimming 276

talk 277
taxation 279
tears and weeping 279
temptation 280
thanks 281
thieves 281
thoughts 281
threats 282
thrift 282
time 283
time, wasting 286
timeliness 286
tomorrow 286
transience 287
traps and tricks 287
travel 288
treason and treachery 289
trifles 289
Trojan war, the 290
trouble 290
truancy 290
trust 290
truth 290
tyranny 291

uncertainty 292
usury 292

value 293
vanity 293
victory 294
violence 294
virtue 294

vows 296

waiting 296
Wales and the Welsh 296
war 297
war, civil 301
weakness 302
weapons 302
weariness 302
weather 303
wild behaviour 303
wilfulness 304
winter 304
wisdom 305
wise sayings 305
wishing 305
wit 306

witches 307
women 308
women, loose 313
wooing 313
words 314
work 316
working people 316
world, the 317
worldliness 318
worst, the 319
worth 319
worthless people 320
wounds 320
writing 320
wrongs 321

youth 321

✤ Keyword Index ✤

—A—

absolute
How a. the knave is 277.7
abstinence
A. engenders maladies 134.9
abused
He hath been most notoriously a. 133.8
academe
A little a. 72.3
accent
the a. of reproof 229.10
accidents
moving a. by flood and field 271.8
accomplish
a. as you may 2.4
account
sent to my a. With all my imperfections 260.1
achievements
How my a. mock me 84.6
acorn
like a dropped a. 62.8
act
did the a. of darkness 318.10
the a. a slave to limit 256.8
the a. of darkness 255.3
acting
Between the a. of a dreadful thing 43.9
action
A. is eloquence 1.5
All out of work and cold for a. 25.5
lose the name of a. 136.3
Suit the a. to the word 217.3
actions
Our necessary a. 1.6
actor
a well-graced a. 220.4
Like a dull a. 216.5
Adam
A. was a gardener 213.8
A.'s profession 316.10
th'offending A. 175.10
adamant
hard-hearted a. 166.11
adder
bright day that brings forth the a. 9.1
adders
a. fanged 104.9
ears more deaf than a. 236.6
Adonis
Rose-cheeked A. 179.5

adored
I was a. once too 166.3
advantage
A. feeds him fat 60.4
A. is a better soldier than rashness 272.6
I spy a. 6.2
let not a. slip 286.9
adversaries
as a. do in law 155.1
adversary
stony a. 215.8
adversity
A.'s sweet milk, philosophy 214.11
sour A. 3.3
Sweet are the uses of a. 2.11
wretched soul bruised with a 3.1
affliction
Henceforth I'll bear A. 271.2
again
Lo, where it comes a. 10.9
age
a. cannot wither her 34.4
A. is unnecessary 204.7
Crabbed a. and youth 205.5
dust and injury of a. 206.1
homely a. th'alluring beauty took 173.9
no a. between ten and three-and-twenty 323.10
None but in this iron a. 17.4
some smack of a. 183.1
That which should accompany old a. 205.1
thou a. unbred 206.9
Unregarded a. 203.1
warns my old a. to a sepulchre 57.5
When the a. is in 205.3
agent
trust no a. 38.7
ages
all a. smack of this vice 233.9
air
I scent the morning a. 187.8
Slight a., and purging fire 282.6
The a. bites shrewdly 35.1
this most excellent canopy the a. 61.5
Ajax
A. employed 246.2
ale
pot of a. and safety 298.9
Alexander
noble dust of A. 189.6

[347]

Alexandrian
  Our A. revels   216.3
  This is not yet an A. feast   99.1
allegiance
  I did pluck a. from men's hearts   224.7
alms
  a. for oblivion   285.5
alone
  Who a. suffers   266.1
alteration
  a. of honour   227.3
ambition
  a. should be made of sterner stuff   7.2
  A.'s debt is paid   148.10
  Art not without a.   7.6
  Caesar's a.   147.9
  Fling away a.   6.7
  makes a. virtue   300.5
  vaulting a.   7.7
  Virtue is choked with foul a.   17.3
  Who doth a. shun   5.9, 40.4
  with divine a. puffed   5.11
ambitious
  as he was a., I slew him   7.1
  very substance of the a.   5.10
amen
  'A.' stuck in my throat   228.3
amity
  a., and painted peace   212.11
ancestors
  When I am sleeping with my a.   100.6
ancientry
  wronging the a.   323.10
angel
  A minist'ring a. shall my sister be   73.4
  As if an a. dropped down from the clouds
    119.7
  Let's write good a. on the devil's horn
    13.9
angels
  A. and ministers of grace   11.1
  a. of light   313.1
  By that sin fell the a.   6.7
  few are a.   126.1
  flights of a. sing thee to thy rest   73.5
  like a., trumpet-tongued   295.6
  Women are a., wooing   313.9
angry
  Who is man that is not a.   8.5
anguish
  ease the a. of a torturing hour   219.7
animal
  bare, forked a.   126.7
antic
  a. disposition   170.2
  there the a. sits   57.3
antiquity
  blasted with a.   203.9
Antony
  A., Enthroned i'th' market-place   265.9
  none but A. Should conquer A.   125.9

Not Caesar's valour hath o'erthrown A.
    173.3
anything
  No man is the lord of a.   35.8
ape
  like an angry a.   126.8
apes
  lead a. in hell   144.6
Apollo
  A.'s lute, strung with his hair   193.2
  songs of A.   193.3
apparel
  the a. oft proclaims the man   3.7
appetite
  a. had grown By what it fed on   254.5
  a., an universal wolf   292.7
apprehension
  sense of death is most in a.   56.1
April
  he smells A. and May   323.3
  lovely A. of her prime   30.10
  men are A. when they woo   179.6
  proud pied A.   269.9
  uncertain glory of an A. day   164.3
Arabian
  O thou A. bird   173.2
  She is alone th'A. bird   295.1
arbitrement
  a. of swords   234.4
argument
  All the a. is a whore and a cuckold   290.2
  not to stir without great a.   122.1
arguments
  Let thy tongue tang a. of state   226.1
Ariel
  Approach, my A.   269.1
  Dearly, my delicate A.   167.9
arm
  Though others have the a.   137.5
armed
  Thrice is he a. that hath his quarrel just
    148.7
arms
  take a. against a sea of troubles   274.1
arrogancy
  crammed with a., spleen and pride   229.5
arrow
  I have shot my a. o'er the house   185.1
  Swifter than a. from the Tartar's bow
    268.7
art
  an a. Which does mend nature   71.7
  A. made tongue-tied by authority   15.3
  A. to enchant   228.6
  Desiring this man's a.   79.1
  glib and oily a.   278.6
  I swear I use no a. at all   277.5
  Still and contemplative in living a.   72.3
  The a. itself is nature   71.7
Arthur
  A.'s bosom   87.8

arts
    Fair Padua, nursery of a. 32.7
    had I but followed the a. 286.6
Asia
    clean through the bounds of A. 288.4
    furthest inch of A. 288.8
    Hollow pampered jades of A. 123.9
ass
    enamoured of an a. 165.7
    I am such a tender a. 116.6
    You are an a. 223.3
Ate
    With A. by his side come hot from hell 301.3
attempt
    a. and not the deed 84.4
augury
    We defy a. 91.1
author
    He was the a., thou the instrument 108.8
authority
    a little brief a. 126.8
    demi-god, A. 15.8
    Though a. be a stubborn bear 39.10
autumn
    teeming a. 16.1
aweary
    a. of the sun 302.8
    Cassius is a. of the world 61.6

—B—

babe
    Pity, like a naked new-born b. 215.7
bachelor
    a b. of threescore years 260.6
    When I said I would die a b. 260.9
bachelors
    shows me where the b. sit 260.7
bad
    Things b. begun 80.4
badge
    Suff'rance is the b. of all our tribe 145.4
bag
    b. and baggage 258.1
ballad
    I love a b. in print 24.6
balm
    'Tis not the b. 28.5
Ban
    'B., 'B., Cacaliban 103.8
banish
    b. all the world 87.5
banishment
    bitter bread of b. 82.13
bank
    I know a b. 85.3
banquet
    His words are a very fantastical b. 279.3
bar
    Throng to the bar, crying all, 'Guilty' 115.7

Barbary
    My mother had a maid called B 311.8
    Rode he on B. 124.4
barbered
    b. ten times o'er 173.1
barge
    The b. she sat in 34.2
bark
    scarfed b. puts from her native bay 259.2
base
    Who is here so b. 103.7
bastard
    I am a b., too: I love bastards 134.5
    Why b.? Wherefore base 134.2
bastards
    gods, stand up for b. 134.3
    I wish the b. dead 133.11
bastinado
    He gives the b. with his tongue 24.7
battle
    few die well that die in a b. 299.3
bay-trees
    The b. in our country are all withered 208.2
be
    B. that thou know'st thou art 253.1
    Men should b. what they seem 121.5
    the b.-all and the end-all 44.3
    To b., or not to b. 274.1
beadle
    rascal b. 255.5
bear
    Exit, pursued by a b. 9.5
beard
    He that hath a b. 180.2
beast
    a b. that wants discourse of reason 137.6
    b. with many heads 61.1
    The b. with two backs 255.11
beat
    Let's b. him before his whore 294.6
beauteous
    B. thou art, therefore to be assailed 313.7
beauty
    B. dead, black Chaos comes 18.10
    B. herself is black 18.8
    b. is a witch 162.3
    b. itself doth of itself persuade 18.2
    b., like a dial hand 287.4
    b. lives with kindness 312.4
    B. o'ersnowed 305.1
    b. ... purchased by the weight 18.3
    b. starved with her severity 30.3
    b., Till now I never knew thee 18.1
    B. too rich for use 18.7
    B., truth and rarity 74.2
    b.'s canker 112.10
    B.'s ensign 247.4
    dedicate his b. to the sun 251.7
    He hath a daily b. in his life 241.6
    In the holiday-time of my b. 323.2
    If b. have a soul 139.1

beds
    b. i'th' East are soft 70.6
bedtime
    I would 'twere b. 298.1
bee
    Where the b. sucks 87.1
beef
    Give them great meals of b. 77.5
    I am a great eater of b. 99.11
beer
    chronicle small b. 311.7
    to desire small b. 67.7
beetle
    poor b. that we tread upon 9.2
begetter
    To the only b. 60.1
beggar
    The king's a b. 216.2
beggars
    Bedlam b. 18.11
    When b. die there are no comets seen 151.1
beggary
    There's b. in the love that can be reckoned
        160.6
beguile
    b. many and be beguiled by one 313.3
    I do b. The thing I am 182.6
bell
    B., book and candle 186.4
    mock the midnight b. 125.1
    the b. invites me 44.5
belly
    No barricado for a b. 258.1
benefits
    b. forgot 139.4
best
    I am b. When least in company 266.2
    The b. is past 20.4
    the b. sometimes forget 177.4
    We have seen the b. of our time 59.3
better
    b. spared a b. man 104.3
    If ever you have looked on b. days 20.1
    Striving to b. 181.2
    We have seen b. days 20.2
beware
    B. the Thane of Fife 232.2
bird
    b. of loudest lay 21.6
    b. of night did sit 207.2
    this b. of dawning 32.2
birds
    like b. i'the cage 230.8
Birnam
    Great B. wood to high Dunsinane hill 232.2
birth
    Some glory in their b. 229.11
black
    Is b. so base a hue 79.7
blade
    with bloody blameful b. 315.3

blank
    A b., my lord 120.6
blasphemy
    flat b. 33.5
bleed
    if you prick us do we not b. 145.6
blessings
    Tell me what b. I have here alive 58.5
bliss
    B. in our brows' bent 160.7
blood
    a thing of b. 264.2
    B. will have b. 244.2
    he today that sheds his b. with me 299.4
    I am in b. Stepped in so far 44.7
    lay the summer's dust with showers of b.
        301.4
    no sure foundation set on b. 191.10
    Now could I drink hot b. 43.6
    so much b. in him 22.8
bloody
    Be b., bold, and resolute 23.8
    B. thou art, b. will be thy end 232.4
    What b. man is this 265.2
boars
    Eight wild b. roasted whole 98.8
bodies
    Our b. are gardens 23.1
bodkin
    with a bare b. 274.1
body
    all the b.'s members 237.1
    Is this thy b.'s end 190.8
    little b. with a mighty heart 77.1
    my little b. is aweary of this great world
        302.9
    This common b. 232.9
Bohemia
    deserts of B. 289.3
boldness
    B. be my friend 23.3
bond
    'tis not in the b. 38.6
    Let him look to his b. 38.5
bondman
    Every b. in his own hand 103.5
bones
    My old b. ache 206.2
    Of his b. are coral made 250.6
book
    dainties that are bred in a b. 72.6
    I'll drown my book 242.8
    Painfully to pore upon a b. 24.1
    we quarrel in print, by the b. 14.7
books
    b. in the running brooks 40.3
    Burn his b. 24.5
    gentleman is not in your b. 104.5
    Knowing I loved my b. 24.4
borrower
    the b., the arts, the academes 310.10

the b., the academes 310.9
Neither a b. nor a lender be 3.7
borrowing
b. dulls the edge of husbandry 3.7
Bottom
B.'s Dream 66.7
bounty
For his b., There was no winter in't 73.1
My b. is as boundless as the sea 247.1
bourn
from whose b. No traveller returns 274.1
bow-strings
hold, or cut b. 89.3
boy
dangerous and lascivious b. 49.7
little scrubbed b. 323.1
to be b. eternal 30.5
When that I was and a little tiny b. 303.6
wimpled, whining, purblind, wayward b.
161.4
boys
As flies to wanton b. 158.2
b. pursuing summer butterflies 23.2
unrespective b. 292.5
brain
book and volume of my b. 176.9
My b., more busy than the ... spider 221.5
my old b. is troubled 206.3
not more b. than I have in mine elbows
142.12
not so much b. as ear-wax 143.2
brains
Cudgel thy b. no more about it 282.1
I am cut to the b. 65.1
breach
Cure this great b. 65.2
more honoured in the b. 47.8
Once more unto the b. 298.7
breathe
So long as men can b. 222.5
breed
this happy b. of men 78.2
brevity
b. is the soul of wit 306.3
briars
how full of b. is this working-day world
2.10
bride-habited
I am b. 30.4
brief
I will be b. 306.3
Britain
B.'s a world by itself 26.1
liver, heart and brain of B. 26.2
British
I smell the blood of a B. man 271.6
brothels
Keep thy foot out of b. 4.4
brother
I never loved my b. in my life 26.3
like b. and b. 79.4

The b. blindly shed the b.'s blood 301.6
We came into the world like b. and b. 26.4
brothers
heart of b. govern in our loves 5.1
we band of b. 299.4
Brute
Et tu, B. 19.4
Brutus
B. only overcame himself 275.1
budge
I will not b. for no man's pleasure 25.2
buds
darling b. of May 97.6
build
When we mean to b. 216.1
bull
savage b. doth bear the yoke 174.8
burglary
Flat b. 281.8
buried
Beat not the bones of the b. 55.4
burr
I am a kind of b. 214.5
business
It is thy b. that I go about 210.1
My b. was great 82.7
To b. that we love 316.1
butchers
Let's be sacrificers, but not b. 248.6
butchery
furious close of civil b. 301.1
this house is but a b. 80.7
butterflies
laugh At gilded b. 230.8
button
Pray you undo this b. 69.10
buy
I will b. with you 239.5

—C—

Caesar
C. must bleed for it 148.2
C. thou art revenged 243.8
I come to bury C. 73.6
Imperious C., dead and turned to clay
189.7
mighty C.! dost thou lie so low 59.1
My heart is in the coffin there with C. 113.5
Not that I loved C. less 212.1
'Tis paltry to be C. 101.5
When C. says, 'Do this' 227.9
Cain
spirit of the first-born C. 301.2
cakes
no more c. and ale 109.4
calamity
wedded to c. 184.8
calendar
A c., a c.! Look in the almanac 187.3

calumny
    Back-wounding c. 261.3
    thou shalt not escape c. 261.2

came
    I c., saw, and overcame 294.3

camomile
    the c., the more it is trodden on 322.1

candle
    Here burns my c. out 53.8
    must I hold a c. to my shames 258.9
    Out, out, brief c. 158.5

candles
    blessed c. of the night 270.4
    Night's c. are burnt out 270.6

canker
    The c. galls the infants of the spring 321.6

cankers
    c. of a calm world 264.6

cannon
    Even in the c.'s mouth 157.2

canon
    fixed His c. 'gainst self-slaughter 273.10

canons
    Religious c., civil laws 300.8

caper
    I can cut a c. 48.4

caps
    They threw their c. 146.2

captain
    c. of compliments 179.3
    his c.'s c. 5.7
    Our great c.'s c. 129.10

captains
    All my sad c. 125.1

carcass
    c. fit for hounds 191.9

care
    c. is no cure 10.3
    C. keeps his watch 263.5
    c. killed a cat 27.5
    ravelled sleave of c. 262.8
    so wan with c. 27.3
    windy side of c. 27.4

carnations
    c. and streaked gillyvors 98.2

carousing
    c. till the second cock 68.1

carry-tale
    Some c. 141.9

case
    The c. is altered 29.4

castle
    This c. hath a pleasant seat 215.10

cat
    A harmless necessary c. 27.10
    as a c. laps milk 115.9
    as vigilant as a c. 27.7
    Hang off, thou c. 141.13
    I could endure anything ... but a c. 27.6
    poor c. i'th' adage 42.8
    Thrice the brinded c. 27.9

catalogue
    in the c. ye go for men 141.10

caterpillars
    The c. of the commonwealth 225.9

cause
    if the c. be not good 150.6
    it is the c., my soul 236.9
    numbers cannot try the c. 297.9
    our c. is ripe 228.8
    Report me and my c. aright 198.4

caviare
    c. to the general 233.2

celerity
    C. is never more admired 268.2
    such a c. in dying 50.9

centre
    c. of my sinful earth 267.8

century
    c. of prayers 109.6

ceremony
    No c. that to great ones longs 181.5
    Save c., save general c. 28.4
    thrice-gorgeous c. 28.5

certainties
    C. are past remedies 28.7

chambers
    perfumed c. of the great 150.4

chance
    If C. will have me King 29.1
    slaves of c. 29.2

chaos
    C. is come again 167.2

chapmen
    You do as c. do 27.1

charm
    The c. dissolves apace 172.2

charms
    My c. crack not 273.1

chased
    more with spirit c. than enjoyed 62.5

chaste
    As c. as unsunned snow 29.7
    Be thou as c. as ice 29.9

chastity
    More than our brother is our c. 26.6

cheek
    c. by jowl 246.1
    Feed on her damask c. 164.1
    the c. of night 18.7

cheerless
    All's c., dark and deadly 62.10

cheese
    It will toast c. 302.6
    You Banbury c. 141.12

chickens
    all my pretty c., and their dam 92.4

chiding
    Better a little c. 45.5

child
    To have a thankless c. 209.6

Childe
C. Rowland to the dark tower came   271.6
childishness
second c. and mere oblivion   157.2
chimney-sweepers
As c., come to dust   189.3
chisel
What fine c. Could ever yet cut breath   15.5
choice
Since my dear soul was mistress of her c.   104.2
choirs
Bare ruined c.   205.9
chooseth
Who c. me   31.10
christened
no thought of pleasing you when she was c.   195.5
Christian
out o' C. burial   33.2
Christians
What these C. are   32.1
Christmas
At C. I no more desire a rose   251.1
chronicles
abstract and brief c. of the time   216.6
church
so wide as a c. door   320.3
citizens
fat and greasy c.   111.2
civil
C. blood makes c. hands unclean   84.1
Cleopatra
C. hath Nodded him to her   254.2
Some squeaking C. boy my greatness   216.3
climate
Is not their c. foggy, raw and dull   77.3
clothes
soul of this man is in his c.   89.7
To me she's married, not unto my c.   175.5
cloud
yonder c. ... in shape of a camel   170.9
clouds
c. still hang on you   61.3
cockatrice
A c. hast thou hatched   244.10
cocks
country c. do crow   187.10
cogitations
worthy c.   282.3
coil
this mortal c.   274.1
cold
as c. as a snowball   30.2
as c. as any stone   53.1
as c. As is a dead man's nose   276.7
C., c., my girl   56.6
Poor Tom's a-c.   35.2
'Tis bitter c. And I am sick at heart   34.6
Colossus
bestride the narrow world Like a C.   147.10

colt
The c. that's backed   124.8
comedians
quick c. Extemporally will stage us   216.3
comedy
most lamentable c.   218.9
comfort
c. comes too late   35.4
I beg cold c.   35.5
comforter
Let no c. delight mine ear   35.6
comforts
loves and c. should increase   183.4
command
not born to sue, but to c.   151.2
Those he commands move only in c.   155.7
commons
The c., like an angry hive of bees   225.3
wavering c.   279.7
companion
I would not wish Any c. in the world   104.8
company
c., villainous c.   82.4
Let men take heed of their c.   172.6
comparisons
C. are odorous   36.1
compassionate
It boots thee not to be c.   147.8
complexion
His c. is perfect gallows   12.11
Mislike me not for my c.   12.5
compost
Do not spread the c. on the weeds   105.3
concealment
c. Worse than a theft   185.9
conception
I have a young c. in my brain   221.8
conclusions
She hath pursued c. infinite   273.9
concord
true c. of well-tuned sounds   194.9
confession
there is a kind of c. in your looks   114.9
confident
C. against the world in arms   41.2
confusion
C. now hath made his masterpiece   64.1
quick bright things come to c.   76.3
conqueror
proud foot of a c.   77.9
conscience
c. does make cowards of us all   274.1
C. is but a word that cowards use   37.9
c. wide as hell   299.1
Coward c.   37.7
dregs of c.   37.4
Every man's c. is a thousand men   37.6
frozen c.   37.1
still and quiet c.   36.10
Wherein I'll catch the c. of the King   217.1
worm of c.   37.3

consequence
    Some c. yet hanging in the stars 184.11
    trammel up the c. 44.3

consideration
    C. like an angel came 175.10

constancy
    Love and c. is dead 162.7

constant
    I am c. as the northern star 270.1

consummation
    a c. Devoutly to be wished 274.1
    Quiet c. have 51.6

consumption
    c. of the purse 226.6

contemned
    known to be c. 95.3

contempts
    What our c. doth often hurl from us 238.2

content
    He that commends me to mine own c. 3.6
    My crown is called c. 38.1

contents
    some shrewd c. in yond same paper 155.9

contract
    I have no joy of this c. 38.8

cook
    'Tis an ill c. 99.10

copulation
    Let c. thrive 255.4

copy
    leave the world no c. 31.7

Corinthian
    a C., a lad of mettle 119.5

correctioner
    You filthy famished c. 223.2

corruption
    C. wins not more than honesty 39.2
    I have seen c. boil and bubble 32.5
    rank c., mining all within 39.1
    Stewed in c. 255.1

counsel
    c. turns to passion 4.6
    How hard it is for women to keep c. 310.3
    I can keep honest c. 121.1
    I defy all c. 4.2
    To c. deaf, but not to flattery 95.7

counsellors
    Good c. lack no clients 4.5

country
    Alas, poor c. 249.7
    Bleed, bleed, poor c. 212.2
    c. matters 254.9
    death, The undiscovered c. 274.1
    Our c. sinks beneath the yoke 291.13
    slain in your c.'s wars 265.7
    What c., friends, is this 160.3

courage
    c. mounteth with occasion 41.5
    screw your c. to the sticking-place 41.6

courtesan
    brave night to cool a c. 303.4

courtesy
    very pink of c. 223.6

coward
    Foul-spoken c. 43.1

cowardice
    pale cold c. 211.8

cowards
    c. die many times before their deaths 41.4
    Plenty and peace breeds c. 117.6

cowslip
    crimson drops I'th' bottom of a c. 22.10
    hang a pearl in every c.'s ear 84.9

Cressid
    This is, and is not, C. 139.2

crimes
    c. ... Are not inherited 244.6
    With all his c. broad-blown 43.7

Crispian
    This day is called the feast of C. 299.4

cross
    c. him in nothing 96.1

cross-gartered
    wished to see thee ever c. 287.12

crow
    the c. makes wing to th' rooky wood 200.4

crown
    golden c. like a deep well 151.12
    sweet a thing it is to wear a c. 150.9
    The c. o'th' earth doth melt 51.1
    Uneasy lies the head that wears a c. 150.5
    within the hollow c. 57.3

crows
    The c. and choughs that wing the midway air 249.8

cruel
    I must be c. only to be kind 82.3
    Let me be c., not unnatural 45.6

cruelty
    direst c. 45.9

cry
    C., Trojans, c. 232.5
    When we are born we c. 158.3

crying
    We came c. hither 21.10

cuckoo
    C., O word of fear 138.1

cucullus
    C. non facit monachum 14.5

cunning
    c. past man's thought 33.10

Cupid
    C. is a knavish lad 162.1
    C.'s strongest bow 296.2
    Some C. kills with arrows 162.4

cured
    none it ever c. 266.8

currents
    corrupted c. of this world 38.10

curs
    common cry of c. 46.3

curse
  primal eldest c. 115.1
custom
  C. hath made it in him 116.2
  What c. wills 47.7
customs
  Nice c. curtsey to great kings 150.8
cypress
  in sad c. 58.4

—D—

daffodils
  D., That come before the swallow dares 98.5
  When d. begin to peer 269.10
dagger
  Is this a d. 11.5
daggers
  d. in men's smiles 49.2
  I will speak d. 45.6
daintiest
  the d. last 99.8
daisies
  When d. pied 97.3
dalliance
  Do not give d. Too much the rein 256.5
  silken d. in the wardrobe lies 298.6
damnation
  I dare d. 25.1
dance
  d. our ringlets to the whistling wind 85.2
  When you do d. 48.5
dancer
  God match me with a good d. 48.2
dances
  what masques, what d. shall we have 219.7
dancing
  past our d. days 48.3
danger
  go and meet with d. 48.8
  we are in great d. 49.1
dangerous
  such men are d. 49.9
  therefore are they very d. 245.10
  These days are d. 17.3
  Yet have I in me something d. 49.8
dangers
  She loved me for the d. I had passed 162.5
Daniel
  A D. come to judgement 147.4
dare
  Letting 'I d. not' 42.8
  O, what men d. do! 2.1
dark
  poring d. 199.6
  we are for the d. 51.2
darkness
  d. be the burier of the dead 301.2
  d. fleckled like a drunkard 188.4
  I will encounter d. as a bride 56.2

instruments of D. 80.3
prince of d. 63.5
send to d. all that stop me 24.10
This thing of d. 50.4
darling
  the d. buds of May 275.4
darlings
  wealthy, curled d. 33.6
date
  their d. is out 58.10
daughter
  I have another d. 209.7
  My d.! O my ducats 50.8
  Still harping on my d. 50.5
daughters
  d. of the game 313.4
  I am all the d. of my father's house 266.3
  pelican d. 50.6
  Tigers, not d. 50.7
day
  a chronicle of d. by d. 272.2
  gaudy, blabbing, and remorseful d. 199.8
  In the posteriors of this d. 314.9
  jocund d. Stands tiptoe 188.5
  The bright d. is done 51.2
daylight
  We burn d. 286.4
days
  Jesu, the mad d. that I have spent 206.5
dead
  As d. as a door-nail 53.6
  He is d. and gone, lady 52.2
  Hector is d. 58.3
  I know when one is d. 54.9
death
  Be absolute for d. 55.9
  bridegroom in my d. 50.10
  cannot be a pinch in d. 210.12
  Come away d. 58.4
  dateless bargain to engrossing D. 153.1
  D., a necessary end 54.1
  D. and destruction dogs thee 184.7
  D. and Nature do contend about them 55.6
  D., as the Psalmist saith, is certain 52.7
  D. by inches 51.5
  d. of a dear friend 219.10
  D. that dark spirit 264.1
  death will have his day 56.9
  d.'s a great disguiser 56.4
  D.'s dishonourable victory 53.2
  D.'s eternal cold 57.6
  D.'s pale flag 247.4
  D.'s second self 205.9
  d.'s the market-place where each one meets 318.9
  dread of something after d. 274.1
  feast of d. 299.6
  for restful d. I cry 57.7
  Nor shall d. brag 222.5
  Nothing can we call our own but d. 57.2
  secret house of d. 273.5

Seeking for Richmond in the throat of d. 25.9
So bad a d. 53.4
strip myself to d. as to a bed 29.10
sure physician, D. 51.8
The d. of Antony Is not a single doom 149.6
This fell sergeant, D. 52.4
Thou art D.'s fool 55.10
thou owest God a d. 298.1
unburdened crawl toward d. 242.6
we owe God a d. 52.8
Yours in the ranks of d. 296.1

debts
He that dies pays all d. 58.1

decay
d. of lust and late-walking 206.8

December
old D.'s bareness everywhere 305.2

deed
A d. of death done on the innocent 192.8
A d. without a name 80.8
d. of dreadful note 44.6
I have done the d. 1.7
No day without a d. to crown it 232.6
So shines a good d. 108.11
They that set you on To do this d. 292.4
We are but young in d. 81.2

deeds
d. must not be thought 171.8
Unnatural d. 248.4

defence
In cases of d. 272.5

degree
d. being vizarded 14.4
d., priority, and place 209.1
Take but d. away 209.3
when d. is shaked 209.2

delay
coldness and d. 60.7
In d. there lies no plenty 229.1
leaden servitor to dull d. 10.5

delays
d. have dangerous ends 60.5

delight
give d., and hurt not 195.1

delights
His d. Were dolphin-like 73.1

description
A maid That paragons d. 311.5
beggared all d. 34.2

desire
deep d. hath none 257.7
D. my pilot is 255.6
d. sees best of all 202.1
d. should ... outlive performance 255.2

despair
d. and die 47.3

desperate
Tempt not a d. man 63.4

destiny
Hanging and wiving goes by d. 174.6

destruction
by d. dwell in doubtful joy 291.11
Even till d. sicken 64.2

detractions
they that hear their d. 128.2

device
I smell a d. 221.9

devices
our d. still are overthrown 90.11

devil
a born d. 107.2
can the D. speak true 63.6
Give the d. his due 305.9n
he must needs go that the d. drives 253.9
sugar o'er The devil himself 131.1
The D. can cite Scripture 63.7
the devil damn thee black 47.1
The devil hath power T'assume a pleasing shape 13.5
The d. understands Welsh 297.1

dice
The very d. obey him 169.9

dickens
I cannot tell what the d. his name is 196.1

die
d. all, d. merrily 52.6
D. and be damned 46.7
d. upon a kiss 152.3
If I d., no soul will pity me 63.3
If it were now to d. 117.4
let it d. as it was born 234.5
Now d., d., d., d., d. 70.1
That we shall d., we know 54.2
To d. – to sleep 274.1
to d., and go we know not where 56.3

dies
He d. to me again 114.6
He d., and makes no sign 53.3

difference
the d. of man and man 178.7
Lord, the d. of men 179.4

digestion
good d. wait on appetite 99.5

dignity
undeserved d. 182.2

diligence
best of me is d. 316.4

discourse
wench of excellent d. 309.8

discretion
Covering d. with a coat of folly 105.5

disdain
D. and scorn ride sparkling in her eyes 249.3
my dear Lady D. 249.2

disease
Like the owner of a foul d. 134.6
This d. is beyond my practice 65.4

diseases
D. desperate grown 134.7

dish
carve him as a d. fit for the gods 191.9

woman is a d. for the gods   309.1
dishonour
Your d. Mangles true judgement   224.1
disorder
Fear frames d.   63.12
disposition
change my d.   29.6
I fear your d.   16.7
dissemble
I would d. with my nature   36.4
dissension
Civil d. is a viperous worm   83.10
distilment
leperous d.   222.9
distinction
D., with a broad and powerful fan   319.8
distribution
D. should undo excess   79.6
ditty
This d. does remember my drowned father   74.4
divinity
There's a d. that shapes our ends   64.4
There's such d. doth hedge a king   150.3
division
ravishing d. to her lute   296.7
do
That we would d.   2.6
this thing's to d.   60.3
dog
a d.'s obeyed in office   15.7
Ask my d.   66.2
d. will have his day   90.12
I had rather be a d. ... than such a Roman   39.5
I had rather hear my d. bark at a crow   166.12
Mine enemy's d.   215.5
Not one to throw at a d.   176.1
Why should a d., a horse, a rat have life   114.2
dogs
let slip the d. of war   301.3
dolphin
Like Arion on the d.'s back   277.2
done
If it were d., when 'tis d.   2.7
What's d. cannot be undone   238.6
what's d. is d.   238.5
doom
even to the edge of d.   285.3
Doomsday
D. is near   52.6
sick almost to d. with eclipse   206.11
The houses he makes last till d.   109.8
door
The d. is open, sir   239.3
double
D., d. toil and trouble   308.2
doublet
what shall I do with my d. and hose   106.4

doubts
Our d. are traitors   252.6
saucy d. and fears   93.9
urge d. to them that fear   41.8
dove
roar you as gently as any sucking d.   219.2
dragon
Come not between the d. and his wrath   8.1
dream
D. on, d. on   66.9
I have had a dream   66.7
one new risen from a d.   133.7
when I waked, I cried to d. again   67.1
dreams
let us recount our d.   66.6
My life stands in the level of your d.   60.8
such stuff As d. are made on   159.3
were it not that I have bad d.   66.4
drink
We'll teach you to d. deep   67.5
drinking
unhappy brains for d.   68.4
drugs
Thy d. are quick   65.8
drum
A d.! a d.! Macbeth doth come   307.8
drunk
D.? and speak parrot   68.5
That which hath made them d.   67.10
Was the hope d.   67.9
drunken
What's a d. man like   68.8
ducat
Dead for a d.   191.7
duck
Swam ashore ... like a d.   277.1
duke
d. of dark corners   50.3
She bears a d.'s revenues on her back   245.3
durst
They d. not do't   209.4
dust
over-mastered with a piece of valiant d.   180.3
sweep the d. behind the door   86.1
what is this quintessence of d.   126.4
duty
a divided d.   68.11
dyer
like the d.'s hand   316.8
dying
I am d., Egypt, d.   69.1
it had a d. fall   195.2
Thou met'st with things d.   197.11
tongues of d. men   70.2

—E—

eagle
    Like an e. in a dove-cote   41.1

ear
    Give every man thy e.   3.7
    in the e. Of him that hears it   306.7
    reasonable good e. in music   194.2

ears
    Lend me your e.   73.6

earth
    Dear e., I do salute thee   212.3
    e. that's nature's mother   196.8
    this most goodly frame the e.   61.5
    thou bleeding piece of e.   113.4

ease
    What infinite heart's e.   150.7

east
    It is the e. and Juliet is the sun   246.11

ebbing
    E. men   242.5

eclipses
    late e. in the sun and moon   207.4

ecstasy
    Blasted with e.   170.7
    the very e. of love   161.1

Eden
    This other E.   78.2

egg
    He will steal an e. out of a cloister   16.6

eggshell
    Even for an e.   5.11

Egypt
    Melt E. into Nile   46.2

Egyptian
    Rare E.   34.3

elbow-room
    my soul hath e.   69.8

election
    Let desert in pure e. shine   61.2

elements
    I tax you not, you e., with unkindness   303.3
    To the e. Be free   103.9

elsewhere
    Tell me thou lov'st e.   166.2

Elysium
    all night Sleeps in E.   262.4
    My brother he is in E.   160.3

employment
    make love to this e.   48.6

empty
    purse and brain, both e.   67.4

emulation
    E. hath a thousand sons   246.3

end
    Is this the promised e.   55.1
    Let the e. try the man   75.10
    The e. crowns all   76.7
    The e. of this day's business   292.8
    The e. of war's uncertain   297.7
    true beginning of our e.   76.5

we shall never see the e. of it   299.2

ending
    my e. is despair   228.6

endure
    Men must e. Their going hence   54.8
    Must I e. all this   273.3

enemy
    feasting with mine e.   76.9
    You are mine enemy   76.8

engendering
    the e. of toads   230.2

England
    A little herd of E.'s timorous deer   77.6
    all the youth of E. are on fire   298.6
    Do it, E.   136.1
    E. keep my bones   69.7
    E., that was wont to conquer others   78.4
    gentlemen in E. now abed   299.4
    God for Harry! E. and Saint George   298.8
    That island of E.   65.11
    this earth, this realm, this E.   78.2

English
    On, on, you noble E.   77.2
    poor condemned E.   15.1

Englishman
    true-born Englishman   78.1

enskied
    a thing e. and sainted   242.1

enterprise
    The e. is sick   209.2

enterprises
    e. of great pitch and moment   136.3

entertainment
    dull thy palm with e.   3.7
    I spy e. in her   96.3

envy
    e. breeds unkind division   78.8

Epicurean
    E. cooks   98.7

equivocation
    e. will undo us   277.7

Ercles
    E.' vein, a tyrant's vein   219.1

Eros
    Unarm, E.   75.7

error
    What damned e.   239.6

eruption
    bodes some strange e. to our state   206.10

estridges
    plumed like e.   264.4

eternity
    E. was in our lips and eyes   160.7
    Passing through nature to e.   189.4
    Time's thievish progress to e.   285.2
    Who ... sells e. to get a toy   61.8

ever
    For e., and a day   179.6
    I am your own for e.   296.3

evil
    The e. that men do   73.6

evils
Cave-keeping e.   178.9
two weak e., age and hunger   226.3
excellent
an e. thing in woman   310.7
excuse
make the fault the worse by th'e.   82.6
The e. that thou dost make in this delay   82.8
exhalation
Like a bright e. in the evening   110.4
exits
their e. and their entrances   157.2
expectation
e. whirls me round   9.8
Now sits e. in the air   83.3
Oft e. fails   83.1
To mock the e. of the world   83.2
experience
E. is by industry achieved   83.8
e. to make me sad   83.5
exploits
Ripe for e.   322.5
extempore
e., from my mother wit   307.3
extenuate
Nothing e.   74.1
extremity
E., that sharpens sundry wits   113.1
eye
A still soliciting e.   214.8
E. of newt, and toe of frog   308.2
Let every e. negotiate for itself   162.3
The e. of man hath not heard   66.7
the e. wink at the hand   62.2
eyebrow
Made to his mistress' e.   157.2
eyes
From women's e. this doctrine I derive   310.9
It is engendered in the e.   161.7
Men's e. were made to look   25.2
Mine e. are cloyed   292.6
Mine e. smell onions   279.8
My mistress' e. are nothing like the sun   36.2
Not ... in their hearts but in their e.   323.6
silent wonder of still-gazing e.   159.6
worn your e. almost out in the service   317.1
eyesight
Dearer than e., space and liberty   166.9

—F—

face
A woman's f. with nature's own hand painted   106.6
By his f. straight shall you know his heart   14.2
God hath given you one f.   293.8
His f. is the worst thing about him   12.4
I saw his heart in 's f.   14.6
Was this f. the f.   12.9

you have such a February f.   12.8
Your f., my Thane, is as a book   12.3
faces
Bid them wash their f.   33.7
I have seen better f. in my time   12.2
lords and owners of their f.   252.5
Ye have angels' f.   13.6
fail
If we should f.   84.3
fair
every f. from f. sometime declines   275.4
F. is foul, and foul is f.   307.6
I have sworn thee f.   118.5
fairies
They are f.   84.7
fairy
defend me from that Welsh f.   297.6
faith
He wears his f. but as the fashion of his hat   90.1
where is f.   169.7
falcon
f., towering in her pride of place   21.2
fall
what a f. was there, my countrymen   54.4
falling
what a f. off was there   58.8
What think you of f. in love   168.1
false
As f. as Cressid   138.9
As f. as dicers' oaths   137.7
as f. as water   156.7
F. face must hide what the f. heart doth know   131.4
Thou mayst prove f.   231.4
falsehood
bait of f. takes this carp of truth   224.2
F. Is worse in kings   156.1
familiar
Be thou f.   3.7
famine
F. is in thy cheeks   227.2
Lean F.   299.5
famous
too f. to live long   120.3
fancy
buildings of my f.   272.8
So full of shapes is f.   135.10
Tell me where is F. bred   161.7
vie strange forms with f.   135.1
fantastical
it alone is high f.   135.10
fantasy
for a f. and trick of fame   297.9
fardels
Who would f. bear   274.1
farewell
A long f. to all my greatness   110.5
everlasting f. take   89.1
F. the plumed troops and the big wars   300.5
F. the tranquil mind, f. content   63.1

F., thou art too dear   89.5

farewells
    As many f. as be stars in heaven   89.6

fashion
    f. of these times   316.2
    f. wears out more apparel than the man   90.4
    F.'s own knight   89.11
    The f. is the f.   90.2
    Thou art not for the f. of these times   5.8
    What a deformed thief this f. is   90.3

fashion-mongers
    These strange flies, these f.   90.6

fashions
    Old f. please me best   90.7

fast
    F. bind, f. find   252.3
    Play f. and loose with faith   87.2

fat
    Let me have men about me that are f.   12.1

fate
    My f. cries out   90.10
    that one might read the book of f.   91.2

father
    ashamed to be my f.'s child   210.5
    Had he not resembled My f.   92.2
    I would my f. looked but with my eyes   210.7
    I would thou hadst told me of another f.   91.9
    It is a wise f. that knows his own child   210.4
    no more like my father   35.10
    Thy f. slew my f.   243.7
    Who would be a f.   92.7
    your f. should be as a god   92.6

fathers
    foolish over-careful f.   91.10

fathom
    how many f. deep I am in love   165.3

fault
    Condemn the f. and not the actor   115.5
    Do you smell a f.   93.1
    Every man has his f.   121.7
    It was a grievous f.   233.8
    The f., dear Brutus, is not in our stars   242.3
    The f. is thine   258.4
    worst f. you have is to be in love   165.1

faults
    Men's f. do seldom to themselves appear   93.2

favourite
    his f. flies   101.10

fawning
    base spaniel f.   95.1

fawns
    When he f., he bites   81.5

fear
    Extreme f. can neither fight nor fly   93.7
    F. no more the heat o'th' sun   189.3
    I have a faint cold f.   93.12
    Not knowing what they f.   248.3
    pale-hearted f.   93.10
    time to f. when tyrants seem to kiss   292.2

You may f. too far   93.6

fears
    naturally born to f.   310.4
    Present f.   135.4

feast
    great f. of languages   278.9

feasting
    This vault a f. presence   109.11

feather
    I am a f. for each wind that blows   302.3

feel
    Speak what we f.   17.5

felicity
    Absent thee from f. awhile   69.3

fellow
    a f. all in buff   223.1

fellowship
    all the f. I hold now with him   174.5

felt
    more is f. than one hath power to tell   75.1

fever
    life's fitful f.   55.7

few
    Never so f.   5.3
    We f., we happy f.   299.4

fewer
    The f. men, the greater share   122.4

fickle
    f. wavering nation   103.2

fiction
    condemn it as an improbable f.   272.3

fields
    a' babbled of green f.   53.1

fiend
    False f., avoid   276.2
    foul f. bites my back   276.3
    The f. is at mine elbow   63.8

fiery-footed
    f. steeds   9.7

fifteen
    When f. once has found us   108.2

figure
    A foolish f.   277.5

finger
    free from his ambitious f.   6.6

fire
    a woman would run through f. and water   179.1
    as coldly in him as f. in a flint   307.5
    frighted with false f.   114.11
    I am f. and air   273.8
    majestical roof fretted with golden f.   61.5
    steep-down gulfs of liquid f.   119.2
    who can hold a f. in his hand   135.8

fires
    sulphurous and thought-executing f.   303.

first
    I saw her f.   246.4
    Since f. I saw you   251.4

fish
    Thou deboshed f.   142.5

fishes
I marvel how the f. live in the sea 111.4
fishmonger
Excellent well. You are a f. 170.3
five
Full fadom f. 250.6
flame
In a mutual f. 162.7
flatterer
He that loves to be flattered is worthy o'th' f.
95.6
flatterers
A thousand f. sit within my crown 95.5
he hates f. 94.9
flattery
f. in friendship 305.9n
F. is the bellows blows up sin 95.4
flea
Thou f., thou nit 142.4
flesh
this too too sullied f. 273.10
flocks
My f. feed not 71.3
flower
a little western f. 97.4
action is no stronger than a f. 190.7
sweetest f. of all the field 57.4
flowers
Fair f. that are not gathered in their prime
97.9
Fairies use f. for their charactery 84.8
fly
To f., To swim 269.2
fold
The f. stands empty 64.3
follies
so tender o'er his f. 171.11
fool
A f.'s bolt is soon shot 305.9n
A motley f. 100.1
Better a witty f. 100.3
Dost thou call me f. 100.2
I had rather have a f. to make me merry 83.5
I met a f. i'th' forest 100.1
my poor f. is hanged 114.2
They f. me to the top of my bent 170.9
foolish
a very f., fond old man 204.9
fools
fond f. serve mad jealousy 143.7
f. by heavenly compulsion 242.4
iron-witted f. 292.5
these tedious old f. 203.6
what f. these mortals be 127.1
foot
The f. That leaves the print of blood 291.9
football
base f. player 269.6,
like a f. you do spurn me 238.10
force
what f. will have us do 197.5

forge
to the f. with it 2.9
forget
f. and forgive 101.1
F., forgive, conclude and be agreed 101.2
Old men f. 100.11
That I could f. what I have been 177.5
forgetfulness
steep my senses in f. 262.3
form
Dwellers on f. and favour 47.10
fortress
f. built by Nature for herself 78.2
fortune
A good man's f. may grow out at heels 102.4
a pipe for F.'s finger 101.9
all that f., death, and danger dare 5.11
F., good night 102.6
F., on his damned quarrel smiling 102.8
F., that arrant whore 102.7
F. thy foe 102.10
F.'s buffets and rewards 101.8
I am f.'s fool 102.11
In the secret parts of F. 101.6
made tame to f.'s blows 226.10
When in disgrace with f. and men's eyes
184.9
Yield not thy neck To F.'s yoke 102.2
fortunes
He shall not knit a knot in his f. 92.5
Making and marring f. 227.5
My f. and my friends at stake 36.4
My f. have Corrupted honest men 101.4
try our f. To the last man 41.3
foster nurse
f. of nature is repose 64.7
foul
f. and pestilent congregation of vapours
61.5
F. deeds will rise 43.3
I doubt some f. play 43.2
So f. and fair a day 303.5
foulest
tells close offices The f. way 19.8
fountain
like a f. stirred 36.8
like a f. troubled 311.11
fowl
poor hurt f. 165.8
fox
f. hath once got in his nose 289.7
Thou hast entertained A f. 50.1
frail
We are all f. 126.2
frailty
F., thy name is woman 137.6
tempt the f. of our powers 126.3
free
born f. as Caesar 103.4
freedom
fight for f. in your choice 61.2

French
He can speak F.   71.9
Frenchman
Done like a F.   103.1
friend
A f. should bear his f.'s infirmities   104.4
Keep thy f. Under thy own life's key   103.10
friends
a soul remembering my good f.   104.7
as many f. as enemies   214.2
F., Romans, countrymen   73.6
I am ... expected of my f.   82.9
I had rather have Such men as my f.   25.8
Our exiled f. abroad   82.11
Virtue finds no f.   295.5
friendship
band that seems to tie their f.   5.2
F. is constant in all other things   104.6
Most f. is feigning   139.4
fritters
one that makes f. of English   278.11
frost
killing f.   110.5
frosty
F. but kindly   203.3
fruit
Hang there like f., my soul   166.4
ripest f. first falls   56.8
Fulvia
Can F. die   143.6
funeral
f. baked meats   282.9
furious
To be f. Is to be frighted out of fear   93.4
further
We will proceed no f.   37.2

—G—

gall
Let there be g. enough in thy ink   320.8
game
The g. is up   128.3
The g.'s afoot   298.8
garden
sea-walled g.   105.9
This best g. of the world   102.13
'tis an unweeded g.   317.6
gardener
Adam was a g.   105.7
gardeners
no ancient gentlemen but g.   109.7
garland
withered is the g. of the war   51.1
gasp
Fight till the last g.   214.3
Gaunt
Old John of G., time-honoured Lancaster   205.6
geese
wild g. that the creeping fowler eye   21.5

general
Our g.'s wife is now the g.   129.11
genius
Under him My G. is rebuked   241.3
gentleman
a g. on whom I built An absolute trust   290.10
When a g. is disposed to swear   202.5
gentlemen
g. of the shade   199.5
We must be gentle, now we are g.   172.10
ghost
I'll make a g. of him   23.5
Vex not his g.   55.2
ghosts
g. did shriek and squeal about the streets   207.3
giant
a g.'s strength   228.1
gifts
Rich g. wax poor   107.3
girdle
I'll put a g. round about the earth   268.6
to the g. do the gods inherit   310.5
girl
An unlessoned g.   107.8
girls
Those g. of Italy   143.3
giving
I am not in the g. vein   107.6
Glamis
G. thou art, and Cawdor   7.6
glance
I was won ... with the first g.   168.8
glass
the g. Wherein the noble youth did dress   132.9
glisters
All that g. is not gold   13.10
globe
great g. itself   220.7
glories
You may my g. and my state depose   112.8
gloss
set a g. on faint deeds   28.6
Gloucestershire
I am a stranger here in G.   288.9
glow-worm
The g. shows the matin to be near   187.9
go
I g., I g., look how I g.   268.7
God
a g. to punish   229.3
Are you a g.   168.4
G., and not we, hath safely fought today   298.5
G. defend the right   108.7
G. is our fortress   108.6
G., the widow's champion   108.9
O G., thy arm was here   108.5
One ... that G. hath made   127.2

the g. of my idolatry   133.1
We are in G.'s hand   108.4
within the will of G.   108.3

gods
The g. themselves throw incense   248.7

going
seek no colour for your g.   82.1

gold
'Tis g. Which buys admittance   186.2
Saint-seducing g.   186.10

golden
G. lads and girls   189.3

Golgotha
field of G. and dead men's skulls   301.5
memorize another G.   94.2

gone
What's g. and what's past help   113.2

good
Are you g. men and true   295.8
G. alone is g.   79.2
G. night, ladies, g. night   88.8
G. night, sweet prince   73.5
his chief g. and market of his time   126.5
I never did repent for doing g.   108.10
It is not, nor it cannot come to g.   117.7
to do g., sometime Accounted dangerous folly
    317.10

goose
Where gott'st thou that g. look   47.1

grace
her strong toil of g.   34.5
momentary g. of mortal men   18.6

graceless
g. action of a heavy hand   294.8

grandsire
Sit like his g., cut in alabaster   322.10

grapple
G. them unto thy soul   104.1

gratis
fool that lent out money g.   293.3
He lends out money g.   293.2

grave
A little little g., an obscure g.   239.10
Convey me to my bed, then to my g.   70.3
earth can yield me but a common g.   110.1
Gaunt am I for the g.   109.9
You do me wrong to take me out o'the g.
    273.4
you shall find me a g. man   320.3

graves
Let's talk of g.   57.1

gravity
What doth g. out of his bed   203.7

Graymalkin
I come, G.   307.6

great
G. men have reaching hands   227.7
G. men tremble when the lion roars
    227.6
Rightly to be g.   122.1
Some are born g.   111.1

greatness
A long farewell to all my g.   110.5
Be not afraid of g.   111.1
g. that will overwhelm thee   6.1
highest point of all my g.   110.4
I and g. were compelled to kiss   196.11
out of love with g.   127.7
possessed he is with g.   230.3
Th'abuse of g.   291.8

Greek
it was G. to me   314.7

green
How g. you are and fresh   322.6
like a g. girl   321.8
When I was g. in judgement   321.2

greyhounds
like g. in the slips   298.8

grief
Each substance of a g.   10.4
Every one can master a g.   112.6
g. and time   112.11
G. fills the room up of my absent child
    113.7
G. makes one hour ten   112.7
honourable g.   280.5
journeyman to g.   114.3
Let g. convert to anger   8.2
My g. lies all within   114.4
My g. lies onward   267.4
poison of deep g.   112.3
Smiling at g.   211.11
the g., that does not speak   266.9

griefs
our g. heavier than our offences   298.4
What private g. they have ... I know not
    266.7

ground
let us sit upon the g.   57.3
We go to gain a little patch of g.   297.8

groundlings
split the ears of the g.   217.3

guests
the g. are come   125.7

guilty
it shall scarce boot me To say 'not g.'   149.3
Make mad the g.   217.2
started like a g. thing   10.10

guts
clay-brained g.   141.2

—H—

habitation
An h. giddy and unsure   233.4
local h. and a name   222.8

hair
more h. than wit   116.4

hairs
His silver h.   204.3
How ill white h.   204.1

halcyon
Saint Martin's summer, h.'s days   212.8
Halloo
H. your name to the reverberate hills   314.1
Hamlet
H. the Dane   132.2
hand
.that I were a glove upon that h.   167.3
hands
Give me your h., if we be friends   89.4
Great men have reaching h.   227.7
these hangman's h.   115.3
we seize into our h. His plate   292.3
will these h. ne'er be clean   33.9
handsome
h. in three hundred pounds a year   186.8
hang
H. thyself in thine own heir-apparent garters   46.6
H.! Beg! Starve   210.9
That would h. us, every mother's son   44.8
hanging
It is but heading and h.   292.1
happiness
H. courts thee in her best array   117.5
happy
H. man be his dole   116.7
on the top of h. hours   109.2
world of h. days   66.8
haps
Howe'er my h., my joys were ne'er begun   136.1
hard-handed
H. men that work in Athens here   317.2
harebells
h. dim   97.8
Harfleur
Holding due course to H.   258.10
harlot
The h.'s cheek   313.2
harm
to do h. Is often laudable   317.10
harmony
touches of sweet h.   193.5
harness
we'll die with h. on our back   101.3
Harry
A little touch of H. in the night   120.2
I saw young H. with his beaver on   119.7
haste
Those that with h. will make a mighty fire   225.6
wooed in h. and means to wed at leisure   175.4
hate
H. all, curse all   118.6
In time we h. that which we often fear   118.2
just cause of h.   167.6
hats
Their h. are plucked about their ears   221.6

have
H. is h.   226.2
H. more than thou showest   4.3
They well deserve to h.   272.10
To h. what we would h.   62.4
What we h. we prize not   293.5
havoc
Cry h.   301.3
hawk
I know a h. from a handsaw   170.5
hawthorn
Gives not the h. bush   127.8
hawthorn-buds
These lisping h.   323.4
hazard
all is on the h.   300.1
Men that h. all   245.7
head
Off with his h.   234.3
heart
a h. to love   161.6
A merry h. goes all the day   289.4
Arm thy h.   7.8
he was great of h.   202.4
how ill all's here about my h.   184.10
I cannot heave My h. into my mouth   278.3
I would eat his h. in the market-place   244.4
In my h.'s core, ay, in my h. of h.   75.3
Just as high as my h.   164.9
My h. dances, But not for joy   144.8
My h. Leaps to be gone   191.5
My old h. is cracked   113.8
no matter from the h.   315.10
Now cracks a noble h.   73.5
one foolish h.   167.5
The h. is sorely charged   266.10
very firstlings of my h.   2.8
wear my h. upon my sleeve   13.12
What his h. thinks his tongue speaks   121.4
yet do they ease the h.   315.7
heaven
Comfort's in h., and we are on the earth   318.5
He who the sword of h. will bear   233.10
H. hath my empty words   228.4
I will shortly send thy soul to H.   192.5
lark at h.'s gate sings   187.6
more things in h. and earth, Horatio   214.9
patch up thine old body for h.   189.8
sings hymns at h.'s gate   21.8
steep and thorny way to h.   130.6
thank h., fasting, for a good man's love   309.6
Hecuba
What's H. to him   216.7
hedge
I will but look upon the h.   82.10
Hell
dreadful minister of h.   119.3
fill another room in h.   47.2
H. only danceth at so harsh a chime   258.7
H.'s black intelligencer   245.1

married to h.   175.1
too cold for H.   35.3

hell-hound
A h. that doth hunt us all to death   244.11

herbs
Small h. have grace   106.2

Hercules
H. himself must yield to odds   202.7
Let H. himself do what he may   90.12
no more like my father Than I to Hercules   137.6

hereafter
She should have died h.   55.8

heretic
an h. that makes the fire   239.9

Herod
It out-H.s H.   217.3

heyday
heyday in the blood   182.8

Hiems
old H.' thin and icy crown   251.3

hill
heaven-kissing h.   11.6
Over h., over dale   84.9

history
history in all men's lives   120.4
Sir, a whole h.   277.6

hit
A h., a very palpable h.   272.9

hobby-horse
for O, the h. is forgot   123.8

holy
Octavia is of a h., cold and still conversation   253.8

home
Speak to me h.   120.9
When I was at h. I was in a better place   288.1

homely
Home-keeping youth have ever h. wits   127.11

homespuns
What hempen h. have we swaggering here   219.5

honest
An h. man ... is able to speak for himself   154.3
An h. tale speeds best   291.6
I am not naturally h.   121.9
To be direct and h. is not safe   121.6
Where I could not be h.   121.2

honesty
armed so strong in h.   282.8
What a fool H. is   121.8

honey
the h. of thy breath   247.4

honey-bees
So work the h.   8.10

honour
from the book of h. razed   240.8
He lives in fame that died in h.'s cause   88.3
High sparks of h.   123.2

h. bright   214.6
H. for wealth   245.6
H. is the subject of my story   122.8
H., riches, marriage-blessing   175.8
h. travels in a strait so narrow   123.3
I love The name of h.   122.7
If I lose mine h.   121.12
New-made h.   229.6
pluck bright h. from the pale-faced moon   122.2
public h. and proud titles   88.2
sin to covet h.   122.5
staff of h. for mine age   206.4
Take h. from me   123.1
too much h.   122.6
Use them after your own h. and dignity   172.5
What is h.   122.3

honourable
Brutus is an h. man   122.9

honours
H. thrive   121.10
New h. come upon him   198.1

hope
Cozening H. – he is a flatterer   123.6
Past h., and in despair   62.9
Things out of h.   23.10

hopes
tender leaves of h.   110.5

horn
Take thou no scorn to wear the h.   137.3

horror
h.! h.! h.   294.10

horrors
I have supped full with h.   39.7

horse
A h.! A h.! My kingdom for a h.   124.5
a h. of that colour   287.10
He doth nothing but talk of his h.   124.3
I had rather have my h. to my mistress   124.1
O, for a h. with wings   268.3
O happy h., to bear the weight of Antony   123.7
run before my.h. to market   117.9
To h., to h.   41.8

horsemanship
witch the world with noble h.   119.7

horses
Duncan's h.   124.2

hose
your h. should be ungartered   165.2

host
A fashionable h.   125.8
play the humble h.   125.4

hostess
like an h. that hath no arithmetic   26.10

hot
H. blood, h. thoughts   256.7
mounted for the h. encounter   257.9
Not so h.   117.8
these h. days is the mad blood stirring   275.3

Hotspur
the H. of the north   178.3
hour
Take thy fair h., Laertes   283.6
You come most carefully upon your h.   286.7
house
He hath eaten me out of h. and home   99.4
What! in our h.   125.3
housewives
h. in ... Your beds   311.6
howl
H., h., h., h.   114.1
howling
h. of Irish wolves   8.7
hugger-mugger
in h. to inter him   251.5
human
the end of h. misery   52.5
hungry
she makes h., Where most she satisfies   34.4
hunt
The h. is up   128.5
hurt
They that have power to h.   252.5
husband
Get thee a good h.   173.5
Heigh-ho for a h.   260.8
Thy h. is thy lord   130.3
husbandry
There's h. in heaven   200.3
husbands
Fools are as like h.   130.5
Hyperion
H. to a satyr   35.9
hypocrite
Out, scarlet h.   230.6

—I—

I
I am I, howe'er I was begot   133.12
I am not what I am   132.8n
I am that I am   132.8
I should have been that I am   134.4
Who is it that can tell me who I am   132.4
ice
hot i., and wondrous strange snow   219.8
icicles
When i. hang by the wall   304.5
ides
Beware the i. of March   231.9
ignorance
Dull unfeeling barren i.   133.5
I. is the curse of God   133.3
monster I.   133.4
There is no darkness but i.   133.6
valiant i.   36.8n
Ilion
Cloud-kissing I.   32.4
ill
Doubting things go i.   10.1

I. will never said well   305.9
In venturing i.   7.4
nothing i. can dwell in such a temple   13.1
ill-favoured
An i. thing, sir, but mine own   185.8
ill-starred
i. wench, Pale as thy smock   192.1
imagination
i. bodies forth The forms of things unknown
222.8
Prove true, i.   135.11
sweeten my i.   135.3
impediments
i. in fancy's course   95.9
imperial
i. theme   218.7
inch
let her paint an i. thick   189.5
Poor i. of nature   16.3
inch-thick
I., knee-deep   144.9
incorporate
I. then they seem   153.5
Indian
Like the base I.   74.1
indirections
By i. find directions out   224.2
infamy
Never dream on i.   41.11
infancy
Tetchy and wayward was thy i.   22.4
infant
At first the i.   157.2
infants
i. quartered with the hands of war   301.3
infection
Against i. and the hand of war   78.2
infirmity
i. of his age   204.4
ingratitude
I hate i. more in a man   140.1
I. is monstrous   139.5
I., more strong than traitors' arms   54.4
I., thou marble-hearted fiend   139.6
man's i.   139.4
inn
gain the timely i.   200.5
innocence
God and our I.   140.4
i. for i.   140.5
i. shall make False accusation blush
140.7
The silence often of pure i.   140.6
innocents
Some i. 'scape not the thunderbolt   140.2
insolence
i. of office   274.1
instant
The very i. that I saw you   167.8
intemperance
boundless i. In nature   81.9

intents
    Their most absurd i.   221.3
    thwarted our i.   84.5
isle
    i. is full of noises   195.1
    this sceptered i.   78.2
Italy
    Proud I.   143.4
item
    i., two lips   13.2

—J—

Jack
    Banish plump J.   87.5
    I'll be friends with thee, J.   88.10
    J. Falstaff with my familiars   87.7
    J. shall have Jill   76.4
jealous
    not ever j. for the cause   144.3
    one not easily j.   74.1
jealousy
    disturbing j.   144.7
    Green-eyed j.   143.8
    my j. Shapes faults that are not   143.9
jelly
    Out, vile j.   45.8
Jerusalem
    To meet with joy in sweet J.   88.11
jest
    a good j. forever   145.7
    fellow of infinite j.   73.3
    j. unseen, inscrutable   146.1
jesters
    J. do oft prove prophets   231.11
Jew
    Hath not a J. eyes   145.6
jewel
    rich j. in an Ethiop's ear   18.7
    this j. in the world   88.7
    You mend the j. by the wearing it   319.7
jewels
    captain j. in the carcanet   120.8
    Dumb j. often   145.3
    I'll give my j. for a set of beads   239.10
Jewish
    spit upon my J. gaberdine   145.5
Joan
    greasy J. doth keel the pot   304.5
jointress
    imperial j. to this warlike state   149.7
journey
    I have a j., sir, shortly to go   55.3
    then begins a j. in my head   263.6
journeys
    J. end in lovers meeting   163.11
Jove
    J., in his next commodity of hair   17.9
joy
    j.'s soul lies in the doing   2.5

    momentary j. breeds months of pain   255.7
joys
    this great sea of j.   146.3
judge
    An upright j.   147.7
    Forbear to j.   53.5
    When the j. is robbed   147.1
    You are a worthy j.   147.5
judgement
    He, which is the top of j.   147.3
    in j. old   305.7
    j., thou art fled   236.1
    like not in their j. but their eyes   233.3
Juliet
    and J. is the sun   246.11
    Heaven is here Where J. lives   247.3
just
    Be j., and fear not   148.9
    The gods are j.   148.11
justice
    And then, the j.   157.2
    In the course of j.   149.2
    sad-eyed j.   8.10
    which is the j., which is the thief   146.8

—K—

Kate
    I am he am born to tame you, K.   130.1
    K. of K. Hall   196.4
    Kiss me, K.   167.7
kill
    K. Claudio   244.3
    k., k., k., k., k.   244.1
kin
    A little more than k.   88.5
    k. with k., and kind with kind, confound   301.5
kindness
    kill a wife with k.   175.6
    milk of human k.   7.6
king
    Down, court! down k.   59.7
    Every inch a k.   151.2
    How can you say to me, I am a k.   151.9
    mockery k. of snow   152.1
    Never alone Did the K. sigh   150.2
    substitute shines as brightly as a k.   151.4
    this was now a k., and now is clay   190.4
    wash the balm off from an anointed k.   151.8
    What must the k. do now   151.10
kingdom
    For a k. any oath may be broken   6.4
kingdoms
    K. are clay   227.4
    We have kissed away K.   159.8
kings
    K. are earth's gods   151.5
    setter up and plucker down of k.   225.4
    Such is the breath of k.   151.7

this royal throne of k.   78.2

kiss
a single famished k.   89.6
murders with a k.   153.4
Then come k. me, sweet and twenty   229.1
You k. by th' book   152.8

kissed
I k. thee ere I killed thee   152.3

kisses
I'll smother thee with k.   153.3

kissing
it was made For k.   152.5

kite
Detested k., thou liest   156.6

knave
beetle-headed, flap-eared k.   142.3
young k., and begging   322.3

knell
a k, That summons thee to Heaven   44.5

knife
prepare your bosom for his k.   234.1

knock
K., k. Who's there, i'th' name of Belzebub   111.6

knocking
Wake Duncan with thy k.   238.4

knot
this k. intrinsicate Of life   69.2
too hard a k. for me to untie   290.5

knots
strong k. of love   88.6

know
Ask me not what I k.   153.7
I k. thee not, old man   19.3
I k. what I k.   153.10
I k. you all   119.4
I k. you what you are   153.6
Mistress, k. yourself   309.6
We k. what we are   104.10
What you k., you k.   235.2

knowledge
Be innocent of the k.   153.8
The k. of mine own desert   252.8

knowst
because thou k. I love her   144.5

—L—

labour
l. we delight in physics pain   316.6

labourer
I am a true l.   316.9

lacked
I shall be loved when I am l.   1.2

ladder
Thou l.   259.7

ladies
If l. be but young and fair   309.3
Sigh no more, l.   138.2

lads
Where are these l.   111.8

lady
Look to the L.   311.1
The l. doth protest too much   114.10

lambkins
L., we will live   158.1

lamentation
Moderate l. is the right of the dead   112.1

land
this dear dear l.   59.5

land-rats
there be l.   259.1

lane
Every l.'s end   281.10

language
You taught me l.   315.8

lantern
the l. in the poop   11.7

lark
Hark, hark, the l.   187.6
I do hear the morning l.   188.3
I took this l. for a bunting   13.3
It was the l., the herald of the morn   188.5
Stir with the l. tomorrow   286.11

lass
a l. unparalleled   73.2

late
Men must not walk too l.   49.5

Latin
away with him! he speaks L.   72.1
I smell false L.   72.7

lauds
snatches of old l.   52.3

laugh
I shall never l. but in that maid's company   182.3

law
court awards it, and the l. doth give it   147.6
In l., what plea so tainted   154.11
Let the l. go whistle   155.5
make a scarecrow of the l.   154.9
nice sharp quillets of the l.   154.4
Old father Antic the l.   154.2
The l. hath not been dead   154.10
The l., which is past depth   155.3
the l.'s delay   274.1
windy side of the l.   155.4

laws
The l. are mine, not thine   291.10

lawyer
skull of a l.   154.1

lawyers
let's kill all the l.   154.5

lean
Yond Cassius has a l. and hungry look   49.9

leave
He hath ... wrung from me my slow l.   214.1

leaving
Nothing in his life Became him like the l. it   55.5

lechery
Fry, l., fry   257.4

L., l., still wars and l.   257.5
war and l. confound all   47.6

leek
If you can mock a l.   297.5
wear the l.   297.4

legions
I'll fight their l. o'er   41.9

legs
His l. bestrid the ocean   73.1

leisure
After-hours gives l. to repent   238.8

lenity
What makes robbers bold but too much l.
    154.6

letter
chain were longer and the l. shorter   107.4

letters
he hath a thousand of these l.   155.11

leviathan
Ere the l. can swim a league   268.6

libertine
puffed and reckless l.   130.6

liberty
A man is master of his l.   178.1
I must have l.   103.3
L.! Freedom! Tyranny is dead   103.6
L. plucks Justice by the nose   148.12

lie
Shall Caesar send a l.   156.5
the L. Direct   14.7
you l. in your throat   156.3

life
except my l., except my l.   157.4
I bear a charmed l.   169.10
I do not set my l. at a pin's fee   267.6
I have set my l. upon a cast   245.8
I love long l. better than figs   157.1
jewel of l.   54.5
L. is as tedious as a twice-told tale   317.8
L.'s but a walking shadow   158.5
l.'s fitful fever   55.7
L.'s uncertain voyage   159.4
This l. is most jolly   139.4
time of l. is short   159.5
web of our l. is of a mingled yarn   156.12
Where is the l. that late I led   206.7
wine of l. is drawn   158.4

light
l. thickens   200.4
l. wenches will burn   313.1
Put out the l.   158.
what l. through yonder window breaks
    246.11

lightness
heavy l., serious vanity   162.8

lightning
Brief as the l. in the collied night   161.10
swift like l. in the execution   268.8

like
I shall not look upon his l. again
    178.2

lilies
l. that fester   39.9

lily
to paint the l.   81.8

lily-livered
l. boy   141.11

Limehouse
The limbs of L.   30.7

line
father to a l. of kings   241.4

lion
Let me play the l. too   219.2
Now the hungry l. roars   201.3

lips
Take, o take those l. away   19.6

lists
in the very l. of love   257.9

little
a l. More than a l.   99.3
blessedness of being l.   127.10
More than a l. is by much too much   224.7
Though she be but l.   12.7

live
l. we how we can, yet die we must   53.9

lives
music of men's l.   159.1

loathe
my relief Must be to l. her   138.5

locks
never shake Thy gory l. at me   116.5

Lombardy
Fruitful L.   143.5

London
I hope to see L. once   288.6

long
I have lived l. enough   204.12
Live loathed, and l.   183.11

longings
I have Immortal l.   110.3

looks
L. kill love   159.7
Sleek o'er your rugged l.   13.8

lord
l. of the whole world   5.6

loses
Who l. and who wins   225.8

love
chameleon L.   99.12
course of true l. never did run smooth
    161.9
finest part of pure l.   33.10
I did l. you once   165.12
Is l. a tender thing   162.10
Let not my l. be called idolatry   163.5
L. alters not with his brief hours   285.3
L., and be silent   161.2
L. comforteth like sunshine   257.10
L. cools   59.2
L., first learned in a lady's eyes   161.5
L. is a smoke   162.9
L. is blind   169.1

L. is not l.   163.7
L. is too young to know what conscience is
 163.9
L. keeps his revels   164.5
L. looks not with the eyes   161.11
l. may transform me to an oyster   165.9
L. that comes too late   160.5
L. will not be spurred to what it loathes
 164.4
L.'s not Time's fool   285.3
My only l. sprung from my only hate   246.9
she never told her l.   120.6
Speak low, if you speak l.   162.2
Spirit of l., how quick and fresh   163.10
the very wrath of l.   254.4
They do not l. that do not show their l.   164.2
This bud of l.   163.2
What is l.? 'Tis not hereafter   229.1
What l. can do   163.1

loved
 no sooner looked, but they l.   168.3
 Who ever l. that l. not at first sight   168.2

love-in-idleness
 maidens call it l.   97.4

lovely
 thou art more l. and more temperate   275.4

lover
 It was a l. and his lass   269.7
 the l., Sighing like furnace   157.2

lovers
 All l. young   51.6
 How silver-sweet sound l.' tongues   201.4
 L. and madmen have such seething brains
 135.6
 L. break not hours   169.5
 L. can see to do their amorous rites   169.4
 L. ever run before the clock   168.10
 L., to bed   201.2
 star-crossed l.   169.3
 The sight of l.   160.10

loves
 Two l. I have   163.8

lowliness
 l. is young ambition's ladder   6.9

lowly
 Tis better to be l. born   127.9

Lucifer
 he falls like L.   110.5

luck
 As good l. would have it   169.11
 good l. lies in odd numbers   169.12

lucky
 'Tis a l. day, boy   170.1

lump
 foul indigested l.   141.5

lunatic
 The l., the lover, and the poet   135.7

lust
 Careless l.   257.8
 cistern of my l.   255.8
 l. and murder wakes to stain and kill   44.2

l. in action   256.4
l., though to a radiant angel linked   254.7
Worse-than-killing l.   256.6

luxury
 The devil L., with his fat rump   257.3

lying
 as easy as l.   156.2
 Let me have no l.   27.2
 this vice of l.   156.4

—M—

Mab
 I see Queen M. hath been with you   86.2
 This is that very M.   86.3

Macbeth
 All hail, M.   111.5

Macduff
 Lay on, M.   94.5

mad
 As m. as a March hare   171.10
 As m. as the vexed sea   97.2
 do not make me m.   209.8
 I am but m. north-north-west   170.5
 I am not m.   171.2
 let me not be m.   171.3
 masters, are you m.   303.9
 so, it will make us m.   115.4
 There the men are as m. as he   76.10

madcap
 I'll be a m.   303.7

made
 You're a m. old man   273.2

madness
 His m. is poor Hamlet's enemy   171.1
 M. in great ones   170.8
 That way m. lies   171.5

magic
 This rough m.   242.8

maid
 chariest m. is prodigal enough   29.8

maiden
 your m. presence   4.1

maidenheads
 how go m.   257.2

maidenhoods
 Played for a pair of stainless m.   201.6

majesty
 The cess of m.   150.1

malice
 ancient m.   133.9
 Deep m. makes too deep incision   118.4

malicho
 miching m.   184.2

man
 a m. or a fish   127.3
 A poor, infirm, weak and despised old m.
 204.8
 a slight unmeritable m.   141.7
 A was a m., take him for all in all   178.2
 Dispute it like a m.   92.4

He'll make a proper m.   177.9
I play The m. I am   142.7
I smell a m. of middle earth   126.9
Is m. no more than this   126.6
let him pass for a m.   178.11
M. delights not me   126.4
M., more divine, the master   179.8
m., proud m.   126.8
M.'s life is cheap as beast's   226.9
Not yet old enough for a m.   323.7
O God that I were a m.   244.4
place and means for every m. alive   79.3
such a m. As this I dreamt of   177.7
the King is but a m.   79.5
the m. entire   214.7
This was a m.   178.5
Unaccommodated m.   126.7
What a piece of work is a m.   126.4
What a pretty thing m. is   165.10
When you durst do it, then you were a m.
    178.10
manhood
    M. is melted into curtsies   179.2
    power to shake my m. so   178.6
mankind
    How beauteous m. is   127.4
manner
    to the m. born   47.8
manners
    view the m. of the town   288.5
    We are the makers of m.   172.7
mansion
    thy fading m.   181.4
map
    I see, as in a m.   232.3
marble
    I am m.-constant   241.8
    Not m., nor the gilded monuments
        222.6
March
    take The winds of M. with beauty   98.5
marigold
    m., that goes to bed wi'th' sun   98.3
mark
    ever-fixed m.   163.7
markets
    you are not for all m.   309.6
marriage
    coldly furnish forth the m. tables   282.9
    curse of m.   174.12
    Hasty m. seldom proveth well   174.4
    instances that second m. move   174.1
    M. is a matter of more worth   174.2
    m. of true minds   163.6
    no fear in m.   173.6
married
    A young man m.   173.8
Mars
    eye like M. to threaten and command   11.6
martlet
    temple-haunting m.   20.10

Mary-buds
    winking M.   96.5
master
    I will be m. of what is mine own   130.2
    m. mistress of my passion   106.6
    that in your countenance which I would fain
        call m.   15.6
masters
    We cannot all be m.   155.8
matron
    mutine in a m.'s bones   254.10
    sober-suited m., all in black   201.6
matter
    gravelled for lack of m.   152.2
    More matter with less art   277.5
May
    As full of spirit as the month of M.   264.4
    Love, whose month is ever M.   269.8
    More matter for a M. morning   275.6
maypole
    Thou painted m.   12.6
meals
    Unquiet m. make ill digestions   99.2
meaning
    with best m. have incurred the worst   84.2
means
    sight of m. to do ill deeds   208.8
    the m. are gone that buy this praise   95.8
    the m. whereby I live   186.6
    Your m. are very slender   226.5
measure
    M. for m. must be answered   148.8
    M. still for M.   149.1
measures
    I am for other than dancing m.   48.1
medal
    He wears her like her m.   258.2
medicine
    Work on, My m.   221.7
meditating
    m. that she must die once   270.7
meditation
    maiden m., fancy-free   107.9
    wings as swift as m.   268.4
melancholy
    as m. as a lodge in a warren   176.5
    I can suck m. out of a song   176.2
    scholar's m.   176.3
melt
    M. and no more be seen   152.4
memory
    begot in the ventricle of m.   306.6
    in my m. locked   176.8
    M., the warder of the brain   177.2
    Pluck from the m. a rooted sorrow   171.9
men
    M. were deceivers ever   138.2
    We m. may say more   180.8
    you are m. of stones   114.1
men-children
    Bring forth m. only   191.4

mending
m. of highways 181.3
Mercury
words of M. are harsh 193.3
mercy
gates of m. 299.1
How shalt thou hope for m. 181.7
Lawful m. Is nothing kin 181.6
m. seasons justice 181.8
Sweet m. is nobility's true badge 182.1
The quality of m. is not strained 181.8
merit
oft got without m. 240.6
mermaid
m. on a dolphin's back 194.1
merriest
Men are m. when they are from home 178.4
merrily
M., m. shall I live now 87.1
merry
As m. as crickets 116.8
as m. as the day is long 260.7
I am not m. 14.1
rejoicing to see another m. 185.6
message
deliver a plain m. bluntly 121.1
metal
m. more attractive 254.8
method
Though this be madness, yet there is m. in't 170.4
mettle
unimproved m. 23.4
mewling
M. and puking 157.2
midnight
iron tongue of m. 201.2
Not to be abed after m. 109.3
We have heard the chimes at m. 206.6
midsummer
gorgeous as the sun at m. 264.4
m. madness 275.5
milk
take my m. for gall 45.9
mince
ways to m. it in love 166.6
mind
A mote it is to trouble the m.'s eye 183.7
A troubled m. drove me to walk abroad 10.6
I fear I am not in my perfect m. 204.9
I have a man's m. 310.2
In my m.'s eye 183.8
minister to a m. diseased 171.9
My m. misgives 184.11
'Tis the m. that makes the body rich 295.10
To find the m.'s construction in the face 13.7
what a noble m. is here o'erthrown 170.6
mine
What's m. is yours 166.10
ministers
m. and instruments of cruel war 300.9

mint
a m. of phrases in his brain 278.7
minute
not a m. of our lives 221.1
minutes
our m. hasten to their end 284.9
miracles
M. are ceased 276.1
m. are past 275.7
Miranda
Admired M. 311.12
mirror
m. of all Christian kings 120.1
to hold ... the m. up to nature 217.3
mirth
disposed to m. 246.5
he is all m. 182.5
M. becomes a feast 125.5
With m. in funeral 173.11
Misanthropos
I am *M.* 184.1
misbeliever
You call me m. 145.5
Mischief
M., thou art afoot 184.3
miserable
The m. have no other medicine 123.5
misery
m. acquaints a man with strange bed-fellows 3.4
your m. increase with your age 46.4
mistress
My m. when she walks 311.10
O m. mine 163.11
mock
She would m. me into air 249.4
moderation
Why tell you me of m. 185.7
modesty
grace and blush of m 137.7
Have you no m. 23.9
m. may more betray our sense 280.9
mole
tread softly, that the blind m. 235.5
money
If m. go before 186.7
Put m. in thy purse 186.9
money-bags
I did dream of m. 66.5
Monmouth
there is also ... a river at M. 297.3
monster
a m. Begot upon itself 144.3
blunt m. with uncounted heads 248.1
green-eyed m. 144.1
My mistress with a m. is in love 165.6
some m. in thy thought 276.6
month
within a m. 137.6
moon
how the m. sleeps with Endymion 187.1

lantern is the m. 187.4
th'inconstant m. 296.4
The m. shines bright 200.7
very error of the m. 187.5
moonlight
How sweet the m. sleeps upon this bank
193.5
Ill met by m. 187.2
morn
grey-eyed m. 188.4
the m. in russet mantle clad 187.7
morning
Full many a glorious m. have I seen 188.6
morsel
A m. for a monarch 34.1
mortal
desperately m. 190.6
she, being m., of that boy did die 22.3
mortality
it smells of m. 190.5
m.'s strong hand 190.3
nothing serious in m. 158.4
mother
He did it to please his m. 191.2
My m. told me just how he would woo 191.1
So loving to my m. 128.10
motley
made myself a m. to the view 319.1
mouse
not a m. Shall disturb this hallowed house
86.1
Not a m. stirring 235.3
Mousetrap
The M. 287.8
mousing
m. the flesh of men 300.2
mouths
made m. in a glass 294.1
multitude
fool m. that choose by show 233.6
many-headed m. 213.7
wav'ring m. 248.1
multitudes
rank me with the barbarous m. 229.8
murder
M. most foul 191.6
M., stern m. 192.6
M.'s as near to lust 192.3
No place indeed should m. sanctuarize 191.8
murther
Most sacrilegious M. 191.11
muse
O for a m. of fire 218.1
mushrooms
make midnight m. 86.4
music
How sour sweet m. is 194.7
I am never merry when I hear sweet m.
193.6
If m. be the food of love 195.2
In sweet m. is such art 193.1

man that hath no m. in himself 193.7
m. at the close 56.7
M. ho, m., such as charmeth sleep 194.3
m. moody food 192.9
m. of men's lives 194.7
the m. of my hounds 128.4
This m. crept by me upon the waters
194.11
This m. mads me 194.8
Where should this m. be 194.11
myself
I am m. alone 132.3
I follow but m. 252.7
m. would be his wife 313.10
What do I fear? M. 132.6
mystery
pluck out the heart of my m. 172.3
take upon's the m. of things 195.4

—N—

name
Good n. in man and woman 240.7
The n. and not the thing 128.6
What's in a n. 196.2
nation
He hates our sacred n. 118.3
nativity
N., once in the main of light 159.2
natural
He wants the n. touch 92.3
nature
Against the use of n. 280.7
Crack n.'s moulds 303.2
free and open n. 115.8
great N.'s second course 262.8
n. crescent does not grow alone 175.9
n. falls into revolt 111.3
N. never framed a woman's heart 311.4
n.'s infinite book of secrecy 196.5
One touch of n. 127.5
ruined piece of n. 59.4
Thou, N., art my goddess 196.7
to hide the sparks of N. 106.7
vicious mole of n. 106.8
nave
unseamed him from the n. to th' chops
294.9
necessities
art of our n. is strange 197.3
let us meet them like n. 197.1
necessity
Nature must obey n. 262.6
N. so bowed the state 196.11
N.'s sharp pinch 197.2
sworn brother ... To grim N. 197.6
need
reason not the n. 226.9
neglect
we do n. The thing we have 61.7

negligence
 O n.! Fit for a fool   185.2
negligent
 I may be n.   302.2
never
 N., n., n., n., n.   62.11
newness
 fault and glimpse of n.   198.2
news
 father of good n.   199.1
 first bringer of unwelcome n.   198.10
 it is never good To bring bad n.   198.9
 nature of bad n.   198.8
 What n. on the Rialto   198.7
 What's the n. in Rome   198.3
 What's the new n.   89.8
night
 Come, seeling N.   200.4
 comfort-killing n.   200.2
 dark n. strangles the travelling lamp   50.2
 dead waste and middle of the n.   199.3
 foul womb of n.   14.9
 In such a n. as this   200.7
 love-performing n.   201.5
 loving black-browed n.   247.2
 make the n. joint-labourer with the day   316.3
 N. and silence   201.1
 n. doth nightly make grief's length   112.9
 N.'s black agents   200.4
 N.'s candles are burnt out   188.5
 N.'s swift dragons   276.4
 one other gaudy n.   125.1
 soft stillness and the n.   193.5
 swift, you dragons of the n.   199.2
 The n. has been unruly   207.6
 Things that love n.   200.1
 This is the n.   2.2
 very witching time of n.   199.4
nightingale
 It was the n. and not the lark   188.5
 no music in the n.   167.10
night-owls
 n. shriek   59.7
Niobe
 Like N., all tears   137.6
noble
 this nature is too n. for the world   142.6
nobleness
 The n. of life is to do thus   254.1
nobly
 Was not that n. done   1.8
noise
 Sneak's n.   192.11
nose
 led by th' n.   115.8
nothing
 Demand me n.   235.2
 He was a kind of n.   243.1
 infinite deal of n.   278.10
 N. will come of n.   136.5

 there is n. left remarkable   51.1
 Thinking of n. else   165.5
 To be thus is n.   93.8
 To have seen much and to have n.   83.4
nought
 N.'s had, all's spent   62.3
nourisher
 Chief n. in life's feast   262.8
now
 If it be n. 'tis not to come   91.1
nunnery
 Get thee to a n.   31.2
nurture
 N. can never stick   107.2
nutshell
 I could be bounded in a n.   66.4

—O—

O
 Within this wooden O   218.2
oath
 good mouth-filling o.   202.6
oaths
 full of strange o.   157.2
 strongest o. are straw   256.5
obedience
 our o. to the King   82.5
object
 o. poisons sight   192.2
objects
 one that feeds On o., arts, and imitations   320.2
oblivion
 dust of old o.   283.8
 formless ruin of o.   286.1
obscenely
 most o. and courageously   219.3
observation
 strange places crammed With o.   71.1
occasion
 He married but his o. here   5.5
 rough torrent of o.   79.9
occasions
 frame my face to all o.   131.2
 How all o. do inform against me   243.3
 on the wing of all o.   161.8
occupation
 Othello's o.'s gone   26.9
odds
 Almost at o. with morning   188.2
 the o. is gone   51.1
offence
 my o. is rank   115.1
 Where th'o. is, let the great axe fall   148.5
office
 a losing o.   198.10
old
 An o. man, broken with the storms of state   69.5

I am o., I am o. 203.10
I am too o. to learn 204.5
If to be o. and merry be a sin 203.8
O. folks 205.8
O. men forget 299.4
She is not yet so o. But she may learn 128.1
when he's o., cashiered 42.4
Why art thou o. and not yet wise 204.11
you never can be o. 205.11

oldest
The o. hath borne most 17.5

one
O. for all 5.4

onions
eat no o. nor garlic 219.6

Ophelia
I loved O. 26.5
The fair O. 208.3

opinion
His own o. was his law 6.8

opinions
I have bought golden o. 240.3

opportunity
o., thy guilt is great 208.9

opposite
Be o. with a kinsman 230.5

oppressor
Th'o.'s wrong 274.1

orange
Civil as an o. 172.9

orator
I am no o. 267.11

order
Let o. die 63.11
Stand not upon the o. of your going 239.1

orisons
Nymph, in thy o. 208.3

ornament
world is still deceived with o. 13.11

Orpheus
O. with his lute made trees 193.1

Othello
O.'s occupation's gone 159.9

other
I crave no o. nor no better man 129.6

out
This will o. 45.1

outside
swashing and a martial o. 177.8

oven
An o. that is stopped 257.6

owl
It was the o. that shrieked 21.1
nightly sings the staring o. 304.5

ox
that roast Manningtree o. 87.4

oyster
world's mine o. 318.3

pace
Creeps in this petty p. 78.5

packs
P. and sects of great ones 287.1

pageant
this insubstantial p. 220.7

pain
What p. it was to drown 250.3

palm
an itching p. 39.4
bear the p. alone 227.10
p. to p. is holy palmers' kiss 152.7

palms
Paddling p., and pinching fingers 257.11

pangs
p. of disprized love 274.1

pansies
p., that's for thoughts 96.7

pantaloon
lean and slippered p. 157.2

paper
He hath not eat p. 72.6
p. bullets of the brain 315.4

paradoxes
old fond p. 307.2

paragon
the p. of animals 126.4

parallels
delves the p. in beauty's brow 284.11

pard
bearded like the p. 157.2

parks
Disparked my p. 71.4

partial
Nature makes them p. 191.3

partner
My dearest p. of greatness 129.4

parts
one man in his time plays many p. 157.2

passion
her p. ends the play 220.1
that man That is not p.'s slave 75.3

past
P. and to come seems best 228.9
Things that are p. 211.2

pat
Now might I do it p. 208.6

patches
P. set upon a little breach 181.1

patens
thick inlaid with p. of bright gold 193.5

path
tread the p. that thou shalt ne'er return 192.4

patience
Call it not p. 63.2
Have p. and endure 271.3
laughed him out of p. 96.2
Like P. gazing on kings' graves 211.7

like P. on a monument 164.1
P. is for poltroons 211.4
P. is stale 211.9

pattern
A p. to all princes 74.6

peace
merry songs of p. 212.10
naked, poor and mangled p. 212.7
P. ..., and love, and quiet life 175.7
p. proclaims olives of endless age 213.6
p. With no less honour 212.6
reap the harvest of perpetual p. 213.4
set phrase of p. 265.5
This p. is nothing but to rust iron 212.5
time of universal p. 212.4
weak piping time of p. 213.3

peacemakers
Blessed are the p. 212.9

pearl
a p. Whose price hath launched a thousand
ships 118.8

pearls
Those are p. that were his eyes 250.6

Pegasus
fiery P. 119.7

pen
Devise, wit, write p. 320.5

pencils
Ware p., ho 320.6

pens
quirks of blazoning p. 311.5

people
common p. swarm like summer flies
213.9
the p. had more absolute power 60.9
What is the city but the p. 60.10

peopled
The world must be p. 31.3

perdition
Ling'ring p. 58.2
p. catch my soul 167.2

perfect
Take pains, be p. 219.3

perfection
Holds in p. but a little moment 287.2

performance
lovers swear more p. than they are able 257.1
provokes the desire, but it takes away the p.
68.2

perfumes
all the p. of Arabia 22.9

perjuries
lovers' p. 156.9

perjury,
p., in the highest degree 156.8

perseverance
P., dear my lord Keeps honour bright 214.6

person
Thus play I in one p. 132.5

perturbation
polished p. 10.2

petard
Hoist with his own p. 148.4

Phaeton
like glist'ring P. 59.7

philosophy
dreamt of in your p. 214.9
Preach some p. to make me mad 214.10
Unfit to hear moral p. 215.1

Phoebus
P. gins arise 187.6

phoenix
maiden p. 75.2

phrase
an ill p., a vile p. 45.3
crack the wind of the poor p. 314.2

phrases
Taffeta p. 315.1

physic
Throw p. to the dogs 65.5

physician
Kill thy p. 64.6
Trust not the p. 65.10

pickers
p. and stealers 43.5

pickle
How cam'st thou in this p. 290.4

pigeon-livered
I am p. and lack gall 42.5

pilgrims
lips, two blushing p. 152.6

pin
with a little p. Bores through his castle wall
57.3

pinch
a lover's p. 254.3

pinches
Phoebus' amorous p. 34.1

pipe
easier to be played on than a p. 172.3

pippins
there's p. and cheese 99.6

pitch
They that touch p. 80.6

pitchers
P. have ears 30.9, 248.5

pity
As small a drop of p. 215.3
Her life was beastly and devoid of p. 81.6
p. choked with custom of fell deeds 301.3
P. is the virtue of the law 155.2
the p. of it, Iago 215.9

plague
A p. o' both your houses 47.4

plain
'tis my occupation to be p. 12.2

plainness
To p. honour's bound 120.10

planet
It is a bawdy p. 257.12

plants
p., herbs, stones, and their true qualities 196.9

plates
As p. dropped from his pocket   73.1

play
The p.'s the thing   217.1
this p. can never please   218.5
your p. needs no excuse   220.2

player
Like a strutting p.   220.8

pleasure
I'th' East my p. lies   70.5
P. and action make the hours seem short   284.4
private p. of some one   151.3
the p. of the fleeting year   1.3

pleasures
Their p. here are past   51.7

plodders
Small have continual p. ever won   72.5

plot
The p. is laid   221.4

poet
The p.'s eye   -222.8

poetical
I would the gods had made thee p.   222.1

poison
In p. there is physic   134.8
sweet, sweet p. for the age's tooth   95.2

policy
more in p. than in malice   234.2
P., ... Which works on leases   225.10
They tax our p.   225.12
trail of p.   224.3

politician
pate of a p.   224.5
scurvy p.   225.7
vile p.   224.6

pomp
All p. and majesty I do forswear   240.1
let the candied tongue lick absurd p.   94.6
Pride, p. and circumstance of glorious war   300.5
Take physic, p.   229.7

pond
his p. fished by his next neighbour   139.3

poniards
She speaks p.   279.1

poor
as p. as Job   226.4

porpentine
quills upon the fretful p.   271.5

ports
p. and happy havens   38.2

pound
an equal p. Of your fair flesh   38.3

poverty
all-shunned poverty   19.2

power
If p. change purpose   227.11

praise
I will not p.   185.11
she will outstrip all p.   312.2

thine shall be the p.   60.2

pray
When I would p. and think   228.4

prayer
he is given to p.   228.5
relieved by p.   228.6

prayers
P. and wishes Are all I can return   226.7
They have said their p.   265.1

precepts
These few p. in thy memory   3.7

precise
Lord Angelo is p.   252.4

preferment
P. goes by letter   39.8

preparation
to fool their p.   221.3

presagers
dumb p. of my speaking breast   320.7

present
P. mirth hath p. laughter   229.1
things p. worst   228.9

presume
p. not that I am the thing I was   29.3

Priam
Had doting P. checked his son's desire   210.2

price
The p. is, to ask it kindly   223.5

pricking
By the p. of my thumbs   80.5

pride
his p. Peep through each part of him   229.4
maiden p., adieu   260.10
My p. fell with my fortunes   229.2
p. is his own glass   230.1

priest
churlish p.   73.4
This meddling p.   230.7

primrose
go the p. way to th'everlasting bonfire   119.1
P., first-born child of Ver   97.8
p. path of dalliance   130.6

primroses
pale p.   98.6

prince
a p. out of thy star   33.1
Good night, sweet p.   73.5
It is the p. of palfreys   123.10
nimble-footed madcap P. of Wales   119.6
P. of Cats   179.3
the p. of darkness is a gentleman   63.5

princes
sweet aspect of p.   42.3

prison
let's away to p.   230.8
This p. where I live   230.9

private
the p. wound is deepest   19.7

prize
p. of all-too-precious you   163.4

prodigal
  like the p. doth she return 259.2

profit
  'Tis not my p. that does lead mine honour,
  121.11
  no p. but the name 297.8
  No p. grows where is no pleasure ta'en 221.2

Promethean
  right P. fire 310.10
  that P. heat 158.7
  true P. fire 310.9

promise
  To p. is most courtly and fashionable 231.5

promises
  His p. were as he then was 231.3

promontory
  Once I sat upon a p. 194.1
  one that stands upon a p. 6.5

promotion
  none will sweat but for p. 316.2

proof
  give me the ocular p. 28.8

Proserpina
  O P., For the flowers 98.4

prosper
  I grow, I p. 7.3

prosperity
  a jest's p. 306.7
  P.'s the very bond of love 164.7

protestations
  Stuffed with p. 231.7

proud
  I am very p., revengeful 253.3
  you are too p. 18.9

prove
  I knew what you would p. 179.7

providence
  special p. in the fall of a sparrow 232.7

prune
  no more faith in thee than in a stewed p.
  141.3

prunes
  longing for stewed p. 22.2

public
  The body p. is A horse 213.10

publican
  how like a fawning p. 118.3

punishment
  pleasing p. that women bear 21.9

puppy
  One that I brought up of a p. 66.3n

purgers
  We shall be called p., not murderers 237.5

purpose
  Infirm of p. 41.7
  P. is but the slave to memory 100.10
  p. that makes strong the vow 231.6

purses
  Our p. shall be proud 282.11

Pyramus
  What is P. 169.2

Pythagoras
  hold opinion with P. 9.3

—Q—

quarrel
  Beware Of entrance to a q. 3.7
  find q. in a straw 122.1
  In a false q. there is no true valour 234.7

quarrels
  as full of q. as an egg is full of meat 234.8
  busy giddy minds With foreign q. 225.1

queen
  I would not be a q. 150.10
  q. of curds and cream 40.6
  The mobbled q. 45.4

question
  are you aught that man may q. 11.4
  Ask me what q. thou canst possible 235.1
  that is the q. 274.1

quicksilver
  rogue fled from me like q. 268.5

quiddities
  Where be his q. now 154.1

—R—

rack
  leave not a r. behind 220.7
  The r. dislimns 213.11
  the r. of this tough world 55.2

rackets
  matched our r. to these balls 269.5

rage
  hard-favoured r. 298.7
  Harsh r. 16.4
  tiger-footed r. 7.10

raggedness
  looped and windowed r. 19.1

rain
  Much r. wears the marble 214.4
  the r. it raineth every day 303.6
  With hey, ho, the wind and the r. 303.6

ram
  old black r. Is tupping your white ewe
  255.10

rancour
  R. will out 133.10

rash
  too r., too unadvised 117.10

rashness
  Who cannot condemn r. in cold blood 118.1

rat
  How now? A r. 191.7

rats
  r. instinctively have quit it 259.5

raven
  croaking r. doth bellow for revenge 20.8
  The r. himself is hoarse 207.5

readiness
  The r. is all 91.1

reading
    to reason against r.   24.2
reads
    He r. much   49.9
ready
    All things are r., if our minds be so   183.9
reason
    godlike r.   235.8
    men have lost their r.   236.1
    my r. Sits in the wind against me   146.6
    My r., the physician to my love   236.4
    no other but a woman's r.   236.11
    noble and most sovereign r.   170.7
    pales and forts of r.   106.8
    R. in madness   171.7
    r. is past care   236.5
    r. panders will   254.10
    r. to cool our raging motions   236.3
    You cannot speak of r. to the Dane   235.7
reasons
    If r. were as plentiful as blackberries
        236.8
    My r. are too deep and dead   236.10
    r. find of settled gravity   166.1
rebellion
    R. lay in his way   237.2
    R., flat r.   237.7
reckoning
    great r. in a little room   221.10
record
    living r. of your memory   222.7
recordation
    To make a r. to my soul   177.6
recreation
    Sweet r. barred   173.10
redress
    Things past r.   238.7
region
    She is a r. in Guiana   311.3
relief
    For this r. much thanks   281.3
remedies
    Our r. oft in ourselves do lie   242.2
remedy
    Things without all r.   238.5
remember
    I cannot but r. such things were   177.3
    Must I r.   176.7
    R. me   176.9
remembrance
    Let us not burthen our r.   197.10
    Makes the r. dear   176.6
    r. of things past   211.3
    rosemary, that's for r.   177.1
    Writ in r. more than things long past   56.7
removed
    The life r.   242.7
remuneration
    R.! O that's the Latin word   186.5
report
    they have committed false r.   223.4

reputation
    bubble r.   157.2
    I have lost my r.   240.5
    my r. is at stake   241.1
    spotless r.   240.4
resolution
    How high a pitch his r. soars   241.10
    My r.'s placed   241.8
    native hue of r.   136.3
    r. and the briefest end   273.7
respect
    Is there no r. of place   303.9
    throw away r.   47.9
    too much r. upon the world   318.1
rest
    debarred the benefit of r.   263.7
restoration
    R. hang Thy medicine on my lips   65.3
revels
    Our r. now are ended   220.7
revenge
    capable and wide r.   244.5
    croaking raven doth bellow for r.   243.2
    R. should have no bounds   243.5
    spur my dull r.   243.3
revenged
    I'll be r. on the whole pack of you   244.8
revenges
    I will have such r. on you   243.9
reverence
    none so poor to do him r.   190.2
rhyme
    it hath taught me to r.   222.3
rhyming
    I was not born under a r. planet   222.4
ribbon
    A very r. in the cap of youth   321.9
rich
    R. she shall be, that's certain   180.4
    something r. and strange   250.6
right
    To do a great r.   149.5
ripeness
    R. is all   54.8
roarers
    What cares these r. for the name of King
        250.4
rob
    Who, I r.   281.5
robes
    borrowed r.   136.6
    R. and furred gowns hide all   245.5
Robin
    bonny sweet R. is all my joy   96.7
rogue
    what a r. and peasant slave   253.2
Roman
    A R. thought hath struck him   246.5
    after the high R. fashion   273.6
    more an antique R. than a Dane   246.6
    play the R. fool   275.2

This was the noblest R. of them all   73.7

Romans
    last of all the R.   89.2

Rome
    Am I R.'s slave   239.4
    Let R. in Tiber melt   227.4
    most high and palmy state of R.   206.11
    sun of R. is set   246.7

Romeo
    Come night, come R.   247.2
    R., R., wherefore art thou R.   246.12

ronyon
    rump-fed r.   307.7

root
    I cannot delve him to the r.   195.3

Rosalind
    Heavenly R.   309.2

rose
    a r. By any other word   196.2
    a r. in his grace   241.5
    beauty's r.   31.4
    expectancy and r. of the fair state   89.10
    Gloss on the r.   74.5
    He wears the r. Of youth   321.3
    r. of May   208.4
    the r. distilled   30.1
    The r. looks fair   97.7

rosemary
    For you, there's r., and rue   98.1
    There's r., that's for remembrance   96.7

rot
    a man may r. even here   54.7

rotten
    Something is r. in the state of Denmark   38.9

rub
    there's the r.   274.1

rudely
    I that am r. stamped   12.10

rue
    Nought shall make us r.   77.10
    wear your r. with a difference   96.7

rule
    all be done by th' r.   108.12

Rumour
    loud R.   247.7
    R. doth double ... the numbers   248.2
    R. is a pipe   248.1

Russia
    This will last out a night in R.   200.6

rust
    eaten to death with a r.   70.8

—S—

sack
    If s. and sugar be a fault   67.6

sacrifices
    like s. in their trim   264.5

sad
    I know not why I am so s.   249.1
    nor s. nor merry   185.4

saffron
    I must have s.   99.13

saint
    able to corrupt a s.   280.6
    Such an injury would vex a s.   142.2
    to catch a s.   281.1

salad
    My s. days   321.2

samphire
    one that gathers s., dreadful trade   249.8

sands
    Come unto these yellow s.   250.5
    The s. are numbered   53.7

sans
    S. teeth, s. eyes   157.2

saws
    Full of wise s., and modern instances   157.2

say
    I hear, yet s. not much   40.1
    what was I about to s.   100.9

scar
    Show me one s.   28.3

scene
    our lofty s.   218.6

sceptre
    A s. snatched with an unruly hand   227.8
    barren s.   241.4

scholar
    He was a s., and a ripe and good one   72.2
    Th'art a s.   72.10
    Thou art a s., speak to it Horatio   71.8

school
    Unwillingly to s.   157.2

school-boy
    whining s.   157.2

scorn
    What a deal of s. looks beautiful   249.5

Scot
    That sprightly S. of Scots   249.6

scruple
    Some craven s.   28.2

scythe
    Even with his pestilent s.   24.11

sea
    light foam of the s.   110.2
    Like to the Pontic s.   244.5

sea-change
    suffer a s.   250.6

sea-coal
    latter end of a s. fire   68.3

sea-nymphs
    S. hourly ring his knell   250.6

seas
    backed with God and with the s.   77.7
    multitudinous s. incarnadine   22.6

season
    each thing that in s. grows   251.1
    the s. of all natures, sleep   263.2
    things by s., seasoned are   251.2

seasons
    The s. alter   251.3

secret
    as s. as maidenhead   252.2
    most still, most s., and most grave   224.4
secrets
    trust the air with s.   252.1
seduced
    Who so firm that cannot be s.   39.3
seek
    S. to know no more   153.9
seeks
    Who s. and will not take   208.5
seeming
    Out on thee, s.   131.6
seems
    S., madam? Nay, it is   13.4
seen
    T'have s. what I have s.   83.7
seldom
    when they s. come, they wished-for come   120.7
self
    to thine own s. be true   3.7
self-love
    S. ... is not so vile a sin   253.5
self-trust
    Where is truth if there be no s.   142.10
sell
    S. when you can   309.6
sentences
    Good s., and well pronounced   1.9
    sweet and honeyed s.   278.1
sermons
    s. in stones   40.3
serpent
    s. of old Nile   33.11
    sharper than a s.'s tooth   30.8
    The s. that did sting thy father's life   43.4
    There the grown s. lies   49.4
    Think him as a s.'s egg   286.8
    this gilded s.   81.1
service
    He did look far Into the s. of the time   25.3
    I have lost my teeth in your s.   169.6
    s. of sweet silent thought   211.3
    To make the s. greater than the god   133.2
shadow
    'Tis but the s. of a wife   128.6
shadows
    Be not afraid of s.   93.11
    best in this kind are but s.   219.9
    Come like s.   308.3
    If we s. have offended   220.3
shame
    s., where is thy blush   254.10
    unseen s., invisible disgrace   258.6
she
    You are the cruellest s. alive   31.7
sheets
    incestuous s.   117.7
shepherd
    Dick the s. blows his nail   304.5

    the s., blowing of his nails   188.1
sherris-sack
    A good s.   67.8
shocks
    thousand natural s. That flesh is heir to   274.1
shore
    Darkling stand The varying s. o'th' world   75.8
    That pale, that white-faced s.   77.8
shroud
    In remembrance of a s.   201.3
sick
    Testy s. men   65.9
sigh
    in the likeness of a s.   246.10
    s. away Sundays   78.6
    What a s. is there   266.10
sighing
    A plague of s. and grief   266.6
sighs
    She gave me for my pains a world of s.   272.1
sight
    At the first s. They have changed eyes   168.6
    My soul's imaginary s.   135.9
silence
    S. is the perfectest herald of joy   117.2
    The rest is s.   69.4
    With s. ... be thou politic   225.2
silent
    No tongue! all eyes! be s.   235.4
Silvia
    Except I be by S. in the night   167.10
    What light is light, if S. be not seen   167.10
    Who is S.   312.4
simpleness
    s. and duty   68.10
simplicity
    s. of Venus' doves   296.2
sin
    every s. That has a name   81.3
    foul s. gathering head   260.5
    If to be old and merry be a s.   109.1
    no s. but to be rich   226.8
    S., death, and hell   244.9
    s. will pluck on s.   45.2
    Some rise by s.   102.9
    stifled with this smell of s.   260.3
    that foul s., gathering head   231.8
sinews
    Stiffen the s.   298.7
single
    Die s., and thine image dies with thee   31.5
    lives, and dies, in s. blessedness   30.1
    The s. and peculiar life   253.6
sinned
    More s. against than sinning   140.3
sins
    Be all my s. remembered   208.3
    Commit The oldest s.   260.2
    Few love to hear the s. they love to act   260.4

s. of the father 210.6

sister
   live a barren s. all your life 239.7
skies
   s. are painted with unnumbered sparks 270.1
slander
   no s. in an allowed fool 100.4
   S. lives upon succession 260.12
   S.'s mark was ever yet the fair 261.5
slave
   This yellow s. 186.11
sleep
   an after-dinner's s. 158.6
   exposition of s. 263.3
   gentle s., Nature's soft nurse 262.3
   Glamis hath murthered S. 263.1
   Macbeth does murther S. 262.7
   our little life Is rounded with a s. 159.3
   S. no more 262.7
   s., thou ape of death 261.10
   To s., perchance to dream 264.1
   yet we s., we dream 263.4
sleeve
   What's this? A s. 90.8
slings
   s. and arrows of outrageous fortune 274.1
slow
   I am s. of study 142.11
   Wisely and s. 117.11
slumber
   honey-heavy dew of s. 262.5
small
   S. things make base men proud 289.9
   S. winds shake him 289.11
   These things seem s. and undistinguishable 135.5
smile
   I can s., and murder whiles I s. 131.2
   one may s., and s. 80.9
   We love it not so long as we can s. 241.7
smiles
   making practised s. 257.11
snail
   creeping like s. Unwillingly to school 157.2
snake
   Love hath made thee a tame s. 165.4
   scorched the s., not killed it 49.3
snakes
   You spotted s. with double tongue 85.4
snapper-up
   A s. of unconsidered trifles 290.1
society
   S. is no comfort 265.10
soldier
   a s., and afeard 265.3
   a s.'s debt 265.4
   greatest s. of the world 263.8
   Thou art a s. only 263.9
   Th'unconsidered s. 265.8
song
   A French s. and a fiddle 192.12

sonnet
   I shall turn s. 222.2
sons
   father unto many s. 92.1
sorrow
   Come what s. can 146.4
   Give s. words 266.9
   Gnarling s. 266.12
   More in s. than in anger 266.4
   my s. hath destroyed my face 267.2
   Parting is such sweet s. 211.1
   S. breaks seasons 267.3
   s. flouted at 267.5
   Th'offender's s. lends but weak relief 238.9
   To show an unfelt s. 131.5
   wear a golden s. 127.9
sorrows
   I will instruct my s. to be proud 113.6
soul
   Hear my s. speak 167.8
   I have an ill-divining s. 100.7
   Lay not that flattering unction to your s. 82.2
   Mount, mount, my s. 70.4
   O my prophetic s. 267.7
   Since my dear s. was mistress of her choice 31.8
   something in his soul 176.4
   The poor s. sat sighing 266.11
   The prophetic s. Of the wide world 104.12
   the s. of our grandam 215.2
   the very s. of bounty 107.7
   Thou art a s. in bliss 273.4
   Thou turn'st my eyes into my very s. 253.4
sound
   full of s. and fury 158.5
sounds
   the s. of music Creep in our ears 193.5
south-fog
   the s. rot him 46.5
sovereignty
   I do but dream on s. 6.5
space
   Here is my s. 227.4
   king of infinite s. 66.4
sparrow
   providence in the fall of a s. 91.1
   providently caters for the s. 203.2
speak
   S. of me as I am 291.4
   S. what we feel 121.3
   When I think I must s. 309.5
speaking
   s. is for beggars 230.4
speech
   loath to cast away my s. 268.1
   Mend your s. a little 278.4
   Speak the s., I pray you 217.3
speeches
   Your large s. may your deeds approve 278.5
speed
   most wicked s. 117.7

spider
    That bottled s.   245.2
spies
    come not single s., But in battalions   266.5
spinsters
    The s. and the knitters in the sun   312.3
spirit
    bold s. in a loyal breast   169.8
    Curbing his lavish s.   94.3
    foolish extravagant s.   306.6
    How now, mad s.   268.9
    How now, s.   84.9
    I am thy father's s.   11.2
    invincible unconquered s.   25.7
    Love is a s. all compact of fire   164.6
    My brave s.   269.3
    rest, perturbed s.   11.3
    Th'expense of s. in a waste of shame   256.4
    Th'extravagant and erring s.   10.10
spirits
    choice and master s. of this age   155.6
    I can call s. from the vasty deep   275.9
spoils
    sluttish s. of opportunity   313.4
sponge
    Take you me for a s.   42.2
sport
    She is s. for Jove   256.1
    there was good s. at his making   134.1
sports
    He is given To s., to wildness   173.4
spot
    Out, damned s.   22.7
spring
    apparelled like the s.   90.5
    From you have I been absent in the s.   269.9
    Sweet lovers love the s.   269.7
    this s. of love   164.3
springes
    s. to catch woodcocks   287.7
spring-time
    Faster than s. showers   282.2
    In s., the only pretty ring-time   269.7
spur
    What need we any s.   28.1
square
    I have not kept my s.   231.2
squeak
    s. and gibber in the Roman streets   206.11
staff
    I'll break my s.   242.8
    the very s. of my age   210.3
stage
    A s., where every man must play a part   318.1
    All the world's a s.   157.2
    this great s. of fools   21.11
    to s. me to their eyes   233.5
stair-work
    some s., some trunk-work   258.3
stalking-horse
    He uses his folly like a s.   306.2

stand
    You see me Lord Bassanio where I s.   185.10
star
    bright particular s.   160.4
    fortunate bright s.   312.5
    most auspicious s.   91.7
    s. to every wand'ring bark   163.7
    There was a s. danced   117.3
    To thee no s. be dark   111.10
Star Chamber
    I will make a S. matter of it   154.12
stars
    art thou bragging to the s.   24.8
    certain s. shot madly from their spheres
        194.1
    cut him out in little s.   247.2
    Doubt that the s. are fire   166.5
    Earth-treading s.   125.6
    I defy you, s.   91.6
    my s. shine darkly   91.8
    not in our s., But in ourselves   242.3
    s. above us govern our conditions   91.3
    S., hide your fires   62.2
    those who are in favour with their s.   88.2
    Two s. keep not their motion   245.9
starve
    I'll s. ere I'll rob a foot further   281.6
state
    I have done the s. some service   74.1
statutes
    strict s. and most biting laws   154.8
steel
    s. my soldiers' hearts   264.7
    s. to the very back   241.11
step
    a s. On which I must fall down   7.5
stitches
    laugh yourselves into s.   182.7
stockings
    Remember who commended thy yellow s.
        287.12
stoics
    Let's be no s.   295.9
stomach
    no s. to this fight   42.7
stomachs
    They are all but s.   180.5
stone
    precious s. set in the silver sea   78.2
stones
    very s. prate of my where-about   44.4
    You blocks, you s.   141.6
stories
    sad s. of the death of kings   57.3
storm
    The s. is up   303.1
storms
    Witnessing s. to come   59.6
story
    draw thy breath in pain To tell my s.   198.5
    Never was a s. of more woe   247.5

strange
There is s. things toward   290.3
strangers
we may be better s.   141.1
strife
fierce civil s.   301.3
string
one s., sweet husband to another   194.10
strumpet
transformed Into a s.'s fool   253.10
study
S. is like the heaven's glorious sun   72.5
S. what you most affect   72.9
stuff
silliest stuff that ever I heard   219.9
stumbled
I s. when I saw   185.3
subject
Every s.'s duty is the King's   68.9
What s. can give sentence   151.11
subjects
I am all the s. that you have   261.8
substance
What is your s.   132.7
suburbs
Dwell I but in the s.   129.2
suffered
I have s. With those that I saw suffer   36.3
summer
s.'s flower is to the s. sweet   287.3
s.'s lease   275.4
Shall I compare thee to a s.'s day   275.4
thy eternal s. shall not fade   275.4
sun
The golden s. salutes the morn   188.7
The selfsame s. that shines upon his court
79.8
superfluous
s. branches we lop away   106.1
surfeit
as sick that s.   81.10
surgeon
With the help of a s. with too much   65.6
surges
I saw him beat the s. under him   276.8
suspicion
S. always haunts the guilty mind   115.2
what a ready tongue s. hath   276.5
swain
no better than a homely s.   190.1
swan
I will play the s.   194.6
pale faint s.   54.6
swan-like
he makes a s. end   193.4
sweat
rank s. of an enseamed bed   255.1
sweet
Things s. to taste   99.9
sweeting
Trip no further, pretty s.   163.11

sweets
in what s. dost thou thy sins enclose   14.3
S. grown common   88.4
S. to the sweet   97.1
The s. we wish for   62.1
swimmer
Like an unpractised s.   112.5
swimmers
two spent swimmers   94.1
sword
edge is sharper than the s.   261.1
fleshed thy maiden s.   298.2
his s. Hath a sharp edge   225.5
His s. Philippan   302.4
My voice is in my s.   94.4
sting is sharper than the s.'s   261.7
The s. is out That must destroy thee   302.7
swords
Keep up your bright s.   212.12
measured s. and parted   302.5

—T—

take
T. her or leave her   31.9
Talbot
A T.! a T.   25.6
tale
A sad t.'s best for winter   272.4
a t. Told by an idiot   158.5
I could a t. unfold   271.5
round unvarnished t.   291.3
thereby hangs a t.   283.3
talk
I t. of that, that know it   83.6
loves to hear himself t.   279.6
Talkers
T. are no good doers   2.3
talking
I wonder that you will still be t.   278.12
Tarquin
Lust-breathed T.   178.8
tarry
You men will never t.   180.7
task
long day's t. is done   75.7
Thou thy worldly t. has done   189.3
tasks
gentle means and easy t.   72.8
These are barren t.   72.4
tear
Fall not a t.   279.9
He hath a t. for pity   215.4
tears
drown the stage with t.   217.2
If you have t., prepare to shed them now
279.12
Like Niobe, all t.   279.10
store of parting t.   280.4
strangled His language in his t.   279.11
T. harden lust   258.5

teeth
keep their t. clean 33.7

temperance
you can guess what t. should be 185.5

tempest
after every t. come such calms 250.1

tempted
'Tis one thing to be t. 280.8

tender
How t. 'tis to love the babe that milks me
46.1

tennis-balls
T., my liege 269.4

terms
I like not fair t. 38.4

thankless
to have a t. child 139.7

theatre
wide and universal t. 317.5

thee
For t. watch I 138.7
I have done nothing but in care of t. 210.10

thieves
not t., but men that much do want 281.9
when t. cannot be true to one another
281.7

thing
A t. slipped idly from me 186.1
has this t. appeared again tonight 10.7
Not to be other than one t. 264.3
Simply the t. I am 132.1
this t.'s to do 136.4
Thou art the t. itself 126.7

think
T., and die 62.7
What I t., I utter 277.4

thinking
t. makes it so 281.12
t. too precisely on th'event 28.2

this
That it should come to t. 75.9

thorns
t. and dangers of this world 317.9
t. that in her bosom lodge 114.8

thought
more momentary-swift than t. 201.7
no less celerity Than that of t. 218.4
pale cast of t. 136.3
sessions of sweet silent t. 211.3
T. is free 238.1
t. on t. 282.2

thoughts
Dive, t., down to my soul 282.4
Give thy t. no tongue 3.7
I do begin to have bloody t. 192.7
I think good t. 282.7
Love's heralds should be t. 282.5
My t. are ripe in mischief 184.5
My t. be bloody 243.4
Our t. are ours 281.13
So do all t., they are winged 281.11

So should my t. be severed from my griefs
113.9

threaten
T. the threat'ner 23.7

three
When shall we t. meet again 307.6

thrift
How i'th' name of t. 282.10
T., t., Horatio 282.9

thumb
Do you bite your t. at us 24.9

thumbs
By the pricking of my t. 208.1

thunder
In t., lightning, or in rain 307.6

tide
t. in the affairs of men 208.7

tiger
imitate the action of the t. 298.7
t.'s heart wrapped in a woman's hide 310.1

time
bank and shoal of t. 284.3
chronicle of wasted t. 120.5
Cormorant devouring T. 283.10
demand the t. of day 283.7
Devouring t. 284.6
envious and calumniating T. 285.6
Every t. Serves for the matter 283.2
great gap of t. 1.1
He weighs t. Even to the utmost grain 283.9
how slow t. goes In t. of sorrow 238.3
I wasted t. 286.5
idly to profane the precious t. 286.3
inaudible and noiseless foot of t. 202.8
Injurious T. now with a robber's haste 285.7
last syllable of recorded t. 158.5
Let t. shape 76.1
Let the t. run on 283.5
saltness of t. 183.1
seeds of t. 284.1
Some t. I shall sleep out 211.6
the seeds of t. 232.1
the stream of t. 79.9
The t. is out of joint 17.2
Thou canst help t. to furrow me 205.7
T. and the hour runs through the roughest day
284.2
t. be thine 283.6
T. decays 285.1
T. goes on crutches 9.6
t. Goes upright with his carriage 273.1
T. hath ... a wallet at his back 285.5
T. is like a fashionable host 285.6
t. is old 285.4
T. qualifies the spark 165.13
T., that gave 284.10
t., thou must untangle this 290.5
T. travels in divers paces 283.4
t. will bring it out 44.1
T. will come and take my love away 160.2
T.'s injurious hand 284.12

T.'s the king of men   284.5
very age and body of the t.   217.3
We must obey the t.   68.12
weight of this sad t.   17.5
when in thee t.'s furrows I behold   284.8
whirligig of t.   286.2
womb of t.   104.11
wrinkled deep in t.   34.1
times
    nature of the t. deceased   120.4
    The t. are wild   63.10
    the t. conspire with you   102.4
tired
    T. with all these   302.11
title
    his t. Hang loose about him   136.7
toad
    foul bunch-backed t.   245.2
toe
    He rises on the t.   7.9
toil
    Weary with t., I haste me to my bed   263.6
tomorrow
    T., and t., and t.   158.5
    T. is a busy day   286.10
tongs
    Let's have the t. and the bones   194.2
tongue
    I cannot endure my Lady T.   279.2
    That man that hath a t.   180.9
tongues
    Done to death by slanderous t.   261.4
tooth
    His venom t.   81.5
toothache
    endure the t. patiently   134.10
torches
    she doth teach the torches to burn bright   18.7
touch
    t. of his nether lip   256.2
towers
    cloud-capped t.   220.7
toy
    A foolish thing was but a t.   303.6
traffic
    T. confound thee   71.6
    two hours' t. of our stage   220.6
tragedian
    counterfeit the deep t.   220.5
traitors
    nest of t.   289.8
    What a brood of t.   289.6
translated
    Thou art t.   29.5
trappings
    t. and the suits of woe   113.3
travel
    Having known no t. in his youth   289.2
    to t. for it too   288.2

traveller
    Farewell Monsieur T.   288.3
    from whose bourn No t. returns   52.1
    Now spurs the lated t. apace   200.5
travellers
    t. must be content   288.1
treachery
    T.! Seek it out   289.5
treason
    t. can but peep to what it would   150.3
treasons
    t., stratagems, and spoils   193.7
tree
    Under the greenwood t.   40.4
trees
    These t. shall be my books   109.5
tremble
    You t. and look pale   93.5
trencher-man
    He is a very valiant t.   99.7
Trey
    T., Blanch and Sweetheart   66.1
trick
    I know a t. worth two   287.9
    into the t. of singularity   71.2
    wild t. of his ancestors   8.9
tricks
    T. he hath had in him   95.10
trifles
    Dispense with t.   289.10
    T. light as air   144.2
trout
    t. that must be caught with tickling   287.11
trouts
    Groping for t. in a peculiar river   255.9
trowel
    That was laid on with a t.   81.7
truant
    a t. disposition   290.6
true
    As t. as Troilus   87.3
    How should I your t. love know   52.2
    Not t. in love   160   9
    That he is mad, 'tis t.   277.5
    'tis t. 'tis pity   277.5
trust
    Love all, t. a few   3.5
    on whom I built An absolute t.   13.7
    There's no t., No faith   156.10
    What t. is in these times   290.8
truth
    I have looked on t. Askance   319.1
    my love swears that she is made of t.   156.11
    naked t. of it is   227.1
    Simple t. miscalled simplicity   291.7
    Tell t., and shame the devil   290.11
    That t. should be silent, I had almost forgot   263.9
    To seek the light of t.   24.1
    T. hath a quiet breast   291.5
    T. is t.   291.1

t. of girls and boys   321.4
T. shall nurse her   75.1
T. will come to light   191.12, 291.2
T.'s a dog   290.12

Tu-whit
T.; Tu-who, a merry note   304.5

tyrant
A plague upon the t. that I serve   261.9

—U—

uncle
I will go with thee to thy u.'s   167.1
u. me no u.   111.9

unexpressive
fair, the chaste, and u. she   309.4

ungained
the thing u.   180.6

universe
wide vessel of the u.   199.6

unjust
u. man doth thrive   17.6

unkind
Young, and so u.   323.9

unkindest
most u. cut of all   19.5

unknown
not to leave't undone, but keep't u.   138.4

unmannerly
Be Kent u. When Lear is mad   231.10

unsex
u. me here   45.9

untalked-of
u. and unseen   201.5

upbraidings
sauced with thy u.   173.10

use
How u. doth breed a habit in a man   116.3
u. almost can change the stamp of nature   116.1

uses
all the u. of this world   317.6
To what base u. we may return   189.6

usurp'st
What art thou that u. this time of night   10.8

—V—

vale
Into the v. of years   183.5

valour
Adieu, v.   161.3
better part of v. is discretion   63.9
no more v. ... than in a wild duck   42.6
So full of v. that they smote the air   68.7
v. is the chiefest virtue   25.4
your dormouse v.   41.10

value
V. dwells not in particular will   293.7

valued
What's aught but as 'tis v.   293.6

vanity
What a sweep of v.   294.2

variety
Her infinite v.   34.4

vein
this fierce v.   8.3

vengeance
V. is in my heart   244.7

verbosity
the thread of his v.   14.8

verge
on the very v. Of her confine   204.6

verily
A lady's V.   312.6

Verona
fair V., where we lay our scene   32.6

vessel
comfort the weaker v.   106.3
You are the weaker v.   309.12

victory
laurel v., and smooth success   272.7
v. is twice itself   294.4

villain
a serviceable v.   16.8
Bloody, bawdy v.   80.10
every tale condemns me for a v.   37.8
honeysuckle v.   141.4
I am determined to prove a v.   81.4
one may smile, and smile, and be a v.   80.9
smiling, damned v.   80.9
Which is the v.   17.1

villains
When rich v. have need of poor ones   44.9

villainy
my naked v.   131.7

vine
The v. shall grow   190.9

violet
A v. in the youth of primy nature   96.6

violets
V., dim   98.6

vipers
Is love a generation of v.   256.7

virginity
Crack the glass of her v.   258.8

virtue
Assume a v. if you have it not   295.3
infinite v.   294.12
let not v. seek Remuneration   285.6
no v. like necessity   197.4
To make a v. of necessity   197.7
V. is beauty   295.12
V. itself scapes not calumnious strokes   295.2

virtues
If our v. Did not go forth   35.7

visions
what v. have I seen   165.7

vixen
She was a v. when she went to school   108.1

voice
For my v., I have lost it   192.10
Her v. was ever soft, Gentle and low   310.7
vow
plain single v.   231.1
vows
Men's v. are women's traitors   180.1
v. made in wine   67.3
voyage
she would serve after a long v.   311.9
Vulcan
as foul as V.'s stithy   135.2

—W—

wait
I am to w.   165.11
waiting
though w. so be hell   165.11
wall
You can never bring in a w.   219.4
wanderer
merry w. of the night   85.1
war
dogged w.   300.4
grappling vigour and rough frown of w.   212.11
Grim-visaged W.   213.2
I know the disciplines of w.   298.10
purple testament of bleeding w.   300.7
W. and lechery confound all   300.10
W.! w.! no peace   300.3
warriors
w. for the working-day   15.2
wars
For God's sake, go not to these w.   298.3
go to the w., would you   300.6
We must all to the w.   297.10
water
A little w. clears us of this deed   33.8
More w. glideth by the mill   138.8
Smooth runs the w.   58.6
waterfly
Dost know this w.   33.3
waves
w. make towards the pebbled shore   284.9
way
all the world's my w.   82.12
flow'ry w. that leads to the broad gate   118.10
Take the instant w.   123.3
Thou marshall'st me the w. that I was going   91.5
w. to dusty death   158.5
weakest
The w. goes to the wall   302.1
weakness
Troy in our w. stands   225.11
With mine own w. being best acquainted   252.9
weariness
W. Can snore upon the flint   262.2

weary
w., stale, flat, and unprofitable   317.6
weasel
as a w. sucks eggs   176.2
backed like a w.   170.9
wedlock
what is w. forced but a hell   174.3
weeds
Most subject is the fattest soil to w.   105.4
w. are shallow-rooted   105.6
weep
No, I'll not w.   280.2
weeping
Doth that bode w.   280.3
I am not prone to w.   280.5
weeping-ripe
w. for a good word   62.12
welcome
Small cheer and great w.   125.2
W. hither, As is the spring   111.11
welkin
out of my w.   315.11
well
All's w. that ends w.   75.6
Welsh
hear the lady sing in W.   297.2
there's no man speaks better W.   296.6
westward
Then w. ho   289.1
wether
I am a tainted w.   248.8
whale
belching w.   250.2
wheel
I am bound Upon a w. of fire   273.4
My thoughts are whirled like a potter's w.   36.7
The w. is come full circle   91.4
whipping
who shall scape w.   148.3
whips
w. and scorns of time   274.1
whisp'rings
Foul w. are abroad   248.4
whisper
a w. in the ears of death   259.3
whispering
Is w. nothing   144.10
whit
Not a whit   91.1
whore
like a w. unpack my heart with words   314.4
why
Every w. hath a wherefore   236.7
wicked
Something w. this way comes   208.1
widows
New w. howl   291.12
wife
almost damned in a fair w.   174.11
dark house and the detested w.   173.7

fittest time to corrupt a man's w.   128.9
get thee a w.   174.10
light w. doth make a heavy husband   129.7
my true and honourable w.   129.3
Portia is Brutus' harlot, not his w.   129.2
The Thane of Fife had a w.   129.5
W. and child   88.6

wild
If I chance to talk a little w.   107.1

wilderness
a w. of monkeys   145.1
Rome is but a w. of tigers   246.8

will
a w. most incorrect to heaven   112.2
his w. is not his own   149.8
make his w. Lord of his reason   304.1
My good w. is great   107.5
my name is W.   196.3
The w. of man is by his reason swayed   236.2
Whoever hath her wish, thou hast thy W.   62.6

willow
Make me a w. cabin at your gate   314.1
She had a song of 'w.'   194.5
Sing all a green w.   266.11
There is a w. grows askant the brook   96.8

wills
Let's choose executors and talk of w.   57.1
Our w. and fates do so contrary run   90.11

win
They laugh that w.   294.5

wind
Blow, blow, thou winter w.   139.4
Ill blows the w. that profits nobody   102.1

winds
Blow w. and crack your cheeks   303.2
imprisoned in the viewless w.   56.3

wine
Good w. is a good familiar creature   68.6

wink
I have not slept one w.   262.1

winter
Barren w.   304.2
haunch of w.   20.9
How like a w. hath my absence been   1.3
Now is the w. of our discontent   213.1
w. and rough weather   40.4
W. tames man, woman and beast   305.3
W.'s not gone yet   304.4

winters
When forty w. shall besiege thy brow   183.6

wisdom
a w. that doth guide his valour   305.6
Herein lives w.   31.6
W. cries out in the streets   305.5

wise
Every w. man's son   163.11
Exceeding w., fair-spoken and persuading   172.8
fool doth think he is w.   305.4
So w. so young ... do never live long   323.5

Who can be w., amazed   136.2
w. enough to play the fool   100.5

wisely
loved not w., but too well   74.1

wish
He comes upon a w.   102.3
w. deserves a welcome   111.7
w. was father ... to that thought   209.5

wishers
W. were ever fools   305.10

wit
cause that w. is in other men   306.4
Her w. Values itself so highly   306.11
his w. in his belly   143.1
Make the doors upon a woman's w.   309.7
She would ... press me to death with w.   307.1
skirmish of w. between them   306.9
some sparks that are like w.   306.10
the cause that w. is in other men   87.6
winding up the watch of his w.   307.4
Your w.'s too hot   306.5

witchcraft
w. in your lips   166.7

wits
his w. are gone   171.6
My w. begin to turn   171.4
whetstone of the w.   306.1

wive
To w. and thrive   175.2
to w. it wealthily in Padua   175.3

wives
W. may be merry   129.9

woe
One w. doth tread upon another's heel   184.6

wolf
Wake not a sleeping w.   48.7

woman
A w.'s general   309.13
Frailty, thy name is w.   309.10
indistinguished space of w.'s will   310.6
let not me play a w.   17.7
No more but e'en a w.   308.4
None of w. born   232.2
poor lone w.   265.11
says the married w. you may go   128.7
She is a w., therefore may be wooed   313.8
speaks small like a w.   311.2
Was ever w. in this humour wooed   313.6
Who is't can read a w.   309.9

womb
into her w. convey sterility   46.8
kennel of thy w.   244.11
Macduff was from his mother's w.   198.11
teeming w. of royal kings   78.3

wombs
Good w. have borne bad sons   210.11

women
Have I liked several w.   312.1
W. are angels, wooing: Things won are done   313.9
W. are as roses   287.6

W. are made to bear   142.1
W. will love her   312.7
w.'s weapons, water-drops   280.1

womenkind
way of w.   256.3

won
Things w. are done; joy's soul lies in the doing   2.5

wonder
No w., sir, but certainly a maid   168.5

wood
You are not w., you are not stones   75.4

woodcock
As a w. to mine own springe   148.6

woodland
I am a w. fellow   40.2

wooed
We should be w.   313.5

woollen
I had rather lie in the w.   17.8

word
Answer me in one w.   164.8
every fool can play upon the w.   306.8
every w. stabs   279.1
How long a time lies in one little w.   315.5
I never will speak w.   279   4
You are not worth another w.   140.10

words
fill the world with w.   314.5
He w. me, girls   277.3
Honest plain w.   112.4
I understand a fury in your w.   8.4
man of fire-new w.   314.8
Men of few w.   278.2
My w. fly up   228.2
Out idle w.   315.2
unpleasant'st w. That ever blotted paper   155.10
Where w. are scarce   315.6
wild and whirling w.   314.3
W. are no deeds   314.6
W. pay no debts   315.9
W. without thoughts never to heaven go   228.2
W., w., mere w.   315.10
w., w., w.   235.6

work
If it be man's w.   316.5
w. we have in hand   43.8

world
a w. ransomed, or one destroyed   146.5
He doth bestride the narrow w.   147.10
How goes the w.   318.7
how the w. wags   283.3
in this harsh w. draw thy breath in pain   69.3
It never was merry w. in England   33.4
Let me tell the w.   198.7
Mad w.! mad kings   317.7
O brave new w.   127.4
sick of this false w.   318.8

The third o'th' w. is yours   128.8
The w. affords no law to make thee rich   318.6
the w. is broad and wide   211.10
The w. is not thy friend   318.6
There is a w. elsewhere   197.8
triple pillar of the w.   253.10
'Twas never merry w.   293.1
where thou art, there is the w. itself   166.8
wicked, wicked w.   318.2

worm
concealment like a w. i'th' bud   164.1
smallest w. will turn   237.4

worms
w. have eaten them   177.10

worst
Do thy w., old Time   284.7
reason with the w. that may befall   271.1
The w. is not   319.4
The w. returns to laughter   319.2
The w. that men can breathe   261.6
To fear the w. oft cures the w.   319.5
Who is't can say 'I am at the w.'   319.3

worth
To her own w. She shall be prized   320.1
w. the whistling   319.6

would
We w., and we w. not   137.1

wound
He jests at scars that never felt a w.   137.2

wounds
Now civil w. are stopped   213.5

wrath
the measure of my w.   8.6

wren
The poor w.   21.4

wretches
Poor naked w.   19.1

wrinkles
With mirth and laughter let the w. come   205.2

wrong
a greater grief To bear love's w.   163.3
To persist In doing w.   16.5

wrongs
Still to remember w.   321.1
Those pretty w. that liberty commits   138.6

—Y—

yea-forsooth
rascally y. knave   64.5

year
ever-running y.   250.7
That time of y. thou mayst in me behold   205.9

years
His y. but young   83.9
more command with y.   205.4
y. on my back forty-eight   183.2

yeoman
y.'s service   320.4

yesterdays
  all our y.   158.5
Yorick
  Alas, poor Y.   73.3
you
  Y. alone are y.   167.4
young
  so y. a body with so old a head   322.11
  So y. and so untender   322.7
  So y., my lord, and true   322.7
  We that are y.   322.9
  y. limbs and lechery   322.4
younger
  The y. rises when the old doth fall   322.8
youth
  ashes of his y.   205.10

flourish set on y.   284.11
morn and liquid dew of y.   321.6
not clean past your y.   183.1
salt of our y.   183.3
y. and freshness Wrinkles Apollo's   118.7
Y. to itself rebels   321.7
Y.'s a stuff will not endure   229.1
youths
  y. that thunder at a playhouse   267.9

—Z—

zed
  Thou whoreson z.   141.8

❧ Index of ❧ References to Plays

All's Well That Ends Well **1:** 3.5;
25.3; 103.10; 112.1; 160.4;
173.5,6; 242.2; 253.9;
282.1N; 290.7; **2:** 13.3;
79.2; 83.1; 89.7; 121.10;
140.10; 143.3; 173.7,8;
275.7; **4:** 16.6; 27.6; 40.2;
49.7; 75.6; 79.3; 118.10;
132.1; 156.12; 191.1; 231.1; **5:**
95.9,10; 128.6; 160.5;
176.6; 202.8; 279.8; 283.1;
Epil.: 216.2

Antony and Cleopatra **1:** 1.1;
33.10,11; 34.1; 50.9; 82.1;
93.3; 96.1; 118.2; 120.9;
123.7; 128.7; 143.6; 157.1;
160.6,7; 185.4; 196.5; 198.8;
211.2; 221.1; 227.4; 232.9;
238.2; 246.5; 253.7,10;
254.1; 263.8; 272.7; 275.8;
321.2; **2:** 5.1,2,5,6; 34.2–4;
46.2; 70.5,6; 96.2; 98.7,8;
99.1; 108.12; 121.11; 128.8;
140.2; 169.9; 173.1; 192.9;
198.9; 208.5; 231.2; 253.8;

263.9; 265.9; 283.2; 302.4;
3: 5.7; 24.10,11; 62.7; 93.4;
121.12; 125.1; 146.6; 159.8;
173.2; 185.5; 227.5; 254.2;
268.2; 279.9; 304.1; 321.3;
4: 50.10; 51.1; 69.1; 75.7,8;
78.7; 101.4; 125.9; 173.3;
212.4; 213.11; 273.5–7;
294.12; 305.10; 308.4; 316.1;
5: 34.5; 51.2; 69.2; 73.1,2;
101.5; 110.3; 135.1; 149.6;
177.7; 216.3; 221.3; 241.8;
254.3; 273.8,9; 277.3; 309.1

As You Like It **1:** 2.10; 81.7; 89.8;
91.9; 168.1; 169.6; 176.1;
177.8; 229.2; 306.1; 309.2;
317.3; **2:** 2.11; 5.8,9; 16.2;
20.1,2; 30.6; 40.3,4; 58.7;
70.7; 71.1; 80.7; 100.1,8;
103.3; 106.3; 111.2; 139.4;
146.7; 157.2; 160.8; 168.9;
176.2; 203.1–5; 216.4;
226.3; 240.2; 263.10; 271.4;
283.3,4; 288.1; 305.8; 309.3;
316.2; 317.4,5; **3:** 26.3,7;

51.3; 62.8; 67.3; 106.4; 109.5; 141.1; 160.9,10; 164.8,9; 165.1,2; 168.2; 177.9; 195.5; 221.10; 222.1; 283.4; 309.4–6; 316.9; **4:** 83.4,5; 137.3; 152.2; 165.3,4; 176.3; 177.10; 179.6,7; 281.11; 288.2,3; 309.7; **5:** 8.7; 14.7; 42.1; 48.1; 106.5; 168.3; 185.8; 254.4; 269.7; 302.5; 305.4; 306.2

Comedy of Errors **1:** 3.6; 21.9; 32.3; 288.4,5; **2:** 3.1; 116.4; 137.4; 143.7; 173.9; 178.1; 179.8; 236.7; 238.10; **3:** 125.2; 137.5; 168.4; 260.12; 309.8; **4:** 223.1; 313.1; **5:** 26.4; 79.4; 99.2; 173.10

Coriolanus **1:** 146.2; 185.9; 191.2; 237.1; 247.6; **2:** 25.4; 33.7; 47.7; 51.4; 139.5; 213.7; 223.5; 233.1; 264.1,2; 272.8; 277.4; **3:** 1.5; 7.10; 36.4; 46.3; 60.9,10; 83.6; 142.6,7; 197.8; 202.2; 214.2; 224.1; 229.3; **4:**1.2; 8.8; 23.2; 61.1; 128.9; 133.9; 142.8; 198.3; 212.5; 264.3; **5:** 41.1; 46.4; 51.5; 212.6; 216.5; 243.1; 297.7; 321.1

Cymbeline **1:** 10.1; 23.3; 28.7; 62.9; 88.7; 195.3; 210.12; 234.4,5; 295.1; **2:** 20.6; 22.10; 29.7; 46.5; 96.5; 186.2; 187.6; 199.2; 202.5; 261.10; **3:** 26.1; 106.7; 117.6; 128.3; 147.9; 156.1; 180.1; 261.1; 262.1,2; 268.3; **4:** 51.6,7; 109.6; 189.3; 215.3; 265.10; **5:** 26.2; 51.8; 67.4; 166.4; 283.5; 309.9; 321.4

Hamlet **1:** 3.7; 4.1; 10.7–10; 11.1–3; 13.4; 17.2; 20.7; 22.11; 23.4,5; 29.8; 32.2; 34.6; 35.1,9–10; 38.9; 43.2–4; 47.8; 58.8; 61.3,4; 67.5; 71.8; 75.9; 80.1,9; 88.5; 89.9; 90.10; 93.5; 96.6; 102.12; 104.1; 105.2; 106.8; 112.2; 113.3; 114.7,8; 117.7; 125.10; 128.10; 130.6; 137.6; 142.9; 149.7,8; 157.3; 170.2; 172.4; 173.11; 175.9; 176.7–9; 178.2; 183.7,8; 186.3; 187.7–9; 189.4; 191.6; 199.3; 206.10,11; 214.1,9; 222.9; 234.6; 235.3,7; 254.5–7; 260.1; 266.4; 267.6,7; 268.4; 271.5; 273.10; 279.10; 281.3; 282.9; 283.6; 286.7; 287.7; 290.6; 292.9; 295.2; 309.10; 314.2,3; 316.3; 317.6; 321.5–8; **2:** 5.10; 13.5; 33.1; 42.5; 45.3,4; 50.5; 61.5; 66.4; 80.10; 100.9; 101.6; 114.9; 126.4; 148.3; 157.4; 161.1; 166.5; 170.3–5; 172.5; 196.6; 199.1; 203.6; 216.6,7; 217.1,2; 224.2,3; 233.2; 235.6; 253.2; 277.5; 281.12; 306.3; 314.4;

3: 3.2; 11.6; 20.8; 29.9;
31.2,8; 36.9; 38.10; 39.1;
43.5–7; 45.6; 51.9; 58.9;
75.3; 82.2,3; 83.7; 89.10;
90.11; 94.6; 100.10; 101.
7–10; 104.2,9; 105.3; 107.3;
114.10,11; 115.1; 116.1; 123.8;
131.1; 135.2; 136.3; 137.7;
148.4; 150.1,2; 153.11; 156.2;
165.12; 170.6–9; 172.3;
174.1; 176.4; 182.8; 184.2;
191.3,7; 199.4; 208.3,6;
217.3; 224.4; 228.2; 234.9;
238.11; 243.2; 253.3,4,6;
254.8–10; 255.1; 261.2;
274.1; 277.6; 281.4,13;
287.8; 293.8; 295.3; 313.2;
4: 2.6; 5.11; 25.1; 28.2; 42.2;
52.2,3; 60.3; 88.8; 96.7,8;
104.10; 106.8; 112.3; 122.1;
126.5; 134.6,7; 136.1,4;
148.5; 150.3; 165.13; 177.1;
184.6; 191.8; 208.4; 233.3,7;
235.8; 243.3–5; 251.5; 266.5;
297.8,9; 321.9; **5:** 26.5;
33.2,3; 48.6; 49.8; 52.4;
64.4; 69.3,4; 73.3–5; 76.10;
88.9; 90.12; 91.1; 94.7; 97.1;
109.7,8; 116.2; 132.2; 140.8;
148.6; 154.1; 171.1; 184.10;
185.1; 189.5–7; 198.4,5;
224.5; 228.7; 232.7; 246.6;
260.1; 272.9; 277.7; 282.1;
289.5; 316.10; 320.4

1 Henry IV **1:** 27.3; 119.4; 120.7;
122.2; 154.2; 199.5; 224.6;

280.6; 281.5; 283.7; 301.1;
303.7; 305.5; **2:** 36.5; 42.6;
46.6; 58.10; 67.6; 87.4,5;
109.1; 116.7,8; 119.5; 141.2;
145.7; 178.3; 203.7,8; 236.8;
249.6; 266.6; 281.6,7;
287.9; 295.4; 297.10; 322.1;
3: 11.7; 16.4; 60.4; 82.4;
99.3; 141.3; 202.6; 207.1;
224.7; 275.9; 290.11;
296.6,7; 297.1,2; **4:** 27.7;
52.6; 119.6,7; 264.4–6;
322.2; **5:** 8.9; 41.2; 63.9;
104.3; 122.3; 159.5; 198.6;
237.2; 245.9; 298.1,2

2 Henry IV **Ind.:** 247.7; 248.1; **1:**
5.3; 48.7; 63.10,11; 64.5;
70.8; 87.6; 134.8; 156.3;
183.1; 192.10; 198.10; 203.9;
216.1; 226.4–6; 228.9;
233.4; 276.5; 290.8; 301.2;
306.4; 322.3,4; **2:** 48.8;
67.7; 75.10; 87.7; 88.10;
99.4; 123.9; 127.7; 132.9;
141.4; 189.8; 192.11; 203.10;
255.2; 265.11; 268.5; 286.3;
294.6; 298.3; 309.11,12; **3:**
52.7,8; 76.1; 91.2; 120.4;
150.4,5; 156.4; 196.11; 197.1;
206.5,6; 231.8; 248.2;
262.3; **4:** 6.1; 10.2; 20.9;
41.3; 67.8; 79.9; 91.10;
100.6; 105.4; 111.3; 149.4;
209.5; 215.4; 225.1; 260.2;
294.3; 298.4,5; 305.11; **5:**
19.3; 29.3; 83.2; 154.3; 165.5;

172.6; 204.1; 206.7; 223.2; 288.6

Henry V **Prol.:** 140.9; 218.1,2; **1:** 8.10; 25.5; 108.3; 175.10; 178.4; 269.4,5; 276.1; 278.1; 322.5; **2:** 53.1; 77.1; 83.3; 87.8; 105.5; 120.1; 158.1; 218.3; 253.5; 272.5; 283.8,9; 298.6; 302.6; **3:** 23.6; 46.7; 65.11; 77.2–5; 108.4; 123.10; 124.1; 218.4; 258.10; 272.6; 278.2; 298.7–10; 299.1; 305.9; **4:** 14.9; 15.1,2; 22.5; 28.4,5; 36.6; 42.7; 49.1; 68.9; 79.5; 82.5; 100.11; 108.5; 120.2; 122.4,5; 150.6,7; 183.9; 187.10; 199.6; 204.2; 250.7; 262.4; 264.7; 265.1; 297.3,4; 299.2–4; **5:** 102.13; 150.8; 166.6,7; 172.7; 212.7; 297.5

1 Henry VI **1:** 25.6; 36.7; 53.2; 88.1; 120.3; 212.8; 214.3; 230.6; 235.1; **2:** 108.6; 154.4; 221.4; 225.2; **3:** 10.3; 52.5; 60.5; 83.10; 103.1; **4:** 25.7; 77.6; 78.8; 103.2; 299.5,6; **5:** 174.2,3

2 Henry VI **1:** 6.1,2; 133.10; 199.7; 245.3; 276.2; **2:** 108.7; 212.9; 304.2; **3:** 6.3; 17.3; 28.3; 53.3–5; 58.6; 105.6; 148.7; 166.8; 221.5; 225.3; 227.6; 282.2; **4:** 33.4; 37.10;

53.6; 71.9; 72.1; 105.7; 133.3; 154.5; 199.8; 213.8; 227.7; 237.3; 289.9; **5:** 63.12; 141.5; 169.7; 289.6

3 Henry VI **1:** 6.4; 53.7; 150.9; 211.4; 243.6,7; 309.13; 310.1; **2:** 53.8; 102.1; 127.8; 129.1; 148.8; 154.6; 188.1; 190.1; 202.7; 213.9; 225.4; 237.4; **3:** 3.3; 6.5; 38.1; 80.11; 92.1; 102.2; 131.2; 214.4; **4:** 29.4; 40.1; 77.7; 108.8; 174.4; 289.7; **5:** 4.7; 53.9; 88.11; 115.2; 132.3; 314.5

Henry VIII **1:** 1.6; 6.6; 18.1; 107.1; 192.12; 211.5; 225.5; 229.4; **2:** 76.8; 127.9; 150.10; 226.7; 229.5; **3:** 6.7; 13.6; 36.10; 39.2; 42.3; 58.11; 110.4,5; 122.6; 123.4; 148.9; 174.5; 185.2; 193.1; 245.4; 282.10; 295.5; 304.3; 314.6; **4:** 6.8; 35.4; 69.5; 72.2; 127.10; 154.7; 172.8; 231.3; **5:** 30.7; 74.6; 75.1,2; 94.8; 126.1; 212.10; 232.6; 267.9; 279.11; **Epil.:** 218.5

Julius Caesar **1:** 12.1; 39.3; 43.8; 49.9; 103.4,5; 122.7,8; 141.6; 147.10; 148.1; 207.2; 214.7; 225.6; 227.9,10; 231.9; 241.9; 242.3; 245.10; 274.2,3; 282.3; 314.7; **2:** 6.9;

9.1; 28.1; 41.4; 43.9; 54.1;
94.9; 129.2,3; 148.2; 151.1;
156.5; 173.4; 191.9; 204.3;
207.3; 221.6; 237.5; 248.6;
262.5; 286.8; 291.8; 303.8;
310.2,3; **3**: 7.1,2; 19.4,5;
54.2–4; 59.1; 69.6; 73.6;
75.4; 80.2; 95.1; 102.3;
103.6,7; 113.4,5; 122.9;
148.10; 155.6; 184.3; 190.2;
212.1; 218.6; 233.8; 236.1;
237.6; 266.7; 267.11; 270.1;
279.12; 294.7; 299.7; 301.3;
4: 39.4,5; 61.6; 104.4; 141.7;
208.7; 228.8; 262.6; 270.7;
273.3; 282.8; 320.2; **5**: 25.8;
73.7; 89.1,2; 178.5; 202.3;
243.8; 246.7; 271.1; 275.1;
292.8; 300.1; 303.1

King John **1**: 95.2; 133.12; 226.2;
229.6; **2**: 24.7; 41.5; 77.8;
113.6; 226.8; 267.10; 300.2;
310.4; 317.7; **3**: 4.2; 87.2;
102.4; 113.7; 171.2; 186.4;
212.11; 214.10; 227.8; 230.7;
237.7; 300.3; 317.8; 322.6;
4: 17.4; 69.7; 81.8; 82.6;
117.1N; 181.1; 190.3; 191.10;
208.8; 248.3; 260.3; 291.9;
294.8; 300.4; 317.9; **5**: 23.7;
35.5; 54.5,6; 69.8,9;
77.9,10; 190.4; 239.4; 251.6

King Lear **1**: 4.3; 7.3; 8.1; 15.6;
20.3; 30.8; 31.9; 46.8;
59.2,3; 64.6; 93.1,6; 100.2;

120.10; 121.1; 132.4; 134.
1–4; 136.5; 139.6,7; 153.6;
156.6; 161.2; 166.9; 171.3;
178.6; 181.2; 183.2; 196.7;
204.4; 207.4; 209.6,7;
214.8; 231.10; 242.4,6;
269.6; 278.3–6; 290.12;
316.4; 322.7; **2**: 12.2; 18.11;
45.7; 102.5–7; 113.8; 141.8;
197.2; 204.5–7; 209.4,8;
211.6; 226.9; 243.9; 280.1;
304.4; **3**: 4.4; 19.1; 35.2;
45.8; 50.6; 63.5; 66.1;
126.6,7; 140.3; 171.4–6;
197.3; 200.1; 204.8; 229.7;
255.3; 266.1; 271.6; 276.3;
290.3,9; 303.2–4,6N;
318.10; 322,8; **4**: 15.7;
16.7,8; 21.10,11; 50.7; 59.4;
64.7; 65.1–3; 79.6; 91.3;
95.3; 97.2; 101.1; 113.9;
131.3; 135.3; 146.8; 151.2;
158.2,3; 171.7; 178.7; 185.3;
190.5; 204.9; 210.1; 215.5;
225.7; 226.10; 244.1; 245.5;
249.8; 255.4,5; 271.2; 273.4;
296.1; 302.7; 310.5,6;
319.2–4,6; **5**: 17.5; 44.1;
54.7–9; 55.1–3; 62.10,11;
69.10; 76.2; 81.1; 84.2; 91.4;
114.1,2; 117.8; 121.2,3; 148.11;
153.7; 195.4; 204.10; 225.8;
230.8; 231.11; 248.7; 287.1;
291.10; 310.7; 316.5; 322.9

Love's Labour's Lost **1**: 24.1,2;
72.3–5; 89.11; 161.3; 222.2;

251.1; 278.7; 283.10; 310.8; 314.8; 320.5; **2:** 123.8N; 306.5; **3:** 161.4; 186.5; **4:** 24.3; 72.6; 133.4; 134.9; 161.5; 193.2; 222.3; 269.8; 306.6; 310.9,10; **5:** 14.8; 55.4; 62.12; 72.7; 97.3; 107.4; 112.4; 138.1; 141.9; 193.3; 227.1; 278.8,9; 304.5; 306.7; 314.9; 315.1; 320.6

Lucrece 5.4; 7.4; 18.2; 32.4; 37.1; 44.2; 61.7,8; 62.1; 75.5; 93.2,7; 112.5; 142.10; 147.1; 151.3; 159.6; 178.8,9; 200.2; 204.11; 208.9; 210.2; 238.3; 245.6; 255.6,7; 258.4–6; 266.8; 315.2

Macbeth **1:** 2.7; 7.5–7; 11.4; 12.3; 13.7; 20.10; 22.1; 27.8; 29.1; 37.2; 41.6; 42.8; 44.3; 45.9; 46.1; 55.5; 60.6; 62.2; 63.6; 67.9; 80.3; 84.3; 94.1–3; 102.8; 111.5; 129.4; 131.4; 135.4; 136.6; 177.2; 178.10; 191.4; 198.1; 207.5; 215.6,7,10; 218.7; 232.1; 240.3; 265.2; 280.7; 284.1–3; 290.10; 294.9; 295.6; 303.5; 307.6–8; 308.1; **2:** 1.7; 11.5; 21.1,2; 22.6; 33.8; 35.3; 41.7; 44.4,5; 49.2; 50.2; 55.6; 64.1; 67.10; 68.1,2; 84.4; 91.5; 92.2; 111.6; 115.3,4; 119.1;124.2; 125.3; 131.5; 136.2; 158.4;

161.6; 171.8; 191.11; 200.3; 207.6; 228.3; 238.4; 262.7,8; 263.1; 270.2; 294.10; 311.1; 316.6; **3:** 1.8; 13.8; 21.3; 39.6; 44.6,7; 49.3–5; 55.7; 62.3; 80.4; 81.2; 93.8,9; 99.5; 116.5; 125.4; 141.10; 153.8; 188.2; 200.4,5; 238.5; 239.1; 241.3,4; 244.2; 263.2; 288.7; 291.11; 305.6; **4:** 2.8; 8.2; 21.4; 23.8; 27.9; 64.2; 80.5,8; 81.3,9; 88.6; 92.3,4; 93.10; 153.9; 177.3; 208.1; 212.2; 232.2; 249.7; 255.8; 266.9; 291.12,13; 308.2,3; 317.10; **5:** 22.7–9; 33.9; 39.7; 47.1; 55.8; 65.4,5; 78.5; 82.11; 94.4,5; 101.3; 129.5; 136.7; 141.11; 155.7; 158.5; 169.10; 171.9; 198.11; 204.12; 205.1; 218.8; 238.6; 248.4; 265.3,4; 266.10; 271.7; 275.2; 302.8

Measure for Measure **1:** 4.5; 15.8; 26.8; 35.7; 148.12; 154.8; 198.2; 213.10; 227.11; 233.5; 242.1,7; 252.4,6; 255.9; 317.1; **2:** 12.4; 13.9; 22.2; 26.6; 29.10; 33.5; 62.4; 102.9; 115.5; 126.2,8; 147.2,3; 154.9,10; 181.5,6; 200.6; 228.1,4; 233.9; 280.8,9; 281.1; 292.1; **3:** 9.2; 55.9,10; 56.1–3; 111.7; 123.5; 153.10; 158.6; 185.6; 233.10;

261.3; 293.1; **4:** 19.6; 50.3; 56.4; 137.1; 190.6; 214.5; **5:** 32.5; 129.6; 149.1; 166.10; 291.1

Merchant of Venice **1:** 1.9,10; 32.1; 38.3,4; 63.7; 81.10; 118.3; 124.3; 145.4,5; 178.11; 198.7; 205.2; 239.5; 249.1; 259.1; 278.10; 293.2; 302.9; 318.1; 322.10; **2:** 12.5; 13.10; 31.10; 50.8; 62.5; 63.8; 66.5; 168.10; 169.1; 174.6; 182.2; 191.12; 210.3–5; 229.8; 233.6; 245.7; 252.3; 258.9; 259.2; 291.2; 293.4; 305.7; **3:** 13.11; 18.3; 38.5; 107.8; 108.10; 128.1; 143.8; 145.1,6; 154.11; 155.9,10; 161.7; 185.10; 193.4; 210.6; 239.6; 293.3; 306.8; **4:** 9.3; 27.10; 38.6; 147.4–7; 149.2,5; 181.7,8; 186.6; 215.8; 234.1; 248.8; 322.11; **5:** 108.11; 129.7; 151.4; 181.3; 186.12; 187.1; 193.5–7; 200.7; 251.2; 270.3,4; 323.1

Merry Wives of Windsor **1:** 68.3; 96.3; 99.6; 141.12; 154.12; 182.3; 184.4; 228.5; 311.2,3; **2:** 129.8; 155.11; 161.8; 182.4; 183.3; 186.7; 208.10; 286.4; 289.10; 318.2,3; 323.2; **3:** 92.5; 102.10; 169.11; 179.1; 186.8; 196.1; 323.3,4; **4:** 2.9; 129.9; **5:** 40.5; 45.5; 84.7,8;

126.9; 169.12; 174.7; 206.8; 278.11; 297.6

Midsummer Night's Dream **1:** 17.7; 30.1; 44.8; 76.3; 89.3; 92.6; 142.11; 161.9–11; 169.2; 210.7; 218.9; 219.1–3; 239.7; 296.2; **2:** 22.3; 64.3; 84.9; 85.1–4; 97.4,5; 107.9; 166.11; 187.2; 194.1; 201.1; 236.2; 251.3; 268.6; 313.5; **3:** 8.3; 12.6,7; 21.5; 23.9; 24.8; 29.5; 76.4; 85.5; 108.1; 127.1; 141.13; 162.1; 165.6; 187.3; 219.4,5; 246.1; 268.7,9; 276.4; **4:** 66.6,7; 111.8; 116.6; 128.4; 135.5; 165.7; 188.3; 194.2,3; 219.6; 263.3,4; **5:** 65.6; 68.10; 70.1; 76.5; 86.1; 89.4; 135.6,7; 187.4; 201.2,3; 219.7–10; 220.1–3; 222.8; 295.7; 315.3; 317.2

Much Ado About Nothing **1:** 78.6; 90.1; 99.7; 104.5; 166.12; 174.8; 210.8; 241.5; 249.2; 260.6; 278.12; 294.4; 306.9; **2:** 9.6; 17.8; 18.4; 27.4; 31.3; 38.7; 48.2; 104.6; 117.1–3; 128.2; 138.2; 162.2,3; 165.8,9; 172.9; 174.9; 176.5; 180.2–4; 194.4; 260.7–9; 279.1–3; 288.8; 306.10; 315.4; **3:** 36.1; 44.9; 80.6; 90.2–4; 112.6; 121.4; 162.4; 182.5;

205.3; 249.3,4; 260.10; 295.8; 307.1,11; 311.4; **4:** 2.1; 131.6; 179.2; 223.3; 244.3,4; 271.3; 281.8; 293.5; **5:** 4.6; 12.8; 17.1; 27.5; 35.6; 134.10; 165.10; 167.1; 174.10; 222.4; 223.4; 234.7; 261.4

Othello **1:** 13.12; 23.1; 33.6; 39.8; 42.4; 49.6; 68.11,12; 92.7; 104.11; 105.8; 115.8; 132.8N; 138.3; 155.8; 162.5; 174.11; 186.9; 205.4; 212.12; 236.3; 241.7; 252.7; 255.10,11; 265.5; 271.8; 272.1; 291.3; **2:** 14.1; 60.7; 68.4–6; 117.4; 129.10,11; 177.4; 182.6; 183.4; 234.2; 240.5,6; 250.1; 256.1; 284.4; 307.2; 311.5–7; **3:** 26.9; 28.8; 63.1; 121.5,6; 138.4,5; 143.9; 144.1–3; 167.2; 174.12; 180.5; 183.5; 240.7; 244.5; 276.6; 296.3; 300.5; **4:** 8.4; 72.8; 129.12; 194.5; 215.9; 221.7; 256.2; 266.11; 280.3; 294.5; 313.3; **5:** 2.2; 18.5; 56.5,6; 74.1; 119.2; 144.4; 152.3; 156.7; 158.7; 162.6; 187.5; 192.1,2; 194.6; 202.4; 235.2; 236.9; 241.6; 265.6; 279.4; 291.4; 311.8

Passionate Pilgrim 71.3; 205.5

Pericles **1:** 90.5; 95.4; 151.5; 192.3; 258.7; 260.4; 292.2; **2:** 111.4; 122.10; 125.5; 284.5; **3:** 16.3; 107.5; 160.1; 250.2; 259.3,4; **4:** 30.2; 239.2; 256.3; 258.8; 300.6; 311.9; 318.4; **5:** 146.3; 152.4; 191.5; 211.7

Phoenix and Turtle 21.6; 74.2; 162.7

Richard II **1:** 38.2; 63.2; 65.7; 78.1; 82.12; 99.8,9; 101.2; 108.9; 112.7; 114.3; 118.4; 123.1; 133.5; 135.8; 147.8; 151.6,7; 169.8; 197.4; 205.6,7; 211.8; 240.4; 241.10; 266.12; 268.8; 280.4; 291.5; 315.5; **2:** 10.4; 41.8; 56.7,8; 59.5,6; 70.2,3; 78.2–4; 95.5; 104.7; 109.9; 111.9; 123.6; 143.4; 208.2; 225.9; 232.8; 238.7; 279.7; 288.9; 292.3; 302.10; 315.6; 318.5; **3:** 21.7; 47.9; 56.9; 57.1–3; 59.7; 71.4; 82.13; 105.9; 106.1; 109.10; 151.8–10; 154.13; 177.5; 197.5; 212.3; 239.10; 272.10; 300.7; 301.4; **4:** 12.9; 112.8; 114.4; 151.11,12; 152.1; 229.9; 240.1; 267.1,2; 301.5; **5:** 47.2; 70.4; 123.2; 124.4; 132.5; 159.1; 194.7,8; 197.6; 211.9; 220.4; 230.9; 259.7; 260.5; 286.5

Richard III **1:** 2.3; 12.10; 37.3–5; 45.1; 66.8; 81.4,5; 115.6; 117.9; 119.3; 131.7; 145.2;

152.5; 192.4,5; 213.1–3; 244.9; 250.3; 267.3; 279.5; 282.4; 292.4; 313.6; **2:** 30.9; 106.2; 232.3; **3:** 14.2; 18.6; 131.8; 140.4; 220.5; 234.3; 323.5; **4:** 10.5; 22.4; 45.2; 107.6; 133.11; 184.7; 229.10; 232.4; 236.10; 238.8; 244.10,11; 245.1,2; 291.6; 292.5; 294.11; **5:** 25.9; 37.6–9; 47.3; 63.3; 66.9; 93.11; 115.7; 124.5; 132.6; 156.8; 192.6; 213.4,5; 245.8; 286.10,11; 301.6

Romeo and Juliet **Prol.:** 32.6; 84.1; 169.3; 220; **1:** 10.6; 18.7; 24.9; 30.3; 48.3; 86.2,3; 125.6,7; 152.6–8; 162.8–10; 184.11; 186.10; 246.9; 251.7; 302.1; **2:** 38.8; 71.5; 76.9; 82.7,8; 90.6; 117.10,11; 127.2; 133.1; 137.2; 146.4; 156.9; 163.1,2; 167.3; 179.3; 188.4; 196.2,8,9; 201.4; 205.8; 211.1; 223.6; 231.4; 246.10–12; 247.1; 263.5; 279.6; 282.5; 296.4; 323.6; **3:** 9.7; 25.2; 47.4; 100.7; 102.11; 117.5; 156.10; 169.4; 184.8; 188.5; 201.5,6; 210.9; 211.10; 214.11; 234.8; 247.2,3; 270.5,6; 275.3; 320.3; **4:** 57.4; 93.12; 99.10; **5:** 57.5; 63.4; 65.8; 84.5; 91.6; 109.11; 153.1; 227.2; 247.4,5; 281.2; 318.6

Sonnets 1.3,4; 14.3; 15.3; 16.1; 18.8; 21.8; 30.10; 31.4–6; 36.2; 39.9; 47.10; 57.6,7; 59.8; 60.1,2; 62.6; 65.9; 74.3; 79.1; 88.2,4; 89.5; 97.6,7; 104.12; 106.6; 109.2; 110.1; 112.9; 118.5; 120.5,8; 132.7,8; 135.9; 138.6,7; 144.5; 156.11; 159.2; 160.2; 163.3–9; 165.11; 166.1,2; 167.4–6; 181.4; 183.6; 184.9; 185.11; 188.6; 190.7,8; 194.9,10; 196.3; 205.9–11; 206.1,9; 211.3; 213.6; 222.5–7; 225.10; 229.11; 236.4,5; 238.9; 240.8; 251.4; 252.5,8,9; 256.4; 261.5; 263.6,7; 267.4,8; 269.9; 275.4; 282.6,7; 284.6–12; 285.1–3; 287.2–4; 291.7; 296.5; 302.11; 305.1,2; 311.10; 313.7; 316.7,8; 319.1; 320.7

Taming of the Shrew **1:** 32.7; 72.9; 143.5; 155.1; 175.1–3; 221.2; 295.9; **2:** 130.1; 142.1; 144.6; 167.7; 196.4; 307.3; **3:** 90.7; 124.6; 130.2; 142.2; 175.4,5; 239.3; **4:** 90.8; 133.7; 142.3,4; 175.6; 248.5; 260.11; 282.11; 295.10; 305.3; **5:** 130.3,4; 175.7; 311.11

Tempest **1:** 12.11; 13.1; 24.4; 36.3; 74.4; 91.7; 112.10; 168.5,6;

194.11; 210.10,11; 250.4,5; 259.5; 261.8; 269.1–3; 315.8; **2:** 3.4; 35.5N; 47.5; 103.8; 115.9; 127.3; 242.5; 261.9; 276.8; 277.1; 307.4; **3:** 20.4; 24.5; 41.9; 58.1,2; 67.1; 104.8; 142.5; 167.8; 168.7; 195.1; 206.2; 238.1; 311.12; 312.1; **4:** 67.2; 68.7; 107.2; 159.3; 167.9; 175.8; 192.7; 206.3; 220.7; 235.4,5; 256.5; 312.2; **5:** 50.4; 86.4; 87.1; 103.9; 127.4; 172.1,2; 197.9,10; 242.8; 272.2; 273.1; 290.4; **Epil.:** 76.6; 228.6

Timon of Athens **1:** 28.6; 71.6; 95.6,7; 107.7; 186.1; 294.2; 318.7; 319.7; **2:** 95.8; **3:** 8.5; 118.1; 121.7; 155.2,3; 183.11; 261.6; **4:** 19.2; 20.5; 65.10; 105.1; 110.2; 118.6; 184.1; 186.11; 227.3; 281.9; 300.8; 318.8; **5:** 159.4; 231.5; 244.6

Titus Andronicus **1:** 2.4; 7.8; 43.1; 61.2; 88.3; 138.8; 182.1; 188.7; 206.4; 265.7; 313.8; **2:** 128.5; 244.7; 256.6; **3:** 192.8; 246.8; 267.5; 292.6; **4:** 79.7; 241.11; 252.1; **5:** 81.6

Troilus and Cressida **Prol.:** 300.9; **1:** 2.5; 14.4; 180.6; 209.1–3; 220.8; 221.8; 225.11,12; 246.2; 292.7; 313.9; 319.8; **2:** 16.5; 47.6;

114.5; 118.7,8; 133.2; 142.12; 143.1; 215.1; 230.1–3; 232.5; 236.6; 239.8; 290.2; 293.6,7; 300.10; **3:** 9.8; 26.10; 35.8; 36.8; 87.3; 123.3; 125.8; 127.5; 138.9; 168.8; 214.6; 230.4; 241.1; 246.3; 256.7,8; 257.1; 285.4–6; 307.5; 315.9; 319.5; **4:** 7.9; 27.1; 76.7; 84.6; 89.6; 96.4; 118.9; 126.3; 180.7; 185.7; 201.7; 257.2; 285.7; 286.1; 313.4; 320.1; **5:** 58.3; 134.5; 139.1,2; 143.2; 177.6; 231.6; 257.3–5; 315.10

Twelfth Night **1:** 13.2; 14.5; 15.4; 18.9; 31.7; 48.4; 68.8; 99.11; 100.3,4; 135.10; 160.3; 163.10; 195.2; 252.2; 266.2; 268.1; 277.2; 286.6; 313.10; 314.1; 323.7; **2:** 58.4; 71.2; 72.10; 91.8; 109.3,4; 111.1; 120.6; 153.2; 163.11; 164.1; 166.3; 180.8; 211.11; 221.9; 226.1; 229.1; 230.5; 266.3; 287.5,6,10–12; 288.10; 290.5; 295.11; 303.9; 312.3; 323.8; **3:** 17.9; 41.10; 100.5; 130.5; 135.11; 140.1; 155.4; 182.7; 249.5; 272.3; 275.5,6; 289.1; 295.12; 315.11; 320.8; **4:** 133.6; 215.2; **5:** 133.8; 184.5; 244.8; 253.1; 286.2; 303.6

Two Gentlemen of Verona **1:** 83.8; 127.11; 164.2,3; 236.11;

289.2; **2:** 41.11; 66.2; 83.9; 99.12; 146.1; 241.2; **3:** 145.3; 167.10; 180.9; **4:** 50.1; 66.3; 197.7; 231.7; 312.4; **5:** 8.6; 19.7; 116.3; 164.4; 169.5

Two Noble Kinsmen **1:** 97.8; 111.10; 112.11; 113.1; 127.6; 265.8; 289.11; 318.9; **2:** 108.2; 179.4; 190.9; 246.4; **3:** 171.10; 312.5; **5:** 19.8; 30.4

Venus and Adonis 9.4; 18.10; 23.10; 74.5; 82.9; 97.9; 124.7,8; 144.7; 153.3–5; 159.7; 164.5,6; 179.5; 189.1,2; 202.1; 257.6–10; 286.9; 323.9

Winter's Tale **1:** 14.6; 30.5; 31.1; 139.3; 140.5; 144.8–10; 257.11,12; 258.1,2; 302.2; 312.6; **2:** 140.6; 171.11; 239.9; 261.7; 272.4; 276.7; 280.5; 289.8; 302.3; **3:** 9.5; 58.5; 60.8; 113.2; 140.7; 149.3; 170.1; 197.11; 258.3; 259.6; 273.2; 289.3; 323.10; **4:** 17.6; 24.6; 27.2; 29.2,6; 39.10; 40.6; 48.5; 71.7; 79.8; 82.10; 90.9; 98.1–6; 99.13; 121.8,9; 155.5; 164.7; 269.10; 281.10; 289.4; 290.1; **5:** 15.5; 111.11; 114.6; 146.5; 172.10; 196.10; 312.7